UNIX Systems

Advanced Administration and Management Handbook

Bruce H. Hunter
Karen Bradford Hunter

Macmillan Publishing Company
New York

Collier Macmillan Publishers
Toronto

Maxwell Macmillan International
New York   Oxford   Singapore   Sydney

Production Supervisor: Ron Harris
Production Manager: Rick Fischer/Pam Kennedy
Text Designer: Jane Edelstein
Cover designer: Jane Edelstein
Cover illustration: Armen Kojoyian

This book was set in Times Roman by Publication Services, printed and bound by Book Press. The cover was printed by NEBC.

Copyright © 1991 by Macmillan Publishing Company, a division of Macmillan, Inc.

Printed in the United States of America

Macmillan Publishing Company
866 Third Avenue, New York, New York 10022

Collier Macmillan Canada, Inc.

Library of Congress Cataloging in Publication Data

Hunter, Bruce H.
    UNIX systems : advanced administration and management handbook /
Bruce H. Hunter, Karen Bradford Hunter.
        p.   cm.
    ISBN 0-02-358950-7
    1. UNIX (Computer operating system) I. Hunter, Karen Bradford.
II. Title.
QA76.76.063H86 1991
005.4'3–dc20   90-6012
                                                                              CIP

Printing: 1 2 3 4 5 6 7 8   Year: 1 2 3 4 5 6 7 8 9 0

We would like to dedicate this book to our dads.

William Edgar Bradford
Charles Hunter
William W. Duke

The world is a better place because you were here.

P R E F A C E

If you administer UNIX systems, *UNIX Systems: Advanced Administration and Management Handbook* is for you. Whether you are an experienced administrator or relatively new to UNIX system administration, you will find this book a handy reference and guide. You will learn day-to-day UNIX system administration techniques in Section I, and from there the book goes on to cover UNIX subsystems, configuration and tuning, UNIX network administration, and system management.

Whether your systems run SCO XENIX, UNIX System V, Berkeley UNIX, or a combination of all three, you'll find the information you need to administer your UNIX system in this book. It was written from Bruce Hunter's 10 years of personal experience with various micro versions of UNIX (including SCO XENIX), administering UTS (System V UNIX) on Amdahl and IBM mainframes, and running SunOS and DEC ULTRIX on a network of Sun and DEC workstations and Sun and DEC servers. Thus, whether you run mainframes, micros, or minis, and whether your systems are stand-alone or networked, you will learn what you need to know from this book to administer the systems on your site.

There are some excellent books already published on UNIX system administration, but none of these books goes into the detail this book does. For example, seven chapters in Section 3 cover system creation, configuration, and tuning. You will learn how to configure and tune both BSD and AT&T System V UNIX systems to maximize your systems' performance. Configuration methods vary from UNIX version to UNIX version, and so not only will you learn about configuration theory and the differences between BSD and System V configuration, but you will learn how to put that theory to use on specific machines. For instance, how do you configure a Sun workstation running SunOS, and in what ways does that differ from configuring other UNIX systems, such as DEC ULTRIX or a mainframe UNIX system like UTS? What is the difference between setting up a XENIX system on a 386 micro and setting up an ULTRIX system on a DEC VAX Server? You'll learn all this and more in *UNIX Systems: Advanced Administration and Management Handbook*.

Only a few years ago UNIX system administration books were geared to supporting stand-alone UNIX systems, but times have changed, and we work in an entirely different world today. At this writing, most UNIX systems are networked, and many UNIX system administrators are rapidly becoming network administrators out of necessity. Existing network books cover the huge field of general networking, but specific information on UNIX networks is rarely mentioned. For that specialty, look no further than this book, for there is an entire chapter devoted exclusively to UNIX network administration. All UNIX system administrators eventually will need to become intimately familiar with the intricacies of UNIX networking, because that's where the computer world is going, and you can get a head start by reading *UNIX Systems: Advanced Administration and Management Handbook*.

Most system administration books approach UNIX system administration from a theoretical perspective, and that is the best way to become acquainted with the UNIX operating system. But eventually there will come a time when you venture into the business world and find yourself responsible for administering UNIX machines in actual MIS or engineering environments, and then you will have to put that theory into practice. No other UNIX system administration book deals with what it is really like doing system administration for a living. Which parameters will you need to tune when the users on your machines temporarily change over from running 100 small jobs to running CPU-intensive CAD simulations? What's the best way to handle user requests on large sites? How much should you rely on system scripts to do problem determination on your systems? Which operating system updates have the most bugs? What is the UNIX `accounting` subsystem all about, and how can you use it on your site to monitor and manage all processes in use on your UNIX systems? What is the difference between `lp` and `lpr`, and how will these differences affect your system administration techniques? What are service-level agreements, and why should system administrators use them? What are the quickest ways to recover from system crashes so you will not have 100 users breathing down your neck while they wait for you to bring up a down system? How do you set up NFS or YP? How do you diagnose network problems? Not only does this book answer all these questions, but one chapter is devoted exclusively to actual system administration scenarios that are a representative sampling of the kinds of situations you will encounter on various UNIX computer sites. Each scenario relates a specific problem, details the processes involved in solving that problem, and summarizes what can be learned.

System administrators also have to cope with the company management side of their jobs, and there are certain key system management issues that UNIX system administrators must address. For example, to run their UNIX machines at maximum efficiency, it is imperative that technical UNIX managers be able to communicate to nontechnical managers their specific UNIX system administration needs. Equally important, nontechnical managers must learn as much about UNIX as they can in order to manage their UNIX sites effectively. Pertinent system management information can be found in the **Manager's Corner** section at the end of every chapter in this book. In addition, four chapters in Section V address key system management topics. Indeed, UNIX system administration involves a lot more than knowing how to add new users to the system, install software, and handle system maintenance tasks.

Of course one must always be prepared to cope with change in our rapidly developing computer industry, and UNIX System 5.4 is changing UNIX system administration. In this book you will see some of the ways UNIX System 5.4 differs from UNIX System 5.3, BSD 4.3, and SCO XENIX, and how these differences affect system administration.

Because of everything we've said so far, we know you will learn a lot from this book and benefit from the information within, but the best reason for reading it is that you will discover more about how this fascinating, versatile UNIX operating system works and why it is becoming such a dominant force in the computer industry today. That is why we worked hard to make this book as readable as possible, so that not only technical but also nontechnical people can revel in how vital and interesting UNIX really is.

B.H.
K.H.

A C K N O W L E D G M E N T S

Special thanks to our Canadian friend Jim McCormick.

We would also like to acknowledge Simone Auger, Noelle Balbi, Ed Broadbent, Tim Cahill, Claude Duval, David Elliott, Ted Farrant, David Foster, Harry Freedman, Glenn Gould, Joan Grundy, K.H., Ted Johnston, Jim Joska, Toshi Kawamura, Elaine Keillor, Don Kendrick, Gordon Lightfoot, Rich Little, Tim Malroney, Rodolphe Mathieu, Gerry McCormick, Sharon McCormick, Debi McGilvery, Colin Miles, Joni Mitchell, MuShu, Anne Murray, Caroline Schaefer, R. Murray Schafer, Harry Somers, Rosemary Watkins, Healey Willan, and Neil Young.

CONTENTS

Section II
UNIX Subsystems   **115**

Section V
System Management   339

CHAPTER 19   **Critical Services Administration:**
          A New Approach   340

Section VI
System Administration Scenarios   381

SECTION
I

Pedestrian Administration

1

Introduction to UNIX System Administration

WHAT UNIX SYSTEM ADMINISTRATION IS

A UNIX system administrator's job is to keep UNIX systems alive and functioning with optimum efficiency, but that's just the beginning. The system administrator also must guarantee the integrity of the system and its data and must

- Install new systems.
- Maintain existing systems.
- Install new applications.
- Maintain existing applications.
- Upgrade software.
- Upgrade hardware.
- Monitor hardware operation and performance.
- Support system software.
- Maintain system software.
- Create new system software.
- Manage file systems.
- Monitor system security.
- Back up system data.

Performing these tasks requires not only a knowledge of the UNIX operating system but also enough system programming ability to write and maintain system software and enough hardware ability to take a smaller system out of a box, put it together, and get it going.

UNIX system administrators also interact with users to do the following:

- Put users on the system.
- Solve the users' problems.
- Establish user groups.
- Educate the users.
- Educate the operations staff.

Interaction with users is one of the most important system administration tasks. System administrators interact with management as well, to prepare state-of-the-system reports and to advise management on technical aspects of the system so they can make intelligent management decisions about the system.

Furthermore, if the systems are networked, system administrators will do double duty as network administrators by maintaining all network files, caring for network daemons on all machines, monitoring network security, and taking special care of all the domain servers, file servers, printer servers, and mail masters.

People in the company look to the system administrator for help when the system is in trouble, so UNIX system administrators should be familiar with the system's internals and its most obscure functions. Part of a system administration job is supporting whatever company activities are carried out on the UNIX machines. For example, if users do lots of documentation on the site, the administrator will be expected to become an expert on nroff and troff macros, to know all about the latest typesetting software and how to install it, and to be able to pick out the best printer for the documentation.

The system administrator is expected to make all UNIX machines run, whatever version of UNIX happens to be on site. Today's UNIX system administrator should be able to administer System V UNIX, Berkeley UNIX, and XENIX.

This is the "big picture" of UNIX system administration. Let's zero in on some specific system administration tasks.

Day-to-Day Administration

Each day, system administrators do some (or all) of the following:

- Add and delete users.
- Provide daily backups and restore lost files and directories.
- Support users.
- Clean up old system files.
- Clean up unused and unneeded core files.
- Empty spoolers.
- Get rid of unnecessary temporary files.
- Change ownerships and permissions and create links.

Some of these administration tasks can be performed on an organized, daily basis as part of a schedule, but there usually are a lot of interruptions. While attempting a simple morning cleanup, for example, an administrator may be besieged with requests to fix a glitch in last night's backup run, to fix errors in user-created software and scripts, to answer questions from anxious users, and so on. And in one way or another the administrator must take care of all of these.

Periodic Maintenance

The administrator is responsible for scheduling and maintaining the system by doing such tasks as

- Regular periodic full backups.
- Incremental backups.
- Archives.
- Password cleanup.
- Security checks and "hole plugging."
- Disk cleanups.
- Massive spooler cleanups.

These tasks can be planned ahead of time and performed whenever scheduled.

Tasks Performed As Needed

Some system adminstration jobs only occasionally pop up, but the administrator needs to be ready to tackle them when they do. Examples are migrations and installations of new systems, new software, and new hardware. There are several different kinds of system migrations: moving from one version of the operating system to another—such as from AT&T System V Release 3 to System V Release 4—or moving from stand-alone systems like DEC mainframes to a clustered system of workstations and separate file servers.

Network Administration

On many UNIX sites today, network-related administration tasks account for at least half of an administrator's time—for example, adding new users, new systems, and printers to the network and updating `hosts` and `networks` files. Each new user integrated into the network has to be added to numerous network-related files on all the machines. Every time a new machine is added, its host name, Ethernet address, and Internet address must be found or assigned, and all this information must be distributed to all machines on the network.

WHERE UNIX IS TODAY

UNIX was first created at Bell Labs back when AT&T was still The Telephone Company. AT&T was prohibited by its corporate charter from selling computers or software, and so UNIX could not be sold. Instead, it was given to some universities at a nominal installation cost. A few of these universities, particularly the University of California at Berkeley, greatly modified the operating system. Current BSD versions are 4.2, 4.3, and 4.4. Variations are ULTRIX (4.2), Sun OS (4.3) and so on. 4.4 is new enough to exclude commercial versions for a while.

By the time AT&T completed its divestiture and took on a new charter, it was finally free to sell UNIX as well as its internally developed line of computers. However,

AT&T UNIX soon ran into head-on competition with the older UNIX version modified by the University of California at Berkeley. Indeed, Berkeley's enhancements to UNIX were so significant that AT&T couldn't afford to ignore them. So Berkeley UNIX (BSD) is now merged into AT&T UNIX at System V Release 4.

But BSD and AT&T aren't the only UNIX versions in town. Microsoft had one of the earliest successful OEM UNIX ports, called XENIX. The Santa Cruz Operation put Microsoft's UNIX version, XENIX, on the map by selling and supporting the system with such vigor that there are currently more XENIX machines than any other UNIX version. Tandy Corporation also had excellent sales of small UNIX systems running XENIX.

Today's UNIX system administrators should be familiar with all three major UNIX factions—AT&T UNIX, Berkeley UNIX, and XENIX—and this book covers all three. System V Release 4 brings these three UNIX versions together, and we shall examine many 5.4 UNIX features as well.

Some UNIX system administrators today still work on only one version of UNIX, but they are rapidly becoming a minority. Because of the advances in networking, soon most UNIX system administrators will not only have several different kinds of UNIX machines at their sites, but they will also run different versions of UNIX simultaneously. For example, knowledge of XENIX is necessary for most PC-class systems, and XENIX is a hybrid version of Berkeley UNIX and AT&T System V. At this writing, SunOS is a Berkeley 4.3 derivative, and DEC's ULTRIX is a Berkeley 4.2 derivative. Amdahl's UTS V is almost pure System V UNIX. Since it is common for PC systems, Sun workstations, DEC servers, and a mainframe to be networked together, the administrator of such a site would have to be familiar with XENIX, SunOS, ULTRIX, and UTS V.

That brings up another point. Any version of UNIX today is either one of the three UNIX versions—AT&T UNIX, Berkeley UNIX, or XENIX—or some derivative of those three. Once you know how to administer these three UNIX versions, you can jump in and administer virtually any UNIX machine with little additional training. For example, a Sun system running SunOS can be run in a pinch with DEC ULTRIX manuals, because both are Berkeley derivatives. Similarly, you can sit at a Sun 386i and run scripts created for an ULTRIX system. The scripts are almost identical. The DEC manual sections that reflect ULTRIX's dependence on DECnet won't apply to Sun machines, but the commands, file names, and file locations of SunOS and ULTRIX are very similar. Here's an even more radical example: If you are used to AT&T UNIX 5.2 on your AT&T 3B micro, you could sit down at the console of a huge mainframe running UTS V and find yourself surprisingly at home, because both machines run System V UNIX versions. The differences the administrator sees center mostly on the hardware.

COMPUTERS USED TO COME IN THREE SIZES

For a while computers came in three sizes: micro, mini, and mainframe. Each category was distinct from the others. Mainframes were clearly the largest and most powerful computers money could buy, and they were distinguished by being rack-mounted. They were huge, requiring raised floors, water cooling, stand-alone air conditioning, and a crew of 30 people to feed and care for them. Micros were very small and limited in size and ability, but they were the first truly affordable computers. Minis were larger and more powerful than micros, but not as powerful as mainframes.

When people used to sit down and figure out what computers to buy for a computer site, the lines between micros, minis, and mainframes were distinct. Micros were limited, and you could never get any real disk capacity. They were suitable for some purposes, but if you wanted to do any serious work, you started thinking about whether you could get away with buying smaller minis, and you went on from there.

Today the former distinctions between micro, mainframe, and mini are blurred by continuing technological development. Micros have long since passed the older minis in performance, so when looking at a system like a Sun 4/490 or DECstation 5000, it isn't clear whether they could or should be called micros or minis. Meanwhile some micros today have more computing power than mainframes used to have.

Now the first thing you do when you're thinking about major computer purchases for a business is compare the processors offered. While you listen to the different sales engineers, you should think about the following:

- Processor speed.
- Effective number of instructions per second.
- Bus width and throughput.
- Caching.
- Types of controllers and devices for both disks and tapes.

Once you've settled on a processor, you will have an array of machines built around that processor from which to choose, ranging from relatively small to very large. Let's say you decide to go for Sun's SPARC (RISC) processor. You either study the catalog or work with the sales engineer and decide on the size of the machines you will need for your application. This is where you start making your price/performance trade-offs. The terms *micro* or *mini* are nowhere to be found, nor are you thinking in those terms. Instead, you are thinking in terms of which machines to buy for *servers* and which machines to buy for *workstations*. In theory, all of Sun's SPARC machines could be either servers or workstations. But in practice, if you are buying machines that will be servers, you should go for more disk capacity. If you are buying workstations, you should decide whether you want them dataless or diskless, and so on.

FEW COMPUTERS WILL STAND ALONE IN THE 1990s

All computers used to be stand-alone systems; indeed the term *stand-alone* didn't exist, because there was nothing else. Then computers started talking to one another with greater ease. With a high degree of connectivity, users could establish remote logins, transfer files, and send mail. Today entire file systems can be mounted from another system. If you are running stand-alone systems, it is just a matter of time before you will network. And if you are networked but haven't moved to NFS or YP yet, you will eventually.

Stand-alone UNIX systems are most common at the extremes of the computer spectrum. For example, many mainframe UNIX systems are stand-alone systems. A 370 mainframe can run several UNIX systems simultaneously under either VM or a multiple-domain feature. Twelve UTS V UNIX virtual machines all running on an IBM 3090 600E were used for some of this book's UNIX system administration topics.

The smallest stand-alone systems are PC-AT type machines known as *desktops*. Dominated by XENIX, they have become the lowest common denominator of UNIX. Although they can be networked, they also function well as single-user UNIX systems or as small, multiuser machines. This book was written and edited on a four-user 386 micro of this kind.

The stand-alone minicomputer was the progenitor of UNIX, but today's UNIX marketing thrust is networked workstations. A *workstation* is characterized by a fast microprocessor and built-in networking features, such as Ethernet capability. Workstations usually favor graphics processing, so features like graphics accelerators, large screens, small pixels, and the inevitable mouse, are common. Their disk capacities are relatively small. A dataless workstation has enough disk space for the operating system and its swap space, usually fewer than 100 megabytes. Many workstations have no disks at all and are referred to as *diskless workstations*. Workstations need *file servers* to provide disk space. File servers may also have to double as YP servers, mail servers, and so on (see Chapter 18).

It's not so difficult to manufacture a card to plug into a computer's bus so that the computer can talk to the Ethernet, but how do you develop something to plug into a mainframe's channel? The slowness of mainframe system OEMs to come out with fully networked UNIX systems has cost them a substantial share of the rapidly developing networking market. Nevertheless, a large UNIX mainframe is still an object of wonder. Nothing can beat the power of a mainframe when running massive simulations and other disk- and processor-intensive programs. Mainframes will maintain an important niche in the UNIX world for a long time to come, and they are networked on the Ethernet.

Networked systems can run from one workstation attached to another as a file server to a cluster system with so many workstations, bridges, servers, routers, and networked large systems that a map is necessary to comprehend its size and form. One of the sites used to research this book consists of forty Sun 386i systems, even more mixed DEC workstations, two DEC file servers and two Sun file servers, fifty PC-AT-type desktop systems, and three DEC VMS systems. This small data center was subnetted as part of the corporation's massive network.

To accommodate stand-alone systems as well as networked systems, we shall discuss different kinds of computer sites in this book, for the best overall picture of commercial UNIX in today's marketplace.

UNIX STANDARDS

A decade ago no one was concerned with UNIX standards, and when UNIX came into the commercial marketplace, it had to compete in a world dominated by proprietary operating systems. Data General computers ran AOS/VS. DECs ran VMS. Software that was developed on one machine couldn't run on another machine until it was rewritten for that machine. Software that ran on Apples couldn't be run on IBM PCs, and so on. Then UNIX changed all that.

UNIX was designed to be a *portable operating system,* capable of being ported to any piece of hardware. When all machines run the same operating system, they can run one another's software; they can communicate with one another; and they can even mount one another's file systems. It costs a company less to run a UNIX site because the users need to know only one operating system. When all the UNIX machines talk to one another, a job can be run on the smallest machine that can handle it well. UNIX has changed the computer industry forever. We will continue to see exciting hardware developments, but in the future many companies will be concentrating on creating software to run on all these networked UNIX systems.

Because UNIX has become such an important force in the computer industry, it is important to establish UNIX standards. Thus AT&T followed up System V Release 2 with a System V Interface Definition known as SVID. This was one of the first attempts at standardizing UNIX, and it was the cornerstone of many standards that followed. An organization known as /usr/group started a standard that went on to become the POSIX standard. The IEEE started from the POSIX standard and went from there. Its UNIX standard is IEEE 1000.3. With eight committees in all, the system administration committee is POSIX 1000.3.7. Another standard is the European X/Open standard. Slowly but surely, the industry is developing universal UNIX standards, but it's a lengthy process.

Standardizing UNIX sounds like a good idea, but it's difficult to enforce. Even the System V Interface Definition has been slow to be adopted. Volume I consisted of system calls only; volume II defined base extensions, advanced utilities, administration extensions, software development extensions, and the terminal interface; and volume III described base system and terminal interface definitions and some networking. By the time the SVID was reasonably defined for System V Release 2, it needed to be extended for System V Release 4.

The unfortunate part of having a standard that is unfinished is that anyone can claim to adhere to it, with little danger of being caught. I've seen a few major players in the industry advertise "new" UNIX systems based on old BSD ports, and they got a foothold by claiming SVID compatibility. Therefore, before buying a UNIX system that claims compatibility with a standard, be sure that the standard has been written and published. Read the standard and take the time to understand it. The SVID is available at UNIX book stores.

WHERE IS UNIX GOING?

It will be easier to understand the scope of a UNIX system adminstrator's duties if we look at where UNIX has been and where it is going.

In 1990 UNIX had its twentieth birthday, for the first minute of January 1970 was the "official" birthdate of UNIX. Since then UNIX system administration has changed considerably. The early UNIX administrator had to be a miracle worker to keep the operating system alive. Documentation and support were scarce, and there were no books on UNIX system administration. Today UNIX is easier to administer, with many machines offering system administration programs to make life easier. UNIX system administration standards are in the process of being defined at this writing, and when they are complete, system administration will become more standard from UNIX machine to UNIX machine.

There are many changes in the computer industry that will affect the UNIX sites where system administrators work. Money that would have bought high-end computers will go to smaller systems, and in the future less money will buy more computer in terms of features and sheer processing power. The magic of the mainframe is *ECL,* emitter-controlled logic. ECL has found its way to low-end systems with processors like the MIPS R6000 chipset running at 55 MIPS on some systems. At the same time, true multiprocessor hardware in UNIX brings similar power with less expensive processors. The days of the mainframe's dominance on the basis of transaction speed alone is gone, and in the future the mainframe must try to hold its own through its much broader I/O processing capability. Not all applications need that capability, but many do.

A quick review of the 1980s shows the decade starting with stand-alone computers either not connected or, at best, networked homogeneously with proprietary schemes that refused to talk to one another. A few years later, Berkeley UNIX was making the most of TCP/IP and preparing the way for the UNIX-to-UNIX Ethernet connectivity we enjoy today. Now networking is a way of life, and most UNIX system administrators are finding out that they have to become network administrators as well.

Sun, Hewlett Packard, Apollo, and a few others created the concept of the workstation, a monumental move for the computing world. The workstation/server concept opened the way for distributed computing, a major milestone. Distributed computing makes UNIX fully contained, with not only basic networking but remote and networked file systems as well. Even PCs running DOS can join UNIX systems via PC-NFS.

The scope of system networking has broadened and is no longer the care and feeding of stand-alone systems; setting up NFS and Yellow Pages is now a vital skill. System administrators should be able to administer a local area network as well as individual systems. On many UNIX sites system administrators have to live on several servers simultaneously as well as to be able to connect immediately to any one of scores of host systems. The UNIX system administrator is now a major user of windows and workstations.

Where are the 1990s leading us? It took a full decade to get to a functional multiprocessor version of UNIX, but now both AT&T and SCO have commercial versions. True multiprocessors, including the incredible hypercubes, have been with us for a while without a known operating system, but now they have UNIX. UNIX's next move is to put an end to the security problem that its all-or-nothing privilege has created. Because government contracts for UNIX are far too important to allow this market to slip away, new levels of security must be guaranteed.

The major move for UNIX is toward distributed processing. On distributed computing we log in on one system, do our work on another with files from yet another system, and so on. Distributed processing also can take still another step and permit a job to be processed transparently on another system. It will even allow a job to be stopped momentarily on a busy system and moved to a quiescent one.

Hardware will go in many exciting directions in the 1990s. Desktops of 50+ MIPS will be with us soon, just for starters. Something called a *work server* is an exciting new class of computer. Just as a file server provides files for a domain of computers, so the work server will provide memory and CPU-intensive computing for smaller systems on the network. These work servers will start at 50 MIPS and 62 megabytes, but they will quickly move to 200+ MIPS and 1 gigabyte of memory, all at the cost of yesterday's minicomputer. At this point the distributed systems will be free of mainframes except for processes that require channel architecture for disk and I/O intensive tasks.

We also should acknowledge window systems, because they have made UNIX user friendly. That is, with windows the user doesn't have to interface directly with UNIX, a marvelous but complex operating system. Others pioneered the concept of windows, especially Apple, but X Windows was the first windowing system that took hold for UNIX. NeWS and Motif are later developments. The real impact in the immediate future will be seen as applications are written and rewritten to taken advantage of these window systems.

The move from Ethernet-TCP/IP to ISO is significant. The advantages are questionable, but several governments, including ours, have committed to it. TCP/IP was only supposed to be an interim DOD standard.

Look for more complex security, particularly over the network. Gains in security are accompanied by increases in difficulty of administration and complicated internals.

How will all these changes affect UNIX professionals? The demand for educated UNIX users, programmers, and administrators will continue unabated. Networked systems will place an even higher demand on UNIX administration professionals, with the need for trained professional system and network administrators continuing to grow until the end of this century.

UNIX: A SYSTEM ADMINISTRATOR'S VIEW

No matter how much UNIX changes its interface with users, you, as a UNIX system administrator, will always have an esoteric view of UNIX, because you need to know how the system works. To be a truly effective system administrator, you must understand what makes UNIX tick. And the longer you administer a UNIX machine, the more admiration you will develop for this massive, fascinating operating system.

Like doctors, UNIX system administrators must be able to diagnose as well as treat. When diagnosing problems and malfunctions, system administrators often have to work with fairly sketchy user information and cryptic or even misleading error messages. Only with a thorough knowledge of the UNIX system, therefore, can you put the pieces together and figure out what's happening. The best way to learn about UNIX system administration is by doing day-by-day system administration tasks, and so that is where we shall begin.

MANAGER'S CORNER

Staffing Requirements

If you are a nontechnical manager in charge of a UNIX system, you will need specific information about UNIX to manage effectively. I've worked in the computer industry for many years, and I've known many managers who made their "technical bones" before UNIX became such a vital force. Some achieved technical expertise as VM system programmers; others did MIS work on MVS; and others had still different technical training. Whatever your technical background, don't make the mistake of relying on your past knowledge of other operating systems to make management decisions about UNIX. *UNIX is different*.

Time and time again, I've seen ignorance about UNIX result in inappropriate management decisions. A nontechnical manager's time is extremely limited, and so extensive UNIX technical education is probably not a practical option. That's why there are "Manager's Corner" sections in every chapter of this book. Their purpose is to spell out necessary management knowledge about UNIX.

Let's start with one important question. How many people does it take to run a UNIX system? You need to know the staffing requirements of your UNIX system when you request next year's budget. Those requirements depend on the size of your site, the number of users, the kinds of computers you have, and what your site applications are.

Small, stand-alone systems require one user who is able to administer part time. An in-house consultant or outside system guru may be needed occasionally, because unusual problems sometimes arise.[1] Medium-sized systems can survive with an administrator and a few support people. Large systems are challenging, full-time jobs for at least one system administrator and a staff of system programmers.

Let's define these terms: A *large-scale system* has an aggregate of at least 50 MIPs of computational power, several processors and machines, disk storage in decagigabytes, and one or more networks. The term *large-scale systems* can imply large mainframe computers and all the peripheral hardware that goes with them, or a conglomeration of networked stand-alones, workstations, and file servers. In today's era of connectivity there is also the built-in implication that the larger systems are networked to most of the company's smaller computers.

A *small system* is something like a stand-alone system of fewer than 10 MIPs with under 100 megabytes of disk storage. Small systems may be networked, but if the system is a network hub, it can no longer be designated as small. Administering small UNIX systems can be a full-time job for the individual who administers a score of them, or a part-time job for the individual who uses the system for his or her own work.

Specific Requirements of Large UNIX Systems

Large UNIX systems should have at least one full-time administrator or administrator-manager. You will need a minimum of one system programmer as a backup system administrator and to share administration tasks. Both the system administrator and the administering system programmer should be adept at writing their own administrative scripts.

---

[1] If your organization is large enough to support it, it will pay to have a UNIX center of competence that can run a consulting service for separate UNIX groups in the company.

Anywhere from one to three additional system programmers are also required, depending on how much local software needs development, how much local software needs support, and how much direct storage exists. If you intend to develop your own drivers, batch systems, or bill-back accounting systems, you will need at least one system programmer for each task. Expect system programmers to be literate enough to write documentation. Local code without thorough documentation isn't worth the cost of its backup tape.

Workstations and servers are special cases as they act as one large system and are heavily interdependent. The workstations are bound to the servers and cannot function without them. Special knowledge of the environment is needed, because workstations don't behave like separate systems. You will need one system administrator for your first 20 workstations and server, and you will need one more body for each additional twenty to thirty workstations with server.

How many system programmers you will need depends on the size of your UNIX systems. Whether virtual or real, each system requires time to maintain, and the more storage you have, the more time the system takes to administer. A virtual system resides on a host system like VM, and multiple virtual systems can exist on a single physical machine. VM is not only available on mainframes; VM software also exists on other architectures, including some micros.

Since good system programmers are expensive and hard to locate, find ways to offload programming and administrative tasks onto less skilled members of the staff. A *storage administrator* can take care of direct storage devices only. UNIX user administration can be handled by a user support group or a *user hot line*. Given well-written documentation and training, customer support can field all first-line questions, do initial problem resolution, and handle user administration with few problems. Problems too complex to be handled by the front line can be forwarded for resolution to system programmers and administrators. User administration groups should be located close to the system programming staff, to encourage their sharing news and information.

Some system work normally done by the system administrator or system programmers can be offloaded onto the operations staff. Given good documentation, tutorials, and training, operations can handle many arduous system administration tasks during off hours, such as system shutdowns and startups, system restores, and all backups. Restores should be shared between the hot line and operations because the restore request always comes to the hot line. A good backup system like Unitech's Ubackup or System V Release 4's `backup` command can be used to simplify backup tasks, reducing the time and skill required to do backups even further.

Staffing is a balancing act, so hire technical staff carefully. One skilled, knowledgeable employee does the work of three semicompetent ones, so look for the best and the brightest. On the other hand, two talented, junior programmers who are willing to learn can be of far greater use than one brilliant but temperamental "genius." If your budget is limited, it may be more cost effective to rely on outside consultants to do your occasional guru tasks.

CHAPTER

2

Day-to-Day Administration

The length of time spent performing routine system administration tasks varies from day to day, depending on how much time you have available. If you have a system crash or if you have scheduled major installations, you will use up at least a half a day. On some days the users will keep you continuously busy, whereas on other days you will find that you do have time to choose which system administration tasks to carry out. Your approach to system administration thus should be fairly flexible to allow for the varying conditions on your machine.

Your method of hands-on administration also may vary from day to day. On some days you may have to sandwich your routine administration chores in between meetings and "user interrupts." If you have not written your own custom system administration scripts, you will have to rely on typing in commands manually. On other days you may have enough time to write shell scripts to do some of your administration tasks for you. Occasionally you may even experience the luxury of having enough time to refine the scripts into C programs. You should be ready to operate at all levels to maximize the time available to you, for in this way you will be able to complete vital system administration tasks every day.

THE ONGOING TASKS OF DAY-TO-DAY ADMINISTRATION

Day-to-day system administration tasks keep the system alive, and they vary according to the size and nature of the computer site. For example, on sites with numerous networked workstations and servers, the first thing that system administrators should do is check to see if the servers are alive. Then they should check the network response. Finally they should check individual systems for disk fullness. Doing a simple df on each server while logged in accomplishes all three tasks. If the server is alive, it will respond. The speed of its response should indicate the condition of the network, and its response to the df command should supply the needed information about the disk system.

On small sites, system programmers often do double duty as system administrators, and the machine they work on may be the only one on the site. They issue a df first thing in the morning, and the speed of the machine's response is an instant indicator of its availability.

When system administrators of mainframe UNIX machines come to work in the morning, users may have been running background jobs all evening, and international users may have been doing interactive work on the system around the clock. In other words, the system that administrators see in the morning is not the same system they left the evening before. Consequently, there is much more system administration to do on mainframe UNIX sites.

Large-scale systems are interesting to use for studying system administration tasks because they are so big and have so many users. In this chapter many UNIX mainframe administration examples are used, because on a mainframe you will encounter problems daily that you will see only once a year on a midsize machine and probably never will see on a smaller machine. For example, the console log on a mainframe can go from empty to full in a matter of minutes.

UNIX system administration tasks vary from site to site because every UNIX site is different. As a result, presenting an orderly list of UNIX system administration duties would be misleading and would dilute the immediacy of what it is actually like to be a UNIX system administrator. To keep a real-world flavor, most of this chapter is based on my actual experiences as a UNIX system administrator on two sites, one with mainframe UNIX machines and the other with Sun workstations networked to Sun and DEC file servers. The mainframes ran AT&T System V UNIX; the workstations ran Berkeley UNIX 4.3; and the servers ran Berkeley UNIX 4.2. If the day-to-day tasks in this chapter differ a bit from those on your site, don't worry about it. Study the techniques, and extrapolate the pertinent information for your UNIX computer environment. For example, those with computers too small to have console logs can learn some useful techniques for handling their own error logs. Knowing about UNIX system administration for different versions of UNIX and different computer architectures is job insurance.

When I administer UNIX on several mainframe machines, during the first 45 minutes of my day, I run scripts designed to give me feedback about vital areas on all the machines. A "good-morning" script does the following:

- Tests the local network for loading.
- Checks for sign of life in all file servers and large, stand-alone systems.
- Determines the block node and inode count of critical system disks.
- Reads root's mail looking for error messages.
- Determines the current status of critical system daemons.
- Looks for megafiles in /usr.
- Restarts the console log[1] and runs the current console log data for the previous 24 hours through another script in order to categorize errors.

---

[1] By restarting the console log every day, a new file is written every 24 hours, and each file is dated.

On Mondays there is the additional work of weekend trash cleanup and making sure that site-specific programs, such as a bill-back accounting program, have run.

Once I have the information from these scripts, I can gauge the amount of time I will need to allot to each area. I spend at least half a day doing ongoing system administration tasks, and if I have more time, I will spend more time.

Morning Cleanup and Inspection

Whether or not they use scripts, system administrators start their morning cleanup and inspection after verifying the status of various site-specific programs. The first thing they do is see whether the system has enough space to operate. The critical file systems are

- `/` (root)
- `/usr`
- `/usr/spool`
- `/var` (BSD 4.3, AT&T 5.4)
- `/usr/spool/console`
- `/tmp` (not usually a separate partition)

On my machines each critical file system has its own disk partition, and so let's discuss each one.

The `root` Disk

The `root` disk needs both space and inodes to survive. It can't write the little temporary files it needs to operate if it runs out of space, because the system will appear hung. For all practical purposes it is. It's bad news, therefore, if it runs out of inodes, because you can't do a system generation (see Section III).

`/usr`

Keeping `/usr` at a manageable size is important enough. Granted, it may not hang the system when it fills, but it will stop many user processes, because there's no room to write. Also, `accounting` turns off.

`/usr/spool` and `/var/spool`

On networked systems and systems with high printer activity, `/usr/spool` and `/var/spool` bring work to a halt when full. BSD 4.3, AT&T System 5.4, and SunOS use `/var` as the storage place for highly dynamic file systems such as spoolers and logs.

`/usr/spool/console`

The system complains about its errors to the console and to `root`. Some installations have a human being at the console; others send console output to a printing terminal or to a console log file. The large system console's output is redirected to /usr/spool/console. You usually won't find a console file on small systems, and so they complain to files like /usr/adm/messages (BSD and XENIX), /usr/adm/error, or /usr/spool/error.

If there is any danger of error messages filling the disk overnight, give that section of the system its own disk partition. If /usr/spool/console has its own disk and the console disk fills, then only the daemon writing to the disk will be killed.

/tmp, /var/tmp, **and** /usr/tmp

Because /tmp is the system's scratch pad, educated users use /tmp for a scratch file system and write temporary files to it. You may wish that all users would remove those temporary files as their programs terminate, but there always will be some users who won't. As a result, /tmp has to be watched by both a cron-run cleanup script and a system administrator. Later in this chapter we shall look at a script called /etc/cleanup that does exactly that.

Miscellaneous File Systems

If your company has decided to use UNIX mail for company Email, then /usr/mail (Edition 7), /usr/spool/mail (BSD 4.2, XENIX, and UNIX System III), or /var/spool/mail (SVR4 and 4.3 BSD) will become a virtual spooler that deserves its own disk partition and special surveillance. Spoolers have to be able to fill and empty rapidly, and because they are critical to the system and its users, their maintenance is important.

You can't depend on users to read their mail and clean out their own mailboxes. Years ago I got fed up finding user mailboxes constantly clogging up the machine with unread mail, and so I wrote a program that searched daily for mail, sent full mailboxes to the printer, and then erased mail files. Users who didn't read their mail found empty mailboxes on the system and full ones in their physical mail slots. The system ran better, so this solution was successful. But naturally, it works only where computers, printers, and physical mail bins are central and serviced by the same operations staff.

Read root's Mail

If /usr fills, accounting will turn itself off, a disaster if you're using accounting. A lot of error messages are then sent to root. You will hear about the damage in time if you read root's mail, so read it when you start your day and frequently thereafter.

Check System Daemons

The next step in the "good-morning" routine is to see whether the system's critical daemons are still alive. If not, they must be restarted. To see what all processes except gettys are doing on the system, try this:

```
$ ps -ef!grep -v getty
```

If you run Berkeley, SunOS, or ULTRIX, do this:

```
% ps -qax!grep -v tty
```

Here is one way to see a specific process, like cron:

```
$ ps -ef!grep cron
```

In this, by showing its process table information, the command line determines whether cron is alive and well.

In Search of Overgrown Files

Although /usr has more closets, attics, and basements to hide trash than an old farm house has, if you are desperate, you can always do an

```
# ls -1R /usr
```

which not only gives you a long list (-1 option) but also recursively lists subdirectories encountered (-R option). Since you are only looking for very large files, why not let the find command do the searching for you?

```
#  find /usr -type f -size +50000c -print
```

This tells the system, "Look for any files in /usr larger than 50,000 characters, and print the file name."

Network Administration

Don't forget to test local network access. If you can telnet or rlogin in and out, then all's well as far as the wire goes. The network must be tested frequently: ping or spray work well and give good feedback. Sun's traffic command is an excellent tool, giving a graphic look at the network. When a network goes out, the users will tell you quickly, but test it yourself just in case no one needed to access the net. Become familiar with the network commands, and test with them often.

Scripts Do It Better

Clearly, it is easier and faster to roll all this system administration checking into one "good-morning" shell script. This one is called dfall:

```
df -t / /usr /usr/spool /usr/spool/console /tmp
ps -ef!egrep 'cron!telnet'!fgrep -v grep
ls -l /usr/mail/root
echo "large files:"
find /usr -type f -size +50000c -print
```

As your watchdog needs vary, alter the script accordingly. Enlarge the script to cover other needs of your system. You can call a script like the following from your .login or `.profile` when monitoring multiple systems. You can also execute it with `uux` from a single machine across all machines to be checked:

```
:
for system in stalker hunter1 cj root
  do
    uux "${system}!/local/etc/dfall>!/tmp/${system}"
  done
sleep 300
for ${system} in stalker hunter1 cj root
  do
    echo "\n\necho ${system}\n"
    cat "/tmp/${system}"
    rm  "/tmp/${system}"
  done
echo
```

Here the shell passes the list of system node names to the `uux` line, and `uux` then calls each local `dfall` script. The results are written to `/tmp` and then copied to the screen.

If you have emerged from the dark ages of hardwire networking by `uucp` and `uux` and made it to the Ethernet, here is a YP version:

```
#
foreach system (`ypcat hosts!awk '/128.216.53/ { print $2 }'`)
    rsh $system /usr/local/etc/dfall
end
```

This C-shell script obtains its list of systems from the Yellow Pages data base via `ypcat`. It uses `awk`'s pattern-matching ability to get all the systems on this Class B network by using its network number (less the host number) as a pattern. Then `rsh`, the remote shell, executes the system administrator's script on the remote system, and its results are displayed on the local system. Without YP, the hosts can be taken directly from `/etc/host` by `awk` or `grep`.

Search-and-Destroy Mission

After a cursory check of each file system, it is time for a closer look. Find out which areas are filling from the first morning scripts. Now move into these `/usr` or `/var` areas and initiate a search-and-destroy mission. The goal is to remove files that are old or transient.[2] Move from `/usr/spool` to `/usr/adm` to `/usr/spool/uucppublic` to `/usr/spool/uucp/*`, and so on, doing an `ls -l` and removing appropriate files.

Experience tells you which files to classify as old; it depends on where you are in the system:

1. No user files should be left in `uucp` or `uucppublic` for over four days, because they are dropped there by `uucp` when they can't be written to a user's file system. Have the user take them out, and then remove the spooled copy.

---

[2] Transient files are created specifically to be moved somewhere else or to be removed shortly after their creation.

2. Show no mercy in /tmp. Remove all files over an hour old. If you find a user file tree there, destroy it. No directories belong in /tmp. I have an agreement with users stating clearly that /tmp is the system's temporary area, used for transient files only. Users are warned that it will be cleaned out regularly without prior warning.

3. The home of all sorts of error and log files is /usr/adm. Once these files have outlived their usefulness, they are history. Files, like system error files, would grow forever if unchecked. They must be truncated.

4. Any accounting files over two months old can be considered tired enough to trash.

5. [Mainframes only] Console log files over one week old are ancient history. Get rid of them. Spooled file images will be left in /usr/spool/rdr if a file has been transferred to Amdahl's UTS UNIX by the vmread command. If they are over an hour old, destroy them; they already have been delivered to the user's file system.

In Search of Errors

After your initial search-and-destroy mission, move to the console logs for the period since you were last on the system. Console logs are error logs. If your system doesn't have a console log, try /usr/adm. If the log or error files are small, parse them visually with the editor in read-only mode.[3] If you find a 100-kilobyte console log, start at the end and search backward with regular expressions on key words like space, overflow, too large, and error.

Specific machines have specific errors. I had one set of mainframe systems running a language called MAINSAIL, which could throw 10 megabytes of stack too large errors in an evening. Another problem I had was that whenever the users got to the final stages of their projects, the console log filled with out of disk space errors. For problems like this, the system administrator needs to note the errors, contact the users or their managers, report the problems, and determine how they can be corrected.

Reading a few thousand lines of the console log can be such a discouraging proposition that sometimes it's tempting to put it off. You never have time to read every last line of the console log, but you also know that you can easily miss something important if you rush through it. So why not write a script to read the log for you and summarize into a few lines of output the errors you need to see? Here is one of the scripts that I have used. The key lines are those that count errors:

```
$ cat /local/etc/consck
:
if [ $# -eq 0 ]; then
    echo "usage: consck cons_file [anything]"
    echo "any character gives filtered output"
    exit 1
 fi
if [ -f $1 ]; then
    echo "\t\tConsole file: $1"
    else
      echo "${1} is not a legitimate file"
        exit 1
 fi
```

---

[3] You parse them in *read-only* mode because they are already being written to by the process that created them. You should never allow a file to be held open for a write by two processes!

```
echo "stack errors: \c"
 grep stack $1;wc -l
echo "disk full errors: \c"
 grep space $1;wc -l
echo "ethernet errors: \c"
 grep unknown $1;wc -l
echo "not found errors: \c"
 grep found $1;wc -l
echo "find errors: \c"
 grep find $1;wc -l
echo "CPMSG messages: \c"
 grep CPMSG $1;wc -l
echo "\nout of space on disk: \c"
 addr=`grep space $1;sort -u +9`
 echo ${addr}
if [ $# -eq 2 ] ; then
    echo "\n\tOther errors: \c"
    grep -v ACCT $1;egrep 'find;found;unknown;space;stack;CPMSG;LOGIN'
 fi
fi
exit 0
#
# consck
# a script to count error types and optionally output uncommon errors
# BHH 8/2/88
# UTS UNIX
```

The following lines test for the argument:

```
if [ $# -eq 0]; then
    echo "usage: consck cons_file [anything]"
    echo "any character gives filtered output"
    exit 1
 fi
```

This if-then-else construct tests for a legitimate console file:

```
if [ -f $1 ]; then
    echo "\t\t Console file: $1"
    else
      echo "${1} is not a legitimate file"
        exit 1
 fi
```

The next part of the code searches for specific errors and pipes them to wc for a line count:

```
echo "stack errors: \c"
 grep stack $1;wc -l
echo "disk full errors: \c"
 grep space $1;wc -l
echo "ethernet errors: \c"
 grep unknown $1;wc -l
echo "not found errors: \c"
 grep found $1;wc -l
echo "find errors: \c"
 grep find $1;wc -l
echo "CPMSG messages: \c"
 grep CPMSG $1;wc -l
```

Then the code finds the address of the filled disk:

```
echo "\n out of space on disk: \c"
addr=`grep space $1|sort -u +9`
echo ${addr}
```

Now if there is a second argument, the program will filter out all previously covered errors and print out any remaining errors:

```
if [ $# -eq 2 ] ; then
    echo "\n\tOther errors: \c"
    grep -v ACCT $1|egrep 'find|found|unknown|space|stack|CPMSG|LOGIN'
fi
```

Typical consck output looks like this:

```
$ cd /usr/spool/console
$ /local/etc/consck Sep06
    Console file: Sep06
stack errors:       2
disk full errors:   88
ethernet errors:    62
not found errors:   0
find errors:        28
CPMSG messages:     14

out of disk space on disk(s): W os/alloc.c(alloc): no space on disk 772s0
```

Notice that consck not only breaks down the error messages but also outputs how many times each kind of error has occurred. This is important. Once I caught a channel check error message with this program (channel check are key IBM words that raise a system administrator's blood pressure instantly). Immediately I contacted the field engineer—someone who does most of the hardware work on the machine—and gave him the channel address. The system was saved before any damage was done.

Mainframe console logs normally have 16 to 30 kilobytes of information, but on a bad day I've seen it go as high as 3 megabytes. The odds of catching a one-line channel check error message are slim if you look through each line of the console log. The consck program filters out the error messages, however, so problems stand out like sore thumbs.

Users and Disk Space

When users have full disks, it may not be your *job* to clean out the disks, but it will be your *problem* if users don't clean them. Notify the group representative or each user whose user disk is full. They will already know it unless they are batching a job or running a job in the background with their standard error redirected to /dev/null. Remind them that disk space is a finite resource and that they need to clean out some of their stuff. Make helpful suggestions, like telling them they can request a backup or special archive.

Users need to know that their data are going to be safe. If you say, "Don't worry, I've backed up all your data," that may be only as reassuring as "Your check is in the mail," or one of those other famous promises. On the other hand, how can they help but know their data are safe if the backup tape is in their own desk drawer? On systems in which tape security is not a problem, I make a tape archive of the users' files and give it to them or their manager. The physical possession of the tape gives them a sense of security, and so they will be more willing to clean house.

This solution is a maverick approach, but what can a scratch tape cost? A new 2200-foot tape is worth $17. A scratch tape is probably worth less than $5. Now what does a fast-access 800-megabyte disk drive and controller cost? It doesn't take an accountant to tell you that tape is cheap compared with direct-access storage.

ELECTIVE TIME OR OTHER DAILY TASKS

Once you have finished the morning's administration chores, you have elective time. You usually will use that time to do other pressing system administration tasks, tie up miscellaneous loose ends, or even catch up on some needed programming. The following are some of the system administration chores that you might do during elective time.

Unscheduled Cleanup Areas

Morning cleanup takes care of the daily spill-and-mop-up problems, but there are always unscheduled cleanup areas that you should attend to whenever you have the chance, such as

- /usr/spool/uucp and /usr/spool/uucppublic
- /usr/spool/mail or /usr/mail
- /usr/adm
- /usr/spool/log
- all monitors
- all logs
- miscellaneous system mailboxes for users like lp and bin

Systems without a console log rely heavily on their error log. A good example is ULTRIX's /etc/uerf data file /usr/adm/syserr/syserr* (uerf is the ULTRIX error formatter). Its log can grow quickly when the system is troubled, and if it is left uncleaned, it will get the system into even more trouble for lack of disk space. Regularly clean out or truncate all such files.

You can also cruise around the systems looking for core files and old a.outs files: core files are created when an interrupt forces a core dump. Say a user executes a bad program, called badprog. This is what she will see:

```
$ badprog
core dumped
```

She then will see the following in her directory when she does an ls:

```
$ ls
  badprog
  core
```

Why users don't remove these files is a mystery, but you find them everywhere. Not to worry. A pedestrian UNIX system script run by `cron` is well suited to this cleanup task:

```
$ cat /etc/cleanup
(
 find / -type f \( -name core -o -name a.out -o -name dead.letter \)\
   -atime +1  -exec rm -f {} \;
 find /usr/spool/console -type f -mtime +7 -exec rm -f {} \;
 find /usr/preserve -type f -mtime +15 -exec rm -f {} \;
 find /usr/mail -type f -atime +14 -exec rm -f {} \;
) >/dev/cons 2>&1
```

Remember that there are small differences among UNIX systems. For example, the file name /usr/spool is /usr/spool/mail on pre-UNIX 5.2 systems, XENIX, and BSD.

Use the `find` command interactively if you have to do the cleanup manually:

```
$ su
$ password:
# find / -name core -type f -exec rm {} \;
```

Console Log

Sending all system error output or redirected /dev/cons output to a console log is a good idea. The preceding `cleanup` script shows how to direct command output to the console log by way of /dev/cons. Your system may not have a console log, but it is easy enough to make and support.

The console log tells you who has come and gone, what devices complained, what error messages were sent to `root`, and other such information. The log becomes so large on large systems that it's unreadable in the editor, and so it must be closed periodically and a new log file reopened. Find the console log daemon and kill it. In the following example, the daemon is /etc/osmcat:

```
$ su
password:
# ps -ef|grep osm|grep -v grep
root  213     1 0  07:45 ?  0:00 cat -u /dev/osm
# kill -9 213
# /etc/osmcat
console logging started
```

The names and places may vary from system to system, but the method is the same. The `ps` command is `grep`ed to find the process-ID number of the console logging daemon. Once found, the number is used to kill the daemon, and once killed, the daemon is restarted to create a new log file.

On systems with no console log file, from time to time the error log or message log must be either truncated or cleaned out:

```
$ cd /usr/adm
$ ls -l messages
-rw-r--r--  1  bin  bin   48926 May 28 11:48  messages
$ su
password:
# cp messages Omessages
# >messages
# vi Omessages
```

By using the shell redirection metacharacter, **>**, either to create a file if one doesn't exist or to overwrite one if it does, messages are overwritten with nothing:

```
# >messages
```

The end effect is to remove the contents while leaving the file name and permissions. The inode and directory entries remain.

This kind of blank redirection won't work on BSD, so you have to redirect /dev/null to the file:

```
# cat /dev/null>messages
```

sendmail

If sendmail is active on your systems, it has to be cleaned regularly. Watch and clean its log file. All mail and message facilities require constant cleaning, particularly those that access a network. If you hate to pick up after others, system administration may not be the job for you.

Making lost+found

Have you had a system crash lately? You ran fsck and the system was a mess. Did you remember to clean out lost+found? (Create lost+found directories on every mounted file system.) When fsck cannot reconcile an inode with a directory entry, fsck puts the orphaned file in lost+found. Thus if root writes a temporary file on the root disk and the system dies without its final sync, the file will still exist, even though there may be no directory entry for it. Then fsck makes an entry in /lost+found with the inode number as a name.

An ls -l of each lost+found directory shows the size and owner of all entries. The file command tells you the type of file:

- data
- executable
- text
- nroff
- troff

If they are system-owned files, it will be up to you either to keep or discard them. Most system-owned files in lost+found are trash. Take a quick look, and then either move or remove them. Files owned by users should be identified and the owners called or mailed. Give them a few days. If uncollected, trash the files.

There may still be one more task after recovering from a crash. Did the kernel dump? If so, move the dump to 0dump so that the next crash won't overwrite it. Read it if you can. If not, send it to the supporting vendor with a copy of the current kernel as it was at the time of the crash, and let him read the tea leaves. Then tail the end of your console, error, or message log at the end of the crash. Find out either the reason for the crash or the events leading up to it. *The cost of not understanding history is having to repeat it.*

A few last words about lost + found: The lost + found directory must be *slot-ted* with about 50 entries in its directory file. Here is the end of an od dump of lost + found:

```
          \0  \0    x   z    2 \0   \0 \0   \0 \0   \0 \0   \0 \0   \0 \0
0001700   0000     7a78     0033   0000    0000    0000    0000    0000
          \0  \0    x   z    3 \0   \0 \0   \0 \0   \0 \0   \0 \0   \0 \0
0001720   0000     7a78     0034   0000    0000    0000    0000    0000
          \0  \0    x   z    4 \0   \0 \0   \0 \0   \0 \0   \0 \0   \0 \0
0001740   0000     7a78     0035   0000    0000    0000    0000    0000
          \0  \0    x   z    5 \0   \0 \0   \0 \0   \0 \0   \0 \0   \0 \0
0001760   0000     7a78     0036   0000    0000    0000    0000    0000
          \0  \0    x   z    6 \0   \0 \0   \0 \0   \0 \0   \0 \0   \0 \0
0002000
```

Notice that there are no inode numbers, only file names like xz6. The inode number was removed by the rm command.

Next we're going to look at a C program to create lost + found. The strategy is to get past the usual argument checking and to use mknod(2) to make the lost + found directory. System V Release 3 provides a mkdir(2) command to avoid the clumsiness of passing path, mode, and special arguments to the system call.[4] The program loops 255 times to make a 4096-byte directory, opening a new file on each pass through the loop. In fact, it is so good at loops that it does another 255 to remove each newly created file. As a result, the file names are left in the directory file, but the inode numbers are removed:

```c
/*
    mklf.c
    makes lost+found
    b h hunter 10/2/88
*/

#include <stdio.h>
#include <fcntl.h>
#include <sys/types.h>
#include <sys/stat.h>

main (argc, argv)
int argc;
char *argv [];
{
    int i, fd;
    char f_name[128];

    if (argc != 3)
    {
        fprintf (stderr, "usage: mklf /path/dir_name /dev/special\n");
        exit (-1);
    }
```

---

[4] The argument special is a device special file such as /dev/dsk/*s?.

```
    if ((mknod (argv[1], S_IFDIR:0700, argv[2])) == -1)
    {
        fprintf (stderr, "cannot make directory %s\n", argv[1]);
        exit (-1);
    }

    for (i = 0; i <= 254; i++)
    {
        sprintf (f_name, "%s/%d", argv[1], i);
        if ((fd = open (f_name, O_CREAT, 0600)) == -1)
        {
            fprintf (stderr, "cannot create %s%d\n", argv[1], i);
            close (fd);
        }
        close (fd);
    }
    for (i = 0; i <= 254; i++);
    {
        sprintf (f_name, "%s/%d", argv[1], i);
        if (unlink (f_name) == -1)
            fprintf (stderr, "mklf:  cannot remove %s\n", f_name);
    }
}
/**/
```

The program will be a little easier to read if you drop /usr/include/sys/types.h and /usr/include/sys/stat.h and do this:

```
mknod (argv[1], 0040774, argv[2])
```

instead of this:

```
mknod (argv[1], S_IFDIR:0700, argv[2])
```

*Or*ing bit masks with constants is not necessarily the cleanest way to go.

Note that mklf can be written in script as well. Most system code is not critical to performance, but mklf is an exception. It takes time to open 255 files and then remove them, and there is a definite performance hit with repetitious operations.[5] On lightly loaded systems it may make little difference; just run it as a background task:

```
$ cat /local/etc/mklf
:
if test $# -lt 1
    then
        echo "usage: mklf /path/dir_name"
        exit 1
 fi
if test -d $1
    then
        N_SLOTS=254
        cd $1
        mkdir lost+found
        cd lost+found
        i=0
```

---

[5] A performance hit occurs when CPU usage goes up markedly.

```
            while [ `expr $i` -le $N_SLOTS ]
                do
                    >$i
                    rm $i
                    i=`expr $i + 1`
                done
        exit 0
        else
            echo "${1} is not a legitimate directory"
            exit 1
fi
#    mklf -- make lost+found
#    BHH 10/4/88
```

A word on the scripts and programs in this book. Some of them were actual running programs on various machines that I have administered. A few I have simplified for this book to make their reading easier, and others are still in a rough state, similar to a sketch. I'm deliberately including them in this chapter, warts and all, to give you a realistic picture of doing UNIX system administration for a living. Many of the scripts and programs that you will write are not "picture perfect" but "quick and dirty." Often you will not have time to write truly finished code, with all the programmatic t's crossed and i's dotted. For instance, the last script will not have any protection if lost+found is already present. Other errors may befuddle your system as well. As long as a little script like this does the job in what precious little time you usually have, you can often make do with unfinished code for system administration tasks until you can find some spare time to bulletproof and polish it. If a piece of lightweight code like mklf script fails on an error condition, run it with the -x option of /bin/sh:

```
# sh -x /local/etc/mklf
```

If your code has to pass a peer-review programming committee, then protect it against all boundary conditions, and trap it well. Adding all the necessary error protection tends to obscure the original algorithm and make the logic of the code a bit harder for others to follow.

CPU Hogs

Watch out for CPU hogs. This command line

```
$ps -ef|grep -v getty
```

shows all the pertinent processes. Watch the next-to-last field, TIME, the time accumulated by each process:

```
  UID    PID  PPID   C    STIME TTY   TIME COMMAND
  root      0     0   0 21:08:12   ?   0:00 swapper
  root      1     0   0 21:08:12   ?   0:01 /etc/init
 bruce     33     1   0 08:58:14  01   0:02 -sh
 bruce     34     1   0 08:58:14  02   0:02 -sh
    lp     28     1   0 08:58:12   ?   0:00 /usr/lib/lpsched
  root     32     1   0 08:58:13   ?   0:00 cron
 bruce     35     1   0 08:58:14  03   0:02 -sh
 karen     36     1   1 08:58:14  04   0:02 -sh
 karen     47     1   0 08:58:14  2c   0:02 -sh
 karen    149   148  18 14:07:58  04   0:00 ps -ef
```

A large number shows a CPU hog or a process in trouble. Once I found `sendmail` accumulating half the total CPU time, clearly not a normal condition.

From time to time, users write their own monitors. Some of them not only eat up disk space but also consume vast amounts of CPU time. Seek out the process first, then the owner, and his manager. Have the user remove the process. If he won't, you will have to put your foot down. Kill the process, and give notice to the owner or his manager. There is no room on a system for an abuser; he will only steal the resource from the other users.

The act of killing processes is easy enough. With privilege you can do anything that skill allows you to do, but beware of abusing your own power. Don't kill users' processes without notifying the users first, and be courteous if possible. Naturally you can't be polite in an emergency when a process is threatening the system. Kill it first without remorse. Then notify the owner. If he can't be reached by phone, send him your regrets by system mail.

Some processes *cannot* be killed. They may operate at a kernel priority level below the "killable" threshold, but most of these unkillable processes fall into an interesting, curious category. Because of the way the UNIX kernel is written, a sleeping process will not awaken until a specific event occurs. It continues to sleep, waiting on an event called a *channel*. But what if that event never happens? The process cannot be killed until it has been awakened, so it will never be assassinated!

System administrators are a lot like police officers. They keep law and order on the system, which doesn't necessarily make them popular. They thus need all the good PR they can get. You'll keep a few feet ahead of user problems if you keep in touch with your users, are polite, and give a good guru service.

ADMINISTRATION THAT COMES TO YOU

Most system administration problems land in your lap unbidden. Usually you have to drop everything and deal with whatever comes your way.

Performance Watch

The minute you detect a degradation in system time, check the system. It is either at peak usage or there is a nasty problem lurking about. If your system is peaking, you must monitor its performance. Only during high-usage periods can the system administrator gather meaningful system statistics for system configuration and tuning. Watch particularly for the following:

- Buffer cache hit ratios.
- Buffer cache write-behind ratio.
- Kernel time versus user time.
- Page wait.
- Page rate.
- Fullness of certain vital kernel tables or buffers, such as process tables, file tables, inode tables, and clists.

Wherever the system consistently shows crowding, make it a little larger at the next system generation.[6] Conversely, wherever there is room to spare, cut back the system at the next sysgen. Large tables and buffers rob the users of memory and therefore needlessly increase paging. You must constantly strive for a balanced system.

Most UNIX system administrators have more work than they can handle, so give yourself a break and write a monitor script. Drive it during prime peak times from cron; then you can read it when time permits. This way you will "work smarter, not harder." Naturally you must remember to clean the monitor log regularly.

User Administration

User administration consists of the following tasks:

- Making user directories.
- Creating password and group entries.
- Getting disk space.
- Taking care of all login functions (adding, deleting, modifying).
- Handling group permissions and the group file, /etc/group.
- Changing ownerships and permissions.
- Moving users and user files.
- Updating the YP data base source files.

User-interrupt tasks can seem annoying in a crisis. When a user calls and stops you from doing "important" work, it is easy to forget that users are the reason that system administrators have a job. A system administrator is the only entity on earth that has to process more interruptions than an operating system does. It is to that end we serve.

Planned user administration requires something beyond adding and removing users. Small stand-alone systems have few user administration problems, so first-name user names are no trouble. But clearly, this casual approach is impossible on a large-scale system. The general rule for a log name is the first initial concatenated to seven or fewer letters of the last name. User Mike Woolhiser must settle for mwool, but he is used to it, and that is the way it must be.

On sites with many computers, you must be careful to keep user IDs constant across systems. For instance, if mwool has a user-ID number of 255 on one machine and 127 on another, he will lose ownership of his files when moving them from one system to the other. Thus a system must be created for uniform logins and user IDs. The Yellow Pages facility handles most of this. You just give it a little help:

```
% ypcat passwd!awk -F: '$3>99 { print $3 }'
```

Since there is only one password file source on the entire YP domain, all you need to do is filter its output for the user-ID number. With RFS, log names are resolved, and user-ID numbers are ignored.

---

[6] System V Release 4 allocates kernel table space dynamically, unlike all UNIX versions before it.

Password and User-ID Control

User password administration on multiple machines without YP requires the creation of a user-ID data base. Minimum requirements for the data base are fields for the user's real name, user-ID name, user-ID number, and group number. Check the data base to see whether the user exists before you issue him or her a user ID. If the user does exist, extract the user-ID number, user name, and user group.

Return the user IDs to the free pool when users leave the company. User-ID numbers are taken chronologically from low to high. Numbers returned to the free pool are held briefly and then used again. User-ID numbers from 0 to 100 are not given to specific individuals, but they are reserved for nonhumans, such as `root`, `lpadmin`, `bin`, and `unknown`. Number 100 frequently is reserved for the administrator, and numbers 101 to 199 similarly are saved for the system staff. It's nice to be able to see at a glance whether or not a process belongs to a person, by looking at the user-ID number.

Most systems have scripts that do menu-driven user additions, which have to be modified to access a central data base. If an OEM version exists, disable it by renaming it, and then replace it with a script instructing how to use the local version. Be sure that your local add-a-user script gathers information for an identity file. On System V Release 4 the user configuration management commands are `useradd`, `usermod`, and `userdel`.

Identity Files

There is not enough user information in `passwd`[7] and `group`, and therefore identity files are created. An identity file contains user information that can be used to locate users and bill back their usage to a specific group. The minimal necessary information is

- Log name.
- User-ID number.
- Real name.
- Group.
- Group-ID number.
- Phone number.
- Location (things like site, mail stop, and office number).
- Department number.
- Miscellaneous (such as temporary, contractor, FE, or SE).

The identity file is keyed to your `adduser` program, and it may be used by many programs on your system to give instant user data, like `whois`.

moduser

Your `moduser` program allows everything to be changed except the user's name and ID. Users' data must be changed when their working circumstances change. If they move to a different site, their phone numbers change, or they switch groups, the data in `passwd`, `group`, and `identity` must be changed by `moduser`.

---

[7] Recent releases use two password-related files, `passwd` and `shadow`. `shadow` is used to house the password encryption.

Once in place, the policing of the identity file is essential. Neglect this task, and bill-back accounting information will have errors. Unresolved charges will be dumped into overhead until overhead equals real charges, and your users will be charged unreasonably high overhead costs. Should that occur, depend on them to uphold a true American tradition: They will start a revolution.

MANAGER'S CORNER

Hiring System Programmers

Amazing as it may seem, when a nontechnical manager hires people to fill system programming positions, the decision to hire is not always based on their ability to program.

I know one company that had a strict management hiring policy. They only acquired people who had a 3.8 GPA or higher from an accredited school, and the better the school, the better the candidate's chances. This same company was more than happy to move their operators to UNIX system programmer positions without giving them classes in programming. Perhaps the rationale was that operators were steady workers who were good at their jobs in operations. Interviewing is time-consuming, and the operators were known quantities. Besides, the system programmers who applied for the jobs wanted much higher salaries! These nontechnical managers assumed that operators could be trained on the job fairly quickly by the other UNIX programmers and administrators, but they were dead wrong. UNIX is so complex, it takes several years of study to administer it proficiently. Programming is a craft that requires intense study and years of practice to master. Most of the operators who were promoted only had a superficial understanding of UNIX and they didn't know how to program, so they were completely out of their element as system programmers. This company trusted their precious data and all of their applications to the very people they wouldn't hire to create the data in the first place!

At another site I saw a key system programming position open up. Phil installed 55 workstations at that site in one year. Ed spent most of his time doing "something or other" at the terminal. Phil couldn't program his way out of a paper bag, but it was easy to see what he had accomplished. There were no workstations running when he started, but after a year the computer site was full of them. Ed was the first-class programmer who automated most of the systems, but his work didn't show. The manager at this site wasn't educated enough about workstations, UNIX, or programming to make the logical choice, so Phil was promoted instead of Ed. But you can't run a networked system without modifying some make files, and you can't do that without understanding how to program make, a Bourne-shell-like language used to maintain programs and systems like Yellow Pages. Ed the programmer could have taken it in stride, but Phil couldn't handle the job. It wasn't his fault; it was a poor management decision. This promotion was based on *perceived* performance. The manager had no concept of the importance of programming, nor did he understand the contributions made by his programmers.

In this chapter we have seen how maintaining current system scripts is not the most cost-effective way to do UNIX system administration. Creating new system scripts to automate as many system administration tasks as possible is the most efficent way to do the job, because the computer does the work that otherwise has to be done by several costly administrators.

In fact, the only way many UNIX systems can be maintained with a minimum number of support people is by creating custom system scripts, and only someone who knows how to program can do that.

System programming is a skill that should be highly prized. To run a UNIX system well, you must study some of the source code written in C, a sophisticated, extremely powerful programming language that can be learned and understood only by *people who already know how to program*. System programmers must be equally proficient in Bourne shell to understand vital scripts like rc and to do quick, efficient system administration work. If you are going to give your operators the chance to become system programmers, do them, yourself, and your company a favor and give them the education and training they need before they are expected to fill those jobs. Make sure they have several classes in UNIX, give them at least one class in UNIX networking, and above all give them the time they need to learn how to program. Be as careful in your choice of system programmers as you would be in choosing a comptroller or product engineer. Your company's future may depend on it.

3

Commands

CREATIVE USES OF COMMON COMMANDS

This chapter is not going to be a command-by-command tutorial. Many good UNIX books already do that, and you always have your manual for reference. Instead, we shall examine some of the commands a system administrator uses every day. Of all the hundreds of UNIX commands available, a select number are used repeatedly to administer the machine. You will already be intimately acquainted with most of the commands in this chapter if you do UNIX system administration for a living.

UNIX commands are potentially powerful tools for the system administrator. I don't mean that each command packs particular power and versatility. To the contrary, UNIX commands are inherently simple and single purposed, although sometimes commands are used to special advantage by means of specific flags. Naturally, as a system administrator you use some UNIX commands alone, but frequently you use commands in combination with other commands, because the overall power of each command is enhanced when you combine it with others for your particular use. The result is a custom administration tool set.

The plot thickens when you use the interesting assortment of filters built into UNIX, like grep or sed, to minimize command output or to convert data into information as the data are piped to another command. The grep command is an intriguing filter that converts data into specific information. You must *have* data before you can filter, and the most important system and user process data come from the ps command.

ps

The ps command reports process status, and it gets its information from the kernel's process table. Here are some of the members of the process table structure:

p_pri	The process priority: The lower the number is, the higher the priority will be.
p_time	Residence time used by the scheduler.
p_cpu	CPU usage, used for scheduling.
p_nice	The nice value, also used for scheduling.
p_euid	Effective (not real) user ID.
p_gid	Effective (not real) group ID.
p_pgrp	The process group leader.
p_pid	The process-ID number.
p_ppid	The parent process ID.
p_sig	Signals waiting on this process.

The ps command has 12 possible flags, which vary with the UNIX version. The combinations -ef and -efl get you most of the system administration information you need on UNIX System V and XENIX, and -ax and -lxa are the corresponding flags on Berkeley versions of UNIX. However, whether BSD or System V, the ps command gives you more information than you want.

Wouldn't it be nice if you didn't have to look at 100 gettys every time you typed in ps? Filter the data by combining ps with grep, and you won't have to. For System V use this:

```
$ ps -ef!fgrep -v getty
```

For BSD this does the trick:

```
% ps -qax!grep -v getty
```

Either way, the -v flag is a grep option that cancels every line with the string or substring that you use as an argument, which in these examples is getty. In the System V version, fgrep stands for *fast grep*, a smaller and quicker version of grep that does no metacharacter expansion.

What if you are looking for something specific in the process table? You need to look at the cron daemon to see whether the system's user-level scheduler is alive:

```
$ ps -ef!fgrep cron!fgrep -v grep
root  36  1  0  10:31:10  ?  0:00 cron
```

The second fgrep in the command line kills the line of ps output showing the grep process itself, fgrep cron.

The system administrator frequently needs process table information, and the command lines ps -ef (SV) or ps -ax (BSD) are useful:

UID	This is the user.
PID	This is the process-ID number. If you don't know it, you can't kill it.

| PPID | This is the parent process-ID number. If the process you are trying to kill keeps respawning under another number, kill the parent. |
| STIME and TIME | STIME is the start time. TIME is the accumulated time. Processes starting a long time ago and accumulating a lot of CPU time are suspect. Check these processes right away. |

You may not be familiar with the process table unless you have some knowledge of internals, the scheduler, and the scheduling algorithm. If you do understand internals, you can rely on the command lines ps -elf (SV) or ps -lax (BSD), because they generate even more important process table information, including

process flags	These tell you if processes are swapped, in core, or in some other condition.
process state	This tells you if the process is sleeping, waiting, or in some other state.
WCHAN	This is the wait channel, the *event* on which the process is waiting or sleeping.

You also get this handy information:

- The current scheduler value for "sandbagging" the process.
- The priority number (the highest number has the lowest priority).
- The process nice number.
- The memory address of the process pointer.
- The process block size.
- The tty (terminal or console) of the process (? means none).
- The time accumulated by the process.
- The command name.

Take a look at the /usr/include/sys/proc.h header file on your machine. It defines the process table. You'll see the correspondence between the proc structure members and the long output of the ps command pop right out at you.

Here's a sample of some ps -elf (SV) output:

```
$ ps -elf
F   S UID   PID PPID C PRI NI ADDR SZ   WCHA  STIME    TTY   TIME CMD
3   S root  0     0  0  0 20  4c  0   140d0 21:40:12   ?    0:00 swapper
101 S root  1     0  0 30 20  6d 16   afa8  21:40:12   ?    0:01 /etc/init
101 S bruce 43    1  0 30 20  76 20   b050  10:27:22   01   0:02 -sh
```

The second field, S, shows that all three processes are sleeping.

grep

A nifty filter, grep is not only useful but also fun to play with. Imagine looking for all references to the lp spooling system in the system initiation files. Where do you start? Take advantage of grep's ability to use a metacharacter's meaning in grep's file argument.[1] You can obtain specific system administration information when you substring-search the files.

Here `grep` is used to examine multiple files:

```
$ grep lp /etc/rc.d/*
/etc/rc.d/printers:/usr/lib/lpsched
```

The `/rc.d` directory is peculiar to AT&T machines. Do a `grep` of `*rc*` in the `/etc` directory on other systems.

Furthermore, `grep` isn't thrown by non-ASCII (data) files. The `lp` initialization file is `/etc/rc.d/printers`, and `rc.d` is the local rc directory on AT&T 3B micros. On other machines the initialization material is in a pair of files, `rc` and `local.rc`. Thus the following finds `lp` information on most UNIX systems:

```
$ grep lp /etc/rc
rm -f /usr/spool/lp/SCHEDLOCK
rm -f /usr/spool/lpd/lock
[ -x /usr/lib/lpsched ] && /usr/lib/lpsched
```

Here `grep` pulls out all lines with the substring `lp`.

If you want to have the line number where the substring occurs, the `-n` flag will do the trick nicely:

```
$ grep -n lp /etc/rc
64:rm -f /usr/spool/lp/SCHEDLOCK
65:rm -f /usr/spool/lpd/lock
66:[ -x /usr/lib/lpsched ] && /usr/lib/lpsched
```

Sometimes you use `grep` to do unusual things, such as finding the spelling of a word. To find out how to spell *scenario*, use `grep` with `look` to find a word that starts with *sc* and has the letters *io* in it:

```
look sc!fgrep io
```

Whereas this command line returns only the word *scenario*, `look sc` fills your screen nine times, generating over two hundred words.

Piping to `grep` while using the `ps` command saves you search time. The time saved in an eight-hour day is enough for an extra coffee break.

Read-Only Editor

Searching a writable file with an editor can be dangerous, especially if you've had a long, stressful day. One slip on a line, say an accidental delete or insert, and you will have changed the file. Also, files that may be written to by another process should never be needlessly opened for writing by the editor: `/etc/passwd` is the prime example. When you are a superuser with access to protected system files, you can get into a world of trouble when you least expect it.

Knowing how to use the right flag is very important. On most editors the `-R` flag gives you *read-only* access and removes the danger. Again, this is particularly true when reading the `/etc/passwd` file. Just being in the `/etc/passwd` file in *write* mode

---

[1] Metacharacters refer to the characters used in regular expressions such as wildcard characters, pipes, and redirection.

is dangerous. Irreparable corruption is a strong possibility if another write is attempted while you are accessing passwd.

Once I hired a consultant who was supposed to be a system administrator. She spent a full morning editing the passwd file directory in *write* mode on an active machine. She not only corrupted the password file, but by the time she left the editor, the system was no longer accessible! If you have to modify /etc/passwd, avoid this catastrophe by copying passwd to another file called Npasswd, or some similar name. Edit the new file. Check it with pwck to see whether it is good. Copy the passwd file to Opasswd to be safe. *Then* copy Npasswd to passwd.

ed

As system administrator you must bite the bullet and learn to use the primitive editor, ed.[2] It doesn't make any difference which editor you prefer. Your favorite editor probably won't be available when the system is in single-user mode, init level s, so sometimes you will be stuck with ed. When system administrators have to revive a crippled machine, their resources are limited, and ed will be the only show in town. You will make a miserable situation worse if you wait until you are under fire to learn the ed editor, so take a few minutes every so often to practice using ed. During your next emergency you'll be very glad you did.

The ed editor can be particularly useful in scripts using a *here document*. A here document uses the metacharacter << followed by a user-defined character to read everything following in the script as if it came from the user's terminal.

In my early days as a novice system administrator I once requested that all users add a command to their .profile file to query the host system console log. About one-third of them did. When the scheduled shutdowns were posted in the console log, the rest of the users complained that they had been hit by "unscheduled" shutdowns. I learned a valuable administration lesson from this: *Never leave up to the users what you need to do yourself.*

In response I wrote a script to go down the list of user IDs and write q log to the end of each .profile and .login, using the ed editor with a here document.[3] A few hundred files were modified in a few seconds:

```
$ cat qlog
:
for homes in `awk -F: '$3>99 { print $6 } ' /etc/passwd`
  do
    echo $home
    ed $home/\.profile<<!
    a
q log
.
    w
    q
!
    done
exit
```

---

[2] There are a few good tutorials on ed, and one of the best is in the back of Brian Kernighan and Rob Pike, *The UNIX Programming Environment* (Englewood Cliffs, NJ: Prentice-Hall, 1984).

[3] I could have used sed, the streaming editor, but that would have required the use of a temporary file and thus an extra *write* and an erase operation that ed avoids.

Note that q log, !, and . are deliberately placed squarely against the left margin. I prefer indented, structured code within the do-done construct, but /bin/sh is syntactically picky and doesn't allow it. Furthermore, sh expects to find the *bang*, the *dot*, and the *here-document* escape right after a newline. Everything from the << to the ! becomes the standard input for the ed editor. Granted, adding q log to /etc/profile would have been faster, but that takes away the user's option of being able to remove it at a later date.

fsck

Regular use of fsck is a system administration ritual. It's your first line of defense against file system corruption. You check the system with fsck whenever it comes up, and if you have the faintest suspicion that a file system has been corrupted during the day, you should fsck-check it again. Most contemporary UNIX systems have a file showing the status of the last shutdown. If the shutdown was not graceful, such as when a system crashes, fsck will be run automatically. Let's take a look at some useful fsck options for the system administrator.

The -n Flag

Instead of unmounting a file system to make it quiescent, first test it with fsck -n. This checks a file system without modifying it or even asking if you want to do so. If your suspicions are confirmed and the disk is corrupted, *then* you can unmount and correct it.

The -y Flag

When you bring up a crashed system, the root file system probably won't pass fsck. The root directory constantly writes temporary files to its own disk, but the files fail to get written properly to disk when the system crashes, which is how inconsistencies creep in and cause trouble. Know your root disk address. When initiating the crashed system, clear the root disk *only*:

```
fsck -y /dev/dsk/c1d0s0
```

You will end up with this message:

```
***** BOOT UNIX (NO SYNC) *****
```

All should be ready to go on the second booting. Then you can check the entire file system.

Because the -y option is a blanket yes to everything, be careful when using it. It scrolls data up the screen before you can read all of them. If you use fsck interactively without -y, you will have all the time you need to jot down file system errors noted by fsck, because the system waits for your answer. This information is invaluable, particularly if it is found to be repeating. Running fsck output to the console log is even more helpful. Insist that your operations staff note and inform you of all such errors. The only exceptions are errors generated by fsck on a separate /usr/spool (SV) or /var/spool (AT&T 5.4, SunOS, and Berkeley 4.3). In this case, spooler errors usually can be ignored, except as a reminder to clean `/usr/spool/lost+found` or `/var/spool/lost+found`.

df

The first command to run each morning on every UNIX system is `df`. The `df` command reports the number of free blocks on any mountable file system. System V `df -t` (`df` on XENIX) gives you the total number of available blocks, particularly useful for the system administrator. Berkeley does this without any flags. Overflowing system files can cripple a system, so it is necessary to monitor system files regularly. On large or active systems it is advantageous to give each critical file system its own disk partition. Some critical file systems are `/`, `/usr/spool` or `/var/spool`, `/usr/spool/console`, and `/tmp`. Give the base or the system's portion of `/usr` its own disk also.

Issuing a `df` command to each partition separately, either manually or with a script, gives warning of pending system problems. The technique of issuing a `df` command to each partition separately is covered in numerous places in the book. The following `df` line shows at a glance the condition of the system's critical, mountable file systems:

```
df -t / /usr /usr/spool /usr/spool/console /tmp
.
.
```

In Chapter 2 we saw these lines displaying five file systems in the "good morning" script.

od

Editors and the `cat` command process file information in an orderly, prearranged, canonical fashion. A screen-oriented editor goes down to the next line when it sees a newline, and it expands to the next multiple of eight when it sees a tab. Editors and the `cat` command print ASCII characters 32 through 127, and they interpret newlines, returns, and tabs.

Other UNIX commands are not so polite. The `od` command is an underrated tool in the system administrator's bag of tricks, but it is brutally literal; so is the System V `dump` command that reads core.[4] Both print exactly what is in the file and act on nothing. Sometimes this is to your advantage.

Picture a scenario in which you are trying to remove a file, but it won't go away:

```
$ ls
file1
file2
bar
$ rm bar
rm: bar nonexistent
$ su
password:
# rm bar
rm: bar nonexistent
```

---

[4] There are two UNIX commands called `dump`. One is the UNIX backup command on Edition 7, BSD, XENIX, and AT&T 5.4, but `dump` was not present as a backup command on AT&T UNIX 5.2 and 5.3 UNIX. Those versions used the `dump` command for reading core.

```
# ls
file1
file2
bar
# rm bar*
rm: bar* nonexistent
```

Clearly, the only thing you are accomplishing is getting frustrated. Intuition tells you there is more than the eye can see.

Before you panic, do an octal dump with character display on bar's directory:

```
# cd ..
# pwd
/usr/snark
# od -c snark
0000000 006 186 . \0 ...
0000020 006 200 .  . \0 \0
0000040 006 217 f i l e 1 \0 \0 \0 ....
0000060 006 252 f i l e 2 \0 \0 \0 ...
0000080 006 307 f o o ^H ^H ^H b a r
00000A0
```

There it is! The bar file was originally foo, but the user backspaced three times and wrote bar, and his stty settings interpreted the backspace literally. When the system prints this file name, it prints foo, and faster than the eye can see, it backspaces and overwrites bar.

Now all you need to do is

```
# rm foo*bar
```

and the offending file will be gone.

Use the od command anyplace you need to sprinkle "magic dust" on the invisible to make it visible. When the manual talks about creating a lost-and-found directory and filling or slotting the directory, do you understand what is being said? It is crystal clear when you do an od -xc on the /lost + found directory. The directory has more than 4000 characters, including null bytes. They are file names without inodes, what I call *fileless files*. lost + found was created to initialize *slots*, entries in the directory, to make it easy for fsck to write to it; and od comes to the rescue again by making the invisible visible.

We've seen how rm can be used in conjunction with od. Let's look into the rm command further.

rm Command Humility Lessons

If you haven't accidentally erased more data than you originally intended, you haven't been on the system long. The rm command kills files. Used wisely, it does what it was designed for. Used carelessly, it kills without discretion. Wildcarding turns rm from a single-shot target gun into a fully automatic assault rifle. It lays down a rain of fire that destroys everything in a specific directory section. If you are going to use a wildcard character, be sure to use the -i flag to give you the interactive option:

```
rm -i snark*
```

At least this allows you the opportunity to preview a file name before committing to its destruction.

A little care and caution help. Watch how you can get in deeper trouble than you ever dreamed possible:

```
$ su
password:
# cd /etc
# ls local.junk
lp.tmp
garbage1
foo.tmp
# rm *
```

The expression "shooting yourself in the foot" doesn't even come close to what just happened. A system programmer lists a local repository of trash in a subdirectory of /etc. She forgot to cd to /etc/local.junk before typing in rm *, however, and as a result she absentmindedly killed everything in /etc. She either should have changed directories or used this syntax:

```
% su
password:
# pwd
/etc/local.junk
# rm /etc/local.junk/*
```

Let this be a solemn reminder to all of us. When removing files with a wildcard character, remember these rules:

- Always move to the directory where the file that you want to remove lives.
- Don't use wildcards without being extremely cautious.
- Do an ls with the same file name argument first so that you can preview the removal.

This is a happier scenario:

```
$ cd /usr/spool/rdr
ls *
file
file0
file1
.
.
.
$ su
password:
# rm file file?
```

Here the files to be removed are system-created spool files called /usr/spool/file*. Wildcarding is minimized by using the file name and a question mark. Use file? to take out file0 through file9.

Other metacharacters are helpful. Files are named by date in /usr/spool/console. For example, if it is March 30 and you want to clean out files from earlier in the month, here's what you do:

```
# cd /usr/spool/console
# ls
```

```
Mar01
Mar04
 .
 .
Mar11
Mar14
 .
 .
Mar30
# rm Mar[01]? Mar2[0-5]
```

This leaves the March files for the twenty-sixth and beyond.

Avoid the indiscriminate use of any command with a file argument starting with a period, known as a *dot*. The shell interprets a .* to mean not only files like .profile and .login but also the current and parent directories, . and .. So when you intend to get rid of a hidden directory, you could do this without thinking:

```
# rm -rf .*
```

Unfortunately, this takes out not only the entire directory you are in but also the one directly below it. To remove .profile and .login, therefore, do this:

```
#rm .[pr]*
```

There are always alternatives in UNIX. The expression .??* is "dot followed by any two printables, followed by anything or nothing." This expresses any dot file, and you could use it. Better yet, why overlook the obvious? Take the time to type out the file name in full.

The rm command isn't the only place to exercise caution with a dot reference. This command line

```
# chown achen * .* */* */*/*
```

was meant to give An-Nan Chen ownership of all files in the current directory, all dot files in the current directory, all files in the directory below it, and finally all files in the directory below that. It does all of that, but it also interprets .* to mean . and .., and so it gives ownership to Mr. Chen of everything in the directory above, as well. If that directory is /usr or some equivalent base for all users on your system, you will now have to spend the entire day and part of the next one straightening out file ownerships. Try

```
# chown achen . .??* * */* */*/*
```

Should this give an argument too long error, you will have to use the find command:

```
# find . -exec chown achen {} \;
```

The real challenge comes when trying to remove a file called *, which is created inadvertently with sloppiness like

```
nroff -mm ../text/foo>>*
```

Here the user intended to append the only file in the directory but instead created a monster. Don't even think of doing an rm * or an rm *. Both are dangerous, and neither will do the trick. The shell won't interpret *, and it will take out everything but * with the first. Instead, do a full listing to ensure that there are no files with a single letter for a name. Now you simply do this:

```
$ rm -i ?
```

This safely removes the only file with the single character name, *.

Be careful with `rm -rf`, as it is a lethal combination. In the following innocent-looking example, Mr. Rieger's home directory and everything else in it, including directories and files, are removed, no questions asked:

```
rm -rf /group1/rrieger
```

If you have just backed him up to tape and are doing the removal at his request, you're fine. Otherwise, I hope you have a current résumé.

Needless to say, `rm` is a loaded gun. *Handle it with care.*

find

Few commands are as well named as `find`, and few are as handy to the system administrator. The `find` command does what it says—it finds things. Imagine having to find a source file for the memory section of the kernel code. Where do you start looking? The `/usr/src` directory has many branches. You may vaguely remember the file name was "mem something dot c," so you try this:

```
$ find /usr/src -type f -name "mem*.c" -print
/usr/src/uts/uts/os/mem2.c
/usr/scr/uts/uts/os/mem3.c
/usr/src/uts/uts/os/mem4.c
```

There you are. The `-type` flag and its `f` argument are used to search for files, not directories. Note that `find` uses about the same metacharacter interpretation as `sh` does.

The `find` command is a little bit of a pain because it is syntactically picky. You must give it a place to start looking. You must quote wildcards. You must tell it to print, or it won't. Without `-print` it will merely return a 0 or 1, depending on whether or not it found something.

The next example uses `find` in all its glory to search for potential su-shell programs. The desired result is to find all `root`-owned executables with the set-user-ID bit on:

```
find / -perm -04000 -user root -type f -exec ls -l {} \;
```

From left to right this `find` command line starts at the `root` directory, `/`. It looks for permissions with at least the set-user-ID bit on. The hyphen before 04000 gives the loosest interpretation. Note the 0 leading the 4000, guaranteeing it will be interpreted as an octal number. This is a UNIX convention. The file must be `root` owned. It must be type `file`. Finally, the information is passed to the `ls` command with the `-l` option to give `find`'s results to exec's command as an argument. The ending { } \; is mandatory, with the exec option to hand off the `find` output to the command in `exec` as an argument. The semicolon is also necessary and must be escaped from the shell.

A typical situation you might face as a system administrator is finding out that a critical system directory like `/usr` is nearly full. Because `/usr` is a huge file system, you could spend a full day manually wandering through the file tree and not finding all the branches. Let `find` do the searching for you. You can `find` on recent dates, files, or a specific size of greater than some number, and there are lots of other tricks. This command line finds all files larger than 10,000 bytes:

```
find /usr -size +10000c -print
```

This shows all files in `/usr` that have been written to in the last two days or less:

```
find /usr -ctime -2 -print
```

Now combine all the options, and you will get the following:

```
find /usr -ctime -2 -size +10000c -exec ls -l {} \;
```

The output of the last two `find` command lines all are files and directories that are greater than 10,000 bytes and have been written to in the last two days. This should go a long way toward finding what has filled `/usr`.

No users reside on `/usr` on my stand-alone systems. I like to keep `/usr` in the same pristine state as it was in the distribution tapes, with few exceptions. Nothing sits on top of it unless it has its own separate disk or disk partition precisely because I *don't* want `/usr` to fill in the way it does in this last scenario.

The results of `find` are also used to feed other commands. The following searches the system for core files left by careless users, and it removes all but `/dev/core`:

```
find / -type f -name core -exec rm {} \;
```

By using `-type f`, the accidental removal of the device special file, `/dev/core`, is avoided.

A classic use of `find` is to feed `cpio`:

```
find . -depth -print|cpio -pdl /grp2/archive/0410
```

Here `find` moves through the current file tree to the end of the branches, giving all the names of the files to `cpio`, a UNIX backup method that depends on other commands for input. The `find` command is ideal for feeding `cpio` backup data.

This brief description of good things to do with `find` hasn't even begun to detail all the uses of this versatile command. Next time you need a good challenge, go through your scripts and look for things that could be done better with the `find` command.

REGULAR EXPRESSIONS

We all use regular expressions in our day-to-day UNIX work. Regular expressions are a marvelous variation on the SNOBOL language, and they make system administration much easier. However, many administrators and system programmers not only keep the same minimal subset of regular expressions in their repertoire, but they also resist adding to their knowledge unless they have to. For example, most administrators I've known avoid learning `sed` and `egrep`. It's odd, because their other skills tend to increase the longer they are system administrators. Most get razor-sharp with `awk`, and many do a passable job with grep. They also are willing to explore the ramifications of shell programming. But I wish I had one hundred blocks of memory for each time someone has told me, "Why learn sed when I can do anything comparable with awk?"

Not everyone has a pioneering spirit, but if you're looking for adventure, relearn sed and revisit the intricacies of egrep. The path to mastering both sed and egrep begins with extending your knowledge of regular expressions. It seems that half the code in scripts is used to filter from one thing or another, so a skillful use of regular expressions is necessary. Then you must learn those important exceptions, the things that work for egrep that don't work for grep, sed, or ed.

The *not* Character

Let's start on a negative note with the *not* character, ^. Think about the kinds of things you do all day as system administrator, like looking through a list of users and finding everyone who does not have a login. Sometimes programming constructs do not give us exactly what we need to do the job. In fact, often what they do give us is the exact opposite of what we need. You could shotgun with

```
grep :: /etc/passwd
```

but that would also output all blank comment fields as well. However, consider the expression [^ :]. This means "a character that is *not* a colon." By saying

```
grep '^[^:]*::' /etc/passwd
```

we are telling grep to find a noncolon character starting a line, followed by zero to any number of repetitions of noncolon characters, followed by a pair of colons, ^[^:]*::. In plain English the full expression says, "Find a bunch of alpha characters followed by the first empty set of colons."

Tricky egrep

The egrep command name stands for extended grep. It does a few tricks that fgrep (fast grep) and grep can't, so it's good to get the hang of it. It can ask for one or more repetitions of a character:

```
egrep '^[^:]+::' /etc/passwd
```

This says, "I want at least one noncolon character, and I'll settle for any number of characters greater than 0."

Brackets are used for grouping as well as helping to parse the *not* character, ^. Alphanumeric characters can be expressed in this way:

```
[A-Za-z0-9]
```

When you print out text, make sure you haven't messed up any troff escapes. A mistake like \fBtroff\fp instead of the correct \fBtroff\fP needlessly wastes time, paper, and ribbon, because \fP stands for *previous font*. If the *previous font* was italic, other fonts in the text will be out of whack. You can use a quick check of text work using this:

```
egrep '\\f[BI][A-Za-z0-9]+\\f[^P]' /u/articles/rep
```

This says, "Look for any expression starting with an \fB (for **bold**) or an \fI (for *italic*), followed by one or more alphanumeric characters, followed by a not uppercase-P." You don't want a printout until you correct troff errors, and this is one way to help you find some of them fast.

Note that egrep can group together *logical or* regular expressions, and this feature comes in handy sometimes. Let's expand on the preceding little troff-checking line and put it into a script:

```
:
if [ $# -ne 1 ]
    then
        echo "usage mmck file_name"
        exit 1
 fi
egrep -n '\\[^BIP]!/f[BIP]!\\[^ef]!\\f[BI][A-Za-z0-9]+\\f[^P]' $1
mmcheck $1
exit 0
#
# mmck -- looks for wrongly formed font escapes
# bhh 1/21/89
#
```

The egrep line says, "Look for all font escapes that are not followed by a B, P, or I, *or* a B, I, or P preceded by a slash (not a backslash), *or* a backslash followed by a non-e character or a non-f character, *or* our previous expression. If any of these errors are found, print the error to the screen with the line number." In short, this line checks for almost any font error generated by fast, inaccurate typing.

You can use egrep to look for live daemons. Take advantage of the fact that egrep is able to *or* its expressions:

```
ps -ef!egrep 'cron!osm!telnet!rlogin!tftp!ftp'!fgrep -v 'grep'
```

Notice the ps output piped to egrep looking for cron, *or* osm, *or* telnet, *or* rlogin, *or* tftp, *or* ftp. The output is piped to fgrep to filter out any lines with the grep string itself.

To sed or Not to sed

Remember that sed can be *or*ed, too. Here is doti, a script that converts dot-I and dot-B -mm macro lines into nroff/troff primitives:

```
:
if [ $# -eq 0 ]
  then echo "usage: doti file_name"
  exit
 fi
cat $1!sed  's/\.I/\.B/p'!sed  's/\.B .*/&\\fP/p'!sed  's/\.B /\\f5/p'!
sed  's/ \\fP/\\fP/p'!sed  's/ ,\\fP/\\fP,/p' !sed  's/ .\\fP/\\fP./p'
exit 0
# doti  "dot I"
# converts old mm macro style files to nroff format
# bhh
```

This quick-and-dirty script looks for dot command lines like .I foo and converts them into \fIfoo\fP.

In a different script we'll see how to make better use of sed with a little script called doth (for "dot H"). This script gets you a listing of .H headers in a document; sed is used by feeding it a series of regular expressions separated by newlines effectively *or*ed:

```
:
egrep '^\.H [1-7]|^\.HU' $1|sed  's/\"//g
        s/\\f[BIP]//g
        s/.H [1-7]/ & /
        s/.HU/ &  /'
#
# doth
# outputs all headers in neat columns with heading levels marked
# bhh 12/1/89
```

In this, egrep starts the output by using the file sent to the script as its argument and filtering all lines starting with an .H (dot-H), followed by a blank, followed by 1 through 7 or a line starting with a dot-HU, .HU. Then sed picks up the data stream and removes all double quotes with an edlike expression:

```
s/\"//g
```

On the next line sed removes all nroff/troff primitive slash \fs followed by a B, I, or P. On the next line sed adds a leading and training blank to dot-H, 1-through-7 headers. On the last line it does the same to dot-HUs, but it adds two trailing blanks. All of this action is performed in the same sed command because the sed expression is separated by a newline. This trick is what makes sed able to deal with multiple expressions. Multiple calls to sed are eliminated.

Because sed was written as a streaming editor, naturally its primary purpose is to edit a data stream. How many times have you wanted to use only the second line of output and eliminate the first? This does the job nicely:

```
sed -n '2p'
```

You can get trickier and show a little more output. This line gets the number of blocks in a file system:

```
blocks=`df-t|sed -n 2p|awk ' { print $2 }'`
```

You end up with the second field of the second line, and sed allows you to get the line of output you want.

Let's look for time hogs, processes that are taking a large amount of CPU time from the system. We want the output of ps cleaned of all getty lines to clear the stream of unnecessary trash. Then we print out the third field:

```
ps -ae|fgrep -v 'grep'| fgrep -v 'getty'\
   |awk '{ print $3 }'|sort -n -r|sed -n '1,5p'
```

The awk output, the CPU time, is handed to sort and sorted as a number in reverse order. Finally, sed prints out the first five lines only.

Let's reach out a little and extend that line. Take the output from that line and capture it with set:

```
set `ps -ae|fgrep -v 'grep'|awk '{ print $3 }'|sort -n -r|sed -n '1,5p'`
```

```
ps -ef!sed -n '1p'
for time
 do
  ps -ef!grep $time!grep -v 'grep'
done
```

Here set is used to take the heaviest CPU times found in the process table output by the
first line, putting them in the positional parameters $1 through $5. In C shell this can
be avoided because its variables are vectors, single-dimensional arrays. Next the second
line, a sed line, simply prints the ps header, the top line of the ps command:

```
ps -ef!sed -n '1p'
```

Finally, the for loop uses the seldom-seen form in which the word in and the list are
omitted:

```
for time
 do
  ps -ef!grep $time!grep -v 'grep'
done
```

Normally we see this longer form:

```
for variable in this that the other
  do
     command $variable
  done
```

The simpler form in our script defaults to the positional parameters for the list that will
feed its values into the variable time.
        Is all of this extra work worth the time and trouble? In the long run, the ad-
vanced use of regular expressions sed, ed, grep, egrep, and fgrep will make your
code shorter and far more efficient. Even more important, it will allow you to do things
that seemed impossible before. Now throw in the use of awk in all its glory, and the world
is yours.

ADVANCED ADMINISTRATION COMMANDS

In this part of the chapter we shall take a look at a selected subset of administrative
commands.

Memory Formatters

Both the crash command and OEM system formatters like UTS UNIX's sysdump format
dump files and core images, such as /usr/adm/crash, /dump/dump, and /dev/kmem, to
make them readable. A *dump file* is a core dump of the kernel, forced when the system
crashes, and /dev/kmem is the virtual memory image of the kernel. Both are binary
images, readable by neither an editor nor by ASCII-oriented commands like cat.
        System formatters normally default to /dev/kmem for the core image and the disk
image of the kernel /unix for the symbol table. They allow examination of memory
contents and system tables. Each formatter is restricted to examining the items defined

in its repertoire of symbols. The extent of the repertoire depends on how much work was done by the system programmers who ported the system. This is why an OEM formatter like UTS UNIX's sysdump may well be more flexible than is a standard AT&T utility like crash (see Chapter 17).

uerf: **An Error Formatter**

Systems like DEC's ULTRIX write error information to a data file rather than to a console log file. The files are hidden in places like /usr/adm/syserr, and data files cannot be read without a formatter. The uerf formatter outputs errors in many ways.

fuser **(not BSD)**

fuser must have been written with system administration in mind, as its function is simple: Identify or kill all processes using a particular file, directory, or disk partition. You will need to get everyone and everything off the disk when you need to unmount the disk or when you need to make the disk quiescent for system activities like fsck, archive, and backup.

You can make fuser passive or active. Either it can politely tell you which users are using the file and take no overt action or it can ruthlessly kill their processes. It can also do both at once, killing user processes and telling you which ones are deceased. Sometimes you will end up in a confusing situation in which a user process generates children quicker than you or fuser can kill them in time to unmount the disk. Here time is of the essence, but don't panic. The following quick succession of commands can get the disk off the system before the next process can access it:

```
# (fuser -uk /dev/dsk/eefs0; umount /dev/dsk/eefs0)
```

killall, halt, **and** haltsys

You won't type the killall command very often, for it normally is used only in the shutdown script. Because it's part of the shutdown, who's going to see it? Whereas killall kills all user processes other than the system programmer's, haltsys kills everything. And killall is only roughly equivalent to the XENIX haltsys or BSD halt commands.

There are times when you will have to force a shutdown manually without the benefit of the shutdown script. The minimum instructions for a fast shutdown are

```
# cd /
# sync;sync
# /etc/killall
# /etc/umountall
# init 0
```

The killall command is the file system's kiss of death.

The final shutdown move varies from system to system. For AT&T 3B systems (System V) it is

```
shutdown -y -g0 -i0
```

which leads to init 0. On Berkeley systems you have

```
shutdown -h now
```

which leads to halt. On a VM/UTS mainframe you use

```
# cpcmd log
```

and the machine is gone. Older UNIX systems die in this way:

```
# kill -15 1 or # kill -3 1 or # kill -9 1
```

These kill command variations depend on the implementation.

link

The original ln command created *hard links*. A hard link can be made only within a mounted file system, and it is used only by su to give a file another name in addition to the one the file already has.

For example, say you have a group of users, new to UNIX, who miss the type command of other operating systems such as AOS/VS. Being a good-natured administrator, you give them a UNIX type command. Here ln links the file name type to the original file /bin/cat:

```
$ su
passwd:
# link /bin/cat /bin/type
^D
$ cd /bin
$ ls -l cat type
-r-xr-xr-x  2  bin  13912  sept 14 1984  cat
-r-xr-xr-x  2  bin  13912  apr  18 1988  type
```

Both the link count of 2 in the second field as well as the identical file sizes show that the link was successful. There is indeed only one file. In a C-shell environment ln's usefulness is somewhat diminished by *alias*es.

A *soft link* is the product of networking, brought to us by Berkeley UNIX. Also called a *symbolic* link, a soft link is a file that contains the name of another file. The manual says that it "contains the name of the file to which it is linked." However, /bin is gone in Berkeley 4.3, System V Release 4, and SunOS. This creates a problem, since many scripts look for commands in /bin, including /bin/sh and /bin/csh. To get around the problem, you can create a symbolic link from /bin to /usr/bin. Symbolic links can cross mounted file systems. If the file or file system is to be mounted, it won't generate an error, making it useful for workstations expecting to be connected to file servers. The -s flag of ln is used to create the symbolic link.

/etc/pwck **(System V only)**

To check /etc/passwd, use /etc/pwck. This marvelous but often overlooked command should be used every time the password file is modified. It should also be used from time to time to test the password file. Not only does pwck check the number of fields in each password record, it also checks to see if the login directory exists, and it complains to the standard error output if the password is blocked or expired.

You should copy /etc/passwd to a separate file before modifying it.[5] Also make a backup copy before touching it with the editor:

```
$ su
password:
# cd /etc
# cp passwd Ipasswd
# cp passwd Opasswd
# vi Ipasswd
```

After modifying Ipasswd, you should check it with pwck before copying it back to /etc/passwd.

Also note that /etc/grpck is /etc/passwd's group counterpart.

sadp

The sadp command is a disk profiler that tells disk access, location, and seek distance. On systems with heavy disk access, it is important to understand the frequency of disk accesses and how far the read/write head must move to make them. The problem, or contention, comes when the read/write head is in one place, and the system asks it to be somewhere else. Disk contention ruins system performance. To avoid contention you must place the most frequently accessed disk partitions at the disk's rotational track center. If, for example, your disk has 880 cylinders, its track center will be track 440. If the system's spool disk is 80 cylinders long and it is the most accessed disk partition on the pack, it should be located as close to cylinder 400 as possible.

whodo

The whodo command, the last in section 1M of the manual, could be the first in your bag of tricks if you want to see what your users are up to:

```
$ whodo
Sun Sep 25 16:40:54 PDT 1988
XENIX
01      bruce      10:27
01      218        0:09 vi
02      bruce      10:28
02      222        0:00 sh
02      223        0:00 ps
02      226        0:00 sh
2c      karen      11:13
2c      221        0:00 cat /u/asa/adm
```

---

[5] System V Release 4 has modified password files to include a separate file for password encryption and aging. This complexity just about eliminates the ability to modify the password file manually. The 5.4 administrator must fall back on configuration management tools like useradd, usermod, userdel, groupadd, groupmod, and groupdel.

SYSTEM V RELEASE 4 ENHANCED ADMINISTRATION

System administration commands have been UNIX orphans for nearly a decade. AT&T has one set of commands, BSD another, and OEMs of both systems added to the confusion by creating both their own commands and their own locations for administration commands, files, and libraries. Even UNIX standards initially ignored system administration. System V Interface Definition, X/OPEN, and POSIX barely mentioned system administration commands. Finally, an IEEE P1003.7 system administration committee was formed to standardize system administration commands. At the same time, some of the System V Release 4 commands were added to the System V Interface Definition. At the same time the Applications Binary Interface was created to fix the names and locations of files and commands not covered by POSIX and X/OPEN.

The following AS_CMD commands have been added to the System V Interface Definition, issue 3, Chapter 8, entitled *Commands and Utilities*:

- `prtconf`
- `setuname`
- `groupadd`
- `groupdel`
- `groupmod`
- `groups`
- `logins`
- `useradd`
- `userdel`
- `usermod`
- `users`
- `getvol`
- `getslot`
- `devaddr`
- `getdev`
- `devfree`
- `getgrp`
- `devreserv`
- `listdgrp`
- `putdev`
- `putdgrp`

Accompanying the commands are the following library routines, designated AS_LIB, the library counterparts of the preceding shell-level commands:

- `memory`
- `getslot`
- `getvol`
- `getdev`
- `getgrp`
- `listdev`
- `listgrp`

- devattr
- devfree
- devserv
- reservdev

   While user and group administration commands have existed for years, they have been OEM enhancements, not official UNIX commands. The addition of a password shadow table to tighten password security made it necessary to create these commands and add them to the System V Interface Definition. Additional function has been added with application-related logins solving the previous failing of not having project-related accounting capability. Now users can belong to several groups.

   System V Release 4 has also recognized some standard device types, such as diskettes. Along with them are friendly device names such as diskette1. Volume labels are used by all standard storage media, and commands like getvol are provided to use them.

   Software installation, management, and removal have always been a case-by-case affair. Good software packages have installation scripts as part of their distribution. They do the software installation, but after that you are on your own. If the software package adds files to /etc, /bin, /usr/etc, /usr/bin, or anywhere in /usr/src, /usr/include, and /usr/lib, you don't stand a chance of removing all the garbage from the system when you have to "deinstall" the software. AT&T System V Release 2 has installation software for 3Bs that will "deinstall" it *if* you remember what you did with the distribution disk. Installation and removal commands are standard on System V Release 4.

   System V Release 4 has installation and removal commands and libraries included in the System V Interface Definition, which appear in the System V Interface Definition with the AS_CMD designation. The commands are

- pkgadd
- pkgask
- pakchk
- pkgparam
- pkgtrans
- pkgrm
- pakmk
- pkgpoto
- installf
- removef

The associated library commands are

- pkginfo
- pkgparam

These are designated as AS_LIB in the System V Interface Definition.

   These additions to the system software base, along with the standardization by way of the System V Interface Definition, POSIX IEEE P1003.7, and the Applications Binary Interface, should standardize and simplify system administration at long last.

MANAGER'S CORNER

The Manager's Role

UNIX administration requirements vary with the system's size and complexity and with a more important but less tangible quality—commitment. If a nontechnical manager is committed to providing quality system services to the users, she will insist on effective, value-added system administration, and the administrative requirements of the system will reflect this commitment.

Without the manager's commitment to quality system service, there is no driving force behind stabilizing the system and running it at peak efficiency. Not enough money is allocated for sufficient administration staff, and an unstable system with a high system overhead is the result. Administering an overloaded system means fighting fires that never go out. Users are unhappy because their processes run slowly, and the system response is slower than the release of vaporware. Unstable systems can crash daily and often do. OEM fixes and new releases sit unopened and unused because the current system staff is so busy using bailing wire and duct tape to hold the system together that they have no time to install them. They also have no time to evaluate potential software purchases that would make the system run more smoothly or time to write system software that would improve the system's overall efficiency. In short, administrators are so busy trying to maintain a less than adequate status quo, little positive work is accomplished, and morale goes down.

Stable systems run from PM period to PM period without much wavering or complaining.[6] A stable system is practically bulletproof, so it seldom crashes, and unscheduled system downtimes are minimized or eliminated. Users have optimal working conditions because the system is working at peak efficiency, so all processes run as quickly as possible. Although the system administrator and staff are always squeezed for time, the more stable the system is, the more time there will be to develop an overall system management strategy that will allow for the creation of system software. Reasonable purchase allowances for software that keeps the system running at its best is money well spent. In addition, the more stable the system is, the fewer staff members it will need to run it and the more work it will produce for its users.

Without management's commitment to providing quality system services, there is no incentive for management or staff to keep abreast of current developments in the computer industry. The computer industry changes continually. It is difficult to keep up with current technical innovations because as a technical manager, your job is time-consuming. On the other hand, if you don't regularly spend some extra time and effort to update your technical knowledge, eventually your management decisions will reflect your ignorance, and your company will pay the price.

I once worked for a defense contractor in Southern California that lost its entire UNIX mainframe strategy because of the lack of management commitment to continuing technical education, specifically UNIX. Two perfectly good Amdahl mainframes, which originally cost millions but sell used for only thousands, were sacrificed for some DEC minis, which ran at a measly 1.4 to 4 MIPS. That's like buying two new sports cars and selling them for $10 each to get some bicycles. This occurred because management was technically ignorant to a scandalous degree. They were ignorant about UNIX, programming languages in general,

---

[6] PM stands for *preventive maintenance*.

and the advantages of mainframes over minis for their installation. The management of this company assumed that their engineers knew what they were doing, so they catered to the engineers' impulses and brand prejudices. Unfortunately, the engineers were as ignorant of mainframe UNIX and its potential advantages for the company as management was. They thought they would prefer the autonomy of the little DECs to working on a mainframe. The engineers should have stuck to their own area of expertise and left the computer decisions to computer professionals. A year was lost on a multimillion-dollar contract, and a year of UNIX mainframe work also went down the tube, including a mountain of `nroff`-formatted documentation. Both the company's mainframes were lost to other departments before the enormity of the error was realized. By then it was too late.

The moral of the story is this: A manager cannot afford to make major decisions solely on the recommendations of others. He or she must become as educated as possible on that subject and make decisions based on knowledgeable evaluation of the data. Although many sites get by with knowledgeable users who administer their machines, generally computer installations cannot be run by the users, although their input is important. In the end most computer installations must be run by a technically educated operations or systems group.

In short, nontechnical managers need to understand where UNIX is today. Each new UNIX release has incorporated significant changes that managers of UNIX sites should know about. For example, how can the best management plans for an installation be made if management doesn't understand that the differences between UNIX Releases 5.2 and 5.4 are like night and day? They should not rely on marketing claims alone. Before committing their company to an expensive old system disguised with brand-new packaging, they should fully realize the cost of kernel-level features versus superficial ones. Some features of BSD and other systems based on early versions of UNIX can be added, but many kernel-dependent changes to UNIX cannot. Decisions made in ignorance will tax a company well into the future.

4

Files

FILE SYSTEM ADMINISTRATION

The mounted file system and the directory hierarchy are two central tenets of UNIX philosophy and design. Neither is without price. Separate mounted file systems require additions such as a kernel mount table. The file system tree structure has certain requirements also, such as inode and file system tables and directories. The price goes well beyond the complexity of the internals. It is felt in the administration of the system.

The correspondence between directory entries and individual inodes must be kept intact. There is an inode for every file. There are inode tables on disk, and a slightly different inode table in the kernel. There is at least one entry in a directory for every file. There is an entry in the kernel file table and another in the kernel inode table for every file in use. It is not only possible but also probable that at any given time there will be a mismatch in the kernel inode information, as opposed to the inode information on disk that is caused by the efficiency of the system in reading ahead and writing behind. Disparity can exist except at the moment a system is synced, and this disparity is permanent when the system crashes. You now have no choice but to reboot the system and repair the inode damage.

The creators of UNIX allow file system corruption to be corrected with several UNIX cleanup tools. Some tools, like clri, are hangovers from Version 6. Occasionally clri is still a useful tool, however, as we shall see in Chapter 23. The command that came and stayed is fsck. Much larger than traditional UNIX tools, it is a true utility, for it both finds problems and corrects them.

fsck **Particulars**

The command fsck checks any file systems for inconsistencies. If no argument is given, fsck will obtain the file system information from /etc/checkall, all the more reason for the system administrator to look at checkall to be sure that all the file systems are noted there. When used, fsck looks for the following inconsistencies:

- Data blocks claimed by more than one inode or found in the free list.
- Data blocks out of range of the file system.
- Bad link count.
- Block number error.
- Directory out of 16-byte alignment.
- Bad inode format.
- Data blocks not accounted for anywhere.
- Error in free block format.
- Error in either free block count or inode count. fsck checks directories for (1) file referenced to an unallocated inode and (2) an inode out of range.
- fsck checks the superblock for (1) over 65536 inodes and (2) more blocks than are available.

There are numerous fsck flags: The -n option allows checking only and is invaluable for determining the status of a live file system. The -y option assumes a yes response to all questions asked by fsck. If I suspect damage, I prefer not to use -y. It's better to answer each fsck question one at a time, to give you a far better idea of the extent and nature of the damage.

There are a few tricks to speed up file system checking on very large file systems. Even a massive 70-MIP machine takes about 10 minutes to check file systems on postboot initiation. Always check the raw file systems. Of course, they must be unmounted, and so fsck is best done when bringing up the system. After checking the root file system, check the remaining file systems with dfck, the dual file system checker, which checks systems two at a time. I do not recommend dfck if you suspect any damage, such as after a system crash.

Every time the system boots, fsck should be run on your file systems. In fact, it should be built into the rc script. If a system has been up for an extended time, say over two weeks, it should be taken down for preventive maintenance. The first order of business is a file system consistency check and repair.

After a crash, fsck also must be run, because a crash guarantees that there is corruption of at least the root and spool disks. The root disk won't even survive the first pass of fsck, and the system has to be rebooted. When you get this message

```
***** BOOT UNIX (NO SYNC) *****
```

don't sync the system, because you will only put the mistakes back.

Either rigidly scheduled downtimes or the option of unscheduled downtimes a minimum of every two weeks should be written into an agreement between your organization and other internal organizations within the company (see Chapter 20). The safest is a clause that allows you to call an unscheduled downtime weekly, whenever you suspect file system corruption. Should root, /etc, or any other system disk actually become corrupted, then you have a different ball game. Now you have a severe problem that is an immediate threat to the system. Give a reasonable warning time, then bring down the system for file system consistency checking.

Remember that `fsck` can be run for information purposes only. The following harmlessly checks the file system:

```
fsck -n /dev/dsk/what_ever
```

This is how you can find out if you have to unmount the disk or bring down the system for repair. Don't ever forget the former option. If it is a user disk, a simple unmount will save a shutdown and disable only a small part of the user population.

Disk Fragmentation

UNIX has a simple system for getting disk space, a *first-fit* algorithm. The kernel drops data into the first open gap big enough to fit. It does no testing for *best fit*. The problem with the first-fit algorithm is that it leaves holes in the disk. Files are contiguous when first written to disk, but gaps are gradually created in the address space of the disks when files are erased. These gaps are the spaces from which files have been removed. New files coming in are dropped into the holes regardless of fit, and so little by little the holes become smaller and harder to fit. This is called *fragmentation*.

From time to time it is wise to reorder directories, rebuild the superblock, and rebuild user file systems to get rid of fragmentation. And you might as well take advantage of this opportunity to expand or contract the system and adjust the number of inodes as well. The process starts with a simple `df -t`:

```
$ df -t /dev/u
(/dev/u   ):    23794 blocks    3031 i-nodes
              (  25110 total blocks,  396 for i-nodes)
```

The file system is vastly oversized in this example. Subtract 23794 from 25110, and you will discover that only 1316 blocks have been used. Unless this is a new file system, its huge size is reason enough to make it smaller.

Create a new file system from the old one. Calculate a reasonable size for the surrogate system. Be sure that the inode ratio is ample for the usage shown in the old disk system. Although `mkproto` is a good guide for a totally new file system, an old one already displays the type of usage the system is getting. A `df -t` should give you all the information you need about the size and makeup of the old file system. Use this information to calculate the block-to-inode ratio of the old file system, and use that ratio to calculate the new block and inode requirements. A good point to remember is when a file system gets within 10 percent of filling, the system must thrash for each inode allocated. There is a performance hit every time a new file is created or appended, so allocate a new disk partition of the size required by your calculations.

Once the disk is allocated, format it and prepare it for use with `mkfs`, the command used to construct a file system. Use or create a `root` mount point such as `mnt0` to mount the new disk:

```
# format /dev/rdsk/ee1s0
# mkfs /dev/dsk/ee1s0 1024:256  6 150
.

.
# mount /dev/dsk/ee1s0 /mnt0
# mklf /mnt0
```

Use your local script to create lost + found on the new disk. If you don't have a script, make a lost + found directory, then create and remove about 50 empty files to slot the directory.

The last step is to copy the files from the old disk to the new one before remounting. A recursive descent copy method gives contiguous allocation. Use the ls command with the -R option. It also can be used to feed cpio:

```
# ls -R /u!cpio -pldv /mnt⎕
```

The find command is the traditional way to feed cpio:

```
# find /u -depth -print ! cpio -pvdmlk /mnt⎕
```

Avoid byte-for-byte copy commands like VM/CP's DDR or UNIX's volcopy or dd, because they don't fix fragmentation.

All you need to do now is move the new file system to the mounting point of the old one, and then throw the old one away. Do a du followed by an ls -lR from the base of both directories while both file systems are still mounted. Now compare them by doing a df -t of both disks. If they are the same, it's nearly Miller time:

```
# umount /dev/dsk/ee1s⎕
# umount /dev/dsk/ddas⎕
# mount /dev/dsk/ee1s⎕ /old/filesys
```

Keep the old disk around for a couple of weeks. If no one complains, it is part of the free disk pool.

root **File Expansion**

Size expansions or inode expansions of the root file system are tests of the system administrator's ingenuity. During the expansion the system has to be under the control of a disk-mounted or memory-resident root system other than the one being altered. UNIX can be booted from a minimal, floppy-disk-resident root system on desktop machines. A PC-type system can be booted with a UNIX disk resident in the first floppy drive. The system runs on this minimal disk. Minis can be booted from tape using either a memory-resident version of UNIX or one written to the swap area. The swap-area version allows more work to be done, but the memory-resident version allows anything to be done to the root disk. On large machines, such as VM mainframe systems, the root disk of one virtual UNIX system can be attached as "just another disk" to another virtual UNIX system.

A variation on the theme is to make a bootable partition on a second hard disk and then to boot from there to modify the original root system. The boot operating system must allow for booting from a specified address if you boot from a second hard or floppy disk. VM/UNIX allows an IPL instruction for initial program load:

```
#cp ipl 220⎕
```

Note that the IBM command IPL is in lowercase letters when called from UNIX. UNIX maintains its conventions. The #cp command from VM/CP means "Do a CP command immediately, without a search"; ipl can be abbreviated as i:

```
#cp i 220⎕
```

Even though CP commands are entered in lowercase letters from UTS, CP immediately translates them into the uppercase letters that it understands.

You can boot to any reasonable address from the prom prompt on minicomputers and many micros that utilize a programmable or nonprogrammable boot prom. With the system halted, the system displays its own distinctive prompt, usually one or more greater-than signs. The conventional boot command is b followed by the boot address. Next we see a DEC ULTRIX system booting to dua0, the traditional disk boot address:

```
>b dua0
```

DEC systems can also boot from the network as well as from the tape of any disk address that has a boot track and a copy of vmunix.

Once you are running on an alternative root disk, the expansion takes place in the same way that all other disk expansions do:

- Format the new root disk.
- Initialize a boot track if required.
- Run mkfs (make a file system).
- Attach the new disk to a temporary mount point.
- Make lost+found.
- Copy old root to the temporary mount point.
- Unmount both file systems.
- Mount the new root to the old root mount point.

Most root file systems require a boot track, traditionally track 0. Check the OEM manual to see how this is done on your system. It probably has a simple name like track0 or mkboot. Others, like SunOS, create the boot track from their enlarged format command. The SunOS format takes care of bad-block repair, partitioning, and formatting.

Unmounting Problems

There will be times when umount doesn't seem to work. The complaint is device busy:

```
# cd /etc
# umount /dev/dsk/7?0s1
device busy
# fuser -u /dev/dsk/7?0s1
```

System V fuser with the -u option shows who is on the disk. In this example, notice that the system administrator changes directories to /etc before doing the umount. You don't want to get caught on the disk yourself!

Using fuser with the -k option kills whatever is on disk. If there is a process spawning children faster than you can kill them, issue the kill and umount commands simultaneously:

```
(fuser -uk /dev/dsk/7?0s1;umount /dev/dsk/7?0s1)
```

There also will be times when you get a device busy message, even though no person or process is on disk. Don't let the obvious escape you. Is there another file system attached to this one? You can't unmount /usr if /usr/spool is a separate disk partition mounted to /usr.

FILE CONVENTIONS

System administrators and system programmers are restricted when it comes to file and directory conventions, but UNIX users have a lot more freedom. They can create a file anywhere as long as they can access the directory in which it resides. A file is what they make it. A few names are unwise, such as test or core, and they should avoid file names with metacharacters like /, \\ , ?, and *, but other than that they can be as creative as they want.

System programmers and administrators do not have this kind of freedom but must adhere to a strict set of rules and conventions. Most system files have names given them by AT&T, Berkeley, Sun, and other OEMs and VARs, which cannot be easily changed.

UNIX has the following file and directory conventions:

- root: home of the essential files needed to get to single-user mode as well as /bin, /etc, and /dev.
- /usr: everything that won't fit into a convenient category.
- /usr/spool: everyone's spool space as well as a few spool libraries.
- /var: BSD, SunOS, and System V Release 4—the area for rapidly expanding and contracting files, such as spooler files.
- /usr/src: source.
- /usr/include: all the system header files.
- /etc: the toolbox for system administrators and system programmers.
- /usr/etc: BSD 4.3 and AT&T 5.4, the executables that used to be in /etc.
- /dev: home of all device nodes, the driver entry points.
- /usr/spool/console: the console log, large systems only.
- /usr/spool/cron/crontabs: home of the system's timetables.
- /usr/spool/uucp*: home of the store-and-forward networking files.
- /usr/spool/lp or lpr: home of the printer spooler system.
- /usr/lib: the libraries.
- /usr/adm: the system log files, crash dumps.
- /bin: the main toolbox of early BSD and of AT&T UNIX 5.2 and 5.3, moved to /usr/bin in Berkeley 4.3 and AT&T 5.4.
- /usr/bin: tools that didn't fit in /bin or tools that migrated from /bin.

System file names and their locations vary from machine to machine, but device special files are in the same location, /dev. Your manual set is the best source of information on most system files. The information in Section 4 of the conventional UNIX manuals is exclusively devoted to them. XENIX has an interesting manual section on file formats that gives more information on the structures (reference /usr/include and /usr/include/sys), but less description than manual(5) does.

DEVICE SPECIAL SYSTEM FILES

In this section we shall only touch on some standard UNIX system files and a few OEM-specific files. Systems administrators should take frequent trips around their system's files, and they should read their manuals often. The more they know, the less research they will have to do during a crisis.

Errors and /dev/error

The device special file /dev/error is the root of the system's error-logging mechanism. Because error is closely related to /dev/osm in function, its output may be read to an error-logging file or to the console log.

/dev/lp*

The /dev/lp* files are the interfaces to printer devices. The lp driver performs the canonical duties for the printer, such as mapping into reasonable output returns, backspaces, line feeds, and form feeds. The control of /dev/lp is through ioctl(2) and can be done with stty(1) (see Chapter 7).

Memory: /dev/mem and /dev/kmem

The device special file mem is an image of the system's absolute memory. The kmem file is similar, but it is for virtual memory; /dev/kmem is handy for examining the system with commands like crash. There are non-AT&T commands that have a similar function, such as Amdahl's sysdump. Actually, sometimes the non-AT&T commands are better, because they often have a larger set of constants and tables that the utility can format and understand. In essence, /dev/kmem is the door if you want to examine the system thoroughly, particularly the system tables, the stacks, and the contents of memory locations. Dump formatters like crash (System V) and Amdahl's sysdump are the keys.

null and /dev/null

The black hole of the system is /dev/null. It takes everything and returns nothing. It is the system's bit bucket used to send data streams to nowhere:

```
$ cat /dev/clock >/dev/null 2>$1
```

Use it to send standout or standerr off to the next world.

Sometimes you cannot make an empty file by redirection. It is traditionally done by touching the file or copying /dev/null to a file:

```
cp /dev/null foo
```

or

```
cat /dev/null>foo
```

stx: /dev/stx/??[0-n]

The pseudodevice driver stx is used to assert disciplines between tty line disciplines and real device drivers. The need for drivers like stx is largely eliminated by streams, System V Release 3. Streams allow the layering of software modules between the stream head, set up at the kernel interface and the device driver.

Magnetic Tape: /dev/tape **and** /dev/rmt

There are as many names for the tape interface as there are types of tape devices. Many device special files are named after the device controller. Disks and tapes require both raw and block interfaces that correspond to the raw I/O's read(2) and write(2) system calls and to the block I/O's fopen(3) and fclose(3) library routines. The classic devices are /dev/mt/* and dev/rmt/*.[1]

Remember that whereas a lot of software using tape drives does not require the device name explicitly, commands like cpio and tar do:

```
find . -depth ¦ cpio -ocdv > /dev/rmt0
```

Here the contents of the current directory are sent directly to tape by way of cpio and the device special file rmt0.

One more tape driver is worthy of mention, nrmt. Whereas a conventional tape driver writes a tape and rewinds it, /dev/nrmt is the tape driver with no rewind. That is, nrmt manipulates the tape, but it doesn't rewind it, thereby allowing multiple files, archives, or trees to be written to tape. To access them, the tape must be manipulated from one tape write to the other by commands like tm, the tape manipulator.

/dev/tty*

If users know only one device, it will be /dev/tty. The who command will remind them each time they use it, and /dev/tty itself is the control terminal that goes with each process and process group; /dev/tty* corresponds to each user's login terminal.

Special addressing conventions are associated with nontraditional terminals, such as remote logins, virtual terminals for windows and sessions, and non-ASCII, synchronous terminals.[2] Typical examples are pseudoterminals, ptys, and windows, wins. The naming conventions are determined by the OEM.

The pseudoterminal is used for remote logins. A real terminal requires a port and therefore a full driver and an entry in /dev, but the pseudotty is created in the software. The connection is made through the Ethernet on both host systems. Windows are pseudodevices existing to satisfy the requirements of multiple window systems like X Windows and SunOS's sunview.

Miscellaneous

As you sort through /dev, you will see files that are unique, such as

- cga
- cmos
- color
- ega
- install
- printer
- floppy

---

[1] Note that mt stands for magnetic tape, and rmt is for raw magnetic tape.
[2] These are bi-sync, IBM 327X devices.

Some files, such as ega, cga, and color, are obviously graphics devices. Others, like install, can leave you talking to yourself.

But /dev/install is a puzzle that can be solved by first doing a long listing of /dev/install. Find its major and minor device number in the fifth and sixth fields:

```
$ ls -l /dev/install
brw-rw-rw-   1 bin       bin        2, 64 Mar  4 07:59 /dev/install
$ ls -l /dev ! grep "2, 64"
brw-rw-rw-   1 bin       bin        2, 64 Mar  4 07:59 install
crw-rw-rw-   1 bin       bin        2, 64 Mar  4 07:59 rinstall
$ ls -l /dev ! grep 2,
brw-rw-rw-   3 bin       bin        2,  4 Mar  4 07:59 fd0
brw-rw-rw-   1 bin       bin        2, 60 Mar  4 10:05 fd0135ds18
brw-rw-rw-   1 bin       bin        2, 36 Mar  4 10:05 fd0135ds9
brw-rw-rw-   3 bin       bin        2,  4 Mar  4 07:59 fd048
brw-rw-rw-   1 bin       bin        2, 12 Mar  4 09:46 fd048ds8
brw-rw-rw-   3 bin       bin        2,  4 Mar  4 07:59 fd048ds9
brw-rw-rw-   1 bin       bin        2,  8 Mar  4 09:46 fd048ss8
brw-rw-rw-   1 bin       bin        2,  0 Mar  4 09:46 fd048ss9
brw-rw-rw-   2 bin       bin        2, 52 Mar  4 09:46 fd096
brw-rw-rw-   2 bin       bin        2, 52 Mar  4 09:46 fd096ds15
brw-rw-rw-   1 bin       bin        2, 60 Mar  4 09:46 fd096ds18
brw-rw-rw-   1 bin       bin        2, 36 Mar  4 09:46 fd096ds9
```

Links and similar devices can be found from the device number. If you still have any doubt, searching on the major device alone will end the mystery. Because the major device number, 2, is the number for floppy device drivers, install is exposed as a floppy device, probably used for software installations. It is evident that install is *the* installation device.

The last step in the detective process is to read the index to find the manual page on install and thus the reference to /dev/install and /dev/rfd0 (XENIX System V).

SYSTEM FILES ON /

The root file system is a paradox: It is the root of all file systems and the attaching point of all second-level directories. A recursive descent listing of root lists every file on the system, yet root proper has as few files as possible. Distributed XENIX systems have only three files on root: the xenix kernel, dos, and boot. AT&T's 3B2 systems also have only three, and even massive mainframe UNIX systems have only a handful of files on root.

unix **or** ???x

The kernel is the primary executable file on /, and its name varies depending on the version of UNIX. Although currently AT&T allows some UNIX OEMs the privilege of having their kernel name be /unix, such as SCO, for years AT&T didn't allow anyone else to use the name UNIX. Kernel names thus varied, including /xenix for XENIX, vmunix on BSD, and /uts for Amdahl's UTS. The old, renamed UNIX kernel is also almost always sitting in root, and its name also varies with the version of UNIX, including outs on UTS and xenix.old on older versions of XENIX.

The old kernel version is bootable: Sometimes the new system fails to come up after creating a new UTS system, but luckily the boot procedure allows you to boot outs to get the old system back.

/etc **FILES**

In terms of executable files and data files, the root file system is as barren as /etc is prolific. The system's toolbox, /etc, is also the home of many critical system data files. In time /etc became so large, BSD 4.3, SunOS (a BSD derivative), and AT&T System V Release 4 moved /etc executables to /usr/etc, leaving data files in /etc. The following is a brief description of some /etc files.

rc

The rc "family" of command files takes UNIX from a single-user system to a fully functional, multiuser, multitasking system. Its role and its interaction with init, inittab, and mnttab are discussed in Chapter 12.

checklist

You won't feel like parceling out every disk system to fsck as arguments, so fsck references a file called /etc/checklist, whose contents are an ASCII list of all the file system roots. Instead of being entered as /u, they are entered as special files, such as /dev/u.

/etc/gettydefs

Clearly gettydefs is one of the most innovative parts of UNIX. It allows an unknown, undefined, terminal-like device to log in and establish a baud rate and line discipline. It allows an initial ioctl setting; then it establishes a second and final ioctl setting; and it also allows for retries at different baud rates if a break is sensed and if a "goto" number is provided at the end of the record.

Some gettydefs entries can look a bit strange:

```
0 # B9600 HUPCL # B9600 CS8 SANE HUPCL TAB3 ECHOE IXANY #\r\n@!login: # 0

1 # B300  HUPCL OPOST CR1 NL1 #
        B300 CS8 SANE HUPCL TAB3 IXANY #\r\n@!login: # 2

2 # B1200 HUPCL OPOST CR1 ECHOE NL1 #
        B1200 CS8 SANE HUPCL TAB3 ECHOE IXANY #\r\n@!login: # 3

3 # B2400  HUPCL OPOST CR1 ECHOE NL1 #
        B2400 CS8 SANE HUPCL TAB3 ECHOE IXANY #\r\n@!login: # 1

4 # B2400 HUPCL # B2400 CS8 SANE HUPCL TAB3 ECHOE IXANY #\r\n@!login: # 6

5 # B4800 HUPCL # B4800 CS8 SANE HUPCL TAB3 ECHOE IXANY #\r\n@!login: # 4

6 # B9600 HUPCL # B9600 CS8 SANE HUPCL TAB3 ECHOE IXANY #\r\n@!login: # 5
```

UNIX makes no hard and fast rules about record delimiters. A pound sign, #, is convenient here. Before we go on, glance at terminfo(7), ioctl(2), and stty(1) to get some background.

Each gettydefs line has four parts. The first part consists of the tty settings for the initial receipt of the logname; the second consists of the tty settings to be used when the login is successfully made; the third is the login string; and the fourth is a numeric "goto." When a BREAK or a good imitation of a BREAK is received, the numeric "goto" tells the line heading to go to another line and therefore another baud rate. This feature is important because it allows modems to come in with a choice of speeds. Each line allows a try at a different baud rate and another attempt at a login. On passing the initial login section, the terminal line discipline and canonical translations are set to SANE in an attempt to find reasonable input parameters. That is where the erase-line character is set to @ and the erase character is set to #. On the modem side, HUPCL is set to allow the line to be hung up automatically on logoff. We will look at gettydefs again at the end of the chapter.

group

The /etc/group file maintains group IDs and group memberships:

```
$ cat /etc/group
root:x:0:root
cron:x:1:cron
bin:x:3:bin,lp
uucp:x:4:uucp
asg:x:6:asg
sysinfo:x:10:uucp
network:x:12:network
edit::50:bruce,karen
program::51:bruce,karen
```

The first field is the group name, and the second field is the password field. Note that it is not encrypted as /etc/passwd is. The third field is the group-ID number, and the last field is a comma-delimited list of user IDs.

Group permissions and file ownerships are weak areas in UNIX. There is no consistent way to set passwords (like /etc/passwd), and accounting is not set up to handle group billing. Although you can make group permissions work, you really have to push it. You can create a password encryption for the group file by creating a dummy password file entry and assigning it a password with passwd. You then cut the password encryption from the dummy login entry and paste it to the group file.

One of the files kept in the YP data base is group. It eliminates separate and different group files on each system and hopeless differences from host to host.

One of the more serious problems that administrators face is keeping system information up-to-date. But /etc/passwd is accurate until a user leaves and fails to tell the system administrator that he or she is no longer on the system.

Identity files have all the information that is missing from passwd, such as the user's telephone number, office location, and last mail stop. Identity files are good for keeping track of users, but only if they are updated regularly.

/etc/inittab

Not only is /etc/inittab cleverly conceived, but it also is as cryptic as gettydef is. Here inittab sets the port initialization parameters for each port:

```
$ cat /etc/inittab
01:2:respawn:/etc/getty tty01 9600
02:2:respawn:/etc/getty tty02 9600
03:2:off:/etc/getty tty03 m
04:2:respawn:/etc/getty -t 60 tty04 1200
05:2:respawn:/usr/lib/uucp/uugetty -r -t 60 tty05 1200
06:2:off:/etc/getty tty06
```

The first field is a symbol related to the device name or number, and co (not shown here) is the symbol for console. The second field is the initiation level at which the entry becomes active.[3] The third field is the action to be taken, such as respawning gettys or turning them off. The fourth field is the command and arguments that will be executed.

motd: **The Message of the Day**

The file /etc/motd is the login bulletin board, which is displayed when a user logs in and often is used by the system administrator to make a greetings message and to display any messages that all users should see. Typically it shows shutdown notices and network outages. Don't attempt to use motd to send a full page of salutations and other information of dubious value. Keep it short, particularly on machines being accessed by slow communications lines or through network logins. Users tend to be intolerant of two screens full of prose printing at an effective rate of 600 baud.

passwd

The file /etc/passwd hardly needs an introduction, as it is the file accessed each time you log onto the system. Here are a few lines taken from passwd:

```
lp:BLOCKED:14:3:Print spooler administration:/usr/spool/lp:
dos:BLOCKED:16:10:Access to Dos devices:/:
bhunter:2VkUv4T4sWoIw:100:50:Bruce Hunter:/u/bhunter:/bin/csh
khunter:1WMvKAtHD9Jws:201:50:Karen Hunter:/u/khunter:/bin/sh
```

The first field is the log name. Except on the smallest systems, it is best entered as the first initial followed immediately by the last name:

```
bhunter
```

The second field is the encrypted password. It is a one-way password encryption, in that it cannot be easily reversed, and there is no way anyone can see the password, not even the system administrator. In System V Release 4 and in SunOS's security package there is a shadow password file for the password encryption. The actual password encryption is kept there, and it is not publicly readable as a password file is.

---

[3] XENIX System V does not support initiation levels and therefore the second field.

The third field is the user-ID number. It should be unique and stored in a data base or some other location that system programmers can access easily. All user-ID numbers must be the same on all systems whose users access more than one machine. For example, as an administrator your user ID might be 100 on all machines you access. This avoids conflicts of ownership when transferring files with `tar` and `cpio`, just to mention a few problems that can be avoided. YP was created for sticky situations like this. Just read the user ID, the user name, and so forth, and YP will propagate it across all machines.

The fourth field is the group ID. Like the user ID, it should be the same across systems within a site. It is always best to maintain a central data base of user-ID and group-ID numbers.

The fifth field is undefined and is usually used for comments. Some OEMs use it for special information storage like a GECOS field, a comment field within the `passwd` file.

The sixth field is the user's home directory. If this area cannot be found, users will find themselves in `/`, a situation frequently discovered by the administrator logging in remote to a user's machine.

The last field is the command to be executed when logging in, usually a shell. If Bourne shell is wanted, the field is usually left blank. Notable exceptions are `sync` and `uucp`, and `sync` isn't even a login, but it is used as an emergency way to `sync` the system without logging in. Also not a login, `uucp` is a call to `uucico`.

Note that `/etc/passwd` presents some unique system administration problems. If the file is lost or corrupted, you'll be out of business. The file becomes corrupted when it is held open for writing, even if only one field delimiter is added or lost. At best it will be corrupted to the point where you made your last change or addition. This is why the system records are *always* at the top and why you *never* sort the password file. Dealing with `/etc/passwd` is like walking on eggs! But you can avoid problems by following a few simple rules and procedures. Always keep a backup copy of `passwd` on disk, and on large machines it is not overkill to copy `passwd` to `Opasswd` and `Opasswd` to `OOpasswd` daily or at least every time it is modified. The sequence is

```
# cp Opasswd OOpasswd
# cp passwd Opasswd
```

This can be done automatically from a couple of entries in `cron`, and `root`'s `cron` file is `/usr/spool/cron/crontabs/root`.

When modifying `/etc/passwd`, make copies of `passwd` to `Ipasswd` and `Opasswd`. Then modify `Ipasswd`. On System V run `/etc/pwck` on `Ipasswd` when you are through. It should give no output. If there are either too many or too few colon delimiters, it will complain. If it cannot find the user login directory, it also will complain. If the password has expired, it will complain some more. Indeed, complaining loud and clear is `pwck`'s job. Once you are sure that `Ipasswd` is good, copy `Ipasswd` to `passwd`.

Suspect `/etc/passwd` if your users have trouble logging on. The culprit will fall out if you run `/etc/pwck` on `/etc/passwd`. Remember that hand-editing `passwd` is sure to corrupt `passwd` sooner or later. It is best to use an adduser script or an `a.out` program, and if one is not supplied with your OEM distribution, write one. Be sure not to let it manipulate data in `passwd`; it should simply append the next record. The open-write-close sequence should occur on three consecutive lines. You shouldn't hold `passwd` open for even one unnecessary machine cycle.

Berkeley systems have a special version of vi, called vipw, expressly designed for editing /etc/passwd. It avoids *race conditions* in writing to the password file. If you're in the editor doing a write in the passwd file and someone simultaneously executes the passwd command, there will be a race condition to see which process writes to the file first. This is trouble waiting to happen.

Password administration changes drastically at System V Release 4, which uses a separate file to hold the password encryption and aging information. Password files are administered with specific tools, such as the users option of the menu-driven Forms and Menu Language Interpreter and the useradd, userdel, and usermod commands.

baddu.c: passwd **File Manipulation**

The following program was created to add /etc/passwd records to a variant UNIX system: A batch UNIX system has been set up as an extension of a Berkeley batch program. The addition to Berkeley batch is a remote batch queue that causes remote command execution on a separate system. The remote batch machine must have all passwords blocked, with root as the only exception. The scheme requires the dynamic mounting and unmounting of disks. That is, if a user is logged onto a disk that needs to be unmounted, the umount will fail, and the batch system will become confused and will fail also.

Note that in the code no user except root or superuser is allowed to use the program. This was added to prevent an illegal-privilege login from being created if this code were ported to an interactive system. Another point to note is the use of a raw write to give rapid, unbuffered writing to /etc/passwd. The file is open for only a few kernel cycles from the open to the write and close system calls, thus preventing passwd corruption.

Not too many years ago, this program would have been written in about a dozen lines of code. As the UNIX system matures, however, it also sags under its own weight. Heavy, well-protected code is the result:

```
/*
     baddu.c
     BHH 4/27/88
*/

#include <stdio.h>
#include <signal.h>
#include <fcntl.h>
#include <errno.h>
#define EVER ;;
#define PW_FILE  "/etc/passwd"

extern int errno, sys_nerr;
extern char *sys_errlist[];
int fd;
void  syserr(), trap();

void main()
{
    char u_name[15],  ans[5], buff[BUFSIZ];
    int  uid, gid, ret;
```

```
        security();
        printf("\n\n\tadduser\n\n");
        for(EVER)
        {
            printf("enter log name: ");
            scanf ("%s", u_name);
            uid = get_uid();
            printf("enter group id number: ");
            scanf ("%d", &gid);
            printf ("logname: %s  UID: %d  GID: %d\n", u_name, uid, gid);
            printf ("is this correct: ");
            scanf  ("%s", ans);
            switch (ans[0])
            {
                case 'y':
                case 'Y':
                    goto end_loop;
                case 'q':
                    exit(9);
                default:
                    continue;
            }
        }
        end_loop:
        if (access(PW_FILE, 06) == -1)
        {
            syserr("can't access passwd");
            errno = 0;
        }
        if ((fd = open(PW_FILE, O_WRONLY !! O_APPEND)) == -1)
        {
            syserr("can't open passwd");
            errno = 0;
        }
        signal (SIGHUP, trap());
        signal (SIGINT, trap());
        signal (SIGQUIT, trap());
        sprintf(buff, "%s:BLOCKED:%d;%d::/u\n", u_name, uid, gid);
        ret = write(fd, buff, sizeof(buff));
        if (ret == -1)
        {
            syserr("can't write to passwd");
            errno = 0;
        }
        close(fd);
        sync();
        exit(0);
}

security()
{
    if ((getuid() !=  0) !! (geteuid() !=  0))
    {
        fprintf (stderr, "you must be superuser\n");
        exit (-1);
    }
}

get_uid()
{
    int u_id;
```

```
        for(EVER)
        {
            printf("enter user id number: ");
            scanf ("%d", &u_id);
            if (u_id < 100)
            {
                printf  ("UID %d is out of range, resubmit\n");
                continue;
            }
            else
                return (u_id);
        }
    }

    void syserr(msg)
    char *msg;
    {
            fprintf(stderr,"ERROR: %s (no %d", msg, errno);
            if ((errno > 0) && (errno  < sys_nerr))
            fprintf(stderr, "%s)\n", sys_errlist[errno]);
            else
                fprintf(stderr, ")\n");
                exit (-1);
    }

    void trap(signo)
    int signo;
    {
        close (fd);
        printf ("\nprocess aborted on signal  %d\n", signo);
        exit(-1);
    }
    /* */
```

On small, quiet systems, passwd can be operated on directly. You can get away with anything when the system is quiescent. Do your user administration directly, then in *maintenance mode*[4] or at init level s.

/etc/passwd **FILE SECURITY**

One final note of caution: /etc/passwd must be readable but not writable except by root. It is best left with root ownership at mode 444, *read-only* by all. Remember, too, that /bin/passwd is an open invitation to penetrate your system security. Keep it *execute-only* to group and others, set-user-ID bit set, and root owned:

```
$ ls -l /bin/passwd
-rws---x--x   root bin  16856 April 16 1987 /bin/passwd
```

Sometimes you will need to stop any users from logging on while the system is in multiuser mode. Here's a typical scenario:

- The local machine's Ethernet device has failed.
- Local users are still logged on and have to finish their work.
- You have warned the users of a pending shutdown with wall or rwall.

---

[4] XENIX, BSD, and old UNIX.

The immediate problem is that some users can log on while you are giving the users a specified grace period. Although a message in /etc/motd keeps off about 80 percent of the users, only 100 percent is effective. This problem has several solutions: You can modify /etc/inittab or ttys on XENIX by replacing each init level 2 getty respawn with off. This has to be restored later. Be sure to copy ttys to Ottys. On XENIX the 1 in ttys's first column is replaced with 0. The problem with this tactic, however, is doing an accurate restore later. A series of inittab files can be kept: inittab, Oinittab, and NOinittab. The inittab version with init gettys off is NOinittab: inittab is copied to Oinittab, and NOinittab is copied to inittab.

My preference is to make a short version of /etc/passwd. System user-ID numbers go from 0 to 99, while the human programming staff has user-ID numbers from 100 to 199. A passwd file is created from /etc/passwd and is truncated at user ID 199. Mine is called Spasswd, for "short password file," and is truncated at user ID 199. Now system personnel can log on as root, operator, bin, and so on, but regular users cannot log on. When needed, /etc/passwd is copied to Opasswd, and Spasswd is copied to passwd:

```
$ su
password:
# cd /etc
# cp Opasswd OOpasswd
# cp passwd Opasswd
# cp Spasswd passwd
```

The follow-up is critical with a modified inittab or passwd file. When you have shut down the system and brought it up again, you must restore the standard /etc/passwd or /etc/inittab file. And in all likelihood you will have put up an emergency message of the day that must be changed as well:

```
$ su
password:
# cd /etc
# cp Opasswd passwd
# cp Omotd motd
```

Now all is as it was before the emergency. Back to business as usual.

YP PASSWORD ADMINISTRATION

The addition of Yellow Pages to a networked system changes the entire complexion of password administration. Before YP, each system had autonomy over its own password data base. In fact, it was only with the greatest of care that any form of reasonable password data base could be created and used constructively among several systems.

Yellow Pages exists to create and share system data bases among networked systems. All systems grouped together sharing a single data base are called a *YP domain*. Clearly, YP's contribution to password management is enormous.

Adding Users

To create a new user login under YP, the first step is to get a usable, unique user-ID number for the new user. Here is where YP comes to the rescue. Without YP you have to remote-copy all the `passwd` files in the cluster to a single directory. They have to be merged and sorted, but not before filtering out all nonhumans like `root`, `daemon`, and `sync`. Since YP maintains a single file, all you have to do is get YP to give you a copy, sort it, and then filter it. The following says, "Give me all the user-ID numbers larger than 99, and sort them numerically":

```
% ypcat passwd!awk -F: '$3>99 { print $3 }'!sort -n
```

Now `awk`'s pattern-matching operation obtains user IDs over 99, the real people. If you are looking for a different range, change this number. The output is a list of used user-ID numbers. Now you have a list of all the numbers that have been used, so all you need to do is pick the next available number.

The second step is to add the user to the YP `passwd` source file on the YP domain server. Unless a lot of work has gone into creating a separate YP source directory, the source file is `/etc/passwd`. Be safe and create both a temporary and an old `passwd` file.

```
% su
password:
# cd /etc
# cp passwd Tpasswd
# cp passwd Opasswd
# vi Tpasswd
```

Append the new user to `Tpasswd`, and double-check your entry. Are there seven fields and six colons? Have you specified the right shell and qualified the path? If it looks good, copy `Tpasswd` to `passwd`. Use Berkeley command `vipw` if you don't need to leave an audit trail.

With a good entry in `/etc/passwd`, move to the base of your YP directory. It may be `/usr/etc/yp` or `/var/yp`, depending on the UNIX implementation. Run `make`, and you're done. The `Makefile` does all the work of creating the new password data base entries and propagating the new data base to the domain slave server.

Now move to the file server that services the user's client system. Move to the base of the directory that hosts the user, and make him or her a directory. Copy all the necessary dot files from the server's source. The locations will vary: On ULTRIX systems they are in `/usr/skel`. Now change ownership, and the user will be in business:

```
# mkdir /u/mplefka
# cd /usr/skel
# ls!cpio -pv /u/mplefka
# cd /u/mplefka
# chown mplefka . .??*
```

Accompanied by the `-p` option, `cpio` is as good a method as any to copy all the dot files. Berkeley's recursive copy option to `cp` is another good choice. BSD's `ls` command lists dot files, but AT&T versions have to use `find`:

```
# find . -type f -name ".??*"  -print!cpio .....
```

The `find` command is about as sophisticated at string searching as `ls` is. The metacharacters, `. .??*`, get the current directory and all files starting with a dot followed by at least two letters, dot files like .cshrc and .login. All of this can be accomplished in less time than it takes to describe the process.

Changing Passwords on YP

Changing passwords under YP is not necessarily a breeze, as /bin/passwd is effectively disabled on YP, and so yppasswd must be used instead. Note also that yppasswdd, the YP password daemon, must be enabled in rc.local. When a new password is handed to yppasswd, it updates the YP domain password source file. Remember that the source file, usually /etc/passwd, is not where passwords are checked under YP. The new password does not take effect until make is run on the YP domain directory.

If a user uses the passwd command, the password entry will be changed in /etc/passwd. However, on YP the system gets information from the YP data base, not /etc/passwd. When a make is run on /usr/etc/YP, then the source password file is read, and the new password has become part of the data base. As a result, scenarios like the following occur: A user changes her password but sees no immediate change. Eventually, when she wonders what on earth is going on, her password changes. This can blow a user's mind. There are homemade cures, of course, such as having cron run a script to confirm that /etc/passwd has been modified. If it has, then the code will make YP. The problem is the granularity of find is one day, and that's not close enough.

utmp **and** wtmp

Both utmp and wtmp are used by accounting and who (see Chapter 10). User accounting information is stored in the following structure:

```
struct utmp
    {
        char ut_user[8] ;          /* User login name */
        char ut_id[4] ;            /* /etc/lines id(usually line #) */
        char ut_line[12] ;         /* device name (console, lnxx) */
        short ut_pid ;             /* process id */
        short ut_type ;            /* type of entry */
        struct exit_status
            {
              short e_termination ;/* Process termination status */
              short e_exit ;  /* Process exit status */
            }
        ut_exit ;                  /* The exit status of a process
                                      marked as DEAD_PROCESS. */
        time_t ut_time ;           /* time entry was made */
    }
```

Also, utmp records are stored in /etc/utmp. User accounting information is written to these files at each user-to-kernel cycle. You will have to access these raw data if you need to use them to create an accounting scheme, such as bill-back accounting.

Sometimes you will see *phantom terminal* problems on systems on which a communications line is broken. The system administrator must go in and kill all user processes, but a who shows that the user logged on. What still must be changed is the ut_line structure member contents in the utmp entry and the user's entry on wtmp.

Good bill-back accounting information can be gathered from accounting records at a higher level with accounting commands in manual(1M). The data can be manipulated with awk for a reasonable output, but usually management wants something that is neither available from accounting nor formattable by awk. The remaining choice is to hire a consultant to write you a bill-back accounting program with the data from utmp and wtmp. My own experience with homegrown, bill-back accounting systems has not been pleasant. The problems become particularly severe when the user data are not up-to-date, which is most of the time.

In addition, utmp is used to store current logins. It is a non-ASCII data file, so it must be read by the octal dump command, od, if you wish to see anything:

```
% od -c /etc/utmp!sed -n '3,15p'
0000100   \0  \0  \0  \0   X 305 371   $   r   o   o   t  \0  \0  \0  \0
0000120    0   1  \0  \0   t   t   y   0   1  \0  \0  \0  \0  \0  \0  \0
0000140  264  \0 007  \0  \0  \0  \0  \0 211 365 371   $   L   O   G   I
0000160    N  \0  \0  \0   1   0  \0  \0   t   t   y   1   0  \0  \0  \0
0000200   \0  \0  \0  \0   ,  \0 006  \0  \0  \0  \0  \0   b 305 371   $
0000220    L   O   G   I   N  \0  \0  \0   2   c  \0  \0   t   t   y   2
0000240    c  \0  \0  \0  \0  \0  \0  \0   1  \0 006  \0  \0  \0  \0  \0
0000260    c 305 371   $   b   r   u   c   e  \0  \0  \0   0   2  \0  \0
0000300    t   t   y   0   2  \0  \0  \0  \0  \0  \0  \0   $  \0 007  \0
0000320   \0  \0  \0  \0 354 353 371   $   b   r   u   c   e  \0  \0  \0
0000340    0   3  \0  \0   t   t   y   0   3  \0  \0  \0  \0  \0  \0  \0
0000360    %  \0 007  \0  \0  \0  \0  \0 341 353 371   $   L   O   G   I
```

If you look carefully, you will see the user root on tty01 and bruce on tty03.

The who command makes extensive use of utmp. Its permissions are usually set at 0622, but permissions must be changed to make utmp publicly writable on systems running SunOS's sunview or any system running X Windows. If not, logins made through the pseudoterminals for the windows are not able to write to utmp.

File and Inode Modes Internals

A knowledge of file system and inode internals often proves invaluable to system administrators. The user interface to files starts at the directory, yet there is very little information there. Rather, the directory is a collection of 16-byte structures of type direct. They contain an inode number of type ino_t and an array of char holding a 14-byte file name. That's it. All the directory entry does is associate a name with an inode number.

The inode itself has an intriguing structure: The disk version and the inode table version differ noticeably. Here is the simpler disk version:

```
struct dinode
{
      ushort di_mode;          /* mode and type of file */
      short   di_nlink;        /* number of links to file */
      ushort di_uid;           /* owner's user id */
      ushort di_gid;           /* owner's group id */
      off_t   di_size;         /* number of bytes in file */
      char    di_addr[40];     /* disk block addresses */
      time_t  di_atime;        /* time last accessed */
      time_t  di_mtime;        /* time last modified */
      time_t  di_ctime;        /* time created */
};
```

The di-mode term requires further definition. We all are familiar with the permissions in octal as shown in chmod(1M).

read	04
write	02
execute	01

They are called permissions bits, and they will make a lot more sense if you think in base 2 instead of octal. In octal the total of 4, 2, and 1 is 7, but in base 2 it is 0111. Each 1 turns on a permission for r, w, or x. Similarly, 777 (*read*, *write*, and *execute* across *owner*, *group*, and *other*) gives a 111111111 or rwxrwxrwx.

Mode bits extend beyond the nine permissions fields. The next bit field sets the "sticky" bit, which holds the text image on the swap disk. It is 001000 octal, but in binary it becomes 1 000 000 000. Now we see a pattern emerging in the tenth through the twelfth bit fields. The set-group ID (EGID) on execution is 2000 octal, and the set-user ID on execution is 4000, finishing out the bit pattern 111 000 000 000.

That isn't all. UNIX isn't about to waste bits in a perfectly good 16-bit, short integer. Unlike the ones before it, the fifth octal position is no longer a mask, because at this point there is just too much to cram in. The fifth and sixth octal positions define the file type. The following is from inode.h, the incore inode structure:

```
IFDIR    0040000  /*directory
IFCHAR   0020000  /*character special
IFBL     0060000  /*block special
IFREG    0100000  /*regular file
IFMPC    0030000  /*multiplexed character special
IFMPB    0070000  /*multiplexed block special
IFIFO    0010000  /*fifo special (pipe)
IFNAM    0050000  /*name special (named pipe)
```

Now it is clear how the system knows what kind of file it is seeing. If the bit fields in the thirteenth through sixteenth positions become corrupted, the system will not be able to talk to the file or directory. There thus is little choice but to clear the inode with clri and remove the directory entry.

BERKELEY TREATMENT OF TERMINALS

The way terminal files are handled by BSD is so different that it merits its own section. In some ways BSD is similar to XENIX: BSD has a ttys file as XENIX does, a vestige of UNIX Editions 6 and 7. The ttys file is not used by the system in later versions of BSD but retains it for compatibility. Also similar to XENIX, BSD has a ttytypes file, although BSD also has a gettytab file, which is similar to the AT&T System V's gettydefs. BSD has no initiation states, so there is no inittab either; it has ttytypes instead.

Let's take a closer look at some BSD files.

ttytab

Remember the old Edition 7 and XENIX /etc/ttys file? It looks like this:

```
% cat /etc/ttys
1mtty01

1mtty02
1mtty03
.
.
.
0mtty2b
0mtty2d
0mtty2e
```

Each /etc/ttys entry acts as if it has three fields. Tear apart the first line 1mtty01:

```
on      baud    tty
off     rate    name

1       m       tty01
```

Now it makes more sense: 1 stands for *on* and 0 for *off*. But the m makes no sense until you look at XENIX's /etc/gettydefs:

```
j # B1800 HUPCL # B1800 CS8 SANE HUPCL TAB3 ECHOE IXANY #\r\n@!login: # j
k # B2400 HUPCL # B2400 CS8 SANE HUPCL TAB3 ECHOE IXANY #\r\n@!login: # k
l # B4800 HUPCL # B4800 CS8 SANE HUPCL TAB3 ECHOE IXANY #\r\n@!login: # l
m # B9600 HUPCL # B9600 CS8 SANE HUPCL TAB3 ECHOE IXANY #\r\n@!login: # m
n # EXTA  HUPCL # EXTA  CS8 SANE HUPCL TAB3 IXANY #\r\n@!login: # n
o # EXTB  HUPCL # EXTB  CS8 SANE HUPCL TAB3 IXANY #\r\n@!login: # o
```

Here we see that m is 9600 baud with all sorts of termio settings.

Now let's contrast this all with Berkeley's /etc/ttytab. Bear in mind that BSD is written to interact with the network, while System V Releases 2 and 3 and XENIX are not:

```
% cat /etc/ttytab
# name   getty                     type     status  comments
#
console  "/usr/etc/getty std.9600"  sun      on      secure
ttyp0    none                       network  off
ttyp1    none                       network  off
ttyp2    none                       network  off
ttyp3    none                       network  off
ttyp4    none                       network  off
ttyp5    none                       network  off
ttyp6    none                       network  off
ttyp7    none                       network  off
.
tty0     "/usr/etc/getty d1200"     dialup   on
```

Here ttytab is read by the gettyent(3) library routine. Note that there is one line in the file for each device special file that is terminal related. Fields are white-space separated, so lines like "/usr/etc/getty std.9600" must be quoted.

The first field is the device special file as it appears in /dev. The second field is a command, usually a getty, and none is a placeholder and does what it says, nothing.

The third field is the terminal type or a descriptor if it is not a conventional terminal. The status field is a flag field, on allowing the command to be executed and off not allowing it.

The comment line does double duty. Besides being available for comments, it is also the security field, with the word secure used to allow root to log in. Otherwise, administrators and system programmers must log on as themselves and su to get user ID 0.

Now let's put everything together and look at line 1: Line 1 is the console /dev/console. The console spawns a getty at 9600 baud. Its terminal type is sun, a Sun 386i monitor in this case. If the status is on, the getty works. The word secure is optimistic, because root may log on directly.

ttys

Descending from old UNIX and present in XENIX and BSD, the file /etc/ttys in all its cryptic glory turns ports on or off to logins and sets the ports' baud rates. It looks like this:

```
12console
02ttyp0
02ttyp1
02ttyp2
.
```

Note that it is identical to XENIX and Edition 7. It is used only to maintain backwards compatability with old versions of BSD software.

gettytab

Since 9600 baud is an old favorite of standard hardwire terminals, let's start looking at gettytab there:

```
% grep '9600' /etc/gettytab
2:std.9600:9600baud:\
    :sp#9600
```

The first line is a *this* or *that* or *the other* proposition:

```
name1:name2:nameN:\
```

Remember printcap's

```
$   lp:lp1:epson:\
```

The gettytab command's entries are reminiscent of printcap and termcap.

The next line uses termcaplike mnemonics, and std.9600's only mnemonic is sp, a numeric, which sets the speed to 9600 baud.

Now let's look at a nastier entry with a *dialup*, a tty port that is open for outside modem entry:

```
d1200:Dial-1200:\
    :nx=d150:fd#1:sp#1200:
```

This 1200 baud dial-up has the following mnemonics:

nx   Type string, the next table for auto speed selection.

fd   Type numeric, form feed delay default 0, now set to 1.

sp   Type numeric, the line speed.

ttytype

Somewhere a file must exist to associate the port or device special file with whatever is attached to it. System V has inittab, which associates the initiation state with the terminal or port, sets a getty with terminals, and allows the line speed to be set:

```
$ cat /etc/inittab
co:123:respawn:/etc/getty console 9600
11:2:respawn/etc/getty -t 60 tty11 1200
.
.
```

Berkeley does the association in ttytype:

```
ansi        tty01
ansi        tty02
.
unknown     tty1a
unknown     tty2a
dialup      tty1A
.
dialup      tty1D
unknown     tty1b
unknown     tty1c
unknown     tty1d
dialup      tty2B
dialup      tty2C
dialup      tty2D
unknown     tty2b
adds        tty2c
unknown     tty2d
```

Here ttytype is read by login and tset, but more recent BSD derivative systems like ULTRIX and SunOS are more tolerant of setting the term variable directly rather than relying on tset:

```
% grep term .cshrc
set term=vt100
```

Nonetheless, tset can be tedious to set, particularly by uninitiated users. At its simplest, it requires aid to prevent character interpretation:

```
set noglob
eval`tset -s2621`
unset noglob
```

Here noglob is used to prevent shell interpretation of any metacharacters on the tset command.

MANAGER'S CORNER

Why UNIX?

You've probably heard that old comedy routine in which the comedian compares every exotic meat he's ever tasted with chicken. Snake tastes like chicken, turtle tastes like chicken, possum tastes like chicken, and so on. One day he is given some unknown meat to try. He puts some in his mouth, rolls his eyes, and says, "Mmmmm, that's the best meat I've ever tasted. What is it?" Naturally the answer is chicken.

For some time now in the press, other operating systems have been compared with UNIX, and indeed, some commercial operating systems are getting more and more like UNIX, such as DOS and OS/2. What, then, makes UNIX the vital computer industry force it is today? It's not clever marketing, aggressive company management, or some other nontechnical ploy. Computer managers should know the actual technical reasons.

UNIX has an innovative operating system design approach. Since all devices are files and since pipes and redirection exist, data can be moved easily in ways limited almost exclusively to the user's imagination. Data can be moved from device to file, file to file, file to device, file to command to device, and so on. Work can be done much faster when you can move data that easily. A special report on a traditional mainframe takes days to program with RPG pulling data from a COBOL-created data base. Under UNIX a special report can be created quickly with `awk` augmented by other filters such as `sort`, `grep`, and `sed`.

UNIX has a hierarchical file structure that allows searching for files and directories from any point in the system. No directories or files are hidden unless their creators deliberately want them to be hidden. The concept of each mountable file system with its own `/root` allows entire mounted file systems to be attached to the UNIX tree.

Hundreds of simple, single-function commands permit users to learn the commands quickly and easily, a philosophy that is markedly different from the massive, do-all commands used by traditional mainframe operating systems. Indeed, VM's `dirmaint` requires one manual for that command alone.

UNIX has three major orientations: programming, writing and text processing, and networking and communications. Programmers are provided with an ideal programming environment that was built into UNIX from the start. I earlier mentioned pipes and redirection, simple function commands, and a hierarchical file structure, but UNIX also has several tools available for program development. UNIX is the only operating system I know that has its own compiler compiler and lexical analyzer. UNIX also has a remarkable collection of filters, programs that add to, delete from, or otherwise modify the data stream, which saves enormous amounts of programming time. Perhaps the most well-known UNIX contribution to the programming environment is the C language and all of its support tools.

UNIX contains abundant document preparation tools, from text entry to final typesetting. The UNIX text-processing environment is radically changing the publishing industry today, and powerful publishing software such as FrameMaker is readily available.

UNIX has always had its own internal Email system, and its communications ability expanded with `uucp`. Berkeley and other contributors created the final touches with the addition of Ethernet TCP/IP. The computer industry was looking for interconnectivity: Most major vendors have their own networking schemes, but few are heterogeneous; besides, Ethernet TCP/IP does it better. This UNIX feature alone is responsible for many of the networking developments in the computer industry today.

This is only a partial list. What I like most about UNIX is that it wasn't designed with a limited, proprietary mentality. My favorite UNIX design feature is that it is a multiuser, multiprocess system with code and user portability. As a "portable operating system," the goal of its design is to have an operating system that runs anywhere, from PC to mainframe. While being retentive is fine for the acquisitive and those who would inhibit progress for their own shortsighted gains, it is not fine for operating systems in a country that is fighting to maintain its technical lead in at least one area. The United States has a chance to retain its software engineering advantage by developing a few universal operating systems that can talk to one another. DOS can fill the notch at the low end because its home is a highly accepted, open architecture. Those operating systems are limited to personal computers, but the rest of the field runs with an array of processors and architectures that defies description. Only UNIX is prepared to span this diversity of applied silicon.

People committed to UNIX should insist that the UNIX kernel, the heart of UNIX, be free to develop. Imagine buying a new Ford fresh off the floor of the dealer's preparation room. It looks good and it smells good, but it moves with the speed of a sick slug. Opening the hood, you find a vintage, side-valve, 6-cylinder, 1932 engine trying to burn unleaded fuel with a rat's nest of air pollution equipment. UNIX's kernel is an engine that must be allowed to develop, uninhibited by the personal gain of a few. What we need is good, independent research. Whether the developments occur in industry or come from university researchers experimenting with innovations, if they are good enough, they will make their way to commercial UNIX, and everyone will benefit. None of us needs UNIX arbitrarily fixed at some old version. For organizations to choose UNIX versions for any reasons other than portability and performance is the height of folly.

5

Backups and Restores

Two of the most important system administration tasks are preserving the system's integrity and preserving its data. To do this well, you must have a viable scheme to back up the system's data. But even that isn't enough. Should the system fail, as they sometimes do, you also must be able to get at specific data and restore them quickly. *Backups and restores go hand in hand: Backup schemes should be planned with ease of data restoration in mind.*

BACKUPS: THEY ARE MORE COMPLEX THAN YOU THINK

There are lots of general things to know about backups. The principle of backups is to copy data from their computer source to portable media and store the media out of harm's way. When you back up data, you either copy everything in sight, a *full backup*, or you copy only some of them, a *partial backup*. There are many kinds of partial backups, including an *incremental backup* used to copy files that have recently had their contents or inode information created or modified. Enough general information. Let's look at some backup specifics.

How Precisely Do You Want to Be Able to Restore the Data?

Once you've decided when to do partial backups and when to do full backups, you should consider some other factors before you go ahead and make the actual backup. Now you have to choose from three more categories.

Nonarchive (No Header File)

A nonarchive backup copies everything, but it doesn't catalog anything for you. It doesn't contain a header file or any other kind of clue to what is in there. The tape simply has an external label, usually just a number. This copy method is great for doing byte-for-byte copies of the root disk and copying multivolume files, but trying to restore anything less than the entire contents from this kind of archive method is like trying to build a house with a 8-ounce hammer. Unless you are into pain, supplement it with some other backup method if you often need to restore data.

Archive (Header File)

An archive backup method creates a header file containing a list of the contents of the copy. When you want to know exactly what you backed up, this method is a vast improvement over the previous method. Should there be any doubt about what's on tape, you have only to read the header file to know precisely what is there.

Catalog (Online Data Base)

With a catalog the administrator has an online data base of each copy's contents, dates, media names, and locations. This method offers you the most specific restores. The only disadvantage is that it isn't currently a part of the standard UNIX distribution, so you have to buy the software or write your own programs.

How Often Do You Need to Back Up Your Data?

You also must consider how *often* to do backups in your overall backup scheme. Backup philosophies and requirements vary from site to site, the most common being

Monthly   Full archives, including the system itself
Weekly   Full backups, not necessarily an archive
Daily   Incremental backups
Hourly   Highly critical backups of rapidly changing system files like /etc/passwd

Tape Storage

With backup storage you don't have the luxury of an on-site or off-site option. Backups *must* exist off-site. A company cannot survive if it loses its entire data base. You also must have some recent backups on your site. The most current full backup and incremental backups must be stored on your site for quick access when data need to be restored in a hurry.

What Kind of Backup Medium Suits Your Site?

There is more to backup media than tapes or diskettes. Currently you have a lot of choices:

Diskette   The backbone of PC backups, but too low in capacity for full UNIX backups

Reel-to-reel	The one-time industry standard
Disk-to-disk	The quickest backup and an interesting option
Cartridge	Huge capacity and a great deal of convenience
Optical	Extreme capacity and speed

Floppy diskettes are not large enough to do complete UNIX backups, but they are a viable choice for partial and incremental backups. They are also a better choice than nothing at all.

Reel-to-reel, ½-inch tape is currently the only fully portable medium available. The only variables you have to cope with are byte ordering and density. Density means that you can make one tape 800, 1600, or 6250 bpi, if your drive allows it. Reel-to-reel tapes were the industry standard for years, but they have disadvantages. They are not easy to load, and the drives are very expensive. People used to think of reel-to-reel tapes as a large-capacity medium, but today their capacity is thought of as limited, and so they are becoming obsolete.

Cartridge tape is taking over. Fortunately, it has passed the gigabyte range, because disk-drive capacity has also. Cartridge tape capacity is so much larger than reel-to-reel tape that most large installations have switched over to cartridge tape.

Optical disks are still a relatively new technology. Most are *WORM* drives, an acronym for *write once read many*.

Quiescent Disks: The Impossible Dream

How can you make perfect copies unless the disks are quiescent? Think about it. Data cannot be guaranteed. If the file is being modified, the copy will be a mix of the old and new versions. The answer seems so obvious. You simply unmount each disk before copying it, and that's that, right? If only it were that simple.

You don't run into as many problems on small or medium sites. Small systems usually run under a benevolent dictatorship. You don't have hundreds of users and dozens of internal organizations to please, so there are no written agreements to abide by, and the system administrator has fewer inhibitions (see Chapter 22). The administrator notifies users on the system in the message of the day, by `wall`, or even by shouting an over-the-office-partition warning, depending on the size of the site. She then brings the system to an initiation level where no users can log on, does her backups, and returns the system to the users.

On larger sites the machines are never entirely your own to administer, because you have so many people and organizations to please. The system administrator is pulled in many directions at once, and the best he can do is try to please most of the people most of the time. Backup methods are negotiated, and written agreements are drawn up to protect all parties involved.

I have never been at a large site that allowed the administrator enough time to unmount disks before copying them, and I probably never will. Assuming that you could get hundreds of users in different organizations within the company to agree on short time periods to back up data—an unlikely assumption—consider the time it would take to schedule each user's partition for backup. Even if it took only about 10 minutes to unmount a partition, back it up, and remount the partition, on a large installation there would be hundreds of partitions, so it would take two full shifts to unmount them all. For hours there would be a ripple effect of one address after another being unavailable. If any users had programs running at the wrong time, their unprotected programs would go down the tubes when you unmounted the disks, and guess who would get the flack for that.

What about backing up the system at night? Large system users usually rely on working around the clock. They batch their time-intensive, noninteractive jobs to run all night, and they depend on the results to be there the next morning. For large machines the upshot is this: *Unmounting a disk for even a short period is prohibitively expensive, day or night, in terms of work hours lost and programs killed or maimed.*

BACKUP MEDIA CONSIDERATIONS

Backups schemes range from the mundane to the complex. We have just seen some backup variables. The backup scheme you develop will encompass most of them, but the type of medium you use is another crucial factor.

UNIX system administrators need to find the ideal combination that guarantees not only that data will be copied but also that they will be restored precisely. The degree of complexity of your backup scheme is a function of site requirements. If the system is small enough and the medium is large enough, a full archive backup can be made nightly. But this is an ideal situation that rarely exists on real sites. Usually you will have to settle for incremental backups, except on the weekend. Your main rule of thumb is *keep backups as simple as possible*. It doesn't take much to make backups complex, and they can go from simple to impossible in short order.

Backups to Floppy Diskette

The simplest backup scheme is one in which the users' area is copied to a single medium with a one-line script:

```
$ cat flop.bak
find /u -depth -print!cpio -ocv>/dev/fd096ds15
```

It doesn't get much simpler than this. The find command is used to get a recursive descent listing of the user directory, /u.[1] The -depth flag guarantees that find won't get sidetracked on its way through the tree, and -print is used to get output. The entire results of find are piped to cpio using the -o option for *output archive*. The -c flag gives an ASCII header for portability. The output is redirected directly to the floppy disk using the 96-tracks-per-inch, 15-sector, double-sided driver options, fd096ds15.

Backups start getting complicated when the contents of the file system exceed the size of the floppy diskette. Then cpio's input must be broken up into diskette or tape-sized pieces when the medium's capacity is exceeded. Backing up dynamic system files

---

[1] A recursive descent search goes from the root base of the entire directory structure to the extremes of all branches. It is sometimes called a *recursive ascent*, depending on whether the tree is visualized with roots at the top or the bottom.

and network files adds an additional complication. The following system backup script takes these factors into consideration by reducing the size of the backup output:

```
$ cat /local/etc/sys.bak
find /etc -type f -mtime -30 -print!cpio -ocv>/dev/fd096ds15
```

Notice this is an incremental backup that makes copies of anything in /etc that has recently been added or modified. The find command uses -type to limit the copy to files and the -mtime option to limit the files copied to those modified in the last thirty days. The cpio command copies to an archive file with an ASCII header, in the verbose mode, -v, printing what it copies to the screen. The destination is a 96-tpi, double-sided floppy, specified by fd096ds15.

Disk-to-Disk Backups

Don't always think in terms of hard-disk-to-floppy or hard-disk-to-tape backups. Hard-disk-to-hard-disk backups on very small systems have an attractive economic incentive. In 1990, a tape unit with controller started at $500, and a good 40-megabyte, SCSI, quick-access, half-height hard disk discounted at around $330. If it's your second hard disk, you will still have room for it on your controller. On SCSI controllers you can extend to 4 to 6 drives, IPI drives up to four per controller and so on. A disk-to-disk backup of an entire project like this book can be done with the following one-liner:

```
$ cat /local/etc/to.disk.bak
find /u -print -depth!cpio -pdvmu /p/local/bak/u
```

There it is in all of its unsophisticated glory. Notice there is no checking for time stamps, no incrementals, and no checking for overwrite protection. Everything is simply written en masse to the other disk. It's enough to make a UNIX purist cringe, but it's fast and clean. It's over in a few seconds on a 386 or 486 system with 28-msecond disk access time. Naturally, archive backups must still be done to tape or diskette.

Not only is this backup technique inexpensive; it also allows for a bootable partition on the backup disk, which can make it a freestanding system should the root disk fail. Then it is truly a complete backup.

Backup to Tapes

Tapes are a more realistic medium for UNIX system backups. UNIX is a large system by definition, and tapes are a larger medium. The industry standard for large machines was ½-inch, reel-to-reel tape, and for many years reel-to-reel tape was Hollywood's standard symbol for the computer. Think back to any movie or television scene involving computers. They all show banks of flashing lights and reel-to-reel tape drives, probably because actual computers are as exciting to film as a row of refrigerators in an appliance store. Now reel-to-reel tape is old news, and I don't know what Hollywood is going to do about that.

In spite of their extended storage capacity, reel-to-reel tapes run out of space before direct storage does, but you can get around this by defining and precalculating zones of storage. Before each backup, have your script go through and calculate blocks of data to be stored, and then create a file of file names of the data to be sent to tape or diskette. The file of file names will be stored with the backup file. You will come close to maintaining an online catalog of backed-up files using this method, necessary if you want to restore data quickly.

Getting data back from secondary tape storage onto disk has its own set of problems. Data restoration problems center on finding the tape or the diskette volume on which the data live. Thus when you make a backup run, there should be some record of which files were copied where and when. You should have some method of displaying what is going to tape. You can use cpio or tar after the data are backed up to tape to verify that a backup has occurred and then list its contents to the printer or to a disk file. This is one way to catalog what is on the tape.

When the size of the area to be backed up exceeds the size of the medium to which it is being written, you must go to multiple-media volumes. It gets very complicated when a single file exceeds the size of the backup medium, because some UNIX commands are capable of doing multiple volume backups, and some are not. We'll examine this issue shortly when we look at backup commands.

Cartridge Tape

Almost everything that works for reel-to-reel tape works for cartridge tape. Reel-to-reel tape was designed as a source of secondary storage. The drives are capable of seeking, stopping, and reversing, but all of this is not necessary today. Smaller reel-to-reel units built in the last ten years have been streamer tapes that operate like cassettes. Cassettes, also called cartridge tapes, have more capacity and convenience than do their reel-to-reel counterparts. Their disadvantage is the lack of a standard and therefore portability.

DATA BASE BACKUP UTILITIES

I have run a few commercial schemes that create a data base tape management system for backups. UTS backup used to be shipped with the operating system, and it used Ingres as its data base manager. It was a good idea, but backup kept corrupting its own data base. Another mainframe backup system I tried was only in its beta stage, and I had more problems with the vendor than with the software. I rejected the system on the basis of product immaturity. The vendors were so upset that they complained to the president of the company I worked for.

Most backup schemes have proved a disappointment in one way or another, but the most efficient one I've seen so far for large-scale systems is a Unitech product called Ubackup,[2] part of the Ucontrol package. Ubackup is a comprehensive tape management system, essentially a backup/restore system with online catalogs coupled with interactive, menu-driven, user-restore screens. It is worth the money for its convenience alone.

Ubackup maintains a disk-resident catalog of files and dates. The entire system is menu driven, and its restores are close to automatic. When a user makes a restore request

---

[2] Ubackup works with diskette or tape of any kind.

to Ubackup, it goes through its online catalog and finds the file reference. Then it sends a message containing the volume number of the tape or diskette to the system console. A medium mount is requested. The tape operator doesn't even need to know what is being restored. He just mounts the medium, and the restore is done by the machine. Tapes or diskettes are internally labeled, and the system does not allow the wrong volume to be mounted for either backup or restore.

Is it worth buying a commercial tape management system or a backup system? Even Ubackup has some faults. It is slow, as one would expect, and it has problems with some odd symbols used in file names. However, according to my experience you can waste more money and time trying to program your own backup system than you will ever spend on a good commercial system. The writer of the commercial system has the advantage of beta tests and the site input of hundreds of customer installations. Although a commercial system may not fit your site like a glove, your money will still be well spent because you will save hours of time otherwise spent restoring data. All of this should be less of a problem at System V Release 4 because the backup/restore system has a friendly interface, an online data base, and many other long-needed additions and improvements.

BACKUP SCHEDULES

There are all sorts of papers on schemes for full backups coupled with varying degrees of incremental backups at periodic intervals. Most are excessively complex. *Remember that your goal is not so much the backup itself but your ultimate ability to restore the data.* The backup is the vehicle for the restore. At most sites a single weekly backup is run on Friday or the weekend, and incremental backups are run Monday through Thursday. At all sites some of the backup media are removed from the site and stored elsewhere. Only the most recent full and incremental backups are kept on the site. At the largest sites a commercial tape storage concern is used to remove and return the tapes. Tapes are returned to the site within a matter of a few hours of a return request.

A full weekly backup should take only minutes for a small, desktop system. There is no need to back up the entire system distribution. Should the system have to be rebuilt, your stored, unused distribution tapes or diskettes will be a better source, because they will not have been corrupted by use and abuse. However, all sites *should* back up dynamic system files such as

- `passwd`
- `group`
- terminal and port files, such as `ttys`, `inittab`, `gettydefs` (if altered), and `ttytypes`.
- uucp files, such as `Devices`, `L-devices`, `Dialers`, and `L.sys`.
- network files, such as `hosts`, `localhosts`, `networks`, `inetd.conf` (standard UNIX) or `NETSTART` (Wollongong), `route`, `hosts.equiv`, `netgroup`, and `/.rhosts`.
- cron (`/usr/spool/cron/crontabs/root`).
- accounting.
- configuration files (`master`, `config.c`, `config.h`, and `devicelist`).

BACKUP, ARCHIVING, AND COPY COMMANDS

So far we have discussed a few possible methods of writing and archiving to another area of storage for the purpose of backups. Now let's look at most of the available methods, command by command.

Basic Backups and Restores with dump and cpio

The cpio command does double duty. You cpio to the archive medium, and when a restore is needed, you cpio it back. Only the flag changes, from -o to -i. The dump command is half of the command pair dump/restore. You dump data out to tape, but you must restore the data back.

A significant difference between cpio and dump is that dump writes only from device to device. If you want to back up a file system to tape, you have to get the name of the disk partition on which the file system resides. Then you have to give dump the name of the tape device. Thus dump must write from a device (a device special file), a disk, or a disk partition, and it can write only one device file system to a tape. The dump command can't back up anything smaller than a disk partition.

The cpio command is not only capable of writing multiple files and directories, but it can also write a single file, a directory, or file trees. This is because cpio has no input; it is fed from another command. For example, the following sends Scott's home bin to the floppy as an archive:

```
# ls /u/scott/bin ! cpio -oc > /dev/floppy
```

Here cpio is fed from the ls command.

The cpio command is very handy for small local backups. In fact, each section of this book was backed up nightly with a simple cpio line:

```
# find /u/asa/section1 -depth -print!cpio -ocv>/dev/fd096ds15
```

The section was in no danger of exceeding 1.5 megabytes, and therefore tape or diskette volume limitations did not exist. Only when backup requirements are larger does exceeding the medium's limits become a problem with cpio.

The cpio command cannot easily do backups to multiple-media volumes. Whereas the contemporary BSD or 5.4 UNIX dump command can back up to multiple-media volumes with ease, cpio doesn't sense the end of the backup medium until it's too late, thereby giving you error messages instead of the backup you wanted. Always remember that you have to be careful with cpio. Although you can use it to back up mounted disk partitions, by all means unmount the disk partitions above it before you use cpio. If you unmount the disks from the hierarchy before you use cpio, there will be no danger of asking for root and getting everything.

Let's look at some program examples to help understand the differences between cpio and dump. An example of a cpio restore is David Fiedler's recover script:

```
$ cat recover
:
```

```
if [ $# -lt 1 ]
  then
    echo usage recover file [file [file,..]]
 fi
cd /
cpio -ivdum $* < /dev/tape
```

Note that the shell metacharacters $* mean all the arguments in the list. The cpio command with the -i flag must be handed a list of the files to be restored. Notice that this script assumes the archive was started from /, but that's not always the case.

Now let's look at how the find command can be used to drive cpio and to write both / and /etc to a single tape:

```
# wall
system coming down
^D
# umount -a
# find / -depth -print ¦ cpio -odlmv > /dev/nrmt1
 .
 .
# find /etc -depth -print ¦ cpio -odlmv > /dev/nrmt1
```

The trick here is the n in the device /dev/nrmt, which stands for *no rewind*. Tape drivers automatically rewind the tape after backing up the data, but the n specifies a different tape-drive driver, one with no rewind. The find command is the pump, sending all the file and directory names in the file system to cpio. The cpio command then creates a tape archive on the device whether it be tape, diskette, or even a partition on a hard disk.

A dump command line looks a lot different. The dump utility goes from device special file to device special file, which amounts to going from one device to another. In the following example, a full dump, level 0, is being taken off the root disk, device ra0a, on a DEC system:

```
# dump 0 /dev/ra0a
```

The data come off one device, a disk, and go to another device, a tape. (In contrast, cpio comes off a file system and goes to a device.) Thus, specifying / is an error

```
# dump 0 /     # error
```

because / is not a device name.

If you don't specify the device name of a tape to send your data to, dump will send data to the default device. Sending a dump to a device other than the default device takes a bit more work, but it still goes from device special file to device special file:

```
# dump 9udf 6250 /dev/rmt1 /dev/ra1c
```

In this example, device rmt1, a reel-to-reel tape on a DEC system with a TK70 square tape as a default, is the target of the level 9 incremental dump. The file system being backed up is a large user disk, ra1c. The d flag alerts dump to the density, 6250. The u flag tells dump to drop a note in the file /etc/dumpdates to let all know that a dump has occurred. The f flag is the key here. It tells dump to write to a specific device, here `rmt1`. Remember that if you don't use the `f` flag, `dump` will go out to the default tape drive.

In spite of `dump`'s ability to do wonders with single-line command invocations, there are advantages to running `dump` from a script. On cluster systems without operations support, backup scripts give each user a consistent script to work from. If you have an operations staff, all that your operators or users will need to do is type the name of the script to do the backup. No technical knowledge is required.

Here is one such script used to back up `root` and `/usr`. The devices in this script, such as `/dev/xd0d`, are particular to Sun systems, but the code can be used for any architecture:

```
:
if [ $# -eq 0 ]
  then
    echo "usage:   system [-r] [-u]"
    echo "where -r is for the root partition and -u is for /usr"
    exit 1
 fi
case $1 in
    -r) dump 0ud 6250 /dev/xd0a
        ;;
    -u) dump 0ud 6250 /dev/xd0d
        ;;
    *) echo "usage [-r] [-u]"
        echo "where -r is for root and -u is for /usr"
        exit 2
        ;;
 esac
exit 0
```

In regard to `cpio`, I once worked with a site where doing backups required all users to maintain in their home directories a file of the files to be backed up. A *file of files* is not uncommon for specialized backup schemes. The `cpio` script goes out, gets the names of the users out of `etc/passwd`, reads the files of files, and does a `cpio` archive to reel-to-reel tape without a rewind. But there is a simpler way to do this, and `cpio` is an ideal UNIX vehicle to do it. The following is a full backup using `cpio`, which backs up each user directory separately:

```
:
for dir in `awk -F:' $3>100 { print $6 }' /etc/passwd`
  do
    echo "$dir \n"
    find $dir -depth -print | cpio -ouvmd > /dev/nrmt0
  done
echo "\n\nbackup complete -- rewind tape"
exit 0
# weekly backup
```

The `awk` line is interesting because it takes advantage of `awk`'s pattern-matching ability, something not often seen. The `$3>100` tells `awk` to get only those `passwd` records in which the third field, the user-ID number, is greater than 100. User IDs greater than 100 are reserved for people, and those smaller than 100 are reserved for `root`, `adm`, `bin`, `nuucp`, and so on. The drawback is that you have to manipulate the tape from one archive to another until you find the one you need.

The following incremental backup script is identical to the preceding script except for the `find`/`cpio` line. The `find` command uses `mtime` to get files written today or yesterday:

```
for dir in `awk -F:' $3>100 { print $ 6 }' /etc/passwd`
  do
      echo "$dir \n"
      find $dir -depth -mtime -2 -type f -print!cpio -ouvmd>/dev/nrmt0
  done
echo "\n\nbackup complete -- rewind tape"
exit 0
```

The problem with relying on `cpio` is that someday your tape may run out before all the data are copied. If that happens, you will have to write a program to presize the data to be written, calculate how much tape is needed, and calculate the break points where the tape (or diskette) write is stopped and a new medium volume is requested.

Why go to all the trouble with `cpio`, when `dump` does all of that for you, whether or not you want it to? The `dump` command does the precalculation, tells you how many volumes and fractions of volumes will be required, and then goes about the business of doing the backup. Here's where a system administrator is wise to have more than one backup strategy up her sleeve. When `cpio` becomes limited, `dump` can take over.

Here's another `dump` script that allows anyone to use it, with little or no training:

```
% cd /u/local/etc
% cat backup
#
if ( $#argv != 1)
    then echo "usage:    backup [daily] [weekly] [root] [usr]"
    exit 1
 endif
switch ( $1 )
   case weekly:
        dump 0udf 6250 /dev/rmt1 /dev/ra2c
        breaksw
   case daily:
        dump 9udf 6250 /dev/rmt1 /dev/ra2c
        breaksw
   case root:
        dump 0udf 6250 /dev/rmt1 /dev/ra0a
        breaksw
   case usr:
        dump 0udf 6250 /dev/rmt1 /dev/ra0d
   default:
        echo "usage    backup [daily] [weekly] [root] [usr]"
        exit 1
        breaksw
   endsw
exit 0
```

For those who prefer the Bourne shell, there are a few syntactic changes:

```
:
if [ $# -ne 1 ]
  then
      echo "usage:    backup [daily] [weekly] [root] [usr]"
      exit 1
  fi
```

```
case $1 in
   weekly)
        dump 0udf 6250 /dev/rmt1 /dev/ra2c
        ;;
   daily)
        dump 9udf 6250 /dev/rmt1 /dev/ra2c
        ;;
   root)
        dump 0udf 6250 /dev/rmt1 /dev/ra0a
        ;;
   usr)
        dump 0udf 6250 /dev/rmt1 /dev/ra0d
        ;;
   *)
        echo "usage    backup [daily] [weekly] [root] [usr]"
        exit 2
esac
exit 0
```

Remember that Bourne-shell programs will execute from C shell if the first character is not a pound sign, #.

The dump command has particular appeal when doing full backups to diskette. If you're going out to a 2400-foot roll of tape, you may make it to the end of the tape, but you certainly aren't going to get a full user area backup on one diskette. If the user area is the same size as the distribution area—and it usually is larger—you will have at least thirteen diskettes to fill!

UNIX system administrators should know that the dump/restore command pair is not the same on all UNIX systems. For example, although SCO XENIX and early AT&T systems run the older version of dump, Berkeley 4.2- and 4.3-based systems like SunOS and ULTRIX-32 have newer versions of dump with an interactive restore command. AT&T has a similar version on the way as a part of System V Release 4. All do full or partial dumps, write across tape or diskette volumes, and restore all or part of the dump on request. We will look at the old version shortly. Now let's take a closer look at restores in general and the restore command in particular.

restore

Restores are the flip side of backups. Part of your backup strategy should include building in the ease of data restoration. Many an organization has fallen for an easy backup method only to find out that the corresponding restore method is a nightmare.

The basic law of any restore method is that it be able to restore anything from a single file to the entire system and all points in between. The corollary to this law is that in the process the restore method should not overwrite good data with bad. A case in point: Imagine an organization foolish enough to do a complete byte-for-byte copy of an entire disk without regard for file organization. Believe it or not, I've seen it done. I know one mainframe site that backs up UNIX from VM using a VM utility called DDR, a byte-for-byte copy of the entire disk. If one or a few files are lost and need to be recovered, all the new data on the disk will be overwritten in the process of restoring the few lost files. One entire free disk pack has to be found and the DDR copied first to the spare disk. Then the data must be methodically and meticulously recopied back to the original location.

The UNIX restore command, however, has none of the failings of this method but can copy all or part of the backup tape's contents to anywhere in the system. The restore can be used as a simple command. However, in BSD 4.2 and 4.3 versions like SunOS and ULTRIX-32 2.2 and up, the restore command can also be an interactive utility. Invoking restore with the i flag is like being in a miniature shell, only instead of being on the disks, you are actually wandering around the tape itself! That's what makes the interactive mode of restore a fascinating utility.

The interactive mode of restore has its own prompt:

```
restore>
```

When you see this, it is ready to do your bidding. It reads in the backup archive header from tape or disk and now will allow you to list, ls, change directories, cd, and get path names, pwd, like a miniature version of UNIX itself. Thus by positioning yourself in the directory, you can make a restore list and mark files or directories for extraction, the restore for putting it back on disk. There is even a help command for the interactive mode. An add command is used to add files to the restore list, and a delete command is there just in case you change your mind. When an ls is done after marking files for extraction, an asterisk appears on each file and directory to be restored. The last step is doing the final extract, and then it's all over.

An interactive session looks something this:

```
# /etc/restore -if /dev/rmt1h
restore> cd home/gsimko/bin
restore> ls
backup bu
restore> add bu
restore> verbose
verbose on
restore> ls
./ 2../ 12209 backup 12290 *bu
restore> extract
Extract requested files
You have not read any tapes yet.
Unless you know which volume your file(s) are on you should
start with the last volume and work toward the first.
Specify next volume #:  1

set owner/mode for '.' [yn] y
```

As you can clearly see, it's like a miniature shell except you are reading tape directories, not the disk. Setting verbose on is not necessary, but it is reminiscent of older versions that needed the inode number in order to work. In this example, only one file was restored, a good illustration of the fine control possible without overwriting good data with potentially old and therefore bad data.

Be careful to position yourself within the file structure of the disk at exactly the point where the dump was taken, or where you want the files or directories to land before invoking restore. Poor positioning in the file system before initiating a restore results in horrendous paths like /home/scott/bin/home/scott/bin/foo, whether you use cpio or dump. Be careful to do your backups and restores from as low in the file tree as possible. For example, /usr/users/sbrock/project/* should be backed up from the `users` directory, not `/`, the root directory, assuming that `/usr/users` is a mounted partition, of course.

If you have to do another full `restore`, all the files will be there, but the `dump/restore` process will have repositioned the files, and the inodes will not be the same. This is no major tragedy, but it does demand attention. Just be sure to follow it up with a full (level 0) `dump`; then the inode number/file relationship will be back on track.

The `dump` Command: preSVR4

Going back to at least Edition 7, `dump` is one of the oldest UNIX backup methods. It has all sorts of bells and whistles for full backups and various stages of incremental backups. The `dump` command is the favored backup method on Berkeley-based systems.

There are other disadvantages to the older `dump` command. It can't keep track of media sequence, that is, the order of tapes or diskettes. Since it does no label checking, it is imperative that the operator be rigorous about affixing external labels. The first tape must be read to get the header information, and then the tapes must be read from *last to first*. Also, the old `dump` command gets rattled when it has to restore data that were being written when the copy was made. Since most backups are made on a "live" system, this can be a major problem.

The old `dump` command's Achilles' heel is its inability to sense the end of the tape. Consequently, this pre-System V Release 4 and pre-BSD 4.2 and 4.3 `dump` command is considered archaic, and it has largely been replaced by the BSD 4.2 version. As of this writing, only XENIX is running without the interactive `restore` feature.

The contemporary `dump` command precalculates the tape (or diskette) requirements and stops well before the end-of-tape marker when it asks that the next tape be mounted. The `dump` command was even eliminated on some AT&T OEM UNIX systems, but it lives on in others. The pure AT&T versions 5.2 and 5.3 have no `dump` backup command, and now the command name `dump` is used for a core-dump formatter on UTS.

Old `dump` is able to handle multiple-volume backups. It has an `s` option that allows the tape length in feet to be input, which, along with the density `d` flag, allows the amount of data to be calculated. The `dump` utility then waits for the reel to be changed; thus, with care, old `dump` writes across volumes. Newer BSD versions of the `dump` command are still nicer, because they precalculate for you.[3]

The Old `restore` Command

The flip side of old `dump` is the old `restore` command. The `dump` command requires great care when making a restore because it has no data base or catalog of files. Restores are best done to a separate disk partition reserved for restores. The additional expense is obvious: Restores are usually done from last-to-first tape or diskette volume. With any nonarchive method, the danger of restoring anything larger than a single missing file is

---

[3] BSD and System V Release 4 put UFS `dump` back into mainstream UNIX, along with some necessary modifications.

overwriting good data with an older version. A directory lost on Friday requires the last full backup to restore the directory and then a search of the week's incrementals for the remaining file update. Fortunately, most of these problems go away with Berkeley's 4.2 and 4.3 interactive `restore` command.

`cpio` **or** `dump`**, That Is the Question**

Enough command descriptions. You can read the manual if you need precise descriptions of what the various backup commands do, but you will learn a lot more about backup commands when you do hands-on system administration. By comparing the strengths and weaknesses of different backup commands for the various kinds of backups that you do, you will gradually gain the experience you need to determine which backup command is best for the job at hand. The `dump` command has good news and bad news. It is simple to use, and it writes across media volumes. On the other hand, it is slower than `cpio`, because `dump` requires time and CPU power to precalculate tape usage. The `cpio` command makes restores easy, and it's best for selective backups. However, `cpio` can't cross media volumes. Your best bet is to analyze the type of data you need to back up and then to choose your backup command accordingly.

`tar` **Versus** `cpio`

The `tar` command is an old UNIX standby that suffers from a fatal backup ailment—it cannot handle anything larger than the tape or diskette medium. If the file, file system, or directory is larger than the storage medium, you will get an `out of disk space` message. The message applies to the backup medium, not the disk being copied.

In spite of its failings, not too many years ago `tar` seemed like a sacred institution that could never be replaced, but it finally was, by `cpio`. AT&T doesn't even include `tar` in its System V Releases 2 and 3, but old standards die hard, and `tar` continues on. The organization /usr/group included `tar` in its UNIX standard, and it may be there to stay.

You can use the latest version of `cpio` to write multiple volume backups if you're careful. The `cpio` command has more flexibility than `tar` does: `tar`'s major failing is that it cannot be fed too long a list of arguments. With too long a list of files to copy, it simply quits. There were ways around this, but `cpio` made them unnecessary.

The `tar` command does have some advantages: It has simple syntax, so it is easy to use. It can create a listing from an archived tape like `cpio`, which is handy for tape verification. After a tape spends long months sitting on the shelf, it's nice to be able to find out what is on it without a major effort.

Copying multiple files and directories with `tar` is easy enough:

```
# cd /etc
# tar cvf /dev/rmt0 /u /local passwd rc ttytype ttys group
```

Pumping a list of files into `tar` is a bit trickier than with `cpio`:

```
# tar cvf /dev/rmt0 `cat tar.file.list`
```

Just remember that when the list is too long, `tar` chokes.

Like cpio, the tar command does its own restores. It reads them in and it reads them out:

```
# tar xv /u/asa/critical
```

The x flag stands for *extract*, and the v flag stands for *verbose*.

SVR4 backup AND restore COMMANDS

The need for a sophisticated backup and restore method has been obvious for years. OEM add-ons like Amdahl's backup with its Ingres data base and Unitech's Ubackup with its online catalogs show clearly that the computer industry acknowledges the need for a method well beyond the tools provided by the basic UNIX system.

System V Release 4 has a fully flexible, user-oriented backup and restore system. The command series allows for full and incremental backups, full file systems, disk partitions, and even migrations. Like Unitech's Ubackup, the command series allows media labeling to prevent accidental writing to the wrong tape or diskette.

Perhaps the most important feature of this backup and restore system is the user-requested restore. A user's request for a restore is sent to the console for action by operations. The request generates an automated restore using an online catalog or history log. System operators with minimal skills can complete a tape mount and let the system satisfy the request. Media label checking ensures a successful mount. To complete the package there are tools to monitor the status of both backup and restore operations.

As a final touch, System V Release 4's backup and restore system can be extended through custom backup and restore scripts. The system has the following service commands:

- backup
- bkreg
- bkoper
- bkhistory
- bkexcept
- bkstatus
- restore
- rsoper
- renotify
- rsstatus
- urestore
- ursstatus
- fdisk
- fdp
- fimage
- incfile

Perhaps the most remarkable feature of the SVR4 backup and restore system is its ability to copy entire file systems, *including* the superblock. The backup system is capable of writing across media volumes, a necessity in this era of large disk capacities and equally large file systems.

finc

The `finc` command is a fast, incremental backup scheme with a simple and direct syntax. There are two things to note: The first is that `finc` uses inode numbers for file references and that its counterpart, `frec`, requires the inode number for a restore. The second is that the tape must be labeled, not a bad idea for any backup system. Here `finc` is doing an incremental backup of all files modified, `-m`, in the last week, `-7`, from the user disk, `/u`, and sending it to tape via the raw tape device driver:

```
# finc -m -7 /dev/u /dev/rmt0
```

The `finc` command produces no catalog, listing, or index, and therefore it is practical to do an `ff` or an `ls -i` on the device special file being backed up in order to create an index. The tape and the `ff` listing can be stored together on systems without the benefit of a tape librarian.

frec

The counterpart of `finc` is `frec`, which recovers files from `finc` and `volcopy` backup tapes. Its syntax and use are not as simple as `finc`'s. Let's see how `frec` is used to recover a file called `/u/asa/command/adm`. The `-p` flag is used to specify the path where the file will be restored:

```
frec -p /u/asa/command /dev/rmt0 21:adm
```

The inode number is `21`, and its name is `adm`. The tape is mounted on a drive associated with `/dev/rmt0`. This command usage is simple enough for a single file, but if you are a masochist, try using it for multiple file restores from a single command-line argument.

A few parting notes on `finc` and `frec`. Although `finc` is fast and convenient, with no catalog or data base, you are dependent on a previously created list of path names and inode numbers. You must be sure to keep the list and tape associated with each other. When you think about it, a fast, convenient backup is not that convenient when you have to make a long, arduous restore.

volcopy

The `volcopy` command is the pickiest copy command. It is fanatical about label checking. Disk and tape labels are a safeguard against the wrong data being written to or from either. In multiple tape copies, a tape label is an absolute necessity to prevent copying the wrong disk partitions or tapes. When doing disk mounts, a disk label is also a necessity. You must use `/etc/labelit` to label the tape before use.

The `volcopy` command uses a from-to argument sequence:

```
volcopy /u /dev/dsk/u tp004 /dev/rmt0
```

Here `volcopy` is copying the user directory, `/u`, residing on device special file, `/dev/dsk/u`, to the raw tape device, `/dev/rmt0`. The tape has a label `tp004`. If the labels do not match, `volcopy` will create havoc with the person who invokes it. What you see is what you get.

ARCHIVING

There is a distinction between archiving and backups. An *archive* is a total copy of something that is *fully portable*. That something may be the system, user files, network files, or anything that needs to be stored or transferred as a whole. An installation or distribution tape is a form of archive.

Archives and backups can be the same if the latter is complete enough. A full cpio or tar copy of all user file systems is a combined archive and backup. This is particularly true of cpio used with the ASCII header option. The advantage of either an archive or a full backup on all systems is that a restore is guaranteed. That is, after all, what a backup/restore cycle really is. The disadvantage on large systems or smaller systems with diskettes is that it takes a lot of time and magnetic media.

CURRENT ISSUES

At the USENIX Large Installation Systems Administration Workshop held in Monterey, California, in November 1988, backups and security were clearly flagged as major system administration problems. Since there are ways to take care of security problems, even if they are work intensive, backups were identified as the most frustrating system administration headache.

Both the speed of the data transfer and the backup media fail to respond to the needs of large systems. The speed of writing to tapes doesn't give sufficient time to complete a backup during nonprime time and off hours. Clustered systems and diskless and dataless workstations send data over the network to the system owning the storage device, substantially aggravating the situation. Network speeds are hampered by multiple protocols and error and parity checking, and so the data transmission from remote systems to tape slows backups intolerably.

Tape media have never kept up with the needs of disk storage. Every time someone builds large capacity tape technology, it always seems to be preceded by a major advance in disk storage technology! As a result, disks always seem to hold more data than tape. Thus backup and archive software *must* be able to cope with writing across tape volume boundaries.

In time, data transfer speeds and tape densities will meet with adequate software and provide a backup solution, but we are still a long way from that goal. The current technology gives us gigabyte-plus tape capacity. Reasonable transfer speeds can be obtained by working directly from the file server or system requiring a backup. It is up to the system's managers and administrators to find the best solution within the confines of current technology. You need to make a software choice that will meet the user's needs for quick and dependable restores rather than basing your decision on the convenience of operations and their continued demands for a fast and simple backup method. Never lose sight of the fact that *backups are the tools and restores are the reason for their existence*.

MANAGER'S CORNER

A Fairy Tale

This is a fairy tale about the management of systems and operations groups. I am deliberately making the specifics fuzzy to protect the guilty.

Once upon a time not too long ago there was an engineering system support group in a major corporation that nurtured a large-scale engineering system. It was a very successful organization in spite of being perpetually understaffed. The group's manager was bright and knowledgeable, and he was well respected by his staff. The group's duties covered both system programming and operations. The operations group reported to the same manager as did the systems group.

One day someone in upper management had an idea. Why not merge the operations group of engineering systems support with the business operations group? The reasoning was *synergy*. If the two operations groups were merged, fewer operators would be needed to take care of both business systems and engineering systems, and fewer operations staff would be needed as well.

Eventually the engineering systems support group was physically moved to another site, where they shared physical resources with the business group. They still owned their hardware, but they shared the floor space. The operations staff of both groups was now under the control of the business operations manager.

The business operations manager was a great guy, but he was not the equal of the engineering systems support manager in either skill or dedication. Although the engineering operations group was used to VM and UNIX, and the business operations group was used to MVS, the business operations manager announced that operators of both groups were now expected to know all three operating systems. When the business operations manager made his announcement, he assumed that his wishes would be carried out. Unfortunately, the operators resisted. If you expect an MVS operator to learn voluntarily about UNIX, then surely you believe in fairy tales.

The operators had many problems adapting to the new work environment, but having to run three different backup systems for three separate operating systems was the last straw. Clearly, MVS would be backed up from MVS, and VM would be backed up from VM, but what about this strange UNIX operating system? Since it lived on a VM host, why not back it up from VM and have only two backup methods? After all, isn't that the true meaning of synergy? Everyone—in operations, that is—agreed. Two backup systems instead of three would be much better.

Now as we all know, fairy tales usually end with "and they lived happily ever after," but our fairy tale doesn't. No one asked the UNIX engineering customers how the changes would affect them, so the poor engineering users ended up with the short end of the stick. Whereas a user file, directory, or even an entire tree used to be restored from a `tar` or `cpio` tape in less than 15 minutes, it now took half an hour just to get the contents of a VM DDR tape onto a VM `temp` disk. From there it had to be attached to a UNIX system. Then after some skillful manipulation by yet another group, the restore was finally transferred to the user's disk. In practice this restore operation took at least half a day, and sometimes it took as much as one full day to do a restore. The restore involved three organizations, and it always led to unhappiness and frustration on the part of all parties concerned.

What is the moral of our story? First of all, the backup method should never be determined by how convenient it is for operations to perform. Backups are necessary for the customers whose data are supposedly being protected. Backups exist in order to restore data rapidly whenever there is a need. Second, *synergy* is merely a word in the dictionary between *synecdoche* and *synesis*. It is not a reality unless it *truly* provides more service with fewer people. While the idea of equal service for less cost was the original, laudable intent of management, what actually occurred was a *marked loss of service* for slightly less cost. The engineering users eventually lost confidence in the engineering systems support group, and they gradually came to expect poor service from the entire MIS organization.

This fairy tale reminds me of a true story about a famous Southern California irrigation equipment manufacturer. Its products were the most expensive on the market, but it had an established reputation for making quality goods, and consequently it had a strong, steady customer base. Then its management redefined *value engineering* to mean "Make the part cheaper, but charge the same money." Management made the decision to make their units more cheaply, and the quality of their merchandise went down, but the price stayed the same. Their long-time customers left in droves. Why pay good money for anything but quality? This irrigation equipment manufacturer lost not only its valuable reputation as a quality manufacturer but also a big chunk of what had been a dependable customer base.

When poor management decisions cause a company to lose sales, it doesn't take more than a single accounting period to sense that something is wrong. Unfortunately, when a company's internal customers are unhappy, there is no immediate indicator. Since internal customers usually cannot take their business elsewhere, their dissatisfaction shows in diminished output, and it takes management longer to realize their error in judgment.

CHAPTER

6

Security

UNIX takes a lot of flack in the area of security. The system's good news is its bad news. The use of permissions bits, user and group ownerships, and the set-user-ID bit are design features in regard to ease of use and accessibility, but they are design flaws in regard to security. *Security is the reciprocal of convenience*. Design is a matter of compromise, and the statement "You can't have it both ways" is relevant here.

Security is dependent on the attitudes of you, as the system administrator, and company management. If you have a clear, enforced policy that unauthorized access or any other system abuse will not be tolerated, you will minimize most system abuse immediately. You will always have to be wary of potential system abuse from your users, but most of them will simply come to work, do their jobs, and go home. They're not interested in causing mischief.

Only the occasional user gets a secret thrill from causing trouble on the system. I have no patience with system abusers. They are a pain in the neck. Some rule infractions at work are a guaranteed, one-way trip to the door, such as gross insubordination, intoxication, and sleeping on the job. Tampering with a company's system falls in the same category, and in most states and under federal law it is a felony.

Abusers tampering from the inside may not be as much of a problem as abusers accessing the system from the outside. Computers no longer stand alone: Not only are they networked, but many also have multiple networks. A system can be on long-haul access running uucp, cu, and uux and also be on the Internet running Wide Area Networks and Local Area Networks. Systems can be accessed from just about anywhere, inside or outside. External tampering is difficult to catch and equally difficult to prosecute. With good security it can be stopped, but the effort is work intensive. The key to UNIX security is to use its existing security features wisely. Maintaining system security is a constant vigil, which starts at /etc/passwd.

PASSWD

The door to the system is /etc/passwd. *Leave it locked*. Consider the permissions for your /etc/passwd file: If they are too loose, your system can be penetrated. If they are too tight, all the software that has to read the password file won't be able to function. The following password file permissions are traditional:

```
$ ls -l /etc/passwd
-r--r--r--   1 root   root     845 May 17 19:07 /etc/passwd
```

This file is root owned with mode 0444. It is readable, but no one except those with root privilege can write to it.

Setting the file permissions is only a start toward a more secure system. Because /etc/passwd can be read by everyone, the security holes should be apparent.[1] Any file without a password encryption can be spotted immediately:

```
$ grep :: /etc/passwd
msnerd::207:83:Mortimer Snerd dept 541:/u/turkey/msnerd:
```

Abuser-users now have a convenient login whenever they need one. The solution is simple: If you don't tolerate empty password encryption fields, then you avoid potential trouble.

You can use grep to search for a specific missing password field. This regular expression reads past all noncolons until it hits the first paired set of colons:

```
$ grep '^[^:]*::' /etc/passwd
msnerd::207:83:Mortimer Snerd dept 541:/u/turkey/msnerd:
```

On finding an entry with an empty encryption field, either give it a password or block the password:

```
msnerd:BLOCKED:207:83:Mortimer Snerd dept 541:/u/turkey/msnerd:
```

The problem with blocking passwords is that now even Mortimer Snerd can't log in. Fortunately, as root you can set passwords for anyone:

```
$ su
password:
# passwd achen
enter new password:
reenter password:
```

A dangerous password entry is one that has been aged and just expired. Clever users find out the login is not being used, and if they ever have the opportunity to get the password from the original user, not an unusual circumstance, they will take advantage of the disk space and use the login.

Check daily for aged passwords. If an aged password is there for two consecutive days, block it:

```
jcroy:BLOCKED:256:128:Jerry Croy CIS/ES:/tech/jcroy:
```

Now this entry can be easily spotted for future reference.

---

[1] System V Release 4 does not put password encryptions and password aging information in /etc/passwd but it has a shadow password file that works with /etc/passwd.

Be consistent with passwd blocking. If you use the full word BLOCKED in uppercase letters, it can easily be searched:

```
$ grep BLOCK /etc/passwd
jcroy:BLOCKED:256:128:Jerry Croy CIS/ES:/tech/jcroy:
```

Blocked password entries should not stay around for long without being questioned. Is the user still with the company? If so, is he still with the same department, and does he still need the login? Removing passwd deadwood makes login time faster, eliminates possible security holes, and keeps your system tidy.

There may be a time when you need to give root privilege to a consultant, hardware service representative, or system programmer from another in-house organization. If you give him *the* system password, you will have to change it as soon as he finishes his job; thus it is safer to make a root-alias login. The user ID is 0, and the name should be something like uadm or sysadm. The account can also be used as a legitimate backdoor entry into the system should the root password be lost or corrupted. Be sure to remove the entry or at least change the password as the visiting guru walks out your door.

BACKDOORS

A *backdoor* is a privileged entry point into the system. It is put there to allow entry if the root password is lost or corrupted. I have had a few experiences in which support personnel have corrupted the password file. They not only changed root's password to an unknown password, but they also removed all administrative logins, including root's. There is no way to issue a privileged command with root's password corrupted. There is also no way to repair or replace the password file on the running system. One way to fix it is to bring down the system and repair the password file while in single-user mode. To complete the repairs, you will probably have to load a memory-resident version of UNIX from tape. The other method is to use a backdoor entry into the system. You gain superuser status through this backdoor and then issue whatever commands are necessary to repair the system.

There are a few alternatives to creating a backdoor to the system. The simplest is to maintain a root-alias passwd entry such as sysadm:

```
$ grep ':0:' /etc/passwd
root:OFkHZqW.GNRj.:0:0:Super user:/:/bin/sh
sysadm:/VLSmc1QqdIsc:0:0:Alternate root login:/usr/sysadm:/bin/sh
```

The root-alias password should be known only to the system administrator and his or her backup, *no one else*.

There is a second method that is more circuitous and secretive. Bury a su-shell program off the root disk, deep in the system's local files. Give it a dot name like .lost. Have the program check the user's user ID, not EUID, to see whether it belongs to the user bin. Have the program write

```
System violated -- SUID program in use
```

to the console, console log, sulog, and root's mail. If it is ever used, it will leave more tracks than an elephant crossing a newly planted lawn. Now set the password for `bin` and give it to your backup only, just as with the preceding `root-alias` password.

These are the only kinds of backdoors that I allow on my systems. If you opt for maximum security, you should have no backdoors at all. To maximize your security, you must first have a plan for restoring a corrupted password file. The plan must be tested and well rehearsed, as there will be precious little time to figure out a plan when the password file is corrupted.

As a system administrator you must be on the lookout for `root` aliases, either those planted by you, as in the preceding `sysadmin` login, or those planted without authorization by a system programmer looking for his or her own backdoor entry. Make clear your policy on backdoors when you hire a system programmer. Then you will have reason to take corrective action if the security policy is violated.

GUEST LOGINS

Many systems have a user `guest` login, which is like leaving the doors to your house unlocked. Issue temporary logins only when you absolutely have to. When the job for which they were created is completed, remove them, and change or block the password immediately.

GROUP LOGINS

Group logins are an invitation to trouble. Why do you need group logins when `/etc/group` and group permissions are used wisely? Watch out for artificial group logins, as they can indicate either a user who has given his password to everyone in the group or a user who left but whose login everyone continues to use. Use a simple `who` or `ps` command from time to time to show abused logins, and immediately remove or block a login if the user leaves the group or company. Likewise, change system passwords whenever a privileged user leaves.

PASSWORD CLEANUPS

In time the password file will become cluttered with all sorts of deadwood, including users who no longer use the system. Unused password records slow down the login process, risk security, and make the `/etc/pwck` output enormous. And a potential security hole can slip by the system administrator, especially if there is a lot of output from the System V password-checking utility, `pwck`. Clean up `/etc/passwd` regularly, and you won't have a problem.

The starting place for a password-file cleanup is to identify all users not using the system. You can make a dead user list in this way:

- Extract the error output of `/etc/pwck`.
- Get the last login data from `accounting`'s daily report.
- Extract all blocked user entries from `/etc/passwd`.

Start with the users no longer with the company and remove their entire login record. Next, remove all of those who are with the company but have no login directory; only this time put a copy of their password records in a disk file for retrieval. The next step is to locate users who haven't logged in for a year—accounting will help you get this last login information. Call all absentee users to see whether they want their logins. Even though they haven't logged on for a year, they probably "can't live" without them. You should archive the user areas of those users you decide to take off the system.

Here's how you do the actual deletion:

- Create a deletion name list.
- Check the list for accuracy against /etc/passwd.
- Separate the password records to be deleted and put them in a safe place.
- Copy /etc/passwd to an intermediate password file, Ipasswd.
- Mark the Ipasswd records for deletion.
- Delete the marked records.
- Clean and test the Ipasswd file.
- Copy passwd to Opasswd.
- Copy Ipasswd to passwd.

I put a minus sign, -, at the beginning of each user passwd record to be deleted. Removal is then a matter of editing Ipasswd in this way:

```
1,$s/^-.*$//
```

The regular expression ^-.* translates as "Look for a minus sign at the beginning of a line followed by any character or any number of repetitions of any characters." The empty substitute expression, //, means replace the recognized regular expression with nothing, so that the entire record will be deleted from the password file.

It pays to have password cleanup scripts on multiple systems without YP. Indeed, one of the first scripts that the reader should write is one to generate a list of users that fall out while checking the password file by /etc/pwck. The output of pwck comes from its stderr, and it is important to redirect the stderr of pwck within the script because stderr cannot be piped:

```
$ cat fpwck
:
if [ $# -ne 1]
    then
        echo "usage: fpwck passwd_file"
        exit 1
 fi
/etc/pwck ${1}>tmp.pwck 2>&1
awk -F: ' { print $1 }  ' tmp.pwck | grep -v Login
rm rwmp.pqxk
exit 0
```

Note that the $1 argument used by the shell as pwck's argument is not the same as the $1 used by awk. The shell's is the first command-line argument, and awk's $1 is the first field of pwck's output. The list of users to be deleted should be checked for accuracy against the password file. It is always better to let the computer do the work, and the following script checks the name list against passwd:

```
$ cat chk.name
:
if [ $# -ne 2 ]
    then
        echo "usage: chk.name name_list passwd_file"
        echo "where name list is the list of names to
        echo "be deleted and passwd_file is the password"
        echo "file"
        exit 1
 fi
for name in `cat $1`
    do
        echo $name
        grep $name $2
    done
exit 0
```

Once you have a list of users to be deleted and have checked it, you should save the passwd entries in a separate file so that you can take them from that file if they ever need to be restored. The following script creates that file from the name list:

```
$cat separate
if [ $# -ne 2 ]
    then
        echo "usage: separate passwd_file name_list"
        exit 1
 fi
for name in `cat $2`
    do
        grep $name $1
    done
exit 0
```

The next script is used with the checked list of names to be deleted in order to mark the intermediate password file. It is called mark:

```
$ cat mark
:
if test $# -ne 2
    then
        echo "usage: mark passwd_file name_list"
        exit
 fi
for name in `cat $2`
    do
        echo $name
        ed $1<<!
        1,\$s/${name}/-${name}/
        w
        q
!
    done
exit
# mark
# marks names for deletion in password files
# bhh 8/8/88
```

This leaves a minus sign before each user's name that is going to be deleted. Although sed would seem a natural candidate for this program, using the streaming editor requires an intermediate file. The line for sed would be

```
sed 's/$name/-$name/' $2 >/usr/tmp/pw.file
```

The deletion process leaves open slots or double newlines in `Ipasswd`. Either remove them manually, or use a filter; `sed` is as good as any with

```
sed 's/^$/d' ipasswd>Ipasswd
```

UNIX is so versatile that you always have more than enough tools and methods to attack a problem. If the pain of using `tr` doesn't bother you, try this:

```
tr -s '\012' '' <ipasswd >Ipasswd
```

On the other hand, if you have to remove newline pairs more then once a year, this humble little C filter is about all it takes to do the job:

```c
include <stdio.h>

main()
{
    int c, c_old = '\0';

    while (( c = getchar ()) != EOF)
    {
        if ( c = = '\n' && c_old = = '\n')
            ;
            else
            putchar (c);
        c_old = c;
    }
}
```

After verifying that `Ipasswd` looks like what you want, run it through `/etc/pwck`. If it passes, check everything one more time, and then copy `Ipasswd` to `/etc/passwd`.

The first commandment of password file maintenance is *never directly edit* `/etc/passwd`. This commandment is repeated many times in the book. Always do something like the following three-way switch that edits, checks, and backs up:

- Copy `/etc/passwd` to `Opasswd`.
- Copy `/etc/passwd` to `Ipasswd`.
- Modify `Ipasswd`.
- Test `Ipasswd` with `/etc/pwck`.
- Copy `Ipasswd` to `/etc/passwd`.

BSD UNIX administrators can use `vipw` to edit `/etc/passwd`, but it leaves no audit trail, and sometimes audit trails are handy if something goes wrong.

/etc/group

The `/etc/group` file has only half the security risk as `/etc/passwd` has, but that is twice as dangerous as it should be. Let's look at group permissions and a typical `group` entry:

```
$ ls -l /etc/group
-rw-r--r--   1 root   root   135 May 17 19:07 /etc/group
$ grep edit /etc/group
edit::50:chad,joanna,eric,alec,heather,scott
```

All user names in an /etc/group record have the same group privileges. Thus Chad, Joanna, and Eric will have group access to Alec's, Heather's, and Scott's files, including executables, if group permissions are set. The rules here are

- Update /etc/group constantly, and remove any users who are no longer in the group.
- Teach users how to use chgrp and the consequences of group permissions.
- Use group password commands wherever the OEM has built them in.

Although standard UNIX offers no way to put a password encryption into the group file, a password encryption can be added by creating a dummy user login: Just cut the known password encryption from the dummy password line, and paste it in the password encryption field of the group line you want to protect.

REMOVING AND UPDATING USERS

Keeping user information up-to-date is a major problem in security and bill-back accounting. Users who have changed their original jobs within the company should have their accounts either moved or removed, and users who left the company must be removed immediately. Their user area should be archived immediately and the tapes stored permanently. Check with their managers to see who is taking over their projects and what is to be done with their data. Any change in status must be reflected in /etc/passwd, /etc/group, and the system identities file, if you have one. Enforcing this is close to impossible without the aid of a central organization. The company's personnel, human resources, and payroll departments are good sources of information. Having one of these organizations give you user information about terminations and transfers should be made a mandatory policy for optimum security on your system.

SUSHI

God protect me from my friends. I already know my enemies.
--OLD ITALIAN SAYING

System administrators generally know who their enemies are. It's the privileged users they need to watch. Serious violation of the system frequently comes from those who currently have, or used to have, root privilege. Sometimes a su-shell program is planted by privileged users to get around system password protection. On our site we call these programs sushi. They have many forms and variations, but the basics are the same. Once invoked, the program changes the effective user ID to 0, root's user ID. It then execs a shell with root privilege. Some well-meaning system programmers put in a line of code to check the user ID and to exit if it is not their user ID, but that still is a violation of privilege. A less clever version of sushi is the one created by nonprivileged users to fork and exec a shell. This version is copied to a command that has root ownership and a set-user-ID bit on.

There is no way to prevent `sushi` programs from being written, but once installed they can be caught. Look at a legitimate root-owned, set-user-ID program:

```
$ ls -l /etc/passwd
-rws--x--x    1 root        bin          16856 Apr 13  1987 /bin/passwd
```

The fourth character of the first field is `s`, showing the set-user-ID bit on. The third field is `root`. Create a script using the `find` command to locate such entries, then run them to a file daily, and check both the number and the size of such programs. This one-liner does the job:

```
# find / -type f -user root -perm -04000 -exec ls -l {} \;
```

The `-04000` gives the loosest interpretation of permissions containing a set-user-ID bit. If you feel that `find`'s syntax is too unwieldy, try this:

```
# ls -lR /!grep '^-r.s.*root'
```

It is not as accurate as the `find` command line, but it is a lot simpler to remember.

Do not allow rampant use of root-owned files with the set-user-ID bit on, as it is like sending out engraved invitations to any lurking `sushi` programs. Scores of system files owned by `root` with the set-user-ID bit on could run just as well with another owner. One system I know had all the `/usr/spool/interface` files owned by `root`. But since the `lp` spooler commands are owned by `lp`, the interface programs should have been owned by `lp`, not `root`. Similarly, change command and data file ownerships away from `root` to minimize the number of root-owned, set-user-ID programs and thus make your system more secure. The smaller the list is, the quicker you will be able to recognize a possible su-shell program.

TROJAN HORSE

The Trojan horse is so old and well known that it merits only a brief mention. It is a false login that waits for a user to log in. It emulates the real login process, captures the user's log name and password, and then destroys itself, but not before shipping the user's name and password to the abuser who installed the program in the first place.

If you never log in correctly on the first pass, you can avoid being nabbed by the Trojan horse. Use commonsense rules to figure out how your system works. On systems that display a particular logo to the screen that must be cleared before logging in, teach your users *always* to look for the logo. If there is no logo in sight, they either should not log in or they should give an erroneous login.

The most dangerous Trojan horse of all is the one set to capture the `root` password. The root-capture script lives in the system programmer's home directory or `$HOME/bin`. The cure is to set your `PATH` to search `/bin` and `/etc/bin` first and your home or current directory last or never. You can take an additional precaution and use the full `/bin/su` instead of `su`. There is a certain safety in not having your current directory in your search path. But `root`'s path does not have a . in it, and without a *dot* directory it won't search the current directory:

```
# who am i
root    tty12    Nov  5  10:50
# echo $PATH
/bin:/usr/bin:/etc
#
```

PRIVILEGE: IT'S ALL OR NOTHING

Privilege is an all-or-nothing proposition in UNIX. There are no IBM-like classes of privilege such as A through G. There have been attempts at making sheltered commands for operators and help-desk personnel that give them a restricted `root` privilege. The problem is that as long as they have any form of `chown` and `chmod` command available with `root` ownership and the set-user-ID bit on, with very little skill they can get the keys to the system.

You can set a separate password to the user `/bin` and restrict it from `/`, and even `/etc`, but that is like giving a police officer only one bullet. The key here is earned trust through education. Those who have been given the privilege must be trained to use it and must be reliable. Those without integrity have no business working as operators, system programmers, or system administrators. The integrity of the personnel at your site is as important as in a bank.

sulog

Every time anyone uses the `/bin/su` command without an argument, it is recorded in `sulog` in `/usr/spool/CHECK`. Read through it frequently to see who is using `su`. Perhaps more pertinent, read it to see who is *not* using it. If your system programmers and operators are logging on as `root`, it is time you have a serious talk with them. Privilege is as dangerous as a loaded gun. Privileged users, the administrator, system programmers, help-desk people, and operators should work with an unprivileged login until they need to issue a privileged command. Then and only then should they invoke `/bin/su`.

MANAGER'S CORNER

Security

Security policy is simple: You can't afford to be without it. The question is, How much security can you afford? Full security is a full-time job, and so it requires additional employees. But buying computer security is like buying insurance. It doesn't seem to make dollars and sense until you suffer a loss. By then it may well be too late.

If you do not opt for full security or cannot convince upper management of the need, at least be sure your staff has protected the machine against internal and external intruders and itself. Ask for evidence of su-shell protection and of no unauthorized backdoors. Most of all, be sure of the integrity of your staff. In the long run the only protection the system has is their personal integrity and honesty. You cannot afford system abusers.

Don't be wishy-washy with violators. Your best protection is a known policy of enforcing security. Years ago I came head-to-head with the biggest security violator in the company a few months after signing on as administrator. I have always had the reputation of being tough, and this was no time to vacillate. I caused the violator deep personal embarrassment, and the word quickly spread around the corporation. There was no further trouble from anyone.

The 1988 Worm Incident

A few days after Halloween 1988, a program was sent on the Arpanet and entered every system it could access on the network. It turned the United States computer world upside down and received wide press coverage.

The havoc this program created was beyond belief. In a knee-jerk reaction to the worm, network managers pulled wires and dropped from the networks in droves. Users were denied access, and for a day or two both work and access were limited. System programmers worked feverishly trying to block entry to the systems.

I know of one administrator who noticed all his systems hitting 100 percent usage and who had the good sense to crash one of them and get a full dump. According to the information gathered, the worm had entered by way of BSD sendmail by taking advantage of the debug option. Unlike UUCP's debug, sendmail's debug option allows some degree of privilege. The worm was planted in /usr/tmp, and from there it was compiled and turned loose to do its damage.

My initial reaction was to protect my systems as quickly as possible. I created a script to haunt my tmp directories and wipe out any C programs that were dropped there:

```
$ cat /local/etc/noc
:
trap '' 1 2 3 15
while sleep 20
    do
        if test -f /tmp/*.c
        then
            file=`ls /tmp/*.c`
            rm /tmp/*.c
            date >>/dev/cons
            echo "removed ${file}">>/dev/cons
        fi
        if test -f /usr/tmp/*.c
        then
            file=`ls /usr/tmp/*.c`
            rm /usr/tmp/*.c
            date >>/dev/cons
            echo "removed ${file}">>/dev/cons
        fi
    done
exit 1
```

This gave me time to fall back and regroup. Other administrators in the company had other temporary solutions. We ordered immediate full backups to augment the evening's incrementals. Groups with network source code modified `sendmail` and either removed the `debug` option or hid it. I had patched Wollongong's WIN/UTS TCP/IP onto my system, so at least my `sendmail` source was not *the* sendmail source. I used a hex editor to zap the `debug` section of `sendmail` and went home for a well-earned rest.

A friend and colleague told me how his company's network and programming staffs reacted to the frightening situation. When the very safety of one's systems are at stake, one sees the best and worst come out in people. Initially the worst prevailed. Hysteria reigned. At his company they had an emergency meeting and discovered to their chagrin that no one had a comprehensive list of the network managers or the system managers. There was no central point to which they could network information. No one moved to create any of these things. Most significant, no senior managers were present at the meeting. (Many holed up in the safety of their offices hoping the problem would go away.) In the hours following the meeting, there was no mass exchange of information. All the relevant personnel either did their best to protect their own systems or frantically called about to find out what the other administrators were doing. From talking with other colleagues in the computer field, this mayhem was more a rule than an exception on that infamous day.

Sanity finally prevailed at a follow-up meeting the next day, and we all can benefit from the lessons learned from this person's experience:

1. The cost of up-front security administration is cheaper than paying for the damage after you have been hit.
2. There should be a central network point of contact for administrators.
3. There also should be a companywide list of computer sites, network nodes, and owners.
4. A disaster recovery plan should be mandatory.
5. It is all too easy to do more damage to yourself than the intruder did.
6. And, of course, your systems should be secured.

How do you secure the barndoor before the horse is stolen? Check and test all network accesses. Assume that UUCP will be used, even if you think that no one is using it. All it takes is a modem and a phone line and a little skill for anyone with privilege to get UUCP going. Enforce the use of call-back devices. Be sure that access is limited to `/usr/spool/uucppublic`.

Test `sendmail` well. Disable the `debug` mode except to your network and system administration staff. If in doubt, disable `sendmail` and use the UUCP `mail` facility. UUCP has better protection. Enforce the maximum protection modes for both files and directories. Stop group logins and instead enforce the use of group privilege. Most important of all, clean out your password files and test for `root` aliases and su-shell programs. You won't be a victim if you fight back.

SECTION

II

UNIX Subsystems

Terminals and Other Asynchronous Chapter Devices, and Terminal I/O Theory

INTRODUCTION

Understanding asynchronous serial character devices, loosely classified as *terminals*, hinges on understanding the character interpretation, canonical processing, line disciplines, and control modes implemented by the system's device drivers or the streams interface to the drivers. These *terminal characteristics* are enabled or disabled at the driver by way of the ioctl(2) system call. They are defined in termio(7) and the header file termio.h. At the shell level they are passed to the driver by the stty(1) command. We shall discuss all of these relationships in this chapter.

First we will define some basic terms. What is the difference between *synchronous* and *asynchronous* data transmission? Synchronous devices run to the beat of the system. The machine's primary clock sets up a pulse, and data are transmitted at that pulse rate. If a machine is running at $16\frac{1}{2}$ megahertz, data are transmitted on the bus at $16\frac{1}{2}$ megahertz. This is called *synchronous data transmission*.

Asynchronous devices listen to the beat of a different drummer. Primarily character devices, asynchronous devices run without the necessity of the clock beat. They run at various speeds, which can be specified through a device, a Universal Asynchronous Receiver Transmitter or UART. In this chapter we will be concerned with asynchronous character devices.

Asynchronous character devices can be classified as terminals, including hardwire terminals, printing terminals, printers, and modems. Both types of terminals are covered later in this chapter. (Printers are covered in Chapter 8, and modems are discussed in Chapter 9.)

The first job tackled in this chapter is covering the theory necessary to understand the underlying concepts of terminals. When most of the "magic" disappears, we shall get down to brass tacks and talk about how to install the terminal.

termio THEORY

Terminal I/O is a general computer concept for input and output to and from the terminal, and `termio` is a UNIX term that refers to the handling of I/O among the system, the user's application, and the hardware itself. Specifically `termio` covers the handling of all device driver flags and definitions of the constants that set these device driver flags.

The overall design of UNIX `termio` is ingenious, particularly the I/O control, the drivers, the shell-level interface, and the interaction with the kernel. At System V Release 4 the streams interface adds yet another level of ingenuity. To appreciate this, you have to remember how it was in the bad old days before UNIX. System programmers had to program in the assembly language of their machines, and naturally they had to know how to write device drivers. Today's UNIX system administrators don't even have to get their hands dirty to install devices. On UNIX it's usually not necessary to write assembly code, nor do special drivers need to be installed very often. In fact, usually you don't even have to know what the drivers look like!

You see the genius of UNIX `termio` when you use it in administering your machines. In addition to its admirable versatility, UNIX `termio` offers the incredible convenience of only one system call, one command, and one set of constants. Let's see how it works.

UNIX Takes Asynchronous I/O Devices in Its Stride

UNIX treats all asynchronous I/O devices as `ttys`, but at the same time it assumes that they are files, too. This isn't schizophrenia: It's enlightened operating system design. Initially asynchronous I/O devices are also considered to be *full duplex*, *ASCII*, *serial*, and *dumb*.

Serial Versus Parallel

In today's world, printers come in two flavors, *parallel* and *serial*. The bus is a parallel device. It gives one data track for each bit of information. If it's a 32-bit bus, there will be thirty-two paths, one for each bit on the bus. A Centronics port is a parallel printer port with an 8-bit data path, essentially one wire for each bit of information.

A serial device treats bits differently than does a parallel device. It queues each bit, one behind the other, before sending them down a single wire. Your telephone lines and the coaxial cable that brings television into the house are serial transmission devices.

Even though UNIX systems have a parallel device driver, UNIX treats devices as if they all are serial, not only because terminals, printers, and modems traditionally are serial, but also because the lower end of the driver can handle a parallel port transparently, so that the upper, high-level portion of the driver treats it like any other serial device.

Dumb Devices

UNIX manuals emphasize that asynchronous serial devices are treated as *dumb*, which means that they do minimal character interpretation on their own. For example, if a dumb device sees a tab character, it won't know how to translate that tab into a series of spaces. Because most terminal devices are dumb devices, UNIX makes life simpler by assuming that they all are dumb.

Full-Duplex Versus Half-Duplex

Full-duplex devices transmit character data over the same line in both directions simultaneously. A telephone is the best example of full-duplex transmission. Two people can talk and listen at the same time, and they frequently do. A half-duplex machine can use a single data line either to transmit or receive, but not both at the same time.

Device Drivers

Your system can't talk to its peripheral devices without device drivers. Although there are many kinds of terminal device drivers, on a small UNIX machine you're likely to run into only three: one for the console, one for serial ports, and one for parallel ports. Do an `ls -l /dev/tty*` and you get something like this on a small UNIX or XENIX machine:

```
crw-rw-rw-  1 bin     bin      3,  0 Aug 31 10:41  /dev/tty
crw--w--w-  2 bruce   edit     0,  0 Sep 4 15:19   /dev/tty01
crw--w--w-  2 karen   edit     0,  1 Sep 4 18:18   /dev/tty02
  .
  .
crw-rw-rw-  2 root    root     0, 10 Apr 23 14:38  /dev/tty11
crw-rw-rw-  2 root    root     0, 11 Apr 23 14:38  /dev/tty12
crw--w--w-  1 root    uucp     5,128 Sep 4 13:15   /dev/tty1A
crw-rw-rw-  1 bin     bin      5,129 May 6 18:54   /dev/tty1B
crw-rw-rw-  1 bin     bin      5,130 May 6 18:54   /dev/tty1C
crw-rw-rw-  1 bin     bin      5,131 May 6 18:54   /dev/tty1D
crw--w--w-  1 root    edit     5,  0 Jul 10 16:49  /dev/tty1a
crw-rw-rw-  1 bin     bin      5,  1 May 8 09:58   /dev/tty1b
crw-rw-rw-  1 bin     bin      5,  2 May 8 09:58   /dev/tty1c
crw-rw-rw-  1 bin     bin      5,  3 May 8 09:58   /dev/tty1d
crw-rw-rw-  1 bin     bin      5,136 May 10 19:21  /dev/tty2A
crw-rw-rw-  1 bin     bin      5,137 May 6 20:22   /dev/tty2B
crw-rw-rw-  1 bin     bin      5,138 May 6 20:22   /dev/tty2C
crw-rw-rw-  1 bin     bin      5,139 May 6 20:22   /dev/tty2D
crw--w--w-  1 root    edit     5,  8 Sep 4 10:39   /dev/tty2a
crw--w--w-  2 root    bin      5,  9 Sep 4 10:39   /dev/tty2b
crw--w--w-  1 bruce   edit     5, 10 Sep 4 19:48   /dev/tty2c
crw-rw-rw-  1 bin     bin      5, 11 May 6 20:22   /dev/tty2d
```

Do a "visual sort" on field 5 and you will see precisely three major numbers: 3, 0, and 5, which tell you how many drivers you have because each device driver is signified by a different major number.

UNIX device drivers are interesting. Think of device drivers living in the lowest stratum of the kernel, talking to the kernel on one side and the hardware device on the other.[1] If the drivers themselves are located in the kernel, what are all those listings in /dev? They are unique, special files that are actually empty, but their directory and inode information point to specific drivers in the kernel. We say that the special files in /dev are *entry points* to a device driver. There are different kinds of special files in /dev, including character special files and block special files. The major number is a number assigned to the driver, and the minor number is a number passed to the driver.

Each character special file in /dev represents a port, except those that are links to other special files or those that are pseudodevices like /dev/mem and /dev/kmem. Ports have two meanings. The first is the mechanical interface to the device such as the DB-25 or DB-9 connections for an RS-232 serial port located on the computer's backplane. The second meaning is the termination of the bus as seen by the driver, such as TCP/IP's "well-known port."

Data Flow

Let's start thinking about data flow in a simple way. The stream of data flows in this way from the kernel's device driver to the tty:

$$driver \rightarrow port \rightarrow tty$$

Going back, it flows like this:

$$driver \leftarrow port \leftarrow tty$$

From the UNIX point of view, the port *is* the tty.

System Calls Revisited

Getting from the application program to the driver is accomplished by a handful of system calls:

- open
- ioctl
- read
- write
- close

System calls make the operating system do things. They are distinctive because they speak to the kernel directly. Anything requested by a system call goes into an entry point into the kernel and causes the kernel to perform a specific task.

System calls, such as read, write, open, close, and ioctl, are primitives. Library functions eventually cause system calls to be executed. A buffered read, such as scanf, or a buffered write, such as printf, are library functions.

Commands are even more complicated, because they operate at the user-interface level through the shell interpreter. They run slowly because they run at the highest level of the machine. In turn, they draw on code utilizing both library calls and system calls, but for themselves, a command is actually a compiled program or shell script.

---

[1] Exceptions are pseudodrivers, but we won't get into those in this book.

Getting to the Device Driver

System calls initiate in any code interacting with the file system, and they are passed through the device switch table. The device switch then passes the system call, with arguments, to the device driver itself:

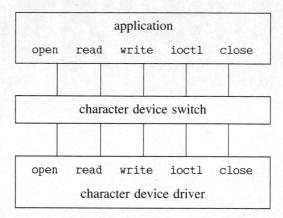

Here `ioctl` stands for I/O control, and of the five character device system calls, `ioctl` will concern you the most as the system's administrator. Its shell-level counterpart is `stty`, and both set terminal device characteristics.

The source of all system information for any terminal-like device is stored in a data structure defined by `/usr/include/sys/termio.h`. The function of `ioctl` is to pass `termio` information to the driver, which can pass back `termio` information about a port to `ioctl` when requested.

How Information Wends Its Way Through Device Drivers

Let's go into the kernel and examine the mechanics of device drivers. Character device drivers have three queues and one flag storage area each:

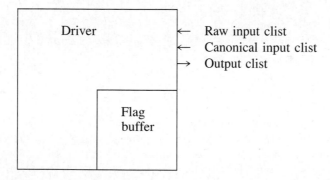

The queues are *clists*, small kernel buffers. There are two input clists and one output clist. The first input clist is the raw input buffer. Raw input can either be translated by passing it to the canonical buffer or used as is. Raw character streams are untranslated. The visual editor, vi, is a program that uses raw character streams. In raw mode, a carriage return has no special meaning.

The second clist, fed by the first, is a canonical clist. Although the general term *canonical* refers to an order or discipline, in the computer sense it refers to the orderly translation of I/O characters. In canonical mode each character is checked for a special meaning, and the carriage return has a very special meaning, indeed.

Look at the flag area of the diagram, the storage for ioctl flags. Here termio characteristics are stored and remembered. The information is stored in the flag area of the driver when you use stty to recognize ^S (Control S) to stop the data flow to the CRT and ^Q (Control Q) to start the data flow back up again. A year from now stty will still remember. The ioctl flags that the driver sees are what determines how it does the canonical processing.

What can be set by ioctl and its shell-level counterpart, stty, is what makes up termio. Terminal characteristics determine the behavior of a physical character device as it relates to the machine.

termio.h

Before you begin reading this section, go to /usr/include/sys and make a copy of termio.h. This is an interesting header file that holds everything that can be set.

Most of termio.h is #define statements, divided into several different groups:

- Control characters.
- Input modes.
- Output modes.
- Control modes.
- Line discipline modes.
- Line disciplines.

Line discipline modes are seldom used because they are open to definition by the applications programmer. We will examine the other categories.

Without termio you have no control over your devices. The termio.h file has over two pages of #define statements, all of which give octal values for terminal characteristics to pass to device drivers. When broken down to base 2, they create masks that work a lot like permissions bits used in chmod.

Control Characters

Control characters require special translation by the driver's canonical section. They start and stop scrolling, send interrupts, and perform many other useful functions:

INTR   This is the interrupt signal, usually a DEL (0x7f). Unless trapped, INTR terminates a process associated with the terminal.

QUIT   This interrupt generates a SIGQUIT signal, normally an FS or ^\ .
It is identical to INTR except that it deliberately causes a core dump.

ERASE   This defaults to the pound sign, #, and is most often substituted by the *backspace*. It erases or removes the preceding character unless it is an \n.

KILL   This interrupt defaults to the *at* character, @, and kills the entire line of input. Most often the user substitutes *delete* (0x7f) as the *kill* character.

EOF   The *end-of-file* character is ^D, Control D. It generates an EOF from the terminal, and it does it without a carriage return.

STOP   The most basic form of xon/xoff, the STOP character suspends terminal output. It is almost always kept as ^S (Control S) or ASCII NULL.

START   This is used in conjunction with STOP. It is normally ^Q (Control Q) or ASCII DC1.

Input Modes

Characters typed at the terminal are sent to the computer as fast as they are entered. They are stored in the device driver's input clist and are not normally processed until a newline (either a line feed or a carriage return interpreted as a line feed) is entered. The *kill* character, EOT, also triggers action on the input clist.

Characters entered into the driver's input clist are not interpreted, but the characters are sent from there to the driver's canonical clist for interpretation. However, the way that the device was set last by ioctl—frequently by way of stty—controls how the characters are interpreted. For example, the *kill* character is set up as @ by an entry in /usr/include/sys/termio.h. As often as not, the *kill* character is reset by stty in the user's .profile or .login to be generated by the *delete* key.

The termio.h file defines a structure called termio:

```
struct termio {
        unsigned short    c_iflag;        /* input modes */
        unsigned short    c_oflag;        /* output modes */
        unsigned short    c_cflag;        /* control modes */
        unsigned short    c_lflag;        /* line discipline modes */
        char              c_line;         /* line discipline */
        unsigned char     c_cc[NCC];      /* control chars */
};
```

The field c_inflag describes input modes. Elsewhere in the structure, octal values of each input mode constant are added. Here is how a few termio.h constants look:

```
IGNBRK 0000001
BRKINT 0000002
IGNPAR 0000004
```

Recognize the bit pattern similarity to chmod (see Chapter 3)?

```
execute 0000001
write   0000002
read    0000004
```

Adding the octal values and then converting them to a base 2 number puts a 0 or 1 in each control field. Octal bit patterns are set up for any one given set of modes so that they comprise a mask when they are added together. True to binary, they are either 1 or 0, true or false.

Here is a brief breakdown of some input modes:

IGNBRK	Ignores break condition. In plain English this tells the machine, "Don't flinch when BREAK is hit." Hitting the *break* key causes a short interruption or space of output from the terminal.
BRKINT	Signals an interrupt on seeing a BREAK, the flip side of IGNBRK. Now BREAK causes an interrupt signal and flushes I/O buffers.
IGNPAR	Ignores parity errors in characters.
PARMARK	Marks parity errors. *Mark* and *space* are modem-oriented bit protocols relating to parity.
INPCK	Enables parity checking of input.
ISTRIP	Strips characters to seven bits.
INLCR	Changes a line feed to a carriage return on input.
IGNCR	Ignores the carriage return.
ICRNL	Changes a carriage return to a line feed.
IUCLC	Translates from uppercase into lowercase characters on input.
IXON	Enables start/stop output control (xon/xoff use of ^S/^Q).
IXANY	Enables any character to restart output.
IXOFF	Enables start/stop input or buffer control of the input queue.

Input modes allow mapping of carriage returns, line feeds, interpretation of the break signal, case mapping, and, most important of all, xon/xoff interpretation of both input and output.

Output Modes

Output processing starts out with the decision to postprocess or not. From there, processing gets into line feed/carriage return mapping, fill characters, and character delays. While we look at a few of the options, remember that these flags are system constants that can be set and are being fed to the device driver by the ioctl system call:

OPOST	Posts process output (canonical output).
OLCUC	Maps lowercase to uppercase characters on output (used with IUCLC).
ONLCR	Maps a line feed to the carriage return/line feed pair on output.
OCRNL	Changes a carriage return to a line feed.
ONLRET	The line feed works as a carriage return.
OFILL	Uses fill characters for delays.
OFDEL	Fill is delete, otherwise a NULL.

Character delays are handled by output mode constants. Although they were created for teletypes, they come in handy for a mechanical printer without buffer control. A few typical constants are

CRDLY	Select carriage return delays.
CR2	Delay approximately 0.1 sec.
CR3	Delay approximately 0.15 sec.

There are more delay constants that allow time killing for tabs, backspaces, and form feeds. The form feed can be dragged out for two full seconds. TAB3 is listed with the output mode constants, but it is not a maximum delay for tabs. It translates tabs into spaces, necessary on most printers and terminals, because they are dumb devices and cannot do the translation themselves.

Control Modes

In UNIX *control modes* govern character transmission or baud rates, character bit size, stop bits, and parity. UNIX terminology differs from general computer terms here, so you can get confused. What UNIX calls control modes, others generally call line disciplines.

B0   This looks like baud rate 0, but it is not a baud rate. It specifies a hang-up.

B50   50 baud

B75   75 baud

The list goes up to 9600 baud and beyond on some systems.

Although a character is defined as eight bits, the entire American ASCII character set can be sent in seven bits, ignoring the high-order bit. When sending in six bits, only the *delete* (0x7f) and the lowercase characters are lost. As odd as it seems, fewer than eight bits can be sent and still preserve intelligence. In fact, it frequently is advantageous to run at seven bits on character devices to prevent data from blowing up the screen or bending the printer out of shape.[2] Here's a look at character bit size:

CS5   5 bits

CS6   6 bits

CS7   7 bits

CS8   8 bits

CSTOPB   Sends 2 stop bits

What's left are the odds and ends that don't neatly fit into any specific category:

CREAD   This enables the receiver. In plain English, it gets characters.

PARNEB   This enables parity generation and detection.

PARODD   This is for odd parity.

HUPCL   This disconnects on close. It disconnects the line when the last process using the line terminates. This sets DTR low.

CLOCAL   This is a local line for a dial-up modem line, so there is no modem control.

Line Disciplines

Line disciplines are used with canonical processing:

ISIG   Enables signal processing for interrupt (INTR) and quit.

ICANNON   Enables canonical processing.

---

[2] If an 8-bit executable or data file is sent to a character device, the device will try to interpret the eighth-order bit, with strange results. Your printer will start printing elaborate extended graphics that resemble native Klingon.

XCASE	Canonical uppercase and lowercase presentation.
ECHO	Enables echo (default).
ECHOE	Makes the *erase* character generate a backspace-space-backspace sequence.
ECHOK	Puts a line feed after the *kill* character.
ECHONL	Echoes a line feed (newline).
NOFLSH	This means "Don't flush the character buffer on SIGINT or SIGQUIT."

stty

The stty command allows all the termio constants to be set at the shell level. The stty arguments are essentially the same as termio's, but in lowercase characters, of course. In stty and ioctl, most termio characteristics can be mapped either way, on or off. For example, echo is enabled or disabled, signal processing is enabled or disabled, and so on.

We are most familiar with using stty to reset tty characteristics. For example,

```
$ stty -hupctl
```

keeps from hanging up the line. If used to set a port other than your own, it will look like this:

```
# stty 300</dev/lp4
```

All of this can be done only if the device is open for reading.

INSTALLING TERMINALS

Now let's go into the practical business of installing a terminal. A terminal is not a difficult device to interface after you've done it a few times. It is not fussy about protocols and does little, if any, signal pin handshaking. It is one of the few peripherals that can survive a three-wire connection, but that's not good practice.[3] Dumb and inexpensive terminals tend to be more tolerant of minimal connections.

You're not likely to run into as many terminal installation problems connecting the hardware. You might have some problems if your device is unknown to UNIX, because getting terminfo or termcap to recognize the terminal is sometimes tricky. Fortunately, all common terminals and most not-so-common terminals are recognized by termcap and termio.

Logins and gettys

The login process is an extension of init. A getty hovers at each active, unused terminal waiting for someone to type in a log name. The getty process sets the terminal type,

---

[3] A three-wire connection consists of *send data* (pin 2), *receive data* (pin 3), and *signal ground* (pin 7). It is preferable, however, to have some minimal signal pin sensing to detect a hang-up (SIGHUP).

modes, speed, and line disciplines. Once the login name is seen, a subprocess is called to verify the user's right to log on.

Once the login section of the code is passed, the next step is to get information about the login terminal. That information comes from /etc/inittab and /etc/gettydefs, except in SunOS, BSD, XENIX, and older UNIX versions that access /etc/ttys and /etc/ttytypes. The terminal System V software interfaces are inittab and gettydefs. The /etc/inittab file associates the port with the device and turns the getty on or off. In the following example respawn tells the system to cause gettys (logins) to be continuously recreated:

```
01:2:respawn:/etc/getty tty1a 9600
02:2:off:/etc/getty tty1b 300
03:2:respawn:/etc/getty tty1c 9600
```

If there is a getty, the baud rate will be set as well. If the third field is off, line disciplines cannot be set in inittab, and there is no getty.[4]

There is an inittab in versions of XENIX before 3.2, but it has only token compatibility with System V. Earlier versions rely on /etc/ttys, /etc/gettydefs, and /etc/ttytypes that function about like inittab and gettydefs in the ways they fix terminal types, line disciplines, and other System V terminal characteristics. The /etc/ttys gets its information about line disciplines from /etc/gettydefs.

/etc/ttys

There is an entry for each port in a XENIX ttys file:

```
1mtty07
1mtty08
0mtty09
0mtty10
0mtty11
0mtty12
0itty1a
1mtty2a
12tty1A
```

The first character in each entry is a binary 1 or 0, on or off. If 1, a login is on the port. If 0, there is no login. The second character is a key taken from /etc/gettydefs, which defines the baud rate and a few primitive local characteristics of the port. The last set of characters is the port name. In the preceding example, there is a getty on ttys 7, 8, 2a, and 1A. The speed on 1a is 1200 baud, and on 1A it also is 1200, but by another definition in gettydefs. All the others are 9600 baud.

SunOS also uses the preceding ttys form. Just for comparison, let's look at the Berkeley BSD 4.3 version, which is more complex. A single record in the 4.3 version looks like this:

```
ttyd1 "/etc/getty std.9600" free100 on #freedom 100
```

Here the fields are the device or port name, command, tty type in termcap-recognizable format, status, and an optional comment. Earlier versions of BSD use a simpler, more cryptic form.

---

[4] System V Release 4 no longer uses gettys.

ttys works with gettydefs. Let's look at an abbreviated version of a gettydefs file:

```
1 # B300  HUPCL OPOST CR1 NL1 # 1
      B300 CS8 SANE HUPCL TAB3 IXANY #\r\n@!login: # 2

2 # B1200 HUPCL OPOST CR1 ECHOE NL1 #
      B1200 CS8 SANE HUPCL TAB3 ECHOE IXANY #\r\n@!login: # 3

3 # B2400  HUPCL OPOST CR1 ECHOE NL1 #
      B2400 CS8 SANE HUPCL TAB3 ECHOE IXANY #\r\n@!login: # 1

g # B300  HUPCL # B300  CS8 SANE HUPCL TAB3 IXANY #\r\n@!login: # g

h # B600  HUPCL # B600  CS8 SANE HUPCL TAB3 IXANY #\r\n@!login: # h

i # B1200 HUPCL # B1200 CS8 SANE HUPCL TAB3 ECHOE IXANY #
      \r\n@!login: # i

j # B1800 HUPCL # B1800 CS8 SANE HUPCL TAB3 ECHOE IXANY #\r\n@!login: # j

k # B2400 HUPCL # B2400 CS8 SANE HUPCL TAB3 ECHOE IXANY #\r\n@!login: # k

l # B4800 HUPCL # B4800 CS8 SANE HUPCL TAB3 ECHOE IXANY #\r\n@!login: # l

m # B9600 HUPCL # B9600 CS8 SANE HUPCL TAB3 ECHOE IXANY #\r\n@!login: # m
```

Note that some speeds such as 300, 600, 1200, and 2400 are repeated, but with different designations in the first field. Also note the termio and stty ioctl constants and the last field, which is a retry to another gettydefs line. In this example the 2 # B1200 login record uses the last field to point to entry 3, the 2400-baud record. Entry 3, the 2400-baud record, points to entry 1, the 300-baud entry, and 300 baud points back to 1200 baud. These entries are set up expecting 2400-baud logins, but they are ready to fall back to 1200 or even 300 if need be. For example, if a 2400-baud login attempt is unsuccessful, the client or sending system will transmit a BREAK, and control will pass to the 300-baud entry. Should that fail, the next BREAK will send control to the second record, and the port will go to 1200 baud.

The first set of termio constants between pound signs are the first settings that receive the attempted login. The second set of termio constants are the characteristics to set the line to if the login is successful. The use of SANE is a good shortcut for setting the port to something sensible without having to set each line characteristic separately.

The /etc/ttytype file is used to make reference between the port and a terminal type. In the following example, the terminals with uppercase letters A through E have modem control and are assigned by default to modem or *dial-up* ports. Then ttys 01 through 12 are virtual terminals taken off an AT motherboard, and they are type ansi:

```
ansi    tty01
  .

  .
ansi    tty11
ansi    tty12
unknown tty1a
unknown tty2a
dialup  tty1A
dialup  tty2A
```

```
dialup   tty1B
dialup   tty1C
dialup   tty1D
dialup   tty1E
unknown  tty1b
unknown  tty1c
unknown  tty1d
unknown  tty1e
dialup   tty2B
dialup   tty2C
dialup   tty2D
unknown  tty2b
wyse30   tty2c
unknown  tty2d
dialup   tty2E
```

The `tty2c` is a Wyse 30; all the others are undefined and therefore unknown. The `/etc/ttytype` file is used in conjunction with the XENIX `tset` command.

tset

The XENIX and BSD `tset` command puts the terminal `/etc/termcap` entries into the user's environment. For example,

```
tset -m ansi:ansi -m tvi925:925
```

sets the environment to TERM=ansi on the motherboard ports to `ansi` or `tvi925` (Tele-video 925), depending on which port is referenced. The terminal port name is picked up from `/etc/ttytype`.

termcap

The `termcap` file is the Berkeley predecessor to AT&T's `terminfo`. Both are used to allow the terminal to do screen-oriented functions such as clearing the screen, positioning the cursor, and handling terminal-specific characteristics like *automatic right*, *margin wrap*, and *backspace*. Not only visual editors, such as `vi`, but also screen-oriented applications software would be impossible without `termcap` or `terminfo`.

Back in the olden days of 8-bit CP/M, text processors like WordStar had to be configured at each installation to interact with specific terminals. When MP/M was introduced, there had to be a separate version of WordStar for each type of terminal on the system, so we can thank our lucky stars for `termcap` and `terminfo`. Today UNIX-resident text processors use `terminfo` and `termcap`, and SCO Lyrix is one of them.

LOOKING FOR A TERMINAL IN `termcap`

Looking for a specific terminal in `termcap` means plowing through the `/etc/termcap` file with an editor or `grep` and searching for the right terminal type:

```
$ grep tvi950 /etc/termcap
v5!tvi950!950!televideo950:\
va!tvi950-ap!tvi 950 w/alt pages:\
        :is=\E\\1:ti=\E-06 :te=\E-16 :tc=tvi950:
```

```
vf:tvi950-4p:tvi 950 w/4 pages:\
        :ti=\E\\1:te=\E\\3:tc=tvi950:
vl:tvi950b:bare tvi950 no is:\
        :is@:ks=\\El:ke=\Ek:tc=tvi950:
vs:tvi950ns:tvi950 w/no standout:\
        :so@:se@:us@:ue@:tc=tvi950:
vt:tvi950-2p:tvi 950 w/2 pages:\
        :ti=\E\\1:te=\E\\2:tc=tvi950:
```

The `termcap` entries are as nasty to read as `troff` and `nroff` macros are.

Terminal characteristics are set by mnemonics. The first mnemonic, `is`, is a terminal initialization string and is set to an *escape one*, `\El`. The last entry, `tc`, is a reference to a similar terminal. The following is an entry for a Televideo 910:

```
VO:tvi910+:televideo 910 PLUS:\
    :ak=\EG%B0+ FRU:al=33*\EE:\
    :dc=\EW:de=\E):dl=33*\ER:ds=\E(:ei=:ic=\EQ:im=:\
    :BS=^B:CL=^U:CR=^J:DK=^V:CO=\E.2:CF=\E.0:tc=tvi910:
```

The names by which the terminal is known are on the first line:

```
VO:tvi910+:televideo 910 PLUS:\
```

`VO` and `tvi910+` are shown to be Televideo 910s with enhancements. Note the name ending with a +, meaning *enhanced*.

The `this=that` notation defines the escape characters and control sequences that make screen handling civilized. In addition, `al` adds a blank line, `dl` deletes a line, and `dc` is a Berkeley *delete* character. Here it is set to an *escape W*:

```
:dc=\EW
```

Uppercase mnemonics like `BS` are control characters. `BS` is backspace, here set to a `^B`, Control B, which is a departure from its usual ASCII backspace, `^H`.

The `termcap` and `terminfo` files also work with a stack. Entries like `%d` (output top of stack as integer) or `%c` (output top of stack as character) are for stack manipulation. For further information on `termcap` and `terminfo`, refer to the BSD manual `termcap`(5), XENIX `termcap`(m), and AT&T `terminfo`(4).

Adding a Terminal to AT&T System V

Adding a terminal to System V starts with the `/etc/inittab` entry. Look at the following line setting port `tty1c`:

```
03:2:respawn:/etc/getty tty1c 9600
```

This line for the specific terminal must be modified to allow a `getty` at terminal speed, usually 9600. Next the terminal's special file is checked in `/dev` for permissions and ownership:

```
$ ls -l /dev/tty1c
crw--w--w-  1 root      bin     5,  0 May 10 19:39 /dev/tty1c
```

The port should be `rw` for the user and `w` only for group and others. If there are no hardware complications, the port will accept a login as soon as the system knows that inittab has been modified to allow a getty. It knows about the getty as soon as the system is rebooted or on issuing an init q.

The last step is to modify the user's .profile or .login to understand the terminal type. Do this to add a Wyse 60 terminal:

```
TERM=wyse60;export TERM
```

For C shell, use

```
setenv term wyse60
```

Adding a Terminal to BSD or XENIX

XENIX makes you jump through a few more hoops than AT&T System V does. First the port must be enabled and the baud rate set in /etc/ttys. Let's do port 1c at 9600 baud, defined as m in /etc/gettydefs. This small piece of information is needed to create the entry for /etc/ttys:

```
1mtty1c
```

Now for /etc/ttytype. Let's go for a simple Wyse 30 terminal again:

```
wyse30 tty1c
```

XENIX has no init command, so init q is out of the question.[5] The ports are enabled and disabled by the XENIX commands of the same name:

```
# enable tty1c
```

Handling the user's .profile entry also is different from System V. The tset command is usually invoked with multiple-terminal types of those likely to be on a particular system or port:

```
eval `tset -m wyse30:wyse30 -m ansi:ansi`
```

If you are looking for System V portability, you can set TERM, but you also have to hand-hold termcap:

```
TERM=wyse30
TERMCAP=/etc/termcap
export TERM TERMCAP
```

But there is another way. The termcap entry can be added to the user's .profile or .login:

```
TERMCAP="wb!wy30!wyse30!Wyse WY-30 in wy30 mode:\
        :is=\E\176"\E\176 \EX\E"\EDF\EC\E`7:\
        :if=/usr/lib/tabset/std:pt:\
        :GG#0:G1=\EH3:G2=\EH2:G3=\EH1:G4=\EH5:GC=\EH8:GD=\
         EH0:GH=\EH\072:\
        :GU=\EH\075:GV=\EH6:GR=\EH4:GL=\EH9:\
```

---

[5] Note that inittab and telint make only a token appearance in XENIX. They do not work with init, because init doesn't exist. Therefore there can be no initiation levels and no reference to inittab.

```
        :al=\EE:am:bs:bt=\EI:cd=EY:ce=\ET:cl=\E+:\
        :cm=Ea%i%dR%dC:co#80:dc=\EW:dl=\ER:ei=\Er:im=\Eq:
        :k1=^A@\r:k2=^AA\r:k3=^AB\r:k4=^ACr:k5=^AD\r:k6=^AE\
         r:k7=^AF\r:\
        :k8=^AG\r:kd=^J:kh=\E(:kl=^H:kr=^L:ku=^K:\
        :li#24:mi:nd=^L:se=\E(:so=\E):sg#0:ug#1:ue=\
          EG0:ul:up=^K:us=\EG8:"
export TERMCAP
```

MANAGER'S CORNER

Terminal Selection

Every nontechnical manager of UNIX systems should know that UNIX loves dumb terminals. Don't get talked into blowing your budget by buying too many extravagantly priced
terminals, unless your budget is unlimited. For the most part, cheaper, simpler terminals
do just fine. You might plan for the future by investing in EGA or VGA graphics terminals
to take advantage of X Windows for future applications, particularly System V Release 4's
version of the X Window System, the OPEN LOOK Graphical User Interface, and the OSF's
Motif. Until then, consider using simple, straightforward terminals for part of your UNIX
installation.

Avoid terminals that have no `terminfo` or `termcap` entries. Your people will tell you
that they can write a `termcap` entry for it, but this is time-consuming and sometimes wastes
valuable project time. On the other hand, if there is a good reason to buy a specialized
terminal, be sure to have a `termcap` entry as part of the purchase agreement. Don't accept
a verbal statement from a sales rep like "I can get you `termcap`."

Be concerned with human engineering when buying terminals. How do the keys feel?
Programmers require a firmer key than do secretarial typists. Key locations also are important;
otherwise, you might keep hitting the keys by accident. CAPS LOCK or FUNCTION keys
located in the lowest left corner of the keyboard are curses you should wish on a competitor,
not your own staff, but jamming a bent paper clip under the offending keys helps.

Color terminals are nice; no one will argue about that. But can your installation take
advantage of them? If not, your money might be better spent on storage than on fancy
terminals. On the other hand, system programmers spending eight hours a day in front of
the screen need some consideration. Also, their environment should be designed for a real
human being, with a desk and chair comfortable enough for nonstop keyboard work. In any
computer installation, people are your biggest investment.

`lp` and `lpr`
Printer Spooling Systems

Both System V and BSD have printer spoolers that are capable of dealing with multiple printers. System V has the `lp` spooling system, and Berkeley has the `lpr` spooling system. Both can be manipulated to allow or disallow print requests, and both have a fair degree of sophistication. System V's `lp` spooler allows *classes* of printers, groups of similar printers that all can take requests as if they are the same printer. Berkeley's `lpr` spooler lacks this feature but more than makes up for it with its ability to send print requests to remote printers. Under BSD a printer does not have to be on the same system, as it does in System V.

In this chapter we shall look at System V's `lp` spooling system first and then the BSD 4.2 `lpr` spooler. The chapter will finish with a discussion of serial and parallel printer ports.

THE SYSTEM V `lp` SPOOLING SYSTEM

The UNIX System V `lp` spooling system is a mature, commercial printing system. Typical of UNIX, it is daemon driven and has a number of special-purpose commands to run it. Up until System V, AT&T UNIX was prepared to deal with one printer, and one printer only.

Before System V there was an AT&T `lpr` command[1] that was simple to administer and easy for users to call, but they could use only one printer. Managers and users wanted

_____

[1] Don't confuse this with the BSD `lpr` spooling system! UNIX Edition 7 had an `lpr` command that allowed for only one printer. But the Berkeley UNIX `lpr` spooling system is highly sophisticated and allows multiple printers.

a more mature UNIX that could handle multiple printers, and the lp spooling system is one of the results.

The old UNIX Edition 7 lpr spooler is a reasonably simple command for a single printer, and its mechanism is straightforward to understand and administer. In contrast, System V's lp spooler is large and complex enough to be considered a UNIX subsystem. Its major capabilities are print spooling, multiple-printer choice, and printer classes. Like UNIX Edition 7's lpr, lp holds multiple files to be printed and sends them serially to the printers. Unlike UNIX Edition 7's lpr, it handles as many printers as are attached to the system. The lp spooler can group similar printers and send print requests to any printer in that class free to take the request, allowing lp to maximize throughput. Clearly, the design intent of lp is to provide a commercially viable print spooling system that can live on a desktop or work in a data center. This was System V's move to what the MIS world calls "operating system maturity."

Glossary

The lp spooling system has a language of its own, and the manuals won't help you much without a knowledge of lp terms.

device   This refers to a physical device, such as a mechanical printer, but it can also mean a file.[2] It most often refers to the /dev entry for the printer port, such as /dev/tty13.

printer   This is a logical name applied to a device.[3] The interface to the device, such as the name epson_1, is the interface to /dev/tty2B. The term *device* most often refers to a printer port, and a *printer* is the name of a specific printer to be found at a particular port.

class   This is a logical name given to a group of similar printers, such as five HP laser printers. AT&T documentation sometimes refers to a class as a *list* of printers.

hardwire A *hardwire* is a printing device that cannot be logged onto, such as conventional printers like Epson FX 850s.

login   A *login* is a printing terminal that can be logged onto, such as an old teletype or Diablo 950. The name comes from its ability to accept gettys or logins.

Actually, the distinction between *hardwire* and *login* is what is most important. A *login* printer must have a getty, and a *hardwire* cannot. The administrative trick is to pass off a baud rate to a port that has no getty, since a getty is guaranteed to respawn and continually guarantee its stty settings. [4]

---

[2] All devices are treated as files in UNIX. Redirection to and from a device would not work without this feature.

[3] The terms *logical* or *virtual* refer to devices that may or may not be real. For example, a virtual address is almost guaranteed not to be the same as the real address, but a real printer has mass, and with luck it can even print!

[4] Set the port characteristics in the files in model and interface in /usr/spool/lp/*.

lp's File System

The lp system is only moderately complex in terms of files and directories. Fortunately, most of the regular files and directories are in the same location, /usr/spool/lp. Most of the executable files are in /usr/lib, but commands that can be used by users are in /bin. Bear in mind that /bin is /usr/bin in System V Release 4.

Here's the first layer of /usr/spool/lp. Notice that the files are owned by lp, not root:

```
$ ls -l /usr/spool/lp
total 26
prw-------   1 lp        bin         0 Jun  4 09:22 FIFO
-r--r--r--   1 lp        bin         2 Jun  4 08:08 SCHEDLOCK
drwxr-xr-x   2 lp        bin        32 Mar  4 10:05 class
-rw-r--r--   1 lp        bin         6 May 30 14:01 default
drwxr-xr-x   2 lp        bin        48 May 30 14:01 interface
-rw-r--r--   1 lp        bin        33 Jun  4 08:08 log
drwxr-xr-x   2 lp        bin        48 May 30 14:01 member
drwxr-xr-x   2 lp        bin       192 Mar  4 09:57 model
-rw-r--r--   1 lp        bin       370 Jun  1 21:55 oldlog
-rw-r--r--   1 lp        bin         0 Jun  4 08:08 outputq
-rw-r--r--   1 lp        bin       124 Jun  1 21:44 pstatus
-rw-r--r--   1 lp        bin       104 May 30 14:01 qstatus
-rw-r--r--   1 lp        bin       394 Apr 13  1987 remote
drwxr-xr-x   3 lp        bin        48 May 30 14:01 request
-rw-r--r--   1 lp        bin         3 Jun  1 21:35 seqfile
```

Let's now describe the files:

FIFO	This named pipe (first in/first out) belongs to lp.
SCHEDLOCK	This is a *lock file*. UNIX uses lock files in many places in the system to prevent the same process from executing two instances of itself simultaneously. SCHEDLOCK is created when lpsched is first invoked, and if lpsched is attempted again, the lock file will prevent it from initializing a live lp system. Make sure your rc or local.rc script removes SCHEDLOCK.
default	This ASCII file contains the name of the default printer.
log	The log file logs all printer requests for all printers. It contains the lp request id, the user log name of the user who sent it, the printer name of the destination, and the time and date. It is headed by the lp start time and ends with the stop time.
oldlog	This is the old log file renamed to oldlog.
outputq	This non-ASCII data file is the list for all devices and classes of printers.
qstatus	This non-ASCII data file holds the printer status for all devices and classes.
seqfile	This file holds the last printer request number.

We delve even deeper when we look at the /usr/spool/lp subdirectories:

request	The /usr/spool/lp/request directory has a subdirectory for each device and printer class where files are spooled on the way to the printer.

class   The class directory holds more information on printer *classes*, similar or identical printers grouped for alternative output, such as a battery of Imagen laser printers.

model   The model directory holds a copy of each potentially executable model interface program that is copied to /usr/spool/interface when selected by lpadmin.

interface   This directory holds the executable files for printer interfaces. When a printer is set up by lpadmin, a copy of a specific interface program is copied from /usr/spool/model to /usr/spool/interface. Characteristics specific to an individual printer are set here, such as the baud rate and other termio characteristics.

member   This directory has a file for each printer. Each file simply has the name of the device destination port:

```
$ cat /usr/spool/lp/member
/dev/lp0
/dev/lp1
```

lp Administration Commands Summary

It takes several commands to make lp work. First, lpsched is the center of the lp system; in fact, it starts the lp system. The lpsched command itself does all the routing requests by sending them to the interface program that initiates the spooling and printing.

lpshut

The lpshut command is lpsched's functional counterpart, shutting down the processes started by lpsched. The lpshut command should be used before modifying the lp system.

lpadmin

The system administrator's primary spooler tool is lpadmin, used to modify and configure the lp system. A typical use is adding or removing printers and classes from the system. We will talk more about lpadmin later in the chapter.

Starting and Stopping Printing

One of the most useful features of the lp system is its ability to gate printing requests. There are three ways it does that. On the user side, it can stop any requests from coming in. On the printer end, it can stop spooled files from going to a printer or class. It can also shut down the entire scheduler. We've already seen that lpsched turns the spooler on and lpshut turns it off. The following commands stop requests before and after they are spooled.

accept

The accept command allows lp to get requests from users and can be applied to any specific printer or class.

reject

The counterpart to accept is reject, which stops any printer or class from receiving print requests from the users. The accept/reject pair either allows or prevents requests from being sent to the spooler. This is useful when the system is running out of spool space and is not able to accept new requests. Naturally the administrator will have the good sense to stop any new requests from going to the spooler.

enable

Devices can be enabled or disabled at the destination. The enable command allows a device to accept files from the spooler.

disable

The counterpart of enable is disable, which prevents spooler requests from going to the printer. An ideal use of the disable command is to stop requests from reaching a printer that needs mechanical attention, such as a paper jam, new paper, or a change of ribbon.

Configuring lp

The lp spooler is far too complex to be altered by hand, so lp configuration is done exclusively with the lpadmin command. A note of caution: Do not attempt to use lpadmin while lpsched is active. Altering lp spooler features while the spooler is running will hopelessly confuse the system. But there are some exceptions, which are noted later in this chapter.

ADDING PRINTERS

A new printer or printer class is also added with lpadmin. Since a printer is a name associated with a logical device, the name is important. There are a few restrictions in the choice of a name:

length   The name must be at least 14 characters long.
character   Only alphanumeric characters and the underscore are permissible, such as epson_850.
duplication   The name must not already exist on the system.

Using lpadmin

The lpadmin command configures lp, its purpose being to describe, install, and remove devices as well as printers and classes. Remember that a *device* most often refers to a printer port, that a *printer* is a name for a specific printer to be found at a particular port, and that a *class* is a group of similar printers. The lpadmin command is used to add and remove devices and to set a default destination, should one be needed.

The major options are

-d   The -d flag is used to make a specific printer the default printer. The -d flag can be used with the system running.

-x   The -x flag is used to remove devices, and it must be used by itself.

-p   The -p flag names the printer to which the other options used with lpadmin refer.

The remaining options can be used with the -p option only.

-m model **Option**

The -m flag selects an interface program from /usr/spool/model. All printers are supplied with a *dumb* interface unless otherwise specified. Since most printers are dumb, this is no problem. In the nondumb arena the Imagen series are the favorites, in that they are well represented in specialized /usr/spool/model files. If your system fails to have full support for your printer of choice, there may be outside software available to do the job. For example, Elan Computer Group makes a desktop typesetting system called Eroff, and Image Network makes one called Xroff. These packages are complete and offer many enhancements beyond troff, eqn, tbl, and pic. They are designed for use with printers like HP LaserJet, and they also handle PostScript printers.

Among standard model programs you can count on finding an HP LaserJet, a TI 820, and a Qume 1155. Beyond that, make sure that the printer manufacturer can give you a model program for lp, unless you can write one yourself. All available model programs are in /usr/spool/lp/model.

-e **Printer Interface Option**

The -e option allows an old, existing printer interface program to be copied to a new program for a specific printer. It allows lpadmin to take an existing interface program and create a new interface program. Why? Imagine you have an interface program that does everything that you want for a Panasonic printer running on a parallel port. You want to add a second Panasonic, but now you need to use a serial port, having run out of parallel ports. You need to set the baud rate at 1200, and so now the original Panasonic interface program will not do. By copying the old interface program with the -i option and adding a line with stty, however, you have a new interface program with minimum effort.

Review

The system administrator can select or create a device interface program. Three options are open for a printer device program:

1.   Through the (-m) model option

$$model \rightarrow interface$$

2.   Through the (-e) interface option

$$interface \rightarrow interface$$

3.   -i created by the administrator

$$new \rightarrow interface \rightarrow model$$

The model interface programs are not particularly complex but enable you to set the baud rate and other stty/ioctl options. This is the only safe place to set the stty characteristics of a hardwire, nonlogin printer.

Other printer attributes are set here, such as graphics, landscape mode, and wide carriage. It is up to you to find the escape sequences for specialized modes. The printer manuals have them, so if you have the time and talent, by all means write your own model programs. If you do write your own, save a little time and use one of the existing model programs from which to "cookbook."

Setting and Removing Classes: -c and -r

To set a class, use the -c option, and to remove a printer from a class, use the -r option.

hardwire and login: -h and -l

Printers are either printing terminals or conventional hardwire printers. The -h option is used for hardwire printers, and -l is used by printing terminals, like teletypes.

Homemade Interface Programs: -i

The last lpadmin option is -i, used to install a new interface program, by putting the path name with the flag:

```
lpadmin -i/u/bhunter/lp_work/interface/new .......
```

Put all this information together, and you can add a printer called ptr5 at address tty2a. It is class1 and uses ptr1's model interface program:

```
# /usr/lib/lpadmin -pptr5 -v/dev/tty2a -eptr1 -cclass1
```

It is a hardwire printer by default.

Modifying Destinations

Recall that the modifiable printer characteristics can be changed with lpadmin as long as the changes are made relative to the printer name. The -p flag must always be used to specify the printer name. The following features are available:

1. The device can be dynamically changed with lpsched running. This feature is done with login terminals in mind.
2. All model interface programs can be modified with the -m, -e, and -i flags.
3. A printer can be added to a class (-c flag).
4. A printer can be removed from a class (-r flag).

Let's put it to work. Here's how you add a printer hp12 to class laser:

```
# /usr/lib/lpadmin -php12 -claser
```

Now let's make the Epson MX-100 a hardwire printer, as if it could be anything else:

```
# /usr/lib/lpadmin -pepson_100 -h
```

But what if you want to remove the Epson from class slow? Here's how you do that:

```
# /usr/lib/lpadmin -pepson_100 -rslow
```

Destinations can be removed only if there are no requests pending. If requests are in the queue, the way out is either to cancel them or to lpmove them. This is how an Okidata 92 is removed:

```
# /usr/lib/lpadmin -xoki92
```

Here's how a class of line printers is removed with lpadmin:

```
# /usr/lib/lpadmin -xlinep
```

Routing Requests

On sites with a lot of printers, the user's greatest frustration is figuring out how to get a print request to a specific printer. A default destination does fine in a small shop or a local site with a single print center. Any other printer choice is necessary only for a speciality printer, such as a laser printer or a wide-carriage printer. How do you get to a specific printer? It's time to look at LPDEST.

LPDEST

A large system can have dozens of printers; there can be no default printer on a multiple-site system. A default printer would have all those users who didn't know where to send their output coming to the same printer, and so each request sent to lp with no p flag destination is an irritant to the operations staff. Usually the default printer is the one in the computer room. The print center or operations staff usually throws away printer output with an unknown origin, print bin, or user name, and they get tired of putting printer output in the trash can.

There is an environment variable called LPDEST that has to be set to the name of the printer of choice for each user in his profile. A list of printers and their locations and names should be made readily available to users, and preferably they should be sent to a README file in a user's home directory when the user's new environment is created. Setting the LPDEST variable uses the same syntax as all other environment variables:

```
LPDEST=fm3;export LPDEST
```

Here the printer destination name, fm3, is being assigned to the LPDEST constant and exported into the environment.

Printers referenced by LPDEST are found in /usr/spool/lp/interface. The following is the printer destination hierarchy:

1. The environment destination set with LPDEST.
2. The (-d) default destination.

Be sure that your users have a list of lp destinations. If you have a news facility, use it. If not, place the list of lp destinations in new users' mail as their first message. Be sure to include instructions on setting LPDEST for their .profile or .login. A line added to their .profile and commented out often helps.

Printer Status and `lpstat`

The spooler status is found with `lpstat`, which gives information about requests, destinations, and scheduler status. The −t flag gets all the device information:

```
$ lpstat -t
scheduler is running
system default destination: 850
device for epson: /dev/tty2b
device for 850: /dev/lp0
epson accepting requests since May 30 14:01
850 accepting requests since Jul  7 21:05
printer epson is idle.  enabled since May 30 14:01
printer 850 is idle.  enabled since Jul  7 21:02
```

A specific printer's information is obtained with the −p option:

```
$ lpstat -p850
printer 850 is idle.  enabled since Jul  7 21:02
```

More than one printer name can be used at the same time. Other flags or options worth mentioning are

-a   Prints acceptance status of destinations (which printers accept which requests).
-c   Prints the class names and their members.
-d   Prints the name of the default printer.
-o   Prints the status of the output requests.
-r   Prints the status of the request scheduler.
-s   Prints a status summary.
-v   Prints the names of printers and the device path names associated with them.

Canceling Requests

A request to send a file to a printer can be canceled with the `cancel` command. The `/usr/bin/cancel` command is owned by `lp`, and it is in either `/bin` or `/usr/bin`.[5] It is set with the set-user-ID bit on, so a user can use it as if he or she is the `lp` administrator. This is typical of most `lp` commands in `/usr/lib`. Look at a listing of the `cancel` command:

```
$ ls -l /usr/bin/cancel
-rws--s--x   1 lp      bin     15999 Apr 13  1987 /usr/bin/cancel
```

Note the set-user-ID bit and `bin` ownership. An individual `print` request can be canceled if the request number is known:

```
$ cancel laser-256
```

A privileged user can cancel all requests:

```
# cancel laser
```

---

[5] For security reasons, don't give `root` ownership to commands and files that can be owned by administrative nonusers, like `bin`, `adm`, `lp`, `admin`, `uucp`, or `lpadmin`.

accept and reject **Requests**

The accept and reject commands gate between the user and the scheduler. The ability to accept print requests can be turned off at the user interface. This is particularly handy when faced with a prolonged printer downtime for repair or lack of supplies. If, for example, you are faced with the paper jam of all times, execute reject with the -r flag to tell the users why:

```
# /usr/lib/reject -r "paper jam" laser
```

The users will see this:

```
# lp -dlaser usage.report
lp: cannot accept requests for destination laser
    -- paper jam
```

enable **and** disable **Requests**

While the accept/reject command pair closes off the user interface to a destination, the enable/disable command pair intervenes between the lp spooler and the device. The difference is a matter of gating, accept before the scheduler, enable after. Any maintenance to a printer requires that the device be disabled. Rejection with the reject command is a matter of current spool space and courtesy to the users. The syntax with a warning is

```
# disable -r "changing ribbons" qume
printer now disabled
```

Note that when creating new printer destinations, all new destinations are automatically rejected and disabled. You must deliberately enable and accept them when they are created.

Changing Destinations: lpmove

Printer requests can be moved about with the lpmove command. If a printer is down for an extended period of time, you will want to change the destination of the print jobs to another printer, provided that the other printer is in the same vicinity. *Use care—*lpmove *cannot be used with the scheduler running*:

```
$ su
password:
# /usr/lib/lpshut
# /usr/lib/lpmove epson oki
# /usr/lib/lpsched
```

Notice that the print daemon is killed with lpshut before issuing the lpmove command. The print daemon is restarted after lpmove is executed.

Another use of lpmove is to move an individual request:

```
# /usr/lib/lpmove epson-32 hpjet
```

In the last example a request is being moved from the printer epson to the printer hpjet with the request number -32.

lpsched **Revisited and Reviewed**

The scheduler lpsched is the heart of the lp spooling system. It is the ultimate arbitrator of all requests, taking requests from lp and putting them through the interface programs. Every printer request is recorded by lpsched in /usr/spool/lplog, and each record contains the user's log name, the time and date, and the printer.

Normally lpsched is started by rc or rc.localwhen the system comes up. It is left up unless maintenance is required or administrative commands have to be issued that require the scheduler to be down. Use lpshut to shut down the scheduler:

```
# /usr/lib/lpshut
```

Use lpstat to check the status of the scheduler:

```
$ lpstat -r
```

The lpsched command creates a lock file to prevent an accidental startup of a second lpsched process. The lock file must be removed after issuing lpshut and before restarting the lp system:

```
# rm -f /usr/spool/lp/SCHEDLOCK
```

In addition, rc, local.rc, or rc.d must contain the line as well.

Printer Interfaces

Every printer requires an interface program, a necessary link in the lp chain, printing to the device associated with it. Interface programs must be executable and can be either a.out files or scripts. They reside in /usr/spool/lp/model and are copied to /usr/spool/interface when a printer is created with lpadmin.

When the lp scheduler, lpsched, sends a request to a printer, that specific printer's interface program is invoked. For example, if the request is to an HP LaserJet, the interface program in the /usr/spool/interface directory will be hpjet. A less sophisticated Panasonic, Epson, or Okidata dot-matrix printer uses an interface program taken from the equally unsophisticated /usr/spool/lp/model/dumb. The interface program passes the following information:

ID   The request (such as epson-256 or linp-1482)

user   The user's log name

copies   The number of copies

options   The class or printer options found in the interface and model programs

file   The fully qualified file path and name

title   An optional title

If you want to explore one of the model files, you will find these assignments at the first five executable lines of most scripts. Here is a command line to print the /etc/motd, the message of the day:

```
$ lp -pepson /etc/motd -oa -ob
```

which produces

```
interface/epson epson-256 mwool ""!"" "a  b" /etc/motd
```

The `-ob` flag used here omits the banner sheet, a handy option, especially if you get upset seeing half a case of paper's worth of `lp` headers going to the wastepaper bin.

The `interface` programs must have the right terminal settings or characteristics. They can be set with `stty`:

```
stty 300 </dev/tty1b
```

This sets port address `1b` to 300 baud. By the way, this can be done only if the device is open for reading.

Device Setup

Hardwire

When setting up a hardwire device, give device ownership to `lp`, and make the device both readable and writable. In the following example, device `tty15` is first linked to `lp3` for convenience:

```
# ln /dev/tty15 /dev/lp3
# chown lp /dev/lp3
# chmod 600 /dev/lp3
```

Since this is a nonlogin terminal, the `getty` in `inittab` must be turned off. Edit `/etc/inittab` in System V. In XENIX use the `disable` command or edit `/etc/ttys`. Here's how to check `inittab` to see that the `getty` is off:

```
$ grep tty15 /etc/inittab
15:2:off:/etc/getty: -t60 tty15 300
```

Use the `q` option of `init` to get `inittab` to recognize the new entry before the next boot:

```
# init q
```

The port must be active before anything can be sent to it. Next, the printer must be associated with the port. In this example, the printer is an Okidata, and it is called `oki`:

```
# /usr/lib/lpadmin -poki -v/dev/tty15 -mdumb
```

Here's an important point about setting baud rates: `inittab` is powerless to set the baud rate with the `getty` turned off. You can try setting it in `rc.local`, but this is neither clean nor effective. The best place is in the `interface` program. Since our fictitious Okidata is a dumb printer, let `lpadmin` copy `/usr/spool/lp/model/dumb` to `/usr/spool/lp/interface/oki`, and put in an `stty` line to set the baud rate. The `/usr/spool/interface` program is called every time a request goes to that printer. Thus the baud rate and any other `ioctl` characteristics are guaranteed to be set at each invocation.

Login Terminals

A printing terminal can be a printer, a terminal, or both. It makes a fair terminal at best, but it is an excellent console. Unlike the hardwire printer, the printing terminal must have a getty. Enter a respawn to the getty line in /etc/inittab (System V), or enable the port (XENIX). Next introduce the printer to lp with lpadmin:

```
# /usr/lib/lpadmin -pdiab -v/dev/tty3 -m1650 -l
# /usr/lib/accept diab
```

The printer in this example is an older Diablo 1650 printing terminal, a login printer. The printer name is diab; its device port is tty3; and the model file to be placed in /usr/spool/interface as diab is 1650. Remember that any new printer is offline when added to the lp system and must be deliberately enabled and accepted before it can be used.

Enabling lp Reviewed

Now let's put it all together. Once you have found a port for the printer, enabled the port, and talked to the printer as a device, you are ready to enable the lp spooling system. First you have to invoke lpadmin to attach the printer to the system:

```
# /usr/lib/lpadmin -pepson -v/dev/lp -mdumb -h
```

Here the printer epson is attached to /dev/lp as a dumb terminal. Note that the model must exist in the /usr/spool/model directory when using the -m model flag.[6] The -h flag is optional; it is the default. The dumb category is here:

```
$ ls -CF /usr/spool/lp/model
crnlmap       hpjet        imagen.rem     imagen.ssp    qume1155
dumb          imagen.pbs   imagen.sbs     network       ti800
```

The old Epson isn't on the list by name, but that's all right. It falls under the dumb category.

   If this is the only printer and you wish to make it the default printer, lpadmin has to go to work again:

```
# /usr/lib/lpadmin -depson
```

The -d flag is the default flag. Adding more printers is just as easy as adding the first:

```
#  /usr/lib/lpadmin -pnec -v/dev/lp1 -mdumb
#  /usr/lib/lpadmin -plaser -v/dev/lp2 -mhpjet
```

One step still remains: The entire lp system must be brought up. The lp daemon is lpsched. You enable it manually the first time:

```
# /usr/lib/lpsched
```

From then on it is done by rc at initiation time. Add these lines to rc or rc.local to remove locks and start the lp daemon, lpsched:

---

[6] The -m model flag is used to associate the printer device with a model file in /usr/spool/model.

```
# clear printer lock, start daemon
rm -f /usr/spool/lp/SCHEDLOCK
/usr/lib/lpsched
```

Let's say you have more than one dumb printer to add. You've already verified that the `model` file exists, so now all you need to do is test the port to see whether it is alive:

```
# echo "hello port">/dev/lp0
```

If it is a `tty` port, turn off the `getty` on the port by editing `/etc/inittab` or using `disable` if it is a XENIX system. The next stop is the scheduler:

```
# /usr/lib/lpshut
```

Here's where the `lp` system is told about the new acquisition:

```
# /usr/lib/lpadmin -p850 -v/dev/lp0 -mdumb
```

Now the `lp` system knows that we have another dumb printer, an Epson FX 850, at port `lp0` called `850`. Since we added a dumb printer earlier, we know that all of the pieces exist for this one. Remember that although the port and printer are now ready, the default creation left the new printer device `disabled` and `rejected`. Being rejected might be depressing to a new device, so:

```
# enable 850; accept 850
```

All that remains is to restart the scheduler

```
# /usr/lib/lpsched
```

and another dot-matrix printer joins the UNIX world.

`lpr`: THE BERKELEY PRINTER SPOOLER

The Berkeley spooler `lpr` is similar to System V's `lp` spooler in concept and in operation, except that `lpr` maintains separate spool areas for files sent to specific printers. Within these areas a queue is maintained that can be manipulated. Like the System V spooler, individual printers can be enabled and disabled and the entire printing mechanism shut down or brought up. Also, `lpr` manipulates the data stream for individual printers to set line disciplines and adjust to printer characteristics, and so does `lp`. However, here there is one difference between the two spooling systems: System V uses a separate `interface` file for each printer type, but Berkeley 4.2 keeps but one file for *all* printers. This file looks and acts very much like `termcap` and is aptly called `printcap`.

There are only a few commands associated with `lpr`: The user's `lpr(1)` command sends files to the printers. Its counterpart is `lprm(1)`, which removes jobs from the printer queue. The printers can be local or remote, and we shall see how to configure `printcap` to make both happen. If you tell `lpr` the name of a printer, the output will get there:

```
% nroff -ms my_text !lpr -Plp1 -h
```

In this example, nroff output is piped to lpr. The -P flag is used to give lpr the name of the printer lp1, and the -h flag is used to omit the banner or header page.

The administrator has several commands to manipulate the queue, administer the entire spooler, and get its status. The workhorse command is lpc, which, with its subcommands, can do the following:

abort   Kills printing by killing the daemon.

clean   Removes files from a printer spool.

enable   Enables a printer's spool queue.

disable   Stops a printer from printing its spool queue.

start   Starts the printer daemon.

restart   Restarts the printer daemon if it has been killed.

status   Gives a printer's daemon and queue status.

stop   Stops a spooler daemon.

topq   Puts a printer job at the top of the queue.

Most of these subcommands to lpc can be used for an individual printer or for all printers:

```
% lpc status all
lp1:
        queueing is enabled
        printing is enabled
        no entries
        no daemon present
lp0:
        queueing is enabled
        printing is enabled
        no entries
        no daemon present
lps:
        queueing is enabled
        printing is enabled
        8 entries in spool area
        waiting for queue to be enabled on fmsvr01
lpx:
        queueing is enabled
        printing is enabled
        no entries
        no daemon present
```

lpr's File System

Like System V's lp spooler, lpr maintains its own spool area, in /usr/spool or /var/spool, depending on the implementation and how close the file systems are to the original BSD 4.3 implementation. A separate spool area must be set up for each printer. Let's say the laser printer you are adding is called lp3 and its spool area is /var/spool/lp3. Every spool area contains lock and status files:

```
% ls -lag /var/spool/lp3
drwxr-sr-x   2  root    daemon 1024 Jun 29 13:43 .
drwxr-sr-x  12  root    daemon  512 Jun 15 14.46 ..
```

```
-rw-r----x   1   root    daemon    4 jun 15 13:32    .seq
-rw-r--r--   1   root    daemon   19 jun 29 13:32    lock
-rw-rw-r--   1   root    daemon   18 jun 29 13:32    status
```

You can also add an error log file when adding a printer, which is traditionally kept in /var/adm or /usr/adm. A separate error log is kept for each printer. To create it, cd to adm, and touch its file name:

```
# cd /usr/adm
# touch error_log1
#
```

Note that touching a file on a BSD-based system is the same as creating a file with indirection on System V:

```
$ >error_log
$
```

or copying /dev/null to a file:

```
% cp /dev/null error_log
%
```

printcap: **The Heart of** lpr

The /etc/printcap file is configured for each printer on the system, with printcap being very similar to termcap. It starts off with a list of names or aliases for each printer:

```
lp1:laser:qms:\
```

The printcap file entries are put in one continuous, colon-delimited list of attributes. A newline can be used between attributes, but it must be escaped:

```
# system default printer
lp:lp0:epson:fx:\
        :lp=/dev/pp0:sd=/var/spool/lpd:\
        :lf=/var/spool/lpd/error_log0:\
        :pl#64:pw#80:br#1200\
        :tc=generic_epson:
#
lp1:laser:qms:\
        :lp=:sd=/usr/spool/lp1:\
        :pw#80:pl#66:\
        :ls/var/spool/lpd/errorlog:\
        :rm=fmserv1:rp=lp1:
```

String constants are set with an equals sign:

```
lp=/dev/tty01
```

Setting lp to tty01 is a good example of a string assignment. Remember that lp is the device name to be opened for output. Numerics are set with the pound sign, #:

```
pw#80
```

Setting the page width, pw, to 80 is an example of a numeric assignment, and it's also a good way to keep your printer's roller clean when using 8-inch paper. In the printcap entry above, we also see the baud rate, br, set to 1200. Boolean variables need only be present to be active:

```
lp1!laser!qms:\
        :lp=/dev/tty01:sd=/usr/spool/lp1:\
        :pw#80:pl#66:\
        :rs:sb:rg:sc:\
        .
        .
```

Here the boolean variables are rs, restricting remote users; sb, short banner; rg, restricted group; and sc, suppress multiple copies. Note how well these boolean variables control both use and access.

Now let's set up a simple printcap entry. The printer is dumb, local, and on a serial port, port 6, and the baud rate is 9600. It is a 132-column printer intended for standard paper. An internal name lp1 is used, but ptr and lp are the same printer:

```
lp!lp1!ptr:\
        :lp=/dev/tty06:sd=/usr/spool/lp1:\
        :lf=/usr/adm/error_log1:\
        :br#9600:
```

You've been clever enough to set up the entry /usr/spool/lp1 as the spooling directory for lp1, so don't forget to make the actual directory. The error log file entry is /usr/adm/errorlog1. The actual file also has to be created. If an error log file is not specified, the console will be the default. Note that 132-column output is the default, so setting pw, the page width, is not required.

The printcap file can also have entries for printer filters. There are a number of system-resident filters, usually stored in /usr/lib/lpdfilters, for special purposes like ditroff output, laser printers, and PostScript. Here is a listing that contains the filters:

```
% ls /usr/lib/lpdfilters
fcv
lcg01of
lj250of
ln010f
ln01pp
lpf
lqf
rotate
rotprt
.
.
vsort
width
xf
```

In the preceding example, of is the filter variable for *output filter*, and tf, rf, cf, and gf codes are other filter codes. A printcap assignment looks like this:

```
:of=/usr/lib/lpdfilters/n01xy:
```

The printcap file also provides for remote printers and printing.

The Default Printer

The `lpr` spooler is more convenient than System V's `lp` spooling system. There is no special command to create a default printer because it is hardcoded into `lpr` itself. The `printcap` entry with the name "lp" is the default printer.

`lpd`, the Printer Daemon

Most of the `lpr` spooling system is run by the printer daemon `/usr/lib/lpd`, which is initiated at boot time by `rc.local` and reads `/etc/printcap`. This is similar to the action of `cron` and most of the network daemons.

Access Control

The `lpd` daemon gains access control through two files, `/etc/hosts.equiv` and `/etc/hosts.lpd`. Requests coming from remote printers must have the printer name in `hosts.equiv`; `hosts.lpd` has a similar function. If an asterisk starts any line, it will allow requests from any system, which is particularly convenient for printer servers. The entries in either file are a simple, newline-delimited list of systems:

```
$ cat /etc/hosts.lpd
stalker
cj
dewey
```

Debugging

The `lpr` spooler is debugged with `lpc`'s status command and the printer daemon's `-L` and `-l` flags. By using the `L` flags, error messages can be redirected from the console to an error log file. The `l` flag causes network requests to be logged as well.

An `lpc` command with the `status` option is probably the handiest debugging tool, because it tells the daemon's status and the condition of the queue. It can be used with the name of a specific printer or `all` and is extremely useful when debugging a recalcitrant, networked printer by executing it at both ends, the client and the machine with the remote printer:

```
% lpc status all
lp1:
        queueing is enabled
        printing is enabled
        no entries
        no daemon present
lp0:
        queueing is enabled
        printing is enabled
        12 entries
        waiting for queue to be enabled on sun_one
```

You may see an interesting conflict, such as the local system claiming that the remote queue is not enabled while the remote system claims that it is. If this is the case, check your daemons at both ends. The chances are that the local system has not started its printer daemon, not an uncommon scenario. If the client gives the `waiting for queue to be enabled` message, but the host system with the printer tells you that the queue is enabled, check the client's printer daemon. It has to be restarted if it is dead. Try `lpc start all`.

Remote Printers

The `lpr` printer spooler system allows for remote printers. A local queue and error log is created for the remote printer. Then a `printcap` entry is made on the local system, clearly defining that the printer is remote by use of the `rp` and `rm` entries. Set the printer port to null in the `printcap` entry, and specify the remote machine name, as it is known to the network, with the `rm` flag:

```
lp2!remote!qms:\
        :lp=:rm=server1:\
        :sd=/var/spool/lp2:\
        :rp=qms:
```

Here the remote machine is `server1`; the name of the printer on the remote system is qms; and the local spool is `/var/spool/lp2`.

After completing the `printcap` entry on the local system, go to the `printcap` entry on the remote system, and be sure it does not have its `rs` flag set, which would restrict it to local requests only. Move to `/etc` on the remote system, and add the name of the client system to both `hosts.equiv` and `hosts.lpd`.

Move back to the client system, and enable the new printer and its daemon with `lpc`:

```
# lpc start qms
# lpc enable qms
```

Now send anything to the remote printer and check the local status:

```
# lpr -P qms /etc/motd
# lpc status qms
qms:
        queueing is enabled
        printing is enabled
        no entries
        no daemon present
```

If you haven't missed anything, the daemon will be alive at both ends, and the remote spool will be accepting.

You can breathe a sigh of relief once it is up and running, because the BSD `lpr` spooler system is reliable and needs little attention. The software is robust, and the system is easy to maintain.

PORTS

Before you can even think about putting a printer on the `lp` spooling system, both the computer and printers must be made ready. The computer ports must be enabled by jumpering, and the printers must be switch-set to the baud rate, nationality, and handshaking expected by the computer.

Parallel Ports

At the computer end there are at least two types of ports that concern you: *parallel* and *serial*. Multiuser computers and aftermarket I/O cards with parallel ports used to be few and far between. The first I remember seeing were on AT&T's five-port I/O cards for the 3B2-300s, four serial and one parallel port each. The unparalleled popularity of the PC made parallel ports commonplace. In regard to cabling there is little to do except plug in each end, and on PC machines the job is to jumper the motherboard to recognize the existence of the ports. The choice is no parallel port, or LPT1 or LPT2, the parallel ports. If you are using the motherboard's port, use LPT1and enable IRQ7 as the corresponding interrupt request line. If you are using a port off an above-board card,[7] use LPT2 and enable IRQ5 as the interrupt request line.

Serial Ports

Serial ports are not as easy, falling under the loose classification of RS-232 connections. The RS-232 specification applies to a terminal-to-modem connection, as long as the terminal is clearly a DTE.[8] If the printer is willing to accept 9200 baud and has DTR buffer control, you can set the port baud rate at 9200 along with all the rest of the devices, modems excluded. Use a much slower rate if you need to slow down the character rate to avoid buffering problems. I have one very early Epson running at 300 baud with delays.

Getting data down the wire to the paper requires a breakout box or its equivalent. Distinguish the "sex" of both the computer and the printer. With voltage on pin 2, it's a DTE, but with voltage on pin 3, it's a DCE. Few printers are without flow control. The printer must signal the computer when its buffer is either full or empty. Handshaking is required for the printer to signal *buffer empty* and the computer to transmit information until it fills the printer buffer. At that point the printer will signal *buffer full*, and the computer will stop sending. There is no standard for signal pins used for this handshaking. Each computer and printer manufacturer has its own ideas on what should be enabled and what should be cross dependent. To narrow down the choice, only pins 4, 5, 6, 8, and 20 are used for flow control. Pin 8, *data carrier detect*, is supposed to be limited to modems, but don't count it out until you have tested it. That leaves 4, *request to send*; 5, *clear to send*; 6, *data set ready*; and 20, *data terminal ready*. In the ideal case, the printer uses pin 5, CTS, to signal *buffer empty*, and the computer uses pin 4, RTS, to signal when it is ready to send data.[9]

Initially hold all signal pins high just to get data to flow. If necessary to get started, you can even go so far as to enable the port with a getty.[10] On XENIX use the enable

---

[7] This is a card attached above the motherboard, much like putting a card on an S-100 backplane. You might say this is the single-board-computer solution to expansion.

[8] DTE stands for *data terminal equipment*, and DCE stands for *data communications equipment*. These were originally defined as a terminal and a modem in terms of function, but the DTE/DCE definitions tend to fall apart when applied to printers, plotters, and computers.

[9] See Martin D. Seyer, *Complete Guide to RS232 and Parallel Connections* (Englewood Cliffs, NJ: Prentice-Hall, 1988).

[10] Yes, this is heresy.

command to get the ball rolling, and on System V set `tty` at the desired baud rate. Set `ttytype` at unknown:

```
$ grep tty01 /etc/ttytype
unknown tty01              # XENIX only
```

Set the port's `inittab` entry to `respawn`. Now check, using the `stty` command, to see what the system thinks about the port:

```
# stty </dev/tty2b
```

If `stty` doesn't show the desired baud rate, use it actively to set the rate:

```
# stty 300 </dev/tty2b
```

Once all of that is in place, push a few bits down the wire:

```
# echo "hello world">/dev/tty2b
```

The next step is a test of logic—the printer's, the computer's, and yours. Remove the signal jumpers from the everything-goes jumpering, and then jumper for buffer control.

You will have reasonable success with short documents if you are depending on baud rate alone to keep the buffer from filling. You may experience garbage from line to line as they get longer, but there is a way out. Remember the reference in the beginning of this chapter to the slowness of the old teletypes? You will be glad to know that `ioctl`, and therefore its shell counterpart `stty`, have ways to cause delays on certain characters like form feeds, line feeds, carriage returns, and tabs. Here is a line for the `interface` program to slow down the printer:

```
stty cr3 nl1 tab3 ff1 vt1 </dev/lp
```

We really have put lead innersoles in the printer's running shoes by putting in maximum delays.

One last trick to remember: You will get tired of remembering and typing the printer's port name long before the computer will get tired of seeing it. So set it as soon as possible to a name associated with the printer, not the port, such as /dev/lp, /dev/line_p, or /dev/model_name. Find the major and minor numbers of the port or driver entry:

```
$ ls -l /dev/tty2b
crw-rw-rw-  1 root     bin          5,  9 May 01:15 /dev/tty2b
```

Now link /dev/lp to tty2b:

```
$ su
password:
# ln /dev/tty2b /dev/lp
```

Check it out with `lp` and `grep`, keying on the major and minor device numbers:

```
# ls -l /dev|fgrep "5,  9"
crw-rw-rw-  2 root     bin          5,  9 May 30 18:52 /dev/lp
crw-rw-rw-  2 root     bin          5,  9 May 30 18:52 /dev/tty2b
```

All you have to deal with is /dev/lp. Use the printer's aliased port name in all printer scripts. If you change ports, you will not have to hunt down each reference to a specific port.

The final steps are to make everything tidy by removing all kludges. If it took a getty to get a hardwire printer started, remove it from `inittab` with an `off` in the `getty` line. Set the baud rates in the `interface` program, as well as `xon` and any other necessary characteristics. There is no joy in administering a kludged system.

MANAGER'S CORNER

A Choice of Printers

I have often been asked, "What is the best UNIX terminal?" and "What is the best UNIX printer?" UNIX's orientation is toward dumb, ASCII, serial, and parallel devices, thereby leaving the entire field open. All dot-matrix printers are dumb, and as such they don't even need any special attention in creating an `interface` program.[11]

Laser printers do, however, require special `interface` programs. The most expensive laser printer in the world won't do you a bit of good without the `interface` program. The choice is to use a laser printer with a `model` or `interface` program that already exists on your system, to persuade the vendor to give you one, or to buy one.

When you buy a printer for your UNIX system, be sure to find out from your system programmers and vendors what is supported before you sign a purchase order for something that isn't going to work. You might even specify in your purchase order that there will be an `interface` program provided with the purchase of a printer. Don't rely on the salesperson's word that there is one.

---

[11] The `/usr/spool/lp/interface` and `/usr/spool/lp/model` directories.

CHAPTER

9

Modems

We're so used to autodialing modems that it's hard to imagine them in any other way. But modems used to be very different. Autodialers and modems were separate devices in the early days of UNIX development, and as originally developed by Nowitz, UUCP required the presence of both a Bell 801 dialer and a modem. The contemporary modem is both an autodialer and a modem. An autodialer, also known as an *automatic calling unit*, dials the number onto the phone line or PBX. The modem acts as an amplifier, signal repeater, and modulator-demodulator. Modems used to be able to transmit a signal over a hardwire, but now they transmit only over a conventional telephone line.

RS-232

The computer-to-modem connection is almost exclusively the domain of RS-232. Actually, the RS-232 standard has only a terminal-to-modem definition, but if you change your mental point of reference, you can understand any form of RS-232 connection.

RS-232 starts by defining the terminal as DTE, *data terminal equipment*. The modem is defined as DCE, *data communications equipment*. The classic cable and connectors for a terminal-to-modem connection are a 25-wire cable with 25-pin DB-25 connectors.

However, of the 25 pins, only a maximum of 9 are ever actually used for conventional computer-to-peripheral attachments:

Pin		Description
pin 1	—	*chassis* or *cable ground* or *frame ground*, not always used
pin 2	→	*transmit data*
pin 3	←	*receive data*
pin 4	→	*request to send*
pin 5	←	*clear to send*
pin 6	←	*data set ready*
pin 7	—	*signal ground*
pin 8	←	*data carrier detect*
pin 20	→	*data terminal ready*
pin 22	←	*ring indicator*

The reference point of this table is from the terminal's point of view, not the modem's. If the arrow symbol points left, ←, it means that data or a signal is coming in to the DTE. If the arrow symbol points right, →, it means that data or a signal is going out from the DTE to the modem.

All of this gets less confusing if we divide the pins into three groups:

data	2 and 3
ground	1 and 7
signal	4, 5, 6, 8, 20, and 22

Data are sent from the DTE to the DCE. The DCE is described as the receiver. The *signal ground* connection is a necessity because it forms a voltage reference for all other pins. The *frame ground* is optional, and there are conflicting stories on how to connect it. Most say to attach the *frame ground* at one end only and to use it as a signal shield. This is particularly handy when fully shielded cable is used over long distances or in noisy environments.

Signal pins are directional. DTR, *data terminal ready*, is the primary signal from the terminal to the modem, saying, "I am alive and ready to work." Set high[1] by a getty, it sleeps, waiting for a DCD event. It is analogous in duty to DSR, *data set ready*, also received by the terminal. Its primary purpose is to tell the DTE that the modem is there, and it is active and ready to do business. DCD, *data carrier detect*, is a signal from the modem to the terminal telling the DTE that an active carrier signal is present, and more than likely there are data ready to come in. RTS, *request to send*, is a signal from the terminal[2] to the modem telling the modem that the terminal is ready to send. CTS, *clear to send*, is received by the terminal telling it that the modem is ready to go.

RS-232 is an existing communications standard, but it is not written for all possible computer connections, such as computer to printer and terminal to computer. You have to be prepared to interpret the standard to fit your particular situation. Terminals and printers

---

[1] When a signal goes high, the voltage is positive, and that is interpreted as a TRUE condition.
[2] Remember that although the RS-232 standard defines this connection as terminal to modem, the "terminal" can be any peripheral, and the "modem" can even be a computer.

seem to write their own rules for handshaking, and computer ports are the signal-pin equivalent of random generation. The computer-to-modem connection is as close to the classic connection as you are going to see today.

It gets complicated quickly once you get away from the terminal-to-modem connection. If the computer port is set up as a DCE (*data send* on pin 3), you have to deal with a null-modem connection, switching pins 2 and 3. Pin 2 goes to pin 3 and 3 to 2 at both ends, making a very long *X*.

The DB-9 Connection

For years the DB-25 connector was the only show in town, but it was finally decided that if only eight or nine pins are used for computer connections, why use a 25-pin connector? A DB-9 connector makes much more sense and is widely used, particularly on PC-type systems. Here are the DB-9 pinouts:

Pin #	Description
1	*data carrier detect*
2	*receive data*
3	*transmit data*
4	*data terminal ready*
5	*signal ground*
6	*data set ready*
7	*request to send*
8	*clear to send*
9	*ring indicator*

Conspicuous by its absence is *frame ground*. Like all RS-232 connections, there is no rule that requires classic pinouts to be followed. Thus if *carrier detect* were needed and *ring detect* were not, rest assured that the switch would be made.

HARDWARE HANDSHAKING: A NONTECHNICAL APPROACH

Picture the engine semaphore and voice tubes on an old steamship. The captain sets the engine semaphore and then hollers instructions down the tube to the engine compartment. The engineer acknowledges both the semaphore signal and the command shouted down the voice tube by hollering back up the voice tube. Modem cable transmission between the computer and the modem is somewhat the same, but with hardware handshaking you have five separate tubes: RTS, CTS, DCD, DTR, and DSR. Think of the engine semaphore as the data lines.

The main thing to remember with hardware handshaking is that there are two givens. The first is that there is a *signal ground*, pin 7, to establish a ground voltage reference. The second is that there are wires over which data are transmitted, pin 2, *transmit data*, and pin 3, *receive data*. That leaves the signal pins used for hardware handshaking, pins 4, 5, 6, 8, and 20. Pin 22 is rarely used.

The first communication step is to go from one end of the wire to the other and to verify the electrical existence of the devices at both ends. The terminal, a DTE, hollers its DTR message, "I'm here!" The modem, a DCE, hollers its DSR message, "I'm here, too!" At this point both pieces of equipment have electrical proof of each other's existence.

Now what? When another system calls, the modem can give a DCD, a *data carrier detect* message, to say, "Hey! Somebody wants to talk to you." However, recall that our terminal-to-modem connection is only the classic RS-232 case. Maybe the two devices communicating with each other are a computer and a printer. We all know a computer sends information to the printer faster than it can possibly be printed. What happens when a computer talks to a printer with buffer control? The computer can use RTS, *request to send*, to tell the printer, "Hey! There is some information coming." How does the printer say it has a mouthful of data it can't swallow? The printer sends CTS, *clear to send*, low,[3] which means, "I'm definitely not ready for more data yet." CTS is a data valve that regulates flow through buffer control.

Here is a nontechnical look at the events and the order of an incoming modem call:

Sequence	Device	Comment	Pin +/−
1	computer	ready	DTR +
2	modem	ready	DSR +
3	modem	call incoming	DCD +
4	computer	I'm ready	RTS +
5	modem	I'm ready	CTS +
6	computer	send	TD
7	modem	receive	RD
8	modem	hold it	CTS −
9	modem	OK	CTS +
10	modem	lost carrier	DCD −
11	computer	I'm gone	DTR −
12	modem	I'm gone	DEC −

This is a simplified idea of hardware handshaking. Done properly, it allows data flow at the quickest possible speed, and it eliminates buffer overflows and the consequent loss of data. The complexity increases when you bear in mind the close association between the software and the hardware created by the `tty` driver. When a carrier drops on the modem, the `tty` device driver knows to send low, and that, in turn, causes the modem to hang up, to simultaneously kill the user shell and all its children, and to remove the reference to the login `tty` in `/etc/utmp`. Note that hardware handshaking is known as *modem control*.

MODEM PORTS: A TECHNICAL APPROACH

A modem port requires maximum handshaking ability, but hardware handshaking is not available on all ports and all computers. On older systems I/O cards have to be manually jumpered to enable or disable full handshaking. Today most machines allow this to be

---

[3] When set low, it means the opposite of the condition. So when *clear to send* is set low, it means *not* clear to send.

done with software. Let's look at the same physical port set up as both a hardwire port with no modem control and a modem port with full handshaking capability:

```
$ ls -l /dev/tty1A
crw--w--w-   1 root    uucp    5,128 Dec 19 10:34 /dev/tty1A
$ ls -l /dev/tty1a
crw-rw-rw-   1 root    root    5,  0 Mar  4  1988 /dev/tty1a
```

For /dev/tty1A, the port with modem control, the major number is 5 and the minor number is 128. Device driver 5 is passed 128 as an argument that tells the port driver to do full hardware handshaking. The major number is 5 and the minor number is 0 for /dev/tty1a. Device driver 5 is passed 0 as an argument that tells the port driver to do no hardware handshaking. It is a hardwire port. Thus PC-like systems allow ports to be configured with or without hardware handshaking. As we saw in Chapter 7, the terminal driver is a great example of how drivers can be written to have it either way, full modem control or no hardware handshaking.

Sometimes you won't want modem control. If you have one terminal hooked up to two computers on an AB switch with modem control enabled, the login will drop when you flip the switch to go from one terminal to another, a disaster if you are in the middle of editing a file. If you turn off the hardware handshaking, nothing will happen when you flip the AB switch. The login will still be there. It's important that the system administrator have the ability to enable or disable hardware handshaking.

The signal pin scenario is supposed to go something like this: The computer (acting as DTE) asserts DTR to show that it, the computer, is ready to do business. The modem as DCE has similarly set DSR to show that it is ready. Neither is signaling anything other than it is there. This condition is literally illustrated by the modem when its MR, Modem Ready, and TR, Terminal Ready, lights are on.

The next phase of the connection starts when the modem gets a call from another modem. DCD is now asserted, and the computer reads this as a signal that data are on the way. At this point theoretically, RTS goes high.

Asserting DTR, the next move, is critical to UUCP and to any connection that wants full handshaking with a guarantee that the phone will hang up when the connection is broken. DCD, *data carrier detect*, must be asserted from the modem side to make the *request to send* assert at the computer port. Even nonmodem connections, such as a hardwire or Ethernet connection, must provide this signal sequence or simulate it. Ethernet connections are notorious for leaving their gettys active when the connection is accidentally broken. Only a reboot takes the terminal off the process table and out of utmp as an active tty.

Now let's back up to the place where DTR and RTS are up, a getty is active, and the modem is *off hook*. What if something goes wrong now? The phone line is open, and the bill continues to grow. The computer keeps the port open, the login fails to drop, and the user will be billed as if she never logged off. Here is where full handshaking comes in: Full handshaking allows the complete interaction that is required to allow the port acting as a terminal to drop the login. If the dial-in/login/process sequence that we have been discussing fails, several things must be allowed to happen. Upon a loss of carrier, the computer must drop the login process and all processes associated with it, such as a user's login and processes from that login. The user processes must be flushed from /etc/utmp and /etc/wtmp to stop any further accounting charges. Finally the port is freed.

Historically, terminals were connected to computers by a pair of modems, similar to the way that computers now use paired repeaters on the Ethernet. This allowed long lines without a conventional network; in a manner of speaking, it *was* a kind of network. Today modemless terminal connections are hardwire connections. As mentioned earlier, it is possible to AB-switch a terminal from computer to computer without dropping the connection with a nondialing modem or a hardwire connection. Thus a user can work sessions on two or more systems and not have to log off and log on every time the switch is made.

CONTACTING THE ACTUAL MODEM

Enough theory. How to you contact a real modem? The modem must be made to operate within the system's capabilities and expectations. Putting it another way, it must be able to give what the computer expects. Since there are very few do-all-fits-all devices in this world, the modem gets its versatility from two sources. The first is by switch settings, and the second is by passing parameters as commands to the modem, which will be stored in the modem's memory and registers.

Switches and Settings

Most modems have 8 to 10 switches. Their switch numbers vary, but the functions are basically the same.

Return Codes

When you flip a modem over on its back so that you can see its belly, you will see two groups of switches. You can set the switches to send *return codes* as words, strings, or single digits. These return codes are the results of terminal commands. Thus when the terminal sends an AT for *attention*, the modem can respond with an OK.

Echo Commands

With this feature enabled, commands are echoed to the screen as they are typed, allowing you to see what you are doing, a helpful feature. The combination of echo commands and return codes makes easy the initial debugging of the modem, and it also makes it easier to use cu to do direct access to ports and then on to other systems.

Auto Answer

Switching *auto answer* allows the modem to automatically answer incoming calls. Turning *auto answer* off makes the modem a send-only unit. Older versions of UUCP required two modems, one to receive and one to send, but uugetty fixed this.

Carrier Detect

This *carrier detect* switch is used to fool the computer into believing that there is a carrier signal present. Full handshaking exists in the ideal situation. The getty makes

DTR on the computer side assert. The modem asserts DSR to let the computer know it's alive, but UNIX ignores it. An incoming call gives a carrier signal to the modem, and DCE, *data carrier detect*, is then asserted. The computers acting on the modem's DCD now sets its RTS high. In the final step, the modem asserts CTS in response to the computer's RTS.

Not all situations are ideal, and sometimes the signal pins are forced by jumpering or switch-setting them to be always asserted. With DCD permanently asserted, commands can be sent to the modem before a connection is made with the answering modem. This is reasonable for an outgoing-only modem, but it is a poor condition for either a two-way or an incoming-only modem.

Telephone Line Connection

The modem can be switched between single-user and multiple-line telephone jacks. The default setting is for single-user RJ-11 connections. The multiuser lines use RJ-12 and J-13 connectors, and they must be switched *on*.

Command Recognition

Command recognition gives you a choice of recognizing or refusing commands typed at the terminal. You may not want an incoming-only modem to respond to line commands, but outgoing-only modems benefit with command recognition.

DTR Monitor

Full handshaking allows the modem to monitor DTR, *data terminal ready*, from the computer. The modem hangs up the connection when DTR goes low. This switch either permits the modem to hang up or prevents the modem from hanging up when DTR goes low. Unless you are fond of large, unexplained phone bills, you definitely want the modem to hang up.

Command Switching

Everything that can be changed permanently by setting switches can also be reset by software or command, which allows modem installation and debugging without altering switch settings. Let's say you need *command recognition*, *echo command*, and *return code* to debug a connection. You can debug the modem by switching only *command recognition* and then software-setting *echo command* and *return codes*.

CONTACTING THE MODEM

Once the modem has been connected and all switches have been set to something reasonable, it is time to contact the device. The software tool is cu for the first try, and we use Hayes protocol. Before any port can be contacted, it must have an entry in /usr/lib/uucp in the device file L-devices or Devices:

```
$ cat /usr/lib/uucp/L-devices
ACU  tty1A   /usr/lib/uucp/dialHA24        300-2400
ACU  tty1B   /usr/lib/uucp/dialVA3450      1200

DIR  tty1A   O    1200
DIR  tty1A   O    2400
DIR  tty1A   O    9600

DIR  tty2a   O    2400
DIR  tty2a   O    1200
DIR  tty2a   O    9600
```

ACU stands for automatic calling unit, an anachronism from the old days when the autodialers and the modems were separate. Notice the lines starting with DIR, which defines a *direct port*, a port allowing direct access with cu. By executing this command line

```
$ cu dir
```

the first port, tty1A at 1200 baud, will be contacted. The next step with a Hayes-compatible modem is to send it an AT, for *attention*, and to wait for it to respond with an OK:

```
$ cu dir
connected
AT
OK
~.

Disconnected
$
```

To disconnect from the port and the modem, send a tilde, ~, to get cu's attention, followed by a period to end the session.

Now if you have made previous arrangements with another computer to get a login and you know its modem-line number, you are ready for the modem's first remote login:

```
$cu dir
connected
ATDT 555 2648
Login:
```

Give the modem ATDT for *attention dial tone* plus the phone number. The modem does the dialing. The next thing you will hear is the calling modem dial out and the called modem pick up. That is the basics of a connection.

If you have done the rest of your homework and set up /usr/lib/uucp/L.Sys or Systems and if the receiving system has a UUCP login set for you, you can reach it by uucp:

```
$ grep unixtoday /usr/spool/uucp/L.sys
unixtoday Any ACU 2400 NJ61234561 ogin: nuucp word: myeditor
$ uucp -u julie next.article unixtoday!~
```

Setting `ioctl`/`termio` **Characteristics**

Just as with any terminal connection, modem connections require the setting of `termio` characteristics. Although `stty` can be used from `rc`, it's only a one-shot deal. You want a permanent setting. The `/usr/lib/uucp/L-devices` file is where the work is initiated for outgoing modem characteristics. On a XENIX system here is where port `1A` has its baud rate set every time it's used by `uucp` or `cu`:

```
$ grep tty1A /usr/lib/uucp/L-devices
ACU   tty1A   /usr/lib/uucp/dialHA24          300-2400
DIR   tty1A   0       1200
DIR   tty1A   0       2400
DIR   tty1A   0       9600
```

Port `tty1A` is set up for both `DIR`, direct access, and `ACU`, modem access. There must be a `DIR` entry for any line with an `ACU`. The first line is for a Hayes 2400-baud compatible modem. The baud rate for the ACU is defined as 300 to 2400 baud, and the range for direct connections is 1200 to 9600 baud. Any other `termio` characteristics that need to be set are done in the interface program `/usr/lib/uucp/dialHA24`.

SETTING `/etc/gettydefs` **FOR MODEM CALLS**

Recall the use of `gettydefs` in Chapter 7, in which `gettydefs` sets terminal characteristics for the login and resets them after the login. The last field in each `gettydefs` line is a "goto" line number for transfer of control on receiving a break. A modem calling in at 1200 baud with the following `gettydefs` lines could reset the baud rate to 2400 by sending a break character. At 1200 baud, the control transfers to line 3, and the login baud rate is then 2400:

```
1 # B300  HUPCL OPOST CR1 NL1 #
    B300 CS8 SANE HUPCL TAB3 IXANY #\r\n@!login: # 2

2 # B1200 HUPCL OPOST CR1 ECHOE NL1 #
    B1200 CS8 SANE HUPCL TAB3 ECHOE IXANY #\r\n@!login: # 3

3 # B2400  HUPCL OPOST CR1 ECHOE NL1 #
    B2400 CS8 SANE HUPCL TAB3 ECHOE IXANY #\r\n@!login: # 1
```

Break characters must be sent from the calling system to cause the line shifting in `gettydefs` on the answering system. The following example is from `/usr/lib/uucp/L.sys`:

```
kwasinski Any ACU 2400 NJ123455 ogin:-BREAK-ogin:-BREAK-ogin:
```

MANAGER'S CORNER

To UUCP or Not to UUCP

Should UUCP be allowed on your UNIX system? It's a manager's dilemma. The benefit to the system's support staff is that they can call in from a terminal at home to support the system. It also permits an administrator to be home ill but still be able to prevent the system from becoming ill. The danger is that the system is now open for abusers to dial into it.

Since every organization would like to establish 7-by-24 service, 7 days a week, 24 hours a day, the ability to UUCP-in cannot be dismissed. The usual solution is a callback device that enables a user to call in and give a password. The user is then called back at a predetermined number. If the device is for the administration staff only, they will be the only people who get both the number and the password.

Avoid circuitous entries to a UNIX system. I know of a number of sites at which the user has to call into the mainframe via a purchased service. Then the user goes into 3270 emulation. Then he has to try to work on UNIX through an emulation program, which, with no editing characters, makes it impossible to use the ned editor. The only show left in town is ed. But this is truly cruel and unusual punishment, especially since no crime has been committed.

Allowing users to dial in via modem must be decided by organizations and their managers. They must be willing to pay for additional equipment, even expensive controllers, if necessary. Also, a full-time security administrator will probably have to be hired if they opt for open-login ability. Managers of the user community must decide whether the service is worth the cost.

CHAPTER

10

accounting

The system administrator doesn't have to spend a great deal of time working on `account-ing`, which must be enabled on a newly installed system by uncommenting or adding lines in `rc`, `shutdown`, and `/usr/spool/cron/crontabs/root`.[1] Once in place and running, `accounting` normally needs only periodic cleaning. It is a full subsystem with a large set of directories, files, and commands, but it is so well planned and executed that it runs nearly trouble free.

The `accounting` subsystem runs in many process states. The system is clever enough to keep track of which state it is in at all times. Whenever the system is stopped, whether by accident or on purpose, the process state is stored on a disk file. On initiation, the system's state is restored automatically; thus `accounting` always knows where it is.

The `accounting` subsystem is one of the least understood areas of UNIX. It is process accounting; it records user usage. It is not the accounts payable/accounts receiv-able kind of accounting we associate with the word *accounting*, although its output can be used to bill users, groups, or projects for time and resources and thus get revenue for system use. At this writing, such bill-back accounting software must be created by the system programmer, but there are some software packages that show promise in this direction, such as SysAdmin by UniSolutions Associates.

The `accounting` output shows terminal use, CPU time consumed by individual processes and individual users, the person who logged on last, and a lot of other valuable

---

[1] Subsystems like `accounting`, `networks`, and `uucp` are initiated in `/etc/rc` and shut down from `/etc/shutdown`. Frequently they also have entries in `/usr/spool/cron/crontabs/root`. These entries are commented with pound signs so they will not execute. In words, their lines start with `#`. They are made executable by removing their pound signs.

164

information. The information produced by accounting is useful both to the system administrator and for bill-back purposes, as we shall see.

In addition to accounting's daily reports, fiscal accounting can make periodic accounting reports of any time specified. Both accounting and fiscal accounting reports include

- Terminal usage.
- Command usage.
- User usage.
- Disk usage.
- Last login dates.

REPORT OUTPUT

The output of accounting fills page after page of 11-inch-by-132-column green bar paper, too much output to show in one piece. We're going to look only at fragments of accounting report output to give you an idea of what kind of information you get.

A typical line of a terminal usage report starts like this:

```
Tues Sep 13 00:15:49 PDT 1988
TOTAL DURATION IS 1233 MINUTES
LINE      MINUTES  PERCENT #SESS     #ON     #OFF
tty601    337      13      1         1       9
tty606    0        0       0         0       16
console   0        0       0         0       16
.
.
TOTALS    2265     --      3         3       784
```

And a command summary report looks like

```
COMMAND   NUMBER  TOTAL     TOTAL   TOTAL     MEAN    MEAN    HOG     CHARS     BLOCKS
NAME      CMDS    KCOREMIN  CPU-MIN REAL-MIN  SIZE-K  CPU-MIN FACTOR  TRANSFD   READ
sh        30550   8669.50   35.71   43861.40  242.78  0.00    0.00    42724496  50584
telnetd   129     3474.09   39.46   13855.55  88.06   0.32    0.00    16984736  1544
vi        437     2449.79   5.66    1946.52   1301.03 0.01    0.00    946990224 24692
awk       6981    1492.61   12.65
```

In a user usage report you see this:

```
          LOGIN   CPU (MINS)      KCPRE-MINS      CONNECT (MINS)  DISK    #OF   #OF   #DISK    FEE
UID       NAME    PRIME  NPRIME   PRIME  NPRIME   PRIME  NPRIME   BLOCKS  PROCS SESS  SAMPLES
0         TOTAL   6      15       13349  704      2348   24       4642880 12369 40    4        0
0         root    3      11       94     367      0      0        635208  2292  2     4        0
1         daemon  0      0        1      7        0      0        0       54    0     0        0
```

The following is a section of output that shows the last time each user logged in, which is very handy for catching people who have accounts but are not using them:

```
00-00-00  adm        87-11-07  achen       88-08-16  mwool
00-00-00  bin        88-04-16  sbrock      88-09-17  jcroy
```

The UNIX accounting system gives a wealth of information about the machine and its activities. You don't need to wait for an official accounting report to extract information about when users logged on last, which programs are using the CPU, or how much connect time is being used. When `accounting` is coupled with UNIX's report-generating programmable filter `awk`, you can get all sorts of useful data just for the asking, in addition to the standard `accounting` reports. System administrators are free to create a report at any time with accounting commands. Also, as a rule, system administrators keep about two months worth of `accounting` data in the directories before the data are destroyed.

AN OVERALL LOOK AT accounting

For a fits-all system, `accounting` does a pretty good job, but unfortunately it has a few glaring weaknesses. The data structure that stores the initial `accounting` data has no internal time stamp, so `accounting` data *must* be gathered and held in time-stamped files, which complicates the separation of time information other than prime and nonprime time. Prime time is usually associated with standard work hours, 8 A.M. to 5 P.M. (08:00 to 17:00 hours), and nonprime time is everything else. What if you have a different billing rate for weekends and holidays, as is often the case? Then prime and nonprime categories won't fit. A weekend or holiday category would help, but it isn't implemented.

The `accounting` subsystem reports strictly on a per-user basis, another weakness, because most real-world internal company billing is done on a group or project basis, not by individual users.[2] If you need more from `accounting` than prime and nonprime time per user, you will find out how well you can program in C, shell, `sed`, and `awk`.

The `accounting` subsystem is a powerful tool for the system administrator, as it is as much of a diagnostic tool as `sar` is. It provides valuable information about CPU time spent in executing binary files, specifically programs and commands, which is a help in finding runaway processes, time hogs, inefficient machine usage, and poorly written code. It exposes users who use the system inefficiently or illegally, and unauthorized program usage can be nipped in the bud. Also, `accounting` pinpoints users who have accounts but are not using the system. Unused accounts take up disk space and cause logins to take longer as `init` wades through unused lines in `/etc/passwd`. Unused accounts also invite unauthorized system break-ins.

UNIX System V accounting differs greatly from XENIX, Berkeley BSD, and earlier versions of UNIX. The last are simpler and more fragile and produce less information. System V's accounting system is well designed and sufficiently complex. You can shut down the machine, and when you bring it up again, `accounting` is automatically at the same state it was in before. If you have a large subsystem like `accounting` that runs in multiple states, it must be able to keep track of what state it's in, even after a system crash. In this way the system administrator doesn't have to straighten out `accounting` before it can be reinitiated.

---

[2] System V Release 4 takes into consideration `accounting` by project and group.

accounting **INTERNALS**

To understand accounting you must know that the kernel writes an accounting record for each process when that process terminates. As each process exits, it leaves a record for accounting. Shell programs are a problem because any shell script is charged to sh, rsh, csh, or ksh. The shell-program name is not entered into accounting, so there's no way to see how much time is used by rc, for example. There is no way around this, since accounting's basic data are created by the kernel and the shells run above the kernel. This oversight should be rectified in future releases of the system.

The kernel writes initial information to /usr/adm/pacct. The structure used to write to it, acct_io, is in /usr/include/acct.h and has the following data:

ai_flag	The record flag
ai_stat	Exit status
ai_uid	The user-ID number
ai_group	The group number
ai_tty	The device number, used only by the tape daemon
ai_btime	Time recorded
ai_utime	Accounting user time in clock ticks
ai_stime	System time in clock ticks
ai_etime	Elapsed time in clock ticks
ai_mem	Memory usage
ai_io	Characters transferred
ai_rw	Blocks, lines, or cards read or written
ai_comm	Command name

The structure looks like this:

```
struct acct_io {
        char    ai_flag;
        char    ai_stat;
        ushort ai_uid;
        ushort ai_gid;
        dev_t  ai_tty;
        time_t ai_tty;
        comp_t ai_btime;
        comp_t ai_utime;
        comp_t ai_stime;
        comp_t ai_etime;
        comp_t ai_mem;
        comp_t ai_io;
        comp_t ai_rw;
        char    ai_comm[8];
}
```

The meanings of the data types are in sys/acct.h.

The accounting subsystem uses the init and login processes to record user sessions in the file /etc/wtmp, and wtmp also holds date changes and shutdown and reboot information. The `wtmp` file is raw data and must be interpreted by the next layers of accounting software. As you can imagine, accounting generates a substantial number of files!

REPORT FIELDS

The most useful information for bill-back purposes comes from the accounting report. Here you can extract your connect-time and CPU-time data to be used to bill back the customer or customer group or project. Some fields are

- User-ID number.
- User login name.
- CPU use in minutes, prime and nonprime.
- Kilobyte-core minutes, prime and nonprime.
- Connect time in minutes, prime and nonprime.
- Disk usage in time blocks.
- Number of processes.
- Sessions.
- Disk sample.
- Fees.

Periodic accounting is called `fiscal`. The assumed `fiscal` time period is monthly, but most organizations want weekly accounting reports. Fortunately the `fiscal` period is easily set by the system administrator.

The `fiscal` accounting process creates summary files and generates a summary report. Like accounting, the files and reports cover terminal usage, user and command time, CPU time, and last login. The `fiscal` process group also cleans out the `sum` directory. Remember that a process group consists of all the processes of the same parent or of any parent that deliberately starts a new process group.

FILES AND DIRECTORIES

The base directory of the accounting system is `/usr/adm/acct`, with acct branching to three major directories: `nite`, `sum`, and `fiscal`.

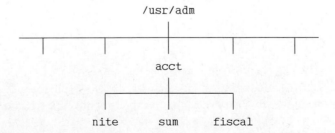

On larger systems I give /usr/adm its own disk partition, because the number of files and directories used and generated by accounting seems overwhelming. It is a massive file system, and when in use on an active machine, it accounts for a big chunk of disk space. If a homegrown bill-back accounting system is appended to standard accounting, as is often necessary, the number of files will grow to unbelievable proportions. Bear this in mind when creating your own bill-back accounting system.

Like all UNIX major subsystems, executable files are kept separate from data files. Executable accounting files live in /usr/lib/acct, with accounting triggered by cron.

Have the accounting lines in cron substitute user ID (su) to acct unless root is running the show. The following fragment shows how to start a line in cron by having /bin/su use acct's user ID for starting the process:

```
/bin/su acct -c "/usr/lib/acct/........"
```

It is always best to have all accounting commands, files, and directories owned by acct, as this minimizes the number of executables that must be owned by root and thus tightens security on your system.

Here are the building blocks of accounting with which you should become familiar:

pacct   Process accounting, the initiation point of accounting

tacct   Total accounting, a sum of accounting records

runacct   The main process-accounting shell program

Now let's examine some files and directories associated with accounting.

/usr/adm

A few regular files are hung directly on the /usr/adm directory itself and contain basic accounting data.

dtmp   acctdusg output

fee   The options output of the chargfee program, an ASCII file

pacct   The active process-accounting file

The initiation point of the accounting process is /usr/adm/pacct. The kernel writes pacct records each time a process finishes, optionally by each user process, by each login, by init through acctwtmp, as well as by disk usage processes like acctdusg and diskusag. Then pacct is accessed by runacct and driven by cron to create summary data.

nite

The nite directory is used to store daily information, and the major files in /usr/adm/acct/nite are

active   Used by runacct to record accounting progress, warning, and error
             messages

cms   Command summary, an ASCII file, used by prdaily, the print daily
             report program

connect.MMDD	Connect-time records
daycms	Daily command summary
dayacct	One-day accounting records in tacct.h format
disktacct	Disk-accounting records
lastdate	The last calendar day that runacct ran
lock, lock1	The lock files for runacct
lineuse	Daily line-usage report
reboots	Begin and end dates from wtmp and a reboot list
wtmp.MMDD	The previous day's wtmp
statefile	Current runacct state: SETUP, WTMPFIX, PROCESS, DISK, MERGEACCT, CMS, and USEREXIT

Pay particular attention to statefile and the process states listed under it. As we mentioned in the beginning of this chapter, accounting stores these process states in statefile to keep track of its current state in case accounting is stopped for any reason. When restarted, the process state information will be here.

sum

The sum directory handles *cumulative* data, and some of its major files are

cms	The command summary for the fiscal period
cmsprev	The old cms file
daycms	Yesterday's cms report
loginlog	Last login date for each user (very handy for finding nonusers taking up space)
pacct.MMDD	Process-accounting files for MMDD date
rept.MMDD	The prdaily report for the date MMDD
tacct	The cumulative total accounting file
tacct.MMDD	The total accounting file for the day MMDD
wtmp.MMDD	A saved copy of wtmp for the day MMDD

fiscal

The fiscal directory is used to store periodic data created from summing daily accounting information. A few of its files are

cms	The command summary file
fisrpt	A prdailylike file for this directory
tacct	The total accounting file

accounting COMMANDS

There are about thirty accounting commands located in /usr/lib/acct, about half of which are in a.out format, compiled C programs. The rest are shell scripts. The main daily shell procedure is runacct, which is initiated by cron and runs daily accounting. Here is a summary of some accounting shell scripts:

runacct   This processes fee-, connect-, disk-, and process-accounting files and also makes a summary file for prdaily.

chargfee   This optional command charges *units* to a log name, used for miscellaneous charges.

ckpacct   This is run by cron to check the size of /usr/adm/pacct. If this file is too large, it will invoke turnacct and eventually turn accounting off.

dodisk   This does disk accounting and is initiated by cron.

lastlogin This creates records of each user's log name and the last date he or she logged in.

moacct   This is the script that generates fiscal reports and is run once per period.

prdaily   This formats a day's accounting, the system administrator's number one accounting tool.

pracct   This formats and prints tacct, the total accounting file.

shutacct   Run by /etc/shutdown, this turns accounting off.

startup   Run by rc, this turns accounting on.

turnacct   This turns accounting on or off, and it is the interface to accton.

These scripts invoke C programs in the same directory. A few of these a.out executables are

acctdisk   Creates total disk accounting records

acctdusg   Computes disk resource consumption

accton   Turns accounting off

acctwtmp   Writes a wtmp record to stdout

Besides these basic commands there are many others, such as

acctcms   Creates a command summary from the per-process files

accton[1,2] Creates connect-time accounting records

acctmerge   Merges or adds total accounting files in tacct format

acctprc[1,2] Processes accounting programs for connect-time accounting, in which users are tracked for the amount of time they are logged on. In this system, acctprc1 feeds acctprc2, reads in wtmp data, and creates tacct data.

SETUP

Now that we have seen where the commands and data files are stored, it's time to see how to set up accounting. Any UNIX subsystem requires permanent changes to rc, shutdown, and cron, and accounting is no exception.

rc

Since rc starts everything, let's start our discussion here. The first accounting command line uses su (substitute user ID) to execute the startup command as if the user acct is issuing the command. The -c flag passes the startup string. As a result, startup is executed in acct's environment as if acct had processed the command:

```
/bin/su acct -c "/usr/lib/acct/startup"
rm -f /usr/adm/acct/nite/lock*
```

The rm command on the second line is executed to remove all the lock files from the nite directory. Then /etc/shutdown has to be appended to shut down the accounting system before the hardware shutdown is completed. Add this line to the shutdown script:

```
/usr/lib/acct/shutdown
```

Shutdowns are always easier than startups.

At intervals you specify, the /etc/cron command fires accounting commands via /usr/spool/cron/crontabs/root. It is best to execute accounting commands a few minutes after midnight to get no more or less than a full accounting, whether in days, weeks, or months:

```
0 4 * * 1-6 /usr/lib/acct/runacct 2>/usr/sdm/acct/nite/fd2log
0 2 * * 1-6 /usr/lib/acct/dodisk >/dev/null
5 * * * *   /usr/lib/acct/ckpacct
```

However, ckpacct is a special case and must be executed every hour. It checks the size of /usr/adm/pacct and turns off data collection if it is too large. Note that dodisk and runacct execute daily and that dodisk must be run ahead of runacct. The commands have a definite sequence. The exact times can vary, but the order must be the same. Note that the first line redirects the standard error 2> to the log: If you want standard error messages when running detached from a terminal, *you have to ask*. On systems serving an international community, it is best to run the system on GMT and set the time zone variable, TZ, on each time-sensitive command executed. It's a lot of work and a pain to administer, but it does keep everyone on time.

Also, /usr/spool/cron/crontabs/adm should have an entry for fiscal accounting:

```
45 0 1 * * /usr/lib/acct/moacct
```

The line gets longer using the time zone constant:

```
45 0 1 * * (TZ=PST8PDT;export TZ;sh /usr/lib/acct/moacct)
```

The parentheses cause all three commands to be executed as the same subshell, putting the new time zone variable into the shell executing moacct.

ADMINISTRATION

Because accounting is written so well, if it is left unmodified and treated with reasonable care, it will run from year to year with normal cleaning and only a minimum amount of attention. You will run into trouble only when you try to combine your own bill-back accounting program with `accounting`. Then `accounting` will become hopelessly complicated, vulnerable to all kinds of problems.

As a system administrator, your biggest job is cleaning out files no longer needed from all the `/usr/adm/acct/*` directories. You must think twice before deleting an accounting file. Will it be needed by another program? Will it be needed for accounting information by the accounting group? If you have enough disk partitions to support it, give `/usr/adm` or `/usr/adm/acct` its own disk partition, and then it won't fill the `/usr` disk if it fills. Check the size of this partition with `df -t` daily.

If the computer system is running 7 days a week and 24 hours a day, you must regularly check the following programs manually to make sure they are running:

- `cron` running (check at 23:45)
- `dodisk` run (03:00)

Even if you set up `fiscal` accounting to be done on a weekly basis, that's no guarantee that you can go blissfully to other tasks secure in the knowledge that `accounting` will run. You need to *make sure* it runs. For example, `week` accounting must be checked at 01:00 on Sunday. If you don't make certain that everything is up and in place, just as sure as `awk` is a funny name, `week` accounting will fail.

It is tedious to reconstruct `accounting`. You are always pressed for time anyway, and accuracy tends to slip under stress. Do yourself a favor and make sure that your operations staff have clear written instructions so they can check `accounting`'s progress (see Chapter 20). They will need either to restart the process that failed or call you up for instructions how. Or check and repair `accounting` first thing Monday morning if you don't have full shift coverage.

INTERPRETING THE DATA

Now we know where `accounting` is, how to start it, how to stop it, and how to administer it, but what does it all mean? Data produced by `accounting` are useful to both the administrator and the bean counters in the accounting department, but first the data must be understood.

The daily report is produced by `prdaily` or `runacct`. Usage portions of these reports have multiple columns of data—we saw some of the output at the beginning of the chapter. Here are the headers of the columns:

UID	The user-ID number from `/etc/passwd`.
LOGIN NAME	The login name from `/etc/passwd`.
CPU (MINS)	The number of central-processor-unit minutes used, broken into prime and nonprime time usage. The constants PRIME and NPRIME are set in `/usr/lib/acct/holidays`.
KCORE_MIN	Kilobytes of memory times minutes used in prime and nonprime time.
CONNECT (MIN)	Real time used (wall time), the amount of time the user was logged on in prime and nonprime time.

DISK BLOCKS	The number of disk blocks used during the session. Don't confuse this with the total blocks of disk storage taken by the user and not recorded by `accounting` .
# OF PROC	This is the number of processes started by the user. Look here for runaway processes or abuses.
# OF SESS	This tells you how many times the user has logged on.
# DISK SAMPLES	This is the number of times disk accounting was run to get disk block data.
FEE	This records optional fees and is frequently unused.

Daily Report

The daily report section starts with a time-period statement followed by any reboots or shutdowns. The first columnar report is line usage:

LINE	`tty` line or port
MINUTES	Total minutes used
PERCENT	Real usage divided by length of login
# SESS	Number of sessions (logins)
# ON	Number of sessions (old version)
# OFF	Logoffs and interrupts

Command Summaries

The `accounting` subsystem produces both `daily` and `fiscal` summaries, which are identical except for the time period: `daily` is a full day's report, and `fiscal` is for a defined period, assumed to be one month unless reset by you. The column headings are

COMMAND NAME	The command names `sh`, `rsh`, `csh`, and `ksh` report all shell activity; therefore, expect the shells to be high.
NUMBER COMMANDS	Total number of invocations.
TOTAL KCOREMEM	Total number of kilobytes of memory used times the number of minutes it was used.
TOTAL CPU-MIN	Total processing time.
TOTAL REAL-MIN	Total number of real or wall time minutes used by the process.
MEAN K-SIZE	Average of `TOTAL KCOREMIN` divided by the number of times invoked.
MEAN CPU-MIN	The average time per command; the figure you want if you are looking for CPU hogs on an individual invocation basis.
HOG FACTOR	The ratio is CPU time divided by elapsed time:

$$\text{HOG FACTOR} = \frac{\text{CPU TIME}}{\text{ELAPSED TIME}}$$

This ratio gives you system availability. The closer to 1, the better, and the smaller the number, the worse shape your system is in.

CHARS TRANSFD	Total number of characters transferred by both *reads* and *writes*.
BLOCKS READ	Total number of physical block *reads* and *writes*.

Last Login

The Last Login section is a listing of the users' names and the last time they logged in. When you want to free up disk space, this is the only place you need to look to find out which people to clean out of /etc/passwd.

STABILITY, STARTS, AND STOPS

We mentioned this before, but it's worth repeating: accounting is designed to be restartable, as it knows that the system may be shut down and rebooted during an accounting period. The entries in /etc/rc and /etc/shutdown guarantee that it will start and stop without harming itself. Because accounting keeps track of its current state by storing it to disk, on restart it will know where to initiate. Note that runacct is the key process and stores its state in statefile.

runacct

Recall that runacct is the heart of the accounting system, the main daily accounting procedure. Initiated by cron, it processes process, disk, and connect data and makes or modifies the following files:

nite/lineuse	The acctcon part of runacct reads /etc/wtmp and makes usage statistics for each tty and port
nite/dayacct	The total accounting file in tacct format
sum/tacct	The sum of /nite/dayacct
sum/daycms	The daily command summary, made by acctcms
sum/cms	The sum of the daily account command summaries, restarted by moacct
sum/loginlog	The record of the last login date made by lastlogin
sum/rptMMDD	The daily report, printed by prdaily

MANAGER'S CORNER

Bill-back Accounting

The accounting subsystem becomes the root of bill-back accounting programs at most sites. Bill-back accounting schemes run from the simple to the impossible, the simplest and probably the best using awk on standard accounting output to generate group bill-back data from accounting data. They are relatively easy to program, and if you don't expect too much in the way of fancy output, you won't be disappointed. Beyond that, bill-back accounting systems can get complicated quickly.

I was once involved in a bill-back accounting scheme that was built on standard UNIX System V Release 2 `accounting`. It ran across several virtual UTS systems that were guests on a VM host. All of this ran on an extremely large mainframe appended to do extra things never intended by the creators of `accounting`. All the UNIX systems sent their information to a central system where it was merged with VM data. Then everything was massaged and sent to another site for final billing.

Because it was so complex, the program ran poorly. The timing was so sensitive that it would run successfully only one time in three. The moral, if there is one, is not to make an already complex system more complex. Use `accounting` well, and it will do well for you.

Stopping just short of being an accounting system for company billing purposes, `accounting` is oriented to individual users, not groups or projects. By sorting on the usage of individual users and assuming that they will work only on one project, it can do a reasonable job of billing. But if you require a full accounting package that does group and project accounting, you will have to have one written or move to System V Release 4. If you write your own bill-back accounting program, the following are a few hints learned the hard way:

- Make bill-back accounting separate from `accounting`.
- Put in a time stamp with the records so that `accounting` can be constructed or reconstructed from and to any date.
- Make the project number a part of every user's environment.

If your organization is committed to a bill-back accounting system, once the system is written, be prepared to invest a fair amount of programming time to support the system. You may even be forced to hire a bill-back administrator if the site is large enough.

Relying on the regular programming staff to support bill-back accounting as part of their regular jobs is asking too much of your staff. Bill-back accounting data are usually delivered on Monday morning, but this is the same time that your programming staff is busy trying to recover from the weekend's damages. Console logs must be read and restarted. Spoolers must be cleaned, and daemons must be checked and restarted if necessary. Although the first few hours of the week are critical to the system, that is the time the bill-back accounting must be out. Do you and your staff a favor and make a choice: Either budget for a dedicated accounting administrator or negotiate a Tuesday bill-back accounting delivery date.

SECTION

III

System Creation, Configuration, and Tuning

11

System Creation and Setup

THE CREATION OF NEW SYSTEMS

One of the most enjoyable system administration tasks is creating new systems. It represents a clean start, an opportunity to throw out the old and look forward to a better system than the last one.

There are numerous reasons to move to another system. Most systems require the addition of software external to the OEM's distribution before the machine can do any useful work, whether the programs are purchased from the outside or developed in-house. Perhaps you are doing a thorough cleaning and revamping of your current system. There are several reasons for creating a new system:

- A new OEM operating system release.
- New in-house releases.
- New OEM software or hardware.
- A massive system expansion.
- A massive system cleanup.
- New hardware.
- Disaster recovery.

Let's examine a few of these categories in detail.

Release Levels: A Word to the Wise

System administrators of smaller UNIX machines tend to think twice before installing new releases of the UNIX operating system. Just because some OEM puts out a release update doesn't necessarily mean that you should be in a hurry to install it. In fact, the smaller the system is, the less likely it is that you will bother installing new operating system versions. You should install a new UNIX release only when major changes to the operating system are made.

It's a different story if you administer large UNIX systems. Installation of new system releases are a common occurrence on mainframe systems. Release tapes come every four to six months, and mainframe OEMs usually insist that you be at the latest release level, because that's where their support group is. That is, if you don't stay current with that support group, you may forfeit vital technical support. Thus, the larger the system is, the more likely it is that you will be installing new operating system updates.

Whether the computers on your site are large or small, the streetwise mainframe UNIX administrator learns what release numbering schemes mean. The number of the operating system release is the key to understanding what kind of changes have been made.

UNIX operating system releases usually have the form X.X.X. An X.0 release tells you that the release is just out of beta test. This "dot 0" release means a large change in the operating system and also that there are going to be quite a few bugs. The next release level is X.1, a bug fix of X.0. By the time you get to X.X.1 you have a relatively stable, almost bug-free system. Mainframe UNIX UTS V 1.1.3 is a stable, bug-free release of what started out as UTS V 1.0, which had more bugs than a compost heap. What if your system is at Release 2.1.3, and you receive a tape for Release 2.2? You now have a release with several new features and a few bugs.

Always read the release description before you decide to install a new release. On sites with smaller machines, you might want to wait until the bug fix of a feature release comes out before you install it on your site.

All UNIX OEMs, large and small, release their particular versions of the UNIX operating system. Not all releases are universally significant in the industry, but when an AT&T or BSD release is announced, sit up and take note. Then you know there will soon be a monumental release for your UNIX system, whatever OEM you may have. The most influential UNIX operating system releases in recent history were AT&T System V Release 2 (5.2), AT&T System V Release 4 (5.4), BSD 4.2, and BSD 4.3. AT&T System V Release 3 did not have as great an impact, but it did pave the way for the 5.4 version.

Releases from smaller OEMs do not necessarily correspond to releases from big leaguers like AT&T, Berkeley, Sun, or IBM. However, when you see major changes in the operating system, such as AT&T 5.4, expect your OEM to do a full rewrite of its version without adding many new features of its own. Naturally, release numbers of smaller OEMs are seldom the same as release numbers of source OEMs like AT&T; that would make life too easy. For example, UNIX System V Release 4 corresponds to SCO's UNIX 3.2.

With experience you will soon become familiar with the release numbers of different OEMs in the industry, and you will know what features each release contains. You will gradually learn whether the OEM UNIX version has Berkeley UNIX features, whether it's an AT&T/Berkeley UNIX blend, or whether it's pure AT&T UNIX. Sometimes you will find out the hard way that no matter what an OEM calls its UNIX version, what counts is how closely that version corresponds to the latest AT&T or BSD UNIX releases.

Some OEM UNIX versions have dated features that go back to an older BSD or AT&T release, so you have to be careful because you don't want to miss out on the latest and greatest features that current UNIX versions offer.

Local Tools

Local tools for users are usually developed by a tool group or the applications staff, but sometimes they are purchased from outside vendors. They are often used in combination with one another, such as a purchased DBMS system supporting a company inventory system that was created by in-house applications programmers.

Be wary. If you haven't learned what the company considers a system programmer's duties, as the system administrator you may be expected to support user tools in addition to your system administration duties. To illustrate this point, imagine that you run a machine that relies on CAD tools. To support those CAD tools you need to become an expert at using all those tools. But you have so much to do as system administrator that if you can, it's best to limit your support to *installing* the software.

Purchased Languages and Tools

Business systems require WYSIWYG[1] editors for semiskilled text work, spread sheets, data base systems, and accounting systems, just for the base applications software. Often additional specialized software is built in as well: Many applications require data base software; scientific systems require special language packages; and CAD systems require graphics packages and CAD, CASE, or CAE tools.

UNIX comes with C, and larger UNIX systems are shipped with FORTRAN, but you must purchase any other programming language that you may want. Each site has its own language preferences. The company's language of choice is usually embedded in thousands of lines of applications programs code, so that language is at the company to stay for the duration of the code.

In addition to system software and installed software, we must also consider software tools available for the system administrator and system programmer, including backup software, monitors, performance tools, bill-back accounting programs, batch systems, network packages, network management programs, and specialized printer tools, to name a few. The longer the system has existed and the more knowledgeable the support staff is, the larger the local administration tool base will have to be.

HARDWARE MISHAPS WITH FIRST-TIME SYSTEM CREATIONS

It's rare to get a squeaky-clean system the first time you create it. Because they are familiar with the hardware, system integrators have few problems getting it to talk, and so installations go quickly. However, most of us make installations infrequently, usually when we purchase a new piece of equipment or when a new operating system release is

---

[1] WYSIWYG: What You See Is What You Get. This term applies to full-screen editors that format directly to the screen.

issued. For some reason there is always something that the manual doesn't cover, some obscure switch or jumper selection to turn a two-hour job into a four-day crisis.

For example, I was setting up a brand-new Intel 301 386 SCO XENIX system and had ordered a FourPORT/XN serial card. It took some time to get the card because it was on special order. But it arrived late one Friday afternoon, and I used the manufacturer's manual to set the switches for the system. The packaging was fine, and the slick manual looked impeccable, but when I set the switches according to the manual's instructions, nothing worked. I tried everything I knew and still came up with nothing. With eight switches there are 256 possible switch settings $(2)^8$, and I wasn't about to try them all.

I called the manufacturer first thing Monday morning after a weekend of frustration. A knowledgeable, helpful gentleman answered the phone and suavely explained that the manual was wrong, so sorry. He gave me the correct switch settings over the phone, with apologies. This kind of scenario is common in the computer business when you bring up a system that is still relatively new, and so be prepared for some inconveniences.

SYSTEMS BECOME COMPLICATED FAST

From the original simple distribution tape or floppy set supplied by the OEM, your basic local system will grow in size and change by one or two orders of magnitude in complexity after you have added all the extra software and hardware needed to do the job at hand. The tasks of maintaining your UNIX system have grown proportionally, and you still haven't added a single user, not to mention data!

If the system is unique, the only one of its kind in the installation, all that needs to be done beyond building the system to this point is to archive the system, add users and their data, and support the system. However, many sites have multiple systems of different sizes and types, and they may be running different versions of UNIX. When NFS is available on all machines, major file systems that have to be shared by everybody can be NFS mounted from a single source. This is an *NFS mount*. In the event that the mount must be in a place other than where it's expected to be, a *symbolic link* can be used. If you don't have NFS, then the files that everyone needs must be installed on each stand-alone system on the site.

WORK SMARTER WITH THE SYSTEM ENGINE APPROACH

If each system in a multicomputer organization were created by adding purchased and local software one piece at a time, thousands of dollars worth of time would be wasted in slow, tedious system installations. Slow, poorly planned system migrations are a drag of company resources. The move to a new system thus must be well planned so it is accomplished swiftly and decisively throughout the site.

If there is no uniformity in your system creation, the resulting mess will be impossible to administer unless you learn the geography of each system. One machine might have /usr/local/bin for local tools, another /local/bin, and yet another /usr/groupname/bin. Many have local tools duplicated in the system programmers' own personal directories. The locations of application software can also be a hide-and-seek proposition. The end result is a repeat of the biblical story of the Tower of Babel, with no one speaking the same language and no one able to work with another.

The prevention and cure for these potential administrative nightmares are the creation of a single UNIX *engine* for each type of system. The engine is substantially preplanned; in fact, it can and should be part of the company's overall computing strategy. In that way specific software and its location are coordinated from desktop to mainframe.

Tools should be in the same area on every machine. Never allow tools to lie in /usr/tools on your micros and in /tools on your minis. Follow UNIX tradition in creating local areas. Users' local tools belong in /local/bin; your tools belong in /local/etc; and local library functions belong in /local/lib. Similarly, using the System V model, manuals belong in /local/man, divided into u_man, p_man, and a_man.

Separate disk partitions—like /local, /app, /cad, and /admin—are easy to administer and to access. Separate disk partitions allow for easy size and inode expansions and rapid backups and restores. They can easily be unmounted for repair because you don't have to bring down the entire system; thus fewer users are inconvenienced. So don't rush out and buy a system that cannot easily partition its disks, whatever you do.

Application areas, CAD tool areas, and similar special-purpose user areas are usually administered by their own work groups. However, as *the* system administrator you still own the machine. Users need to know that it takes a mutually beneficial partnership to create the end product. Negotiate the location and structure of the tool location, and above all, discourage their addition to /usr. Adding everything on the system to /usr creates one awful system to administer. Therefore, /usr should be appended only by traditional directories, such as src, spool, adm, and all of the directories normally found in the standard distribution.

Once your system is planned, create it from the OEM's distribution tape and add software. Give add-on software its own disk partition whenever possible. Unitech recommends that Ubackup go into /usr/bin, but don't rush out and do whatever the vendor says, no questions asked. Create a disk partition large enough to hold the product, and give it the breathing room the vendor recommends. Attach the disk partition to /usr/bin, and then install the tape. Now when difficulties arise, you won't have to worry, because removing and replacing the product will be easy.[2]

A Home for Programmers

The engine takes shape as you add each major product to its own directory partition or to an aggregate partition on a very small system. Only one user disk exists on the engine, your own. Call it /tech or /admin or whatever; the point is that you need a small but safe place to land as yourself, not as root. Without it you will have to log on as root and then scatter junk all over the system. Work with privilege as the superuser only when absolutely necessary.

---

[2] AT&T UNIX 5.2 has an install command that not only installs software but also "deinstalls" it. This feature was made generally available in Release 3. Now System V Release 4 has enhanced installation and removal software called pkeadd that removes software even if it is scattered.

Distributing the Engine

When the engine is complete, examine the system, test it, and archive it. Put it on a safe partition, and copy it to create other systems. Now save it to tape. This tape becomes your master distribution tape that can be *nationalized* throughout the entire organization.[3] Each site now need concern itself only with licensing its own copy of the systems and purchased software, unless your management has made a site or multiple-CPU licensing agreement with the vendor.

Besides forming a method of system distribution, engines are useful in other ways. Under some circumstances they can be attached to a sick system's disks to repair them. This is especially helpful when repairing another system's root disk for special tasks like a disk block or inode expansion of the root file system. It also is helpful when repairing a corrupted password file. You can even ship *system updates* to your customers as ready-to-install system engines. From major releases to point releases, the engine distribution technique saves weeks of installation time, simplifying and standardizing your installations.

SMALL-SYSTEM CREATION

Believe it or not, at this writing there are more active XENIX systems than any other UNIX system version. Few UNIX systems can be installed and set up as easily as SCO XENIX can. The following is how you set up an Intel 301 80386 PC running SCO XENIX System V. The hardware consists of two Seagate 40-megabyte hard disks, 2.5 megabytes of 32-bit memory, and an 80387 math coprocessor. The software is the full SCO XENIX System V distribution run-time environment, text-processing system, software development system, graphics interface, and VP/ix DOS interface, games and all. The installation takes about two hours from start to finish, including putting in the run-time package twice for the practice.

Having all the right hardware is the trick to getting the job done quickly. Standard PC add-ons may not be suitable for UNIX. For example, DOS I/O boards are not configured for UNIX addresses. You also will need at least five serial ports. And the board must have I/O addresses that are recognized by your operating system's driver.

There are a few decisions to make about disk partitioning before installing UNIX. You probably will want to leave a small disk partition for DOS. A moderately tight partition is OK for the base UNIX system itself *if* you don't add unnecessary trash to /usr. Disk partitions can be mounted to /usr, thus keeping the system disk small and uncomplicated. The number of user partitions should run from one to whatever, depending on how many partitions are available and practical and how many make sense to administer. Once the disks are partitioned, load the system, and bring it up.

The strategy for this machine is to create a separate DOS partition, a root partition with a swap area, a separate user area on the first disk, and a second and third XENIX user area on the second hard disk. I have some personal preferences: I don't want any users residing on /usr, and I want the root partition to be able to expand beyond the usual amount of "breathing room."

---

[3] Distributed through the entire organization to establish a house standard.

The hardware comes to life by booting DOS from the system's only floppy disk drive. The installation starts when you put in the XENIX boot floppy disk. SCO ships its installation disks with serial and activation numbers, so take care with this and other contemporary software packages that use an activation key. Be sure to save the paper containing the activation key and the serial number. Then when doing the installation, keep it separate but close at hand, because the serial number and activation key will have to be put in from time to time during the installation.

In a matter of seconds the system will come up in XENIX from its floppy disk. Seeing the pound sign prompt for the first time on a new system is still exciting, even after years in this business. The system replies with its first message:

```
fd(4)XENIX root=fd(4)swap=ram(16)pipe=ram(1)swapllo=o nswap=1000 ronly
```

The system then displays a self-check, sending an uppercase, childlike alphabet recitation to the screen. This is a warm, furry button for the user. Once installed, it continues to do its alphabet recitation to the terminal and to /usr/adm/messages. You're going to see this QRSTUVWXYZdisk[w] drive1 information often in your administration work, so now you don't have to wonder what it is.

When the infant system finally recites to Z, you find yourself in *maintenance mode*. It is single-user mode, the equivalent of init s in AT&T System V UNIX. You now must select the nationality of your keyboard, a gently pleasant reminder that we live in a multinational-UNIX world.

The next step is initializing the hard disks. This is the only time you are able to do so without being nervous about overwriting data. Wouldn't it be nice if there were a uniform method of partitioning and formatting disks? Unfortunately, there is no standard UNIX method. Currently the OEM decides which method to use, but eventually there will be a standard for all phases of system administration. It's in the hands of the POSIX IEEE P1003.7 committee.

Original UNIX systems did their formatting from another operating system, and mainframe versions still get their disk allocations and partitions from a host operating system like VM. Most other UNIX versions do so from a freestanding tape or floppy version.

Disk Initialization and Maintenance

XENIX has its own series of programs for disk initialization and maintenance, including mkdev, dkinit, and divvy. Most are either interactive or command-line driven, your choice. They can be used passively to give back disk information. Coupled with the XENIX conf and configure programs, you have the tools you need to install your XENIX system.

dkinit

The dkinit program creates, modifies, and displays the hard disk parameters. It is particularly useful for nonstandard disks. The program is interactive, displaying current values, and allowing you either to go with default parameters or change them.

fdisk

The fdisk program is used to partition the hard disks, and like dkinit, it can be either interactive or command-line driven. It displays the current disk partitions, status type, start address, end address, and size of the partition. You must remember to feed it the raw disk device name, /dev/rdh??, to make it work. Its default is root's raw disk, which creates, activates, or deletes partitions. You'll be glad to know that it gives no "magic" esoteric data, so it is quick and easy to use. The partition is displayed in tracks (tracks = cylinders x heads).

badtrk

The next step in the installation is the invocation of badtrk, which also is interactive, permitting either display or action on your part. It displays the current bad-track table and can scan the disk in two ways: a *read-only* scan or a *destructive* scan, needed for first-time installations or bad-track repairs. It can add entries to the table by either sector or cylinder and head number. It also deletes individual entries from the table.

Disk drives have some bad tracks; it's a simple fact of life. The manufacturers even acknowledge this reality by shipping new disk drives with a "bad track" record. Part of the initialization procedure is to enter the bad-track information to the formatting software. You *can* let the system look for bad tracks, but the disk drive vendor's testing is much more specialized. (This subject is covered in detail later in the chapter.)

divvy

You have a problem when an operating system doesn't allow the easy partitioning of physical disks into virtual partitions. Disk partitions are a necessity for creating mounted file systems and for being able to mount them where required. Some systems have rigid partitioning. My AT&T 3B offers me two choices: root or /usr. Yes, at System V Release 2, you can split disks into /dev/dsk/c1d0s0 and /dev/dsk/c1d0s1, but this should be reserved for subpartitions. As the sole method of subdividing disk areas, subpartitioning is not as flexible as partitioning, and so it's not the preferred way to make /u or /local or /what_ever. But fortunately, divvy makes partitioning the disks a relatively simple affair. The command syntax is esoteric, with a typical command line invocation looking like

```
# divvy -b 1 -c 1 -p 1 -v 2
```

This is so obscure that you will need the manual handy to translate. The following information has been passed:

- -b block device number
- -c character device number
- -p physical drive number, such as 0 or 1
- -v virtual drive number

The character/block, major/minor categories are old friends to system administrators, because they frequently see long listings of /dev. They are the major and minor numbers seen here in this long listing:

```
$ ls -l /dev/d1110
brw------- 1 sysinfo sysinfo   1,  72    April 30  11:40 /dev/d1110
$ ls -l /dev/rd1110
crw------- 1 sysinfo sysinfo   1,  72    April 30  11:40 /dev/rd1110
```

If you don't like names like /dev/d110, divvy will allow you to give them more creative names, within reason, of course.

Also, divvy gives you the opportunity to size your swap area. Even on the smallest systems, you will want to match real memory size and add a little bit for the size of the swap. The smaller the memory size is, the more likely you'll need to use the swap area.

Most systems permit you to size the swap area. You probably won't push memory too hard on small systems with basic UNIX doing just a little program development and text processing. However, VP/ix, DOS, and UNIX fourth-generation languages, like spread sheets and data base products, push memory to the hilt. SCO recommends the system default *plus* 500 blocks as a minimum for the swap area.

The Installation

The installation of XENIX starts after you have completed partitioning the disk, formatting the disk, making the file systems, and installing bare-bones XENIX. Now XENIX is ready to boot off the hard disk on its own.

Like most uncomplicated systems, XENIX boots simply, by pushing the ENTER button at the boot prompt. To get DOS, all you have to do is type in DOS.

The screen will ask for additional installation floppies. You can install all of the XENIX packages now, or you can omit some things to save space. You can always install them later. However, you will have to install all of the run-time package to get started. Let's say that there are two hard disks on your machine, so you go for it all. As each packet is installed, the system prompts and checks for the next disk. Sometimes there is a pause while it requests the package serial number and software key.

The installation finishes up with the original "N" floppies and a request for a root password. Here you sigh with relief, because you nearly have a system now. A few final nits need to be tended to, like setting time zones (TZ) and setting the system date. Anything that was missed on installation can go in with the XENIX custom command.

Once all this is done, you can go about the system administration business of adding users and creating user directories. If you had the good sense to create at least one additional disk partition, now is the time to make a directory for it, mount the disk, and put whatever you want on it. Don't forget to put a lost+found directory on each mountable file system. Remember that lost+found directories must be slotted by installing and removing a large number of files from the directory.

All in all, a new installation of XENIX is a relatively painless affair. There is enough software added by SCO to take the major headaches out of a new installation. In fact, there are scripts that roll up most of the installation commands for you, like mkdev, so you don't have to understand much of what's going on. On the other hand, if you want to be an ace administrator, you should cultivate the skills needed to do the installation in longhand. In short, either you can go for the defaults and take the easy way out or you can carefully do your homework and preplan your partitions and swap area. Either way, SCO has provided for it.

System Migrations on Small Machines

If you are doing a system migration on this XENIX system, you will need to bring over data from the old system. Tapes and floppies may or may not be compatible between machines. The cleanest way to transfer data is to hardwire the two systems together. The hardwire connection is ground to ground (DB-25 pin 7 to pin 7), TD to RD on both sides.[4] If the systems need handshaking and specific control pins[5] pulled up, you will get to see how creative you can be. Set a getty on the ports of both machines. Now you're ready to start the file transfer.

Single files are easy to transfer with the cu command's ~%get and ~%put, but moving entire directories is best done by archiving. With 1/2-inch, reel-to-reel tape, pick a density compatible with both machines. With floppies you have to hit a match of track density (tpi), sectors per track, and the rotational gap or skew. There is no floppy standard in UNIX. Tape cassettes are also a free-for-all. If you can't match your media, the hardwire will be one of the only options left. Copy the entire directory to an archive file, and send it to the sister machine:

```
# cd /local
# cpio .  -depth -print!cpio -oac >archive
# cu /dev/tty2d
login: ychouinard
password:
$ cd /local
$ ~%put archive
$ su
password:
# cpio -icd <archive
# ^d
$ ~.
#
```

Note that the cu line may be # cu dir on your system. Here cpio is used with the -o option to create an archive. The system that has been hardwired is reached with UUCP's cu command. The archive is then read in with cpio's -i option.

SETTING UP A SUN WORKSTATION

Sun has changed the world's concept of how computing is done. The workstation has two common configurations, *diskless* and *dataless*. The diskless workstation has no disk of its own and relies on the network, and therefore the server, for all of its needs. It even has to boot from the network. The dataless workstation has its own disk for the system, swap area, and /usr, but it relies on the file server for most of its other needs.

---

[4] Pin 2 to 3 on DCE to DCE or DTE to DTE, pin 2 to 2, and pin 3 to 3 on DTE to DCE.
[5] Pins 4, 5, 6, 8, or 20.

Setup and configuration of the workstation are unique. Most workstations run Berkeley-based UNIX because of their need for the Ethernet and NFS. Some examples are Berkeley 4.2 (ULTRIX), Berkeley 4.3 (SunOS), and System 5 Release 4 (AT&T). UNIX 5.4 incorporates most of the Berkeley networking features.

We are going to set up a Sun 386i workstation; Sun 3, Sun 4, and DEC ULTRIX workstation setups are similar.

First Things First

The first step is taking the system out of the boxes. If it is your first installation, open the box with the manual set, and find the installation instructions before you do anything else.

The CPU housing is the first piece of hardware to be worked. Lay it on its side on a table, and remove the side plate to expose the motherboard. The memory modules are not installed at the factory, so you have to do it yourself. The memory board is packed separately with the frame buffer, a board that drives the monitor. Install the memory SIMMs into the memory board, and drop it into the slots recommended by Sun. You also have to install the frame buffer. Be sure to ground your working hand to the system's frame before doing any installation work. Add the box's feet, reinstall the side plate, and you're done with the CPU.

Take the monitor from the box and put it where it will do its work. Plug the monitor cable into the the frame buffer port at the back of the CPU box. It has a massive DB connector that is unmistakable. Attach the *red*, *green*, *blue*, and sync in connectors to the back of the monitor, and ground the monitor to the ground tab.

Attach the keyboard to the monitor cable, and anchor the cable to the monitor's base. Attach the mouse to the keyboard, putting it on the right or left, depending on the user's hand of choice. Grit your teeth, because the cabling is only beginning. Attach the Ethernet cable to the DB-25 connector on the top back of the CPU box, and lock it. If a printer is to be installed, attach it now to the CPU box's parallel port. If a tape cassette expansion unit called a *shoebox* is to be added, remove the tape-port terminator from the CPU box's back, and attach the tape cable. Now all you have to do is attach two or three power cables, one to the monitor, one to the CPU box from the wall, and another from the optional tape unit to the CPU box.

The Smoke Test

The next phase of the install is unofficially called the *smoke test*. You're in deep trouble when you plug in any new appliance if you see smoke and flames. You want the Sun 386i installation to work properly, too. If there is a problem, seize the opportunity to talk to your area service rep. If the smoke test is successful and everything is installed properly, at this stage I prefer to let the system come up and sit on its prompt for about twenty-four hours for a *burn in*, no pun intended.

Configuration

Factory disk partitioning covers 90 percent of everyone's needs, but let's say you are working at a site that belongs in the remaining 10 percent category. Let's imagine that at this site the workstations run extremely memory-intensive jobs. Fifty megabytes of a 91-megabyte drive are devoted to the swap area, not even leaving room for the cluster software. To repartition the workstation, you must boot it from tape or diskette to run under a memory-resident version of UNIX. Let's say that at this site you configure so many units that you have to use a pair of breadbox tape units and load and configure as many as six workstations at a time.

The OEM `format` utility—which allows the current disk partitions to be displayed, resized, or reformatted—repartitions the disk. The disk can be partitioned on the live system and even in multiuser mode on large Sun systems with SMD drives and controllers. Only the `root` disk requires that the memory-resident version of UNIX be used. Smaller units like our Sun 386i workstation do not have the benefit of SMD drives and controller, so they must be done the hard way. They run Western Digital SCSI units.

Whenever you repartition the drive, always create a map of what the partitions are going to look like. It takes a little math to divide the disk into clean cylinder boundaries. The initial output of `format`'s `partition` option shows you the disk layout in number of sectors, writable surfaces (heads), and cylinders. From there you can calculate the remaining figures. The following is a partitioning table that gives the system 50 megabytes of swap at the cost of reducing all other partitions:

```
partition a - start cylinder 0, #blocks  10500(60/0/0)
partition b - start cylinder 318, #blocks 99925(571/0/0)
partition c - start cylinder 0, #blocks 178500(1020/0/0)
partition d - start cylinder 0, #blocks 0(/0/0)
partition e - start cylinder 0, #blocks 0(/0/0)
partition f - start cylinder 0, #blocks 0(/0/0)
partition g - start cylinder 60,#blocks 45150(258/0/0)
partition h - start cylinder 889,#blocks 22925(131/0/0)
```

All partitions must fall on even cylinder boundaries, so there can be nothing but 0 for heads and sectors. The notation (60/0/0) is cylinder 60, head 0, sector 0, and the number 10500 is 10,500 blocks. There are 175 blocks per cylinder, and each block is 512 bytes.

Reloading the System

You will have one small problem once you have completed the repartitioning. The interactive installation software has allowed you to repartition and reformat all of the available disk partitions, a through h, but there is no system on disk! The installation software will ask you if you want to reinstall the system. The answer is yes. You load about twelve diskettes, or with tape you just let it go and stop by from time to time to answer yes to an occasional installation question asked by the software.

Initial Configuration

The workstation's host-ID number is the `root` password. The initial screen of information repeats the host-ID number and gives you the Ethernet address burned into a very small prom on the motherboard. Write them both down, and keep them handy. The workstation must be on the Ethernet when being configured. The only way around this is to bring it up as a freestanding unit, but that would defeat the purpose of a workstation.

Don't worry if you make a mistake during the next part of the installation: The system has a large eraser called `unconfigure`. The installation software will ask if the workstation is going to be a *diskless*, *networked*, or *stand-alone system*. This Sun 386i is a dataless workstation, so *networked* is the correct choice. When the installation software asks for the time zone, give it a simple answer, such as `pst` for Pacific Standard Time or the number of hours away from Greenwich. When it asks for the Internet number, you will have to assign or get one. You will be asked for the system's host name and the name of the YP domain that it serves. Create a host name and name the YP domain if you are creating it. Otherwise, find its name and enter it.

The system reboots at the end of the question-and-answer session. Now is a good time to change the `root` password to something other than the system serial number. It's also a good time to reconfigure the kernel if necessary.

Kernel Reconfiguration

The workstation's configuration file is taken from

`/usr/cluster/devl/config/share/sys/sun386/conf/GENERIC`

a file covered in detail in Chapter 14. The only configurable parameter is `maxusers`, the number of users, factory-set 8 on this machine.[6] This `maxusers` variable is only a multiplier for most of the systems tables, so don't take it literally as the maximum number of users. For sizing anything else, refer to files like `param.h`. When you work from the `GENERIC` file as a model, the main task in a workstation configuration is to rid the system of unnecessary devices. For this you must acquire an intimate knowledge of the bus and the hardware.

rc

The installation software edits the `rc` and `rc.local` files, but you will still need to look through them and edit them manually. Because `rwho`'s convenience isn't worth the overhead, comment the daemon out in `rc.local`. If your software doesn't need file locking, comment out the `lockd` and `statd` daemons. Be sure that you have a reasonable number of `biod` and `nfsd` daemons, as both require a minimum of four and eight instances, respectively, to handle a reasonable amount of network traffic. Your area to configure is `rc.local`; take advantage of your power here.

Configuring for Use

Now that the system is up and on the net, it is time to get it ready for work. Although `/usr` is normally set up as *read only*, you will probably want to make it *read/write*. While you're at it, you may have to make `/etc/utmp` and `/dev/kmem` writable, because `sunview` and X need to write to them. Reboot the system after altering `/etc/fstab` to make `/usr` writable.

---

[6] `MAXUSER` is a parameter, and in UNIX System V it's treated as a constant and so is capitalized. In Berkeley UNIX it's in lowercase letters and is a multiplier for other tables.

/etc/fstab

The file-mounting system's changing point is /etc/fstab. Although the stock OEM copy has no NFS mounts, NFS is precisely why you bought the system. You mount the user's file system here, including his tools and all *cross mounts*, which mount to servers other than the primary one. Be sure to mount all file systems that do not require writing as *read only*. Users may want cluster software mounted as writable, but with a few pointed questions you may find out the *write* link is needed only to use fortunes. Is the access of games worth risking an unauthorized write? It's your decision.

Make all fstab files the same on all workstations if at all possible, as it makes maintenance much easier. You will save yourself much confusion if both sides of the mount have the same name, such as /usr/users on the workstation mounted to /usr/users on the server. The exceptions are system-specific directories on the server. For example, /usr/tools/sun386 on the server is mounted as /usr/tools on the workstation.

Don't forget to make the mount points while you are creating mounts in fstab. On rare occasions you will have to create symbolic links if you are unable to mount to wherever the user software expects to find a file.

YP

Most workstation installations take advantage of Yellow Pages; indeed, I cannot imagine doing user maintenance on networked systems without it. The /etc files taken over by YP must be modified to take advantage of it. For example, /etc/passwd must be cleaned out of all user entries that are in the YP version, and the jump point must be added to get over to the YP version. Perhaps the most important file is /etc/hosts, because the system will never get off the ground if the workstation version doesn't jump to the YP data base version of hosts.

/etc/printcap

Workstations share printers as well as files. As a result, the local printcap file must be changed to access remote printers. I keep copies of all common files like printcap in my home directory on the server so that I can copy them to the workstations when I am setting them up. Also, printcap can be put into the YP data base.

Access Control

Networked UNIX systems allow no access to other systems without deliberately setting up access files. If access is desired, now is the time to make it happen. Get in and modify /etc/hosts.equiv, /.rhosts, /etc/netgroup, hosts.local, and all similar access-control files.

Server Modifications

The server has to be aware of the new workstation. At the very least, the workstation's host name and Ethernet address should be added to the YP master's source file, usually /etc/hosts. If the YP master server is separate from the file server, the YP server is where the change will have to be made. In the unlikely event that the workstation is mounting a unique file system, the server's /etc/exports file will have to be modified as well. Usually all workstations in a work group are configured in the same way. If you know that you are going to add fifteen workstations in the next three months, add their host names and network addresses all at the same time. Then modifications to the file server and YP master will be unnecessary.

sendmail

The last step is to be sure that sendmail is functional. You will want to create a symbolic link from /etc/sendmail.cf to /usr/lib/sendmail.subsidiary.cf for a workstation client. Take little for granted. Be sure that the hosts file makes known the name of mailhost and that the workstation's sendmail.cf file reflects the same system name.

SETTING UP A VAXSERVER

Let's set up a DEC VAXserver 3600 running ULTRIX-32 to get a feel for servers and midsized UNIX systems. The scenario is an upgrade from an older ULTRIX version to a newer one. The migration starts with a full backup of the system, root partition included. This is as good a time as any to note the files you will want restored to the system after the installation.

Your best bet is to let the system make the list for you. A quick and dirty way to get root files by name is bring the system into single-user[7] mode at an appropriate time and to change directories to /usr. Now unmount the disks. On a Berkeley system this will unmount all but root and /usr:

```
# umount -a
```

But /usr will refuse to unmount because you're sitting on it! Although this is a sneaky way to unmount everything but /usr, it works very well. Then cd to / and do a long listing of vmunix, the kernel, to find out when it was made. You will need to search the root and /etc disks for all files modified after that date. Say the kernel was configured 37 days ago. Then you will need to look for all files modified in the last 36 days:

```
# find /etc -mtime -36 -type f -exec ls {} \;>save_list
```

It is necessary to use -type f to prevent recursive listings of entire directories. Nearly all directories will have been touched in the last month or so, and they will give you unwanted data.

Search root and /etc as well as /usr/lib for modified files. If the DECserver is a YP server as well, be sure to take the YP data base. Put all the file names in a *save file* and sort this file with the -u option to get rid of repeats. Here are some of the files to be restored:

```
root:
 .cshrc
 .login
 .profile
 .rhosts
```

---

[7] Use shutdown with no arguments.

```
etc:
 crontab
 fstab
 group
 gettytab
 exports
 hosts
 hosts.eqiv
 inetd.conf
 netgoups (YP server only)
 networks
 passwd
 printcap
 rc.local
 sendmail.cf
 termcap
 ttys
```

Planning Partitions

You may want to use the migration as an opportunity to resize user disks, but pulling off the system disk, resizing it, and reloading the system usually are enough to keep you busy. The OEM's distribution notes give you a recommended size for your new `root` partition. Do not trustingly believe that the old sizes are all right, for most of the time the system will have grown. It rarely stays the same size, and I've never seen it get smaller.

The `/usr` disk takes the most sizing work. You will have to list all the `/usr` software that you intend to load. The size of each package is in the distribution notes. What dynamic file systems live on `/usr`? It depends on the UNIX versions. At this writing, ULTRIX-32 is a BSD 4.2 derivative. In BSD 4.2 there are many, but in BSD 4.3 there are few. On the VAXserver, the `/usr` disk, ra0d, also holds the crash-dump area and dynamic log files. You hand-calculate the totals like this:

Crash	32 M
Logs	15 M
Software	35 M
	82 M

There you have it. The `/usr` disk takes about 82 megabytes, give or take a few blocks to give proper cylinder alignment during repartitioning.

Here are other system file sizes:

File system	Size	Partition
/	7.5 M	a
var	14 M	e
swap	33 M	b

This system uses a DEC RA 82 disk for the system disk and RA 90s for all user disks. The partitioning leaves 460 megabytes on the system disk for additional storage. Swap is minimal because it is a dedicated file server.

Now is the time to line up the distribution tapes. There are three TK 50 tapes for this installation. The first is the stand-alone UNIX tape, which provides a memory-resident UNIX as well as enough goodies to get the installation started. Next is the DEC-supported software tape, followed by the unsupported tape. It is an OEM tradition to give you desirable software but to disclaim responsibility for it by declaring that it is unsupported.

Basic Installation

The actual system installation starts by setting the terminal to 7 bits and space parity. Because it is a DEC system, it's safe to assume that it will have a VT terminal. This terminal can be readily set, but uses DEC control characters. An escape key would make your life a lot easier when you're working in vi.

Take the system down to the halt state, and then boot it from tape:

```
>>> b dua□
```

The installation software asks for the root drive, traditionally ra□a. Next it requests the following:

- System name (host name).
- Time and date.
- Time zone.
- root password.
- Field-service password.[8]

The installation script allows a *default install*, but let's assume that you want the *advanced install* segment because it allows you an educated choice.

Before the system software can be loaded, the disks have to be repartitioned and reformatted. Feed the installation software the sizes you calculated for the □ disk, and it will do the format work for you.

You must know in advance which software packages you want. On this server you don't need the following:

- Accounting package.
- International tools.
- RAND mail.
- Pascal.
- SSCS.

Because servers won't need all the software that stand-alone systems and workstations use, you should save a few megabytes for more useful purposes. No one is ever going to be able to log on, so why bother with the accounting package or Pascal?

Kernel Options

The installation procedure generates a new kernel, and you don't have to edit the GENERIC kernel configuration file. This is the only time that you can avoid manually editing

---

[8] This is a password other than root's that is set up for DEC hardware personnel.

the configuration file. On your next configuration you will have to do the installation longhand. However, let's say you do wish to change some parameters. Answer yes to the parameter changes, and you can manually edit the kernel configuration file. Here you can change system parameters like `maxusers` and `maxuproc`, but let's imagine that you also want to add the following options:

- LAT (local area transport).
- Bisynchronous communications protocol.
- CI, the computer interconnect network.

To add these, you will find it helpful to keep the disk controller information handy. For the server's `ra` disks it is

```
uq0 at uda0 csr 0172150 vector uqintr
```

The `uq0` and `uda0` device addresses are controllers; `csr` is the control status register address; and `vector` is the vector interrupt.

Once past the question-and-answer period, the system regenerates, and a new `/vmunix` is created and installed. Bring the system down and reboot it from disk:

```
>>> b
```

As the system comes up, look for the new version and system name followed by the `login` prompt:

```
ULTRIX-32 V 3.2 (fm01)
login:
```

If you get that prompt, your system generation and installation have been successful.

MAINFRAME CONFIGURATION

It's hard to take a mainframe out of a box; you usually have to take the box off the mainframe. Mainframe UNIX system administrators refer hardware problems to FEs,[9] thereby leaving themselves free to concentrate on the installation and configuration of operating system updates.

Configuring a mainframe system is more complex than configuring smaller UNIX systems, but it is fascinating because of the mainframe's size and complexity. Mainframes need to be configured more often because of all the work done on them. The number of devices on a large system is staggering, up to 4096 devices, or fff hex devices. On 370-architecture you can count on finding EBCDIC terminals and printers. Many variables are unique to 370 mainframe configuration.

You may well go into shock the first time you have to do system work on a UNIX system and find yourself on a 3270 or 3290 terminal. It will be clear right off the bat that they are not ASCII. Many keys are missing, and there are new ones that make no sense at all, like the cent sign, the "golf club," and two very different pipe symbols. To

---

[9] On mainframe sites you buy both software support and hardware support. When you buy hardware support, Field Engineers either work on site or come when you call.

add insult to injury, you will have to find the two-character input sequence to fake the missing ASCII characters in order to have a full set of metacharacters.

Although configuring a mainframe system is complicated, there are some compensations. It usually is a source system, so you don't have to hunt for system parameters the way you do on smaller systems. Even on mainframes with a binary UNIX license (nonsource), there is limited source code. Refer to the configuration source directory, /usr/src/uts/uts/conf, or its Brand-X equivalent (see Chapter 14).

Configuration starts with getting space. Your sysgen will fail if you don't have enough disk blocks or inodes on either your root disk or your /usr/src configuration disk. A large number of inodes are needed to create a /newdev directory, which is on the root disk to create a temporary device directory. On big machines I try to keep at least 3000 spare inodes on the root disks just to be on the safe side.

Mainframe UNIX can be very pure, in spite of being a superset of UNIX and a guest operating system.[10] It relies on its host VM system to handle the real devices, so UTS need concern itself only with virtual devices. UNIX likes virtual memory and virtual devices. It is a good marriage.

Disk Partitions

Disk partitions are taken from the host system. UNIX is free to cut any partition into smaller pieces, such as /dev/dsk/??0s0 and /dev/dsk/??0s1, but the basic disk partition comes from the VM host system. Partitions are called *minidisks*. You can get one by either befriending a VM system programmer or becoming a VM programmer yourself.

A copy of the machine's VM directory is taken from the VM system by using the VM dirmaint facility. Imagine that you are working on a virtual machine called UTSV1. You work from a B-privilege CMS account. Here's how you get a copy of the machine's VM directory into your CMS reader:

```
dirm get UTSV1
```

You have to convince VM that you have the system password. After querying the VM reader and getting the number of the file, it is received into the CMS account's disk space. You receive the file using the VM receive command or with an interactive facility called rdrlist, and you can edit in the new disk address.

It is easier to get the big picture from a dirmap copy of the system's real disks and addresses. The dirmap command puts a copy of the system's DASD in your file system. If you want to see what the bottom of the printer-paper box looks like, you can print it, but it's faster to read it with the XEDIT editor. Look for disk packs that are already assigned to the virtual machine in the dirmaint directory output. The key word to search on is *GAP*. Find a gap either precisely as large as you want or one twice as large as the one you want, so that when you take a piece, you will leave an equally large piece. Try to avoid fragmenting the pack by leaving 5-cylinder gaps all over the disks. It is better to allocate the extra cylinders than to leave them unused and virtually inaccessible.

Once you have located a usable gap on the disk, take the start and end information, and edit the directory obtained from dirmaint. Enter the starting address and cylinder length, and assign it a VM address. Normally it is the same address that the UNIX

---

[10] Amdahl's UTS runs as both a VM guest and a native version.

system uses. If the UNIX device is going to be /dev/dsk/ff0s0, assign the address ff0 to the minidisk. The edited directory is put back into the system and activated with this line:

```
dirm  repl UTSV1
```

Redoing vmap verifies the entry.

It is easy to make an error of 1 on calculating both the length and the ending address, because the beginning address already counts as one cylinder. For example, a starting address of 0 and an ending address of 10 are 11 cylinders. Be sure that you have not overlapped any addresses.

The minidisk is available to UNIX once the directory is updated. Most VM CP commands can be executed by root from UNIX with the UTS prefix command cpcmd. The disk must be linked to the virtual UNIX machine:

```
# cpcmd link \* ff0 ff0 mw
```

Here we link the new disk at VM virtual address ff0 to the UNIX machine as ff0. The asterisk means *this* system, and the backslash is necessary to prevent the shell from wildcarding the asterisk as the entire contents of the current directory. The mw stands for *multiwrite* privilege.

A query will show if the disk has been recognized:

```
# q ff0
```

This may seem complicated if you don't know VM, but it's simple once you get the hang of it. Learning another operating system well enough to gain some degree of proficiency takes a lot of work, but it's worth it. You can observe the virtual UNIX machine and compare it with other virtual UNIX machines on the same physical machine. The system diagnostics available to VM/CP are sophisticated, and they produce good information for tuning. Also, individual UNIX guests can have separate and different share priorities set.

The disk can be formatted once it has been made available to UNIX. Like XENIX, the UTS UNIX format command formats the hard disks. The rest is all standard UNIX, with mkfs making the file system and a UTS command making lost+found. Like all UNIX systems, a directory must be made and the disk mounted:

```
# mkdir /new_group
# /etc/mount /dev/dsk/ff0s0 /new_group
```

Configuration and sysgen

Most items to be configured in the mainframe UNIX system are in a configuration file called /etc/devicelist. Note that devicelist is an ASCII file intended for editing by the system administrator. It starts with VM unit devices, printer, punch, and reader. The addresses are associated here:

```
00c reader
00d punch
00f printer
00e printer
```

Next come the disk devices or DASD:

```
110 dasd /usr
220 dasd
221 dasd /tmp
222 dasd
330 dasd /usr/src
440 dasd /usr/adm
550 dasd /usr/spool
551 dasd /usr/spool/console
660 dasd /usr/man
770 dasd /support
```

The list can run all the way up to address fff. A mainframe system supports a lot of devices!

Next comes the terminals. Ranges are specified, and one entry can generate a half-dozen screenfuls of `ttys`:

```
600-6fff 3278m2 tube 2
600-6fff unshared
```

Now let's look at tape drive addresses. Like all other VM/UTS addresses, they are virtual. The real addresses are `attached` by the console or tape operator when a tape mount is requested:

```
180-184 tape
```

Then `devicelist` goes on with other device addresses and finishes with system constants that can also be found in the system header files in `/usr/include/sys`:

```
timezone = 0*60
localtod = 1
dlimit 522m/512
nproc = 300
nbuf = 300
ncall = 100
nodename = utsv1
```

Note that `timezone` is set to 0, because this machine runs on GMT. Each user is responsible for setting his or her local time zone because this machine serves international users. Even users sharing a state line on a time zone like California to Arizona need time zone resolution. The user `.profile` should contain a `TZ` entry such as

```
TZ=PST8PDT;export TZ
```

Any constants defined in `/etc/devicelist` are sent to appropriate C code when the system is compiled.

sysgen

The system generation procedure, `/etc/sysgen`, pulls all the header files, makes the appropriate C code and intermediate files or object files, and links a new kernel. It also makes an entirely new `/dev`, which it hides in a pocket called `/newdev`. When complete, all is ready, but nothing is installed. It is ready for a `newsys`.

newsys

The newsys program is the partner of sysgen, and it installs the /nuts new kernel, as uts. It also writes the /newdev directory to /dev. The old kernel is copied from /uts to /outs and can be booted in a pinch if the new kernel fails.

HOW TO HANDLE BAD BLOCKS

We need to consider where the hardware meets the software, at the very surface of the disk's platter. Here binary ones and zeros are formed in the microscopically thin surface of iron oxide on the disk's surface.

There probably is no such thing as a perfectly formed disk. Mistakes in chemistry and the thickness of the magnetic medium inevitably cause errors. Similarly, defects in the substrate or the aluminum disk cause errors.

Read/write heads skim over the platter's surface on a thin film of air, and on cheaper disks the heads ride on a sort of nonstick coating. In time the heads will wear through the coating and hit the medium. In the air-bearing heads a hard jolt can cause the heads to contact the medium, with the result being a bad spot in the medium.

Disks also come with bad spots that become even worse with time. If we had to throw out every disk that went bad, we would still be storing data on paper tape and cards. How does the computer industry live with bad spots on disks?

You can always try to ignore bad spots. A list of bad spots is kept on the disk itself, usually on its *boot block* and/or its *label*. The system reads the bad-spot table and stores it. The controller then uses this information to skip over the bad spot, and so the bad spot doesn't seem to exist. This is fine for a new disk, but how about a disk that has seen service for some time?

A better method for dealing with bad spots is to set aside a set of tracks as alternative tracks for storing data that would have been on the blocks marked bad. These tracks are usually at the disk center, and thus the smallest-diameter tracks are near the rotational center of the disk. These are surrogate sectors, and bad tracks are mapped to the surrogate tracks. Then when data are needed, the heads run from the bad track to the surrogate track. Unfortunately, there is also a large hit on performance, and *disk contention* is created.

Berkeley 4.3 came up with a remedy for the rapid head movement caused by surrogate tracking by adding another sector to each track of the cylinder. This sector is called a *slipping sector*. When a bad sector is discovered, its address is mapped over to the slipping sector. Now the head remains literally on track and only has to miss its skew. Slipping is usually combined with surrogate tracks, so if more than one bad sector is on a single track, it can be mapped over to the alternative track.

Disk preparation methods and strategies are largely dependent on the hardware. The choice is a matter of disk and controller type. SCSI (pronounced scuzzy) disks and controllers lack sophistication and settle for the alternative track solution. They simply substitute logical sectors for real ones by mapping a bad sector's read address to an alternative logical sector. ESDI is a more sophisticated controller for the SCSI bus, as its increased performance capabilities allow for slipping. The SMD disk controller is the high end of disk controller intelligence, and it uses both slipping and alternative tracks.

Marking Bad Spots

Good disk maintenance calls for thorough disk cleanup from time to time. At the software level you should take the data off to an archive on either tape or disk. Then you read the data back in to eliminate fragmentation. This is a good opportunity to reformat the disk and do an `mkfs` to recreate the superblock. Actually, the best plan is to go all the way back to basics and start with bad-track maintenance. Here is the sequence of operations:

- Remake the boot track or label by testing and marking all bad spots.
- Format it.
- Make a new file system.
- Read the archive back to disk.

Mapping Bad Spots

Creating a map of a disk's bad spots is a primitive operation, most often done from a memory-resident version of the operating system so that the root disk can be mapped. It can also be done from conventional UNIX when using multiple disks or when using an SMD disk and controller. The SMD controller has sufficient intelligence to allow operations on a disk partition without disturbing the rest of the disk.

When a disk is assembled at the factory, it is thoroughly tested to find bad spots. This bad-spot information is printed to an information sheet and an external disk label, and both are shipped with the drive. Computer OEMs also create a bad-spot map on the disk itself. Never lose the original map. You will acquire new bad spots in time, and you will never lose the original ones.

XENIX has the `fdisk` command to partition the disk. Its options are to display the current bad-track table and to scan the disk for bad tracks. Sun's `suninstall` and `format` commands are similar but broader in scope. All manufacturers have some form of disk-scanning and -mapping utility. Most require running from memory, tape, or a floppy-resident version of UNIX to be able to scan the `root` disk.

If you need to start from scratch, do a disk scan that enables your computer to find its own bad tracks. After the scan, read the bad-track information produced. If necessary, add the bad-track information obtained from the manufacturer. On systems in which the bad-track information is already on disk, do your scan and compare it with the bad-track table on the disk label. If the last scan contains all the original bad-track information plus the new bad spots, save the new data to tape, and write the data to the disk label. Remember that all the diagnostics in the world and editing of the bad-track tables do you no good if you forget to write them to disk.

Bad-Track Maps

Bad tracks are mapped by cylinder, track, and offset, known as *Bytes from Index*, or BFI. Here is the top of a hard error map from a Seagate SCSI drive:

```
HD      CYL     MFM BFI         HITS
----------------------------------------------
0       39      9016            2
0       408     4839            18
1       610     5604            32
1       189     9772            34
2       347     264             19
.
.
```

For comparison, look at the defect list produced by Sun's `format` command:

```
num     cyl     hd      bfi     len     sec
1       86      7       32641   2
2       171     9       2352    2
.
.
-hits return for more-
23      730     0       36468   3       23
.
```

Notice that there is a little more sophistication here, as the length of the defect is noted as well.

The OEM does not use sectors but prefers BFI. You will opt for the cylinder, head, and sector partitioning convention:

```
cyl/head/sector
```

When you ask the system for disk analysis, it responds with information like this:

```
analyze> read
.
    pass 0
24/4/14

    pass 1
Block 10944 (17/5/19), Corrected media error (hard data ecc)
  25/9/23

    pass 2
.
```

Here (17/5/19) refers to cylinder 17, head 5, and sector 19. This format is necessary to permit you to move onto disk repair, which expects this specific information rather than the head, cylinder, and BFI format used for the original tracks. Note the disk repair:

```
format> repair
enter defective block number: /24/4/14
ready to repair defect, continue? y
Repairing /24/4/14
Repair succeed
.
```

See how easy it is when you stick to the cylinder/head/sector format? You don't want to figure BFI, nor does the manufacturer expect you to.

Menu options for OEM disk maintenance commands vary in implementation and method of use. Regardless of name, in order to do disk repair, an OEM disk maintenance command must be able to do the following:

- Print the defect list.
- Search the disk for defects.
- Repair the defects.
- Edit the defect list.
- Write the new defect list to disk.

You cannot edit the defect list with an editor. Also, the new defect list is not in effect until it is written to disk.

With all of this in mind, have ready your system manuals, READMEs, and tutorials. On new disks it is a good idea to run a full disk analysis in spite of the manufacturer's preshipping tests. You never know what damage occurred in shipping. A reformat can't hurt either. On used systems, you will be miles ahead if you do a total disk cleanup from time to time. Take everything off to a clean disk or to tape. If you have a spare disk, simple disk rotation is an effective cure as long as you repair and reformat the old disk before putting it back in service. If you have no spare, after the backup do a thorough surface analysis of the disk. If the number of bad spots is excessive, it may be time for a new disk. At the very least it's time to send out the old disk for a mechanical cleanup and repair.

Once satisfied that the disk is mechanically OK, complete your disk analysis, create a new defect list or append the old one, and write the list back to the disk. Then you can reformat, make new file systems, and bring the data back from tape. Take advantage of the clean disk to recover disk fragmentation by doing a recursive descent read on the way back so that all data are contiguous.

MANAGER'S CORNER

Planning the Installation

Putting in a new system requires much planning. Whether it is a first-time system or an operating system upgrade, the quality of the installation depends on how much preparation time you put into it.

A surprising number of systems are put in "on the fly." You make partitions and parameters as large as you dare, because nobody will know that you could have done a better job. Of course, the users will pay, because they will be short of machine resources. The users get shortchanged whenever you steal disk space and real memory for the system.

If you are a system administrator, take the time to write out a plan for your installations. If you are a manager of UNIX systems, and an installation is coming up, request a copy of the installation outline. Where does this configuration information come from? Some comes from experience, but to start you can fall back on useful system-sizing information from the old system you are replacing, the OEM's recommendations, and the recommendations of other system administrators. The OEM publishes the size of all major software packages and systems in its release notes, with root's size given as a recommended number. The size of /usr must be calculated, but the OEM supplies the size of all packages in /etc as part of the distribution package.

The second step toward a good configuration is an intimate knowledge of the hardware, particularly for larger systems, both minis and mainframes. Why have the kernel carry a huge amount of unwanted junk on devices it doesn't have when you would rather run with a lean and efficient kernel? The purchase order for the system is the best starting place to learn about the system hardware. Next go back to the catalog from which you ordered the system and reread pertinent areas. The old kernel configuration file is another good place to find hardware information.

Watch for features that you either didn't buy or don't want on your system. The last thing you want to do is install software you don't need. For example, of what use is the Source Code Control Program, SSCS, on a system that is a full-time server on which nobody's going to do any programming? You don't need Pascal on that server either. Similarly, if you have a DEC that doesn't happen to need Local Area Transport protocol, why include the LAT package in your /usr area and needlessly configure the kernel for it?

The time of day and the day of the week are critical to installations. Fridays at the end of prime time are a good time to install a small- to medium-sized data center. If anything goes wrong, you will have the entire weekend to straighten out the mess. If you are bound by a service-level agreement (see Chapter 22) to a weekend downtime, start the installation first thing on Saturday morning.

Do two things in the same downtime slot whenever possible, and use installations to leverage other advantages. For example, let's say you have a major bug in the system and need to install a patch. If it's possible to install the new release a little sooner, you can probably avoid installing that patch, because the new release will probably incorporate all the changes that the patch does. Conversely, if you have critical user software that doesn't run on the new operating system release, put off the new-release installation until the users finish up the jobs using that software.

Above all, be sure to allocate enough time for planning the installation as well as for the installation itself. See that you have backed up the system fully before the installation begins, including the old system's root disk. Remember that once you resize and reformat the disks, their entire contents will be erased. Finally, don't leave the installation to one individual but provide backup personnel. You'll never regret it.

12

Startup, Initiation, and Shutdown

BOOTING THE SYSTEM

The initial phase of any UNIX system startup is the *boot*, the process of the system's bringing itself up. The operating system must somehow load enough of itself into memory to be able to take control and bring the remainder of the OS into memory in order to start that continuous process that we call the *kernel*.

You might think that startup should be the same on all UNIX systems, but UNIX made no provisions for booting. It must be booted from another operating system. On most hardware that "operating system" is prom resident, so small that it hardly merits being called an operating system. Nevertheless, it brings itself to life and performs limited but vital functions. For what it does, it is complete.

Not all UNIX systems have to boot from a boot prom; mainframe UNIX systems running on a VM platform are booted by the VM operating system. Systems dedicated to a network existence can be booted from the network itself. Other options include booting from tape or a diskette. Many UNIX systems—such as larger DECs, some MicroVAXs and the larger Suns—have multiple system boot options: tape, network, or prom.

Booting from a prom means powering up and waiting for some sort of prompt at the console. On a PC AT type of system it looks like this:

```
boot:
```

You hit the *return* key to start loading the UNIX system. Enter ᴅos to bring up PC-DOS.

You will see the greater-than prompt on many Suns and DECs:

```
>
```

This prompt invites a simple mnemonic to start the boot from the default disk, usually a b for *boot*. Here's what you do on Suns:

```
> b
```

On DEC systems you respond to three greater-than prompts:

```
>>> b
```

Alternative boot mnemonics can be used:

```
> b fd()
```

On Sun systems this tells the prom-resident program to boot from diskette.

On UTS mainframe UNIX you log on from a CMS prompt as if you are just another user:

```
log UTS1
```

The system is loaded into VM's program space and is booted by *initial program load* to a known disk address:

```
ipl 220
```

On many small UNIX systems the rc script is rewritten by OEMs and VARs to hide the entire boot operation and the single-user phase of initiation. An AT&T 3B 2 comes up in multiuser mode with no stopping along the way. In fact, it is not possible to bring old 3B 2 System V Release 2 systems from a cold start directly to init s without altering rc.

Sun 386i workstations come up in multiuser mode, too. It makes sense for them to do so, as you don't want workstations to come up in single-user mode. Let's say you have a site with fifty workstations. Imagine having a power outage at this site. Do you want to bring up fifty workstations from single-user mode to multiuser mode? Also, the system automatically gives privilege when you come into single-user mode. It assumes that root is logged on, but this allows nonprivileged users way too much power.

To get the prom prompt, a Sun workstation must be brought up and then taken down again and halted deliberately. This is how it's done:

```
# shutdown -h now
```

The only other option is to halt the processor during the first few seconds of initiation to get the boot prompt.

Booting instructions from a prom can get relatively complex for a prom-based program. A particular disk and address can be specified, as seen here on a larger Sun system:

```
> b sd(0,0,0)vmunix
```

This boots /vmunix, the kernel, from the root partition of a disk of type sd. This is an ideal opportunity to boot from an alternative kernel. Sometimes you try a newly created kernel only to find out it is flawed. Then you can boot from the old kernel you saved by specifying `vmunix.save` as the desired system image during the manual boot process.

Going directly to single-user mode takes a little bit of work on some systems. Here a VAX-11/750 is taken to single-user mode only:

```
>>> b/3
```

The variations in UNIX system boot procedures are endless; the point is to know what sort of boot you are looking for and how to get it.

INITIATION LEVELS: A SYSTEM V STATE OF MIND

There is a major division between AT&T System V UNIX and other UNIX versions. System V has initiation levels, and the file `/etc/inittab` clearly defines what is expected at each. All levels can be defined by the administrator, but level `s` and level `2` are traditionally left to the initial system definition of single-user mode and multiuser mode.

System V's `who` command has been modified to show these current and past initiation states:

```
$ who -r
    run level 2 May 23 19:30 2 0 S
```

The `who -r` command is very useful to the system administrator. Let's say you've defined several multiuser states. When you walk up to a machine and you're not sure what state you're in, you not only need to know what state you're in now but also what state you came from to get there.

Edition 7 UNIX, XENIX, and all current BSD systems do not have initiation states. When UNIX is booted, they bring themselves into a single-user process and deliberately do not mount any disks other than `root` and the swap disk. Booting to single-user mode allows the administrator to do any necessary housekeeping before going to multiuser mode. The single-user process is killed with an interrupt, usually a ^D, and is then replaced with the multiuser process. That multiuser process fires the `rc` script, which starts the network, printers, and UUCP; mounts the disks; gets `cron` going; and other things.

OEMs frequently add enough code to the boot prom and `rc` to hide part of the boot process. For example, most XENIX systems boot by simply hitting *return* to the `boot:` query. Then they transparently go through the initial boot process until the disks have been checked, and `fsck` is run automatically if necessary. But this is no guarantee against corruption; it has merely checked to see whether the last shutdown was graceful. If the system was dropped without running `shutdown`, it will run `fsck`. Now, rather than starting out in multiuser mode, the script gives you a chance to enter the `root` password in case you want to do any maintenance. If you do, you will remain in single-user mode. And if you want to go to multiuser mode, you enter a ^D. When a Control D is entered, you kill the single-user interface, start `rc`, and enter the multiuser interface.

XENIX systems are not unusual, for most desktop systems go straight to multiuser mode. At best they pause briefly to give you a fleeting shot at single-user mode. Even larger DEC MicroVAX systems and VAXservers go straight to multiuser mode in the as-configured state.

There is no one best way to come up. The uneducated user needs as simple a boot process as possible, but the knowledgeable user who also administers the system wants a quick boot with the option of doing some light maintenance if necessary. Full-time administrators want to come up directly in single-user mode, thereby allowing them to run fsck and do other system maintenance before letting users on the system.

SYSTEM V INITIATION

UNIX comes up as a single-user system. It usually has one mounted disk partition (the swap area) and one mounted file system (root) with two running processes, the swapper and init. The swapper reads processes in and out of secondary memory, and the portion that reads processes in is the first process started. The init process is the parent of all user processes and the second process started as UNIX comes up.

In single-user mode, with no file systems mounted other than root, the system is used by root only to do necessary housekeeping and maintenance. The system executes the rc family of scripts at the next normal level, init 2.

Not only the parent of all user processes, init also controls its own process level. First let's quickly review the usual init levels:

- init 0: power down (not standard on all UNIX systems).
- init s or S: single-user mode.
- init 2: multiuser mode.

Note that init s is traditionally single-user mode and init 2 is usually multiuser mode. The other modes are whatever they have to be. All init levels, including s and 2, can be defined by the system administrator, for example:

- init 5: firmware mode.
- init 6: return to firmware and reboot.
- init a through c: "pseudo" run states for telinit.

As noted, BSD and XENIX do not use System V initiation levels. XENIX adds new function to System V Release 2's enable/disable command pair, because it uses enable and disable to turn on and off devices such as ttys and printers.

Device initialization and just about everything else takes place in /etc/rc. There is an entire family of rc scripts with names like local.rc or rc.local, bcheckrc, and brc. There also are rc directories on some systems like /etc/rc.d. The traditional script on 90 percent of all systems is simply called rc, with bcheckrc and brc added about the time of System V. They are executed by inittab before rc; if nothing else, they clear /etc/mnttab of mount entries. The brc script is controlled by /etc/inittab:

```
# grep brc /etc/inittab
mt::sysinit:/etc/brc >/dev/console 2>&1
```

The `mnttab` file is a data file that keeps track of mounted file systems. It uses a structure defined in `/usr/include/mnttab.h`:

```
struct mnttab {
  char    mt_dev[32],
  char    mt_filsys[32];
  short   mt_ro_flg;
  time_t  mt_time;
};
```

The contents of `mnttab` can best be seen with a character or hex dump. Here is a character dump:

```
# od -c /etc/mnttab
0000000   /   d   e   v   /   d   s   k   /   c   1   d   0   s   0  \0
0000020  \0  \0  \0  \0  \0  \0  \0  \0  \0  \0  \0  \0  \0  \0  \0  \0
0000040   /  \0  \0  \0  \0  \0  \0  \0  \0  \0  \0  \0  \0  \0  \0  \0
0000060  \0  \0  \0  \0  \0  \0  \0  \0  \0  \0  \0  \0  \0  \0  \0  \0
0000100  \0  \0  \0  \0   "   h  \r 241   c   1   d   0   s   2  \0  \0
0000120  \0  \0  \0  \0  \0  \0  \0  \0  \0  \0  \0  \0  \0  \0  \0  \0
0000140  \0  \0  \0  \0  \0  \0  \0  \0   /   u   s   r  \0  \0  \0  \0
0000160  \0  \0  \0  \0  \0  \0  \0  \0  \0  \0  \0  \0  \0  \0  \0  \0
0000200  \0  \0  \0  \0  \0  \0  \0  \0  \0  \0  \0  \0   "   h 376   K
0000220
```

Now look at a hex dump:

```
# od -x /etc/inittab
0000000 2f64 6576 2f64 736b 2f63 3164 3073 3000
0000020 0000 0000 0000 0000 0000 0000 0000 0000
0000040 2f00 0000 0000 0000 0000 0000 0000 0000
0000060 0000 0000 0000 0000 0000 0000 0000 0000
0000100 0000 0000 2268 0da1 6331 6430 7332 0000
0000120 0000 0000 0000 0000 0000 0000 0000 0000
0000140 0000 0000 0000 0000 2f75 7372 0000 0000
0000160 0000 0000 0000 0000 0000 0000 0000 0000
0000200 0000 0000 0000 0000 0000 0000 2268 fe4b
0000220
```

Examine the two dumps, and you can see the first 32-byte entries showing `/dev/dsk/c1ds0`. This is the `root` device, so there is no second entry on line hex 20. The entry starting at hex 108 shows `c1d0s2`, aka `dev/dsk/c1d0s2`, mounted as `/usr`.

The `/etc/brc` script can be as simple as a single line that calls `setmnt` to create the mount table `mnttab`:

```
/etc/devnm / |grep -v swap|/etc/setmnt
```

The `devnm` command identifies the special file `/dev/dsk/*` where its argument resides. The command line

```
/etc/devnm /usr
```

produces `/dev/dsk/c1d0s2` on an AT&T 3B, or `/dev/dsk/0s1` on a DEC. The `grep` command with the `-v` option removes a line with swap disk information, and `/etc/setmnt` is the final command that establishes the mount table `mnttab`. This all may seem much ado about nothing, but the system won't come up if `mnttab` is not there with the correct information.

Now let's look at bcheckrc, which works in cahoots with brc. It checks the root file system for sanity. On most systems it executes /etc/fsstat first to see whether a check is necessary. The root file system will fail its sanity test if fsstat returns a nonzero exit code. The root file system is checked for sanity, and fsck will be run if fsstat fails in the following bare-bones section from bcheckrc:

```
root='/etc/devnm |grep '[ ]/$'|( read a b;  echo ${a} )'
ret='/etc/fsstat ${root} 2>&1'
if [ $? -ne 0 ]
then
    /etc/fsck -y -D -b ${root}
fi
```

When brc puts the system into init s, S, or 1, and bcheckrc tests root for sanity, the stage is almost set for the move to multiuser mode. The rc script and its rc family of scripts take the system to other init stages,[1] and rc is controlled by lines in /etc/inittab. Here is a 3B version:

```
# grep rc /etc/inittab
fs::sysinit:/etc/bcheckrc </dev/console >/dev/console 2>&1
mt::sysinit:/etc/brc >/dev/console 2>&1
s2:2:wait:/etc/rc2 >/dev/console 2>&1 </dev/console
s0:056:wait:/etc/rc0 >/dev/console 2>&1 </dev/console
```

In this, rc is replaced by rc0 and rc2 for their appropriate initiation levels. The 3B version also goes to an rc.d directory and executes everything in sight.

Other systems call files like local.rc. The AT&T version has more flexibility with an rc directory called rcd. It allows you to create a categorized rc, so that you can have one for network scripts, one for devices, and so on. You can duplicate its flexibility with the following lines of code in rc:

```
for file in /etc/rc.d/*
  do
    if test -f ${file}
      then
        /bin/sh ${file}
  done
```

As a rule, the current and previous initiation states are checked by rc. The following is from a System V DEC rc script:

```
set 'who -r'
cur_mode=$7
no_times=$8
pre_mode=$9
if test ${cur_mode}=2) -a ${no_times}=0
  then
    do
     # everything to be done on entering multiuser mode
    done
fi
```

The test guarantees that the body of code will be executed only on going from init s to init 2 for the first time.

---

[1] An exception is AT&T's rc0 which is used to power down in init 0.

Initiation states are remembered from boot to boot, and are stored in `/etc/utmp` along with active login information. Tasks like mounting the disk systems are accomplished in `rc`'s code. Large machines with many disks execute a separate file like `/etc/mountlist`, which contains the `mount` commands:

```
# head /etc/mountlist
/etc/pagdev /dev/dsk/ee0s0
/etc/mount /dev/dsk/110s0 /usr
/etc/mount /dev/dsk/330so /usr/src
/etc/mount /dev/dsk/660s0 /usr/man
/etc/mount /dev/dsk/771s0 /eng1
```

These mounting chores are done in `/etc/rc.d/MOUNTFILESYS` on 3Bs, a function that is taken up and improved with `fstab` in BSD.

At this point in `rc` it is also a good time to clean up `/tmp`, the system's combination closet and garbage can:

```
rm -rf /tmp
mkdir /tmp
chmod 777 /tmp
chown sys /tmp
```

The `/tmp` dustbin deserves its own disk partition on all but the smallest systems. With `/tmp` on its own disk, the cleanup is saved until after mounting `/tmp`, and the cleanup looks quite different: Instead of making `/tmp`, it is simply cleaned out.

```
rm -rf /tmp/*
```

It is hard to single out the most important task of `rc`, but certainly initiating the `cron` daemon is very important:

```
$ grep 'cron' rc
/etc/cron
```

This daemon checks the `cron` tables at initiation and executes commands in the `cron` tables at the times and dates specified. If an entry is changed in `/usr/spool/cron/crontabs/*`, the cron daemon, `/etc/cron`, will have to be killed and restarted. The tables are in `/usr/spool/cron/crontabs`, and the most important is `/usr/spool/cron/crontabs/root`.

An entry in `/local.rc` or `rc.d`, or their equivalent, sets the node name[2]:

```
uname -S hunter1
```

The machine must have a unique node name, or it will be difficult to do any kind of networking.

Now let's look at some lines that must appear in `rc`, `rc.d/*`, or `local.rc` for the System V `lp` spooling system:

```
if [ -f /usr/spool/SCHEDLOCK ]
  then
     rm /usr/spool/SCHEDLOCK
fi
/usr/lib/lpsched
```

---

[2] Most machines require that the system node name be generated into the kernel.

Remember that we're in the process of bringing a machine up from the state it was left in when it was shut down. Old lock files thus may still exist that may prevent daemons from being started. Lock files *must* be removed:

```
rm -rf /usr/spool/locks/*
```

Network-related daemons must be awakened for TCP/IP, and it is safe to invoke them now that the lock files are removed. This is done by an addition to rc or in a separate script called by rc, such as NETSTART:

```
/etc/ftpd
/etc/tftpd
/etc/rlogind
/etc/rchd
/usr/lib/sendmail -bd -q30m
/etc/telnetd
/etc/rwhod
/etc/rexecd
/etc/fingerd
```

Calling the daemons one at a time works well, but it is relatively crude when compared with the Berkeley inetd daemon. As we shall see, BSD treats network daemons very differently.

BERKELEY rc AND INITIATION

BSD has no initiation states in the sense that System V does. Like UNIX Editions 6 and 7 and XENIX System V, BSD has two modes, single user and multiuser. On going to multiuser mode, the rc scripts are read. There may be an rc.boot that is followed by rc itself, which calls rc.local about halfway through its execution. When rc.local is completed, it returns execution to rc.

The widespread popularity of Berkeley UNIX was largely brought about by BSD's networking ability; indeed, the BSD rc scripts are definitely network oriented. We shall concentrate on some of the network portions of the BSD rc scripts, because should your system hang on initiation, the network section of rc is the most likely culprit.

In a network storm, rc often gets stuck trying to execute ifconfig. The last thing you will see is the portmapper chat lines, and then you will see nothing. The first network daemon invoked is the portmapper daemon, portmap:

```
if [  -f /usr/etc/portmap ]; then
   portmap && chat -n '  portmap'
fi
```

Typical of all rc lines, the daemon is first checked for its existence, and then it is executed. There is a *named function*, chat, whose principal job is to echo the argument portmap to the console.

Next ypserv is invoked, whose lines are commented out on all systems other than on NFS servers. Its counterpart, ypbind, is next in the script. Whereas the ypserv daemon meets the needs of clients requiring YP service, ypbind binds the client to the server for that service. If you have any doubts about how tightly it binds, watch the client's console when the server becomes unavailable. It will cry incessantly for the server. The server also runs ypbind, and it will complain bitterly if it is cut off from the network.

Now that the ports are safely mapped, it's time to assign addresses to the network interface. Anyone who does anything with networking is familiar with the OSI 7-layer network layer model. The network interface is wedged in between the IP layer and the hardware, a job for ifconfig:

```
if [ "NETWORKED" =  yes ]; then
    if ypwhich -m netmasks.byaddr > /dev/null 2>&1
    then
        ifconfig ie0 netmask +
    fi
    if [ -f usr/etc/in.routd ]; then
        in.routd && chat -n ' routd'
    fi
fi
```

The netmask argument of ifconfig specifying + as an option sends ifconfig looking to YP's netmasks.byaddr map for its information. The ie0 device name is the interface parameter, an Intel-Ethernet device. In almost the same breath the system starts the router daemon, routd.

The next two daemons hold hands: rpc.statd is the status daemon, and rpc.lockd is the lock daemon. Most administrators will comment them out if the system and applications software has no immediate need for them. Be sure that rpc.statd is commented out if rpc.lockd is disabled.

The rc.local script is always careful to make sure that the system is networked before it invokes network-specific tasks. The following script looks for the YP directory for the system's domain, but first it tests to see whether the system is networked:

```
if [ -d /var/yp/`domainname` -a "$NETWORKED" = yes ]; then
    chat -n "boot services"
    if [ -f /usr/etc/rpc.ipallocd ]; then
        rpc.ipallocd && chat -n ' ipallocd'
    fi
    if [ -f /usr/etc/rarpd ]; then
        rarpd ie0 && chat ' rarpd (ie0)'
    fi
    if [ -f /usr/etc/rpc.bootparamd ]; then
    .
    .
```

Why a system would have a YP domain data base and not be networked is a mystery, but one can never be too careful when writing system code. This last section of code assures itself that it is a networked system with a YP data base and domain. This being the case, it now goes about starting all the remote procedure calls required by YP.

The balance of network services is started next. NFS has its own particular needs. It uses the network to read files from a disk that is foreign to the local system, and to do this it needs both its own NFS daemons as well as I/O control and buffers similar to the system buffer cache. The biod daemon starts asynchronous block daemons, while nfsd starts the daemons that handle the client file system requests. One daemon is not enough, so both daemons are capable of starting multiple instances of themselves. There are at least four biod daemons and eight NFS daemons.

It is very important for system administrators to know about the next network section of rc, because you probably will want to comment it out. Here lies the infamous rwhod daemon, a champion resource hog. Executing a who on a remote system via rsh is much cheaper in resource.

Let's briefly review what has happened so far. First, init fired rc. When rc got about halfway through its execution, it called rc.local, and when rc.local does what it has to do, it returns execution to rc, and local services are initiated, including the uucp daemon, accounting, and sendmail. The sendmail portion is critical:

```
if [ -f /usr/lib/sendmail -a -f /etc/sendmail.cf ]; then
    (cd /var/spool/mqueue; rm -f nf* lf*)
    /usr/lib/sendmail -bd -q1h && chat -n '  sendmail'
fi
```

The existence of the sendmail command and the sendmail configuration file is checked. If they are there, the sendmail spooler area will be cleaned of unnecessary baggage. Then sendmail is started in daemon mode, with one hour to process any saved messages in the queue.

"Glue-on" versions of UNIX networking like Wollongong rely on a separate script like /etc/NETSTART to start the network daemons. Berkeley systems use inetd for the same purpose, but BSD does it with class. The inetd daemon line is located toward the end of rc itself, long after execution has returned from rc.local. The inetd daemon also is the internet service daemon. Once invoked from rc, it reads the file /usr/etc/inetd.conf or /etc/inetd.conf, the internet configuration file and data base. When inetd receives an internet request from a socket, this information is used to complete the request. In other words, instead of invoking separate daemons, Berkeley's inetd looks in its own configuration file, sees the services that have to be started, and starts them.

The inetd daemon is one of the last network daemons brought up by rc. It is preceded by uucp and followed by the printer daemon, the last rc daemon and the end of the rc script.

KNOWING rc

Most UNIX installations require more than we have outlined, and a few require less. While most are set up by the OEM or VAR that shipped the system, you, as the system administrator, need to know what it all means, because the first time any of it breaks or gets accidentally erased, you will be the one who must either restore it or recreate it.

The most frustrating experience you may ever have as an administrator is to have the machine refuse to come up into multiuser mode. Now your knowledge of rc and all the rc family is invaluable. Let's say the disk partitions on your system haven't mounted. If you know your rc script well, you will immediately know that you need to check for the existence of the /etc/mnttab line in rc:

```
$ fgrep mnttab /etc/*rc*
/etc/mnttab; chmod 644 /etc/mnttab
```

You look through the rc script around that point and search for the missing link. When trying to find out why the system failed to mount all file systems and enable the user facilities, inittab and rc will be your keys to the working of the entire multiuser operation.

SYSTEM V SHUTDOWN

All UNIX systems must be shut down gracefully. Once I was demonstrating to a staff programmer a Microport UNIX system on a 386 Intel PC. When the programmer was through with the system, he hit the power switch and turned off the system. When I asked him why he didn't take the machine through shutdown, he nonchalantly replied, "It's only a PC." Naturally that poor little system had to go through fsck twice before it could come up again.

Systems that have been forced or crashed always have file system damage. Both root and /usr/spool write temporary files that will be left without a directory reference if the system is not synced before shutdown.

The shutdown script enables you to bring down the system gracefully, and the /etc/shutdown scripts do at least the following:

- Warn all users of the impending shutdown.
- Kill all daemon and user tasks.
- Shut down add-on processes like the network.
- Unmount the disks.
- sync the system.
- Halt the processor.

The initial part of a shutdown script is a stall for time. The program tests to see not only whether the user is root but also whether the current directory is root. The most frequent test uses the id command:

```
eval `id!sed  's/[^a-z0-9=].*//'`
if test "${uid:=0}" -ne 0
then
    echo "$0: You must be root to run shutdown"
    exit 2
 fi
```

The id command produces this output:

```
# id
uid=0(root) gid=0(bin)
```

In the first line, the shutdown script passes id's output through sed to get rid of everything after the left parenthesis, (, by looking for the first nonalphanumeric that is not an equals sign and deleting everything from there to the end of the line. The eval command assigns the user-ID number to the variable uid. The test command can now evaluate uid. If it is not 0, the script will complain and quit.

Constructs like

```
${uid:=0}
```

are handy for the programmer, but they are Greek to those not adept in shell programming. With seemingly effortless finesse, the system programmers who created the rc scripts push Bourne shell to its syntactic limits. Translated, it means that if no value has been assigned to uid on the previous line, this test in the if statement will fail:

```
if test "${uid:=0}" -ne 0
```

As a result, the entire shutdown script fails. The ${variable:=value} parameter substitution is used to keep this from happening. If the variable is not set, the value following :$=$ will be substituted.

The test for the root directory is much simpler and more straightforward:

```
if test `pwd` != /
then
    echo "$0 You must be in the / directory"
    exit 1
fi
```

Now the script goes through a series of gyrations to get a time until shutdown. Then it alternates sleeping and passing warning messages to users. There is always a bailout line where you are asked whether you are really serious about bringing the system down. After that the script goes about the business of getting the system ready to come down.

You know the program is serious when it refuses to listen to any external attempts to stop it:

```
trap '' 1 2 3 15
```

Now only a SIG_KILL can terminate the script.

From this point the steps vary from one OEM system to another. Here's where you can add any of your own local code, like an add-on network shutdown:

```
$ cd /etc
$ grep NET shutdown
shutdown: /etc/NETSHUT
$ cat NETSHUT
echo "killing all network daemons"
kill -9 `ps -ae|egrep 'telnetd!rlogind!fingerd!....!ttylink!
   awk '{ print $1 } '`
#
```

The next step is unmounting your file systems. Before you can unmount the disk partitions, you must stop all processes using them. This is the job of killall, and shutdown executes this line:

```
/etc/killall
```

Now all open files are closed, and the disks are quiescent.

It's time to unmount the disk partitions. The code here varies from shutdown script to shutdown script. It's either a matter of OEM preference or your own personal shutdown philosophy. Most shutdown scripts are run by passing the output of mount through sed and a few other loops. My version is a little easier to follow, but like all code, it's a matter of personal coding preference:

```
for fsys in `/etc/mount¦sort -r¦cut -d" " -f3¦egrep -v '220¦vio'`
 do
    echo "unmounting ${fsys}"
    /etc/umount $fsys
 done
```

The importance of filtering `mount`'s output is to *reverse the order* of that output. Normal output puts file systems like `/usr` before `/usr/spool`. This makes `/usr` impossible to unmount, for you cannot unmount a disk that is busy. You also can't mount it if it has another mounted file system on it at the same time. Pass the `mount` output through `sort -r` to get around this. The `egrep` line prevents the `root` disk at address 220 and a memory device, `vio0`, from being unmounted.

The final step is to halt the processor. First a few `sync`s are always in order. The method of the final kill is as varied as the number of UNIX versions out there. Here are a few:

- `haltsys` (XENIX)
- kill `init` itself with `kill -3 1`, `kill -15 1`, or `kill -9 1`
- `init 0`: go to the hardware state
- `/etc/rc0`: go to the hardware state

Here are some typical final lines:

```
sync;sync
sleep 5
kill -3 1
```

Become familiar with your system's shutdown script, and be ready to modify it if necessary. Like `rc`, it is just another tool used to maintain the system.

The `shutdown` command comes in at least two versions. Some use a simple time parameter. But if you want to bring down the system immediately, the command lines are

```
$su
password:
# cd /
# shutdown 0
```

System V is a little more complicated because it gives not only a grace-period option but also allows bypassing of questions like `Do you want to continue?` System V's `shutdown` allows you to bring down the system to yet another initiation level. It can be used to go to `init s` so you can reinitialize `cron` and remount the disks. You must agree to everything to get an immediate shutdown from this version! Tell it 0 grace, and specify an `init` state of 0, the hardware state:

```
$ su
password:
# cd /
# shutdown -y -g0 -i0
```

BSD SHUTDOWN

Berkeley-based systems have a slightly different shutdown command syntax. A flag establishes the shutdown state. You can shut down with a reboot, or you can shut down and halt the processor. If the shutdown is immediate, express the time now. Thus the command line to shut down immediately and halt the processor is this:

```
# shutdown -h now
```

Shutting down with the option of rebooting quickly looks like this:

```
# shutdown -r now
```

MANAGER'S CORNER

Teaching Operations Procedures

The riskiest periods of air travel are the takeoff and landing. Likewise, the riskiest periods for a system are the boot and the shutdown. Both are run at the system's extreme of privilege, and in both ways files and file systems risk damage.

For this reason it is important that the operations and programming staffs be trained in the proper procedures for initiation and shutdown. The system administrator should write complete and accurate procedures for both processes. Periodically, the operations staff should be trained in all phases of caring for the systems, paying particular attention to startup and shutdown.

File system consistency checking must be emphasized when starting up the system. For shutdowns, the method of getting a *graceful* shutdown, recovering from a crash, and getting kernel dumps must be taught. All new procedures must be introduced at reasonable intervals, and repeat classes should be a regular item. Hands-on training is important as well.

Here's a quick war story to drive home a point. We had about a 50 percent turnover in operations, and it had been almost a year since the last training, so it was definitely time for another training session. I had just installed a solid-state paging device on my production mainframe systems, so the training classes were a welcome opportunity to introduce the procedures for booting the systems with the paging device.

In case of a power outage, it is particularly important that the operations staff know how to reformat the disks before allowing the systems to use them. Call it fate, but a week after the training course we had a system crash caused by a power failure. After the crash, two parallel mainframe UTS systems were brought up by two operators. One had attended the training session, and the other had not. Just as we hit prime time at 08:00 the next morning, one of the systems lost its mind and had to be forced into a very hard shutdown. It had been initiated without its page disk by the untrained operator. The sister system that was initialized by the trained operator had a fully functional, formatted page device, just as instructed in class.

The point is clear. Don't let your training classes slide. Training your operations staff is one of the most important system administration tools you have.

13

Custom and Deviant Systems

It is important for managers, system administrators, and system programmers to understand the differences among a standard system, a custom system, and a deviant system.

It is possible to create a UNIX system with minimum effort and minimum quality. You will have a standard, embryo system when you read distribution tapes or diskettes into the computer's hard disk. Make a user directory on top of /usr, add a user or two to the system, and you and a few others can do some useful work. It won't be much of a system, though, because you haven't done anything to tailor it to site-specific needs.

THE CUSTOM SYSTEM

An alternative is to make a value-added, custom system. The custom system precisely fits the needs and requirements of the user community and its administrators. UNIX systems aren't much when they come out of the box. Granted, it is the most wonderful operating system/software combination of all times, but it isn't a fully usable system until you fit it to the needs of your environment and applications. In the process of making UNIX into a user system, you have the opportunity to make a custom system.

A number of rules and traditions are used in the creation of a custom system, starting with building new directories. The rule is to follow UNIX traditions at all times. For example, when creating a local section for manuals, mirror the main system by creating /local/man and dividing that into a_man, u_man, and p_man, like its distribution counterpart, /usr/man.

Don't add anything to /usr unless absolutely necessary, and I mean *anything*, including user trees and local tools. Make a /local directory at root level. Add your user's file systems at root level, because at root level, user file systems have short path names, are easy to archive and back up, and keep /usr from being any more massive or cumbersome than it is already. If you have a small system and you want all users on the same disk partition, create a /u or /us or something similar. If you must put users on /usr, then create a /usr/users as a separate disk partition.

While you are adding directories, make a spare mount point or two, such as /mnt0, /mnt1, . . . , /mntN, to be used for temporary disk mounting. Mount point directories are necessary on PC-sized systems to mount file systems on floppy disk. On larger systems these mount point directories are used to mount hard disk partitions for jobs like restores, mass copies, and disk reorganizations.

rc

The rc files in /etc are the heart of the initiation system used to bring up the system. All additions and modifications to the system must be reflected here. Imagine adding TCP/IP to your XENIX or pre-SVR4 system: You have to start all the internet application daemons, such as telnetd, rlogind, and ftpd, from an rc file. On Berkeley systems it's handled by inetd, as we saw in Chapter 12.

/etc/profile

The environment given to each login even before executing the user's own .profile or .login is set in /etc/profile. Anything that is a default for everyone is set in stone here. Typical entries are

```
$cat /etc/profile
:
# /etc/profile
PATH=:/bin:/usr/bin:.:
export PATH
umask 022
q log
```

This is the place where you can put anything into the user environment or cause any command to be issued in the login process. In some companies it is customary to have each user read the host system console log message to pick up on any scheduled events. Say the command is q log: The line q log is entered last in the .profile given to new users. All users read the console log message when they log in, like it or not. A more subtle and sure way is to add the mandatory command to /etc/profile.

cron

The cron file is where all timed events are initiated. The system administrator's own cron file is /usr/spool/cron/crontabs/root. Bare-bones cron doesn't do much of anything. Rather, it is up to the system administrator to add timed cleanup commands, UUCP cleanup, accounting, and miscellaneous commands required by the local system to make it run well. All local additions have to be in cron. If an accounting process must be initiated at midnight Saturday (00:00 Sunday), the process must have an entry in the crontabs/root file:

```
03 0 * * * /bin/su adm -c " /local/lib/bb_actng"
```

accounting

Distribution tapes usually have `accounting` in `rc` and `cron`, but the entries are commented out:

```
$ tail rc
# If you want process accounting uncomment the following commands,
# mv /usr/adm/pacct /usr/adm/opacct
# > /usr/adm/pacct; chmod 644 /usr/adm/pacct
# [ -x /etc/accton ] && /etc/accton /usr/adm/pacct
```

If you want it to run, at the very least you must remove the comment symbol # from the executable lines:

```
$ tail rc
# If you want process accounting uncomment the following commands,
mv /usr/adm/pacct /usr/adm/opacct
> /usr/adm/pacct; chmod 644 /usr/adm/pacct
[ -x /etc/accton ] && /etc/accton /usr/adm/pacct
```

Every dollar has to be accounted for in a commercial computing environment, and process accounting can be used efficiently to charge users for their use of the resource. It is a great help to you, the system administrator, as well, because you can track users who never use their accounts as well as those who abuse their accounts. It also helps you track commands that are using much too much CPU time.

When you turn `accounting` loose, you have to create a routine that will regularly clean out old files in `/usr/adm` accounting. If you don't, old files will litter the `/adm` directories. You may want to create scripts to clean them out automatically, but every month be sure to traverse all the `/usr/adm` trees to see what was missed.

You will have to write extra scripts to do the work if you want even the smallest amount of sophistication in `accounting`. Although `awk` is a fine tool for extracting and summing information like group usage, beyond that you will have to create your own bill-back software (see Chapter 10).

Networking

Networking used to be UUCP. Like `accounting`, UUCP requires that you either uncomment or add lines in `rc`, initiate `cron` entries for cleanup, and create procedures for running and administering the dial-up network. Files in `/usr/lib/uucp` have to be appended to recognize ports and devices and to understand your network names and numbers. All this is important and is covered in Chapter 18.

Adding TCP/IP software to the system is a major undertaking. So if you are given the choice, buy a version of UNIX that already has TCP/IP as part of its standard software. Installing it well is another area in which the system administrator adds value to the system and truly customizes it, by making up scripts for starting and stopping the Internet daemons and by drawing up schedules and procedures for updating the `hosts` and `networks` files.

Backups

There are as many opinions on how to back up the system as there are commands to do it. Backups are not automatic on a distribution system. As the system administrator you have to define the backup method and schedule and to create operator-friendly scripts and procedures. With care and forethought, your system will also archive. Remember that backups can restore a system but that archives can make the system portable (see Chapter 5).

THE DEVIANT SYSTEM

As we have seen, the custom system modifies buffer and table sizes and makes up directories as needed to suit local requirements. Be careful to change only those system parameters that can be readily altered. First, modify the /etc files, like the rc family, and then add local commands, tools, and software. A custom system meets the special needs and requirements of the users and administrators, whereas a deviant system goes a step further and modifies kernel source code, commands, and utilities. It also alters table and buffer parameters that really shouldn't be touched.

The vendor that supplies your operating system, whether VAR or OEM, supports the system by contractual agreement, but most vendors draw the line of support at deviant systems. That is, if "untouchable" table and buffer sizes are modified, the support agreement will be void. And any modified kernel code will cancel the agreement. Even if the vendor company has good intentions and wants to support you, it really can't when you change your system so much that it fits the classification of *deviant*. The systems used by the vendor's support group no longer respond in the same way as your modified system does. So once you elect to make a deviant system, you're on your own.

But why would anyone want to make a deviant system? Many large-scale UNIX sites were forced to do it, for various reasons. UNIX was born on a computer with less computational power and address space than today's laptop has. The first UNIX was a small, multiuser system, whose hardware restrictions kept it proportionally small and whose open-file limit per user process was 20. In many UNIX versions it still is. The open-file limit wasn't changed to anything reasonable until System V Release 4, which removes open-file limits for root and gives both *hard* and *soft* limits to individual users. They default to 2048 and 64, respectively, and they can be tuned.

Now imagine a mainframe with all the memory that money can buy running with a 20-open-files-per-user process limit. For nearly a decade Amdahl's UTS UNIX was the only commercial UNIX for 370 mainframes. UTS did not open the 20-open-files-per-user process limit until late 1988, in UTS 580. Because the open-file limit was not a tunable parameter, it was not in /etc/devicelist, Amdahl's configuration file. Many site administrators thus found themselves compelled by user pressure to open up the limit by digging into config.c and config.h and altering forbidden table sizes.

Whenever you experiment with forbidden parameters, there will be some repercussions, such as filling the file table and inode table. Until you try it, you won't know if the changes you make will crash the system when too many users open a large number of files.

Whenever you experiment with forbidden parameters on UTS, you also will lose the fine support of Amdahl's hot line. There is no choice, because if a deviant UTS UNIX system crashes, there is no way for the people at Amdahl to duplicate the conditions.

I inherited some deviant systems. It is easy enough to walk into a deviant system, but getting out of it is a trick that defies description. My first move was to find out who required the deviation and why. As it turned out, the CAD tools used on the system were written in an obscure language ported to UNIX as well as CMS and VMS. The work being done required data from many files at a time, well over 20.

My cure was suggesting that virtual files be opened by the language. Files would be opened, buffered, and closed. As long as the buffers had data, it would appear to the application that they were open. The application would open, buffer, close, and maintain fewer than 17 files, plus standard in, standard out, and standard error. The idea was accepted. On moving to AT&T's System V Release 2, the deviant parameter was removed, and the systems were restored to standard distribution parameters.

Another example of the distributed system's not living up to expectations and environment is the old UNIX scheduler. The add-60-and-divide-by-2 scheduler worked fine on a PDP-7, I'm sure, but put it on a system that runs in decamips (10×10^6) and it becomes a bad joke. Three large jobs running at the same time all hit the same "maximum" priority within a few seconds of CPU time. Then they fight one another and all other jobs competing for a piece of the CPU. Big jobs hit the same priority quickly on a large system.

The fair-share scheduler went a long way toward righting the problem, but what was I to do before it arrived? Is bringing the system to its knees by running it with a massive overhead reason enough to alter the source code? How important is it to you? Keep in mind that should you elect a deviant system, you need to know what you and your staff are up to handling. This is no job for the timid. You need the mentality of a pioneer.

In the long run it is faster and cheaper to hire a kernel mechanic. Preferably the firm he works for has a record of this sort of work, and perhaps he has done the same job for someone else. Should there be side effects, make your contract specific, including both guaranteed results and a maintenance clause.

Drivers are an entirely different proposition. Installing a new driver is not considered making a deviant system but, rather, a normal part of UNIX operation. However, writing them is not for the faint of heart or the inexperienced. All UNIX systems, from PCs to mainframes, allow for the installation of drivers.

Should you decide to write your own drivers, heed a few words of advice. There are schools, seminars, and numerous books on drivers.[1] Use them. Don't reinvent the wheel. "Cookbook" the driver by building it from existing code. Everyone else does. Finally, be sure to test it thoroughly before letting it see the light of day on a production system.

SOMETIMES YOU NEED TO FALL BACK AND REGROUP

When you tailor your machine to the needs of your user community within the guidelines of accepted practice, you are customizing your machine. But when you deviate from those guidelines, you are creating a deviant system. Few system administrators go for a deviant

---

[1] Janet I. Egan and Thomas J. Teixeira, *Writing a UNIX Device Driver* (New York: Wiley, 1988).

system willingly. More often they find themselves in uncomfortable situations in which a deviant system is forced on them. Perhaps they come into a group and inherit an existing deviant system, as I did, and they have to support it until they can find a way out.

Companies are not always run in an enlightened way. Occasionally a few individuals use company politics to impose a deviant system on an administrator. Let's imagine that you have a system programmer in your group who is a legend in his own mind. He wants to rewrite `tar` because he claims that he can make it go faster and make it write more out to tape. He not only tells everyone in the group; he also goes over your head to your manager, who doesn't know much about UNIX, and he convinces the manager that the group will function better with his new-and-improved version of `tar`. Suddenly your arguments against a deviant system fall on deaf ears, and you are forced to accommodate his version of `tar`. It never runs that well, but as long as he is around to keep it going with programmatic duct tape and Band-Aids, you grit your teeth and make up your mind to live with the thing.

A year goes by, and you have had to suffer with this Frankenstein version of `tar` all that time. One day the system programmer who caused you all this trouble abruptly leaves your group. Now *you* are stuck with supporting his monster. The OEM won't help you. Whenever a system is changed that radically, you will pay the consequences in loss of support. Don't expect your own people to support it either. As system administrator, the buck stops at your desk every time.

If you ever find yourself in this kind of situation, remember that you can always back out of it by going back to the distribution tape. Don't forget that. As the system administrator it's your job to keep your machines healthy and running at optimum efficiency. When a system modification interferes with the well-being of your system, you have not only the right but also the authority to push for a return to a standard distribution system.

MANAGER'S CORNER

The Dangers of Deviant Systems

How does anyone get stuck with a deviant system? UNIX invites hackers. Hackers love to find out how things work, and that is commendable. System programmers need a reasonable knowledge of internals, but hackers love to go where no programmer has gone before. They want to go one step beyond and discover new horizons. This is where the hacker reigns supreme.

It is tempting to want to yield to users' requests for changes in the operating system. The users are your customers, and we all like satisfied customers. However, when they want you to rewrite the scheduler, you have to ask yourself, "Why didn't Bell Labs do it?" The UNIX kernel is complex now, and it is getting more complex at each release. There is no such thing as a simple change in the kernel anymore.

If you do need to modify the system, consider your options. Contact your system vendor, and see whether he or she is willing to tackle the change. Have your system administrator or system programmer read through the USENIX conference proceedings and find out whether anyone else has attempted the move you are considering. Let's say your users want to move entire processes in midexecution from a busy system to a vacant one. At the 1988 winter USENIX in Dallas, three papers were given in succession on that very subject. There is a Berkeley batch system available and a number of variations that would do the job. The Usenet is another valuable source of information, code, and advice. The last thing you want to do is let an overanxious, underexperienced system programmer jump in and try it because it would be a wonderful challenge.

Should you decide to modify the kernel, hire an experienced kernel mechanic or bring in a consultant who specializes in that *specific* area of the kernel. I have seen a single experienced kernel programmer come in for two weeks, make major modifications in the network portion of the system, and go back home, his work accomplished and tested. I have also seen in-house system "experimenters" spend six months rewriting a single device driver and then leave it with major bugs unfixed, the users' needs unmet. As the manager, the decision is yours. It is possible to have a professionally run, conventional system, modified within approved parameters and geared to the needs of your user community.

14

Configuration

UNIX SYSTEM CONFIGURATION

Most of us buy ready-to-wear clothes, and they fit us well enough. But if we want better-fitting clothes, they have to be tailored. Every piece of a customized garment is precisely measured and sized to fit us perfectly.

The UNIX operating system comes "ready to wear" with internal tables and other adjustable parts of the system presized and preset. For some installations, particularly small ones, presized and preset systems are fine and need no adjustment. On busy systems and on most larger installations, however, system administrators need to tailor the UNIX system to fit the changing needs of the specific installation. Changing the size and form of an operating system so it meets the needs of all the users and the software applications they run is called *configuring the system*.

UNIX is an erector set created with tinkering in mind. When you configure a UNIX system, you set the sizes of some kernel tables and system buffers.[1] You specify devices and assign addresses. The trick to system configuration is assigning the right size to your tables. When you choose too high or too low, your users and your system suffer the consequences. You must also specify the correct number of devices and designate the correct device types.

There are pronounced differences between the system configuration of AT&T UNIX System V and Berkeley UNIX. In System V you concentrate on tuning system parameters, and on Berkeley UNIX you concentrate on setting devices. If you administer

---

[1] The kernel tables expand and contract dynamically in UNIX System V Release 4.

a Berkeley system and you aren't familiar with tuning parameters, you will learn about a whole new world of system parameters when you read about configuring System V systems. If you are on a System V machine and you are not used to setting devices, you will learn when you study the devices section of a Berkeley system configuration file. Because many system administrators have to administer a site full of heterogeneous UNIX machines, some AT&T System V and some Berkeley, UNIX system administrators should be able to configure both versions of UNIX.

AT&T SYSTEM V CONFIGURATION

Configuration parameters are numeric constants that set the sizes of kernel tables or buffers. You will get to know them well as you learn to configure your UNIX system. For example, the kernel process table is constructed as an array of structures of process information. The NPROC parameter is the number of slots or entries in the process table. In other words, NPROC is the maximum number of user processes. Notice that NPROC is capitalized in System V UNIX. Because the kernel is written in C, its program constants are capitalized. Think of parameters as *system constants*.

The two main configuration areas are devices and table sizes. They are interrelated, and you will need to know how they work together to configure your system well.

Making Your System Too Big

When you first start administering UNIX systems, you might be tempted to take a conservative, "safe" approach to system configuration and make all the parameters as large as you think they must be to cover any possible system conditions. Unfortunately, it's not that easy. You can't make everything big enough to cover every possible circumstance because then the kernel will become huge and unwieldy.

Oversized systems waste precious memory space. Remember that *the larger the kernel tables are, the more memory the kernel will take up and the less memory your users will have*. If you don't leave enough memory for your users, you will handicap their performance.

Oversized systems also are more work to administer. If you define 500 ttys, you will get 500 lines of gettys every time you use the ps command. You won't have time to look at all those entries numerous times throughout the day.

Oversized systems waste resources. The more used addresses there are, the longer it will take to do an fsck, read inode tables, and read directory entries. Even a 73-MIP machine takes a long time to run fsck when most of the addresses are used. Creating hundreds of unused devices not only wastes the system's time but it wastes your time as well.

Making Your System Too Small

What happens if you make your superblocks, tables, and buffers too small? When you try to run the system too lean, your performance suffers. When the superblock's free list and many system tables get to about 90 percent full, the kernel must thrash before getting a piece of the resource. Specifically, when a mountable file system has nearly filled its inode limits at the user level, the system keeps reordering the table looking for the next available inode. Making table sizes too small is also a common cause of system crashes and the mark of an inexperienced system administrator. Your goal should be to keep your tables about 70 percent full at peak usage so the system is always free to grab the next available table resource. These activities can be monitored with `sar` and other system activity-reporting software (see Chapter 16).

An Easily Configured System

Configuring is a double-edged sword. You can't make everything big enough to cover all circumstances, and you can't make everything so small that the system will fall down and die. You're constantly trading off. But the more you do it, the better you will get at estimating sizes that work best and reconfiguring with information gathered from system monitors.

Don't get the idea that you configure the system only when you first bring it out of the box. As a system administrator, it is to your advantage to configure your system often to accommodate rapid changes in the work environment. Imagine a UNIX installation at Apex Software Company where hundreds of users open thousands of files each day. That UNIX system needs larger than normal file and inode tables to accommodate these activities. Now imagine that a large block of users at Apex Software Company is temporarily taken off the project on your machine to work on another project somewhere else. Until they come back, it's probably a good idea to reduce those file and inode table sizes to increase available memory and maximize the efficiency of your system.

The point is to size the system so well that you have enough, but not too much, of everything. Your table sizes should be big enough so your system doesn't thrash or crash. Your device directory, /dev, should be big enough for the devices you do have, allowing for a reasonable number of additions, without having so much of a surplus that you can't even list the contents of the directory because you don't have time to look at it. Your goal is to be able to fit the sizes of the configuration parameters carefully and cleverly so that they are neither too big nor too small.

It takes a certain understanding of system internals to estimate table sizes fairly accurately. In this chapter you will learn about the most common tables needed to configure a UNIX system and a simplified picture of the kernel's major tables that relate to user processes. To get your hardware to "talk," you need to understand drivers and how they relate to the /dev files, so you will learn a little bit about how the kernel touches the hardware. For simplicity, the scheduler, memory allocation, and other "nontable" kernel items are left out of the discussion.

Configuration Internals

Being a novice UNIX system administrator can be traumatic during the first few months as you come to grips with this marvelous, complex operating system. There are so many things to learn that you might be tempted to decide, "Right now I'll just concentrate on the day-to-day system administration tasks. I'll put off learning about table sizes until after I take an internals course."

You can't get away with this for long, however, on a real system with a real budget that you and everyone else in the company has to live with. In a perfect world you would always have memory available in unlimited quantities, but in the real world you don't. Maybe you need to wait until it's time for the next budget request before you can get your hands on more memory. Maybe memory just isn't available. Remember the DRAM shortage of 1988? So until you can get more memory, you're stuck with what you have. If your users are bursting the memory's seams, you must pare off a little more memory by fine-tuning the parameter configurations.

Kernel Tables

Kernel tables were fixed in size up until System V Release 4. Dynamic kernel allocation is a fact with Release 4, and many tunable parameters disappear.

On pre-SVR4 UNIX systems only nonkernel areas can be expanded with system calls from C programs such as break and malloc. Once you do a system generation and install the newly configured system, the kernel size is fixed in concrete until you do another configuration and installation. If a table starts to fill, it simply will fill. There's no flexibility.

Configuring and installing the system are important tasks, so it's up to you to make sure your table sizes and device addresses will be workable until the next system generation. Although some installations do a system generation as often as once a day, many installations "get by" with doing a system generation as seldom as twice a year. But if you try to run one of those twice-a-year installations and your size estimates are too far off, will it be worth living with miserable system conditions for six months? Think about it. Don't be afraid to schedule a system generation as often as necessary. First and foremost, you should make friends with the system's tables and structures.

Tables make UNIX run. The kernel is a series of many tables run by a reasonable amount of code, forming a never-ending process. The larger the kernel parameters are, the more memory the kernel will take.

For system administration purposes, a discussion of kernel tables should start with the process table. The process table has an entry for each process that is active, on the way out, and dead but not buried. In UNIX vernacular these processes are called *runable*, *sleeping*, and *zombies*. The process table points at many things, including the file table. In fact, every process starts out with three files assigned to it automatically: stdin, stdout, and stderr. The process can then access more files, up to the user or system limit.

Open-file limits vary among UNIX systems. For years the number of open files per user process was cast in iron at 20 by AT&T, but a few OEMs are changing the limit, conforming to the needs of contemporary processors, which have more speed and addressing capability. For example, two mainframe versions of UNIX, Amdahl's UTS 580 Release 2.0 and IBM's AIX, are going to set the number of open files per user at 200. Pyramid and other OEMs have set the open-file limit at 64. The open-file limit for SCO XENIX is 60. At UNIX System V Release 4, AT&T and Sun finally lifted the open-file limit to the skies with a *soft* limit of 64 and a *hard* limit of 2048. To top it off, rootis not restricted by either limit. The *soft* limit is a tunable, per-process limit. The standard I/O package supports 256 open files per user process.

Whatever the open-file limit is on your system, because each file has an inode associated with it, there must be a slot in another important kernel table, the inode table. There is not necessarily a one-to-one correspondence between active entries in the file table and those in the inode table, however, as multiple file names can point to the same inode.

There are many more kernel tables to deal with, and many of them can be configured. The mount table is a vital one for the system administrator to know. It has entries for every single logical disk, including root. The corresponding parameter, NMOUNT, designates the number of mount structures, and it's based on the number of disk partitions and memory devices.

Each Table Behaves Differently

Each kernel table has its own specific use and its own parameter, and you can learn about them from a good book on system internals. However, you won't understand precisely how each table behaves when it fills until you have experience administering a UNIX system.

There are no hard and fast rules on the behavior of tables when they fill. When the process table fills, it thrashes, slows down the machine, and finally appears to stop the machine cold until one of the processes finishes, opening up a slot for another process. Even superusers can't get a process in edgewise. All they can do is twiddle their thumbs until there is room for their processes.

On the other hand, the callout table is like glass. It has no elasticity. If it fills, it will break, and the machine will kill itself. You're stuck with a dead machine, and that's the way the kernel crumbles. Obviously, you have to think carefully about setting the size of this table!

Configuration Files and Parameters

UNIX is a fascinating operating system. Enormous thought went into the machine at the user level, such as pipes and redirection, the many types of flags, and the innovative way that arguments are handled. Unfortunately, not much was done to make the administrative side of the machine "user friendly." Universal system administration has never been a priority, and so there is little administration consistency from system to system.

In fact, almost anything relative to UNIX administration was missing from current standards until late 1988. Not only POSIX and XOPEN, but even SVID, the System V Interface Definition, had almost nothing about the system administration side of the machine. These standards groups defined the user interface, but administration was the "forgotten area" for a long time. Fortunately, that is changing. IEEE P1003.7 covers UNIX system administration, and System V Release 4 goes a long way toward system administration standardization with its Enhanced Administration set of commands. Also, the Applications Binary Interface has started to enforce system file naming and locations.

In general, on most UNIX systems you are provided with one of two different ways to do a system configuration. Menu-driven configuration systems are the more common, such as those found on System V Release 4 and XENIX. A menu-driven program allows you to read the current parameters on your system and change the parameters where they live. Then you do a system generation and installation and you're set.

The second method is editing a single configuration file, such as `/etc/devicelist` on UTS V, a mainframe version of UNIX.[2] It contains the most common changeable parameters, and configuration is a simple editing job. You go through the file, hand-edit the kernel table parameters you want to change, and modify, add, or remove devices. Then you do a `sysgen` and installation, and you're done.

The Plot Thickens

The only problem with these two configuration methods is that eventually you will need to configure something that goes beyond what the OEM or VAR has provided. Let's consider a real-world example. The open-file limit on many UNIX systems is twenty per user. This is far too small for a mini or mainframe, and the users keep pressuring the UNIX system administrator to change the number of open files per user because their applications require more. The system administrator doesn't find a special-case parameter like this in `/etc/devicelist`. Imagine you are the system administrator at this installation. What would you do?

If you have a UNIX source machine, it's not that difficult. On a source system, configuration materials are kept in a predictable area:

```
/usr/source/uts/*/cf
```

The asterisk indicates the OEM's name for the UNIX version. On an Amdahl the UTS V UNIX source file is called

```
/usr/src/uts/uts/cf
```

Look in this directory, locate the file and parameter for the number of files per user, and change it. Of course, you must bear the consequences of the change, as it can be fatal to the system.

This is fine and dandy if you have a source code machine, but what if you don't? Most UNIX machines are not source code machines; the most common UNIX system runs a binary version of UNIX. Unfortunately, there is no set standard on where to put configuration material if you don't have a source directory. The OEM tries to be as creative as possible, and that's why you end up with strange places for configuration information, such as `/usr/sys/conf` on XENIX or `/etc/master.d` on AT&T UNIX binary systems.

Here's where the hard part of system configuration begins. Your mission, if you choose to accept it, is to go into your system and find where these special-case parameters are set. You must change the parameters where they live.

Although configuration procedures are similar on all UNIX systems, and parameter constants such as `NPROC` are almost the same on all systems, getting your hands on the actual configuration files where you find "size of" parameter information is an exercise in frustration on binary systems. Not only are the locations of configuration files different from UNIX system to UNIX system, but these configuration files have entirely different names as well. Thus there is no way to give you a definitive administration procedure for configuring your binary UNIX system because there is so much variation from OEM

---

[2] Configuration files are called `/sys/conf/`*machine_name* on BSD systems.

to OEM. The only way you can become an expert at finding elusive configuration information is by going through the time and grief of finding it on several different kinds of UNIX systems. After a while, you will be able to make pretty accurate "educated guesses."

If you don't believe this, try finding configuration file information in your numbered manuals. That's the first logical place to look, right? If you're running a conventional AT&T UNIX System V, the manuals will be divided into eight sections:

1. User Reference Manual
   (1M: Administrator's Reference Manual)
2. System Calls
3. Subroutines and Libraries
4. File Formats
5. Miscellany
6. Games
7. Special Files
8. System Maintenance Procedures

Manual 1M is the Administrator's Reference Manual, but amazingly, the configuration information is not available there. If you go on a "configuration information hunt" and you persevere, you'll eventually find little dribbles of information available in obscure manual sections. For example, Manual 7, Special Files, contains fragmentary sections on tuning.

The rest of the system administration information is in the tutorials, the unnumbered manual sections. You have no choice but to flip through all the index markers in the tutorials until you find what you need. Whatever information you can find here is vital. Keep it as a ready reference, because you are going to need all the help you can get.

What if you're doing system administration on XENIX? The AT&T System V manual information won't help you find anything on your XENIX system manuals, because XENIX manuals are indexed in a completely different way. Berkeley UNIX has yet another system manual index format. What's a system administrator to do?

Because parameter constant names remain relatively consistent from system to system, I'm going to give you a list of configuration parameters necessary for viable system administration. There are other parameters I could include, but this minimal list contains what you will need to get started. If some of these parameters aren't readily available on your menu-driven configuration software or in a single configuration file on your system—like UTS V's /etc/devicelist—don't lose heart. The parameter names are valuable information that you can use in your search for the elusive configuration files you must find to change these parameters.

Tunable Parameters

There are some parameters you shouldn't touch with a 10-foot pole, such as parameters found in C source code. But a tunable parameter is a parameter that *can* be changed. You should at least know about the following parameters to do system administration on your UNIX system.

NBUF

NBUF is the number of system buffers. These buffers cache disk data both coming and going. *This is a very important tuning parameter*. If the number of system buffers is sufficiently large, real disk I/O will be cut substantially. When a disk cache is formed, then it, rather than the disk itself, is accessed. Taken to a logical extreme, "read-aheads" anticipate what will be wanted, while "write-behinds" delay disk access. Both reduce the number of immediate disk accesses and thus improve performance.

NHBUF

NHBUF is the number of hash buffers and, to get optimal performance, should be changed whenever NBUF is changed. Five system buffers to one hash buffer is usually an effective ratio.

NPROC

NPROC is the number of process table entries (slots). It holds not only active processes, known as *runable* and *sleeping* processes in traditional UNIX vernacular, but also *zombies*, dead children of live parent processes. If the process table is too small, everything will grind to a halt until one of the processes finishes. Nothing new can be started. Not even a superuser can initiate any course of corrective action. Watch the "percentage-full" figures of the major tables as the system peaks, for only at peak loading will you actually know how well sized your system is.

MAXUP

Be careful not to confuse NPROC with MAXUP. MAXUP is the maximum number of user processes. Notice that it is not a table parameter but relates directly to the size of the process table, because the number of user processes obviously cannot be bigger than NPROC, the number of processes. MAXUP is best kept to some reasonable limit, like 20 to 30. If the maximum number of processes is set at 25, then 20 processes per single user is more than reasonable. Be prepared to fight with users over this one, as users resent restrictions, even when they are imposed for the good of the system.

NCLIST

NCLIST is the number of clist buffers to create, and *clists* are small character list buffers used to character buffering for terminals and ttylike devices. A good number for these buffers is 5 to 10 buffers for each terminal and terminal-like device. Since these buffers are small, you can afford to be moderately generous. If the clists fill, characters will be lost in terminal I/O.

NMOUNT

For each mounted file system, including root, there must be a mount table entry. If there are 50 mounted file systems and another 10 disk addresses are kept in reserve for future needs, define NMOUNT as 60.

NINODE

The NINODE parameter is the number of slots in the inode table. This parameter corresponds to the number of open files (including standard input, standard output, and standard error) for each process attached to a tty and each file opened by system processes. It won't be fatal when the inode table fills, but it will cause system performance to bog down considerably.

NFILE

NFILE is the number of file table entries. There is a correspondence to the number of inode table entries, but not necessarily one to one. When the file table fills, it also will not be fatal to your system, but it will threaten system performance.

Now that you have these precious gems of information, you must be up to the challenge of finding the files where these parameters live on your machine. Bear in mind that these parameters may be different on non-AT&T systems, and some go away at System V Release 4. Next we shall consider the configuration process and some kernel internals to help you in your search. As you read the next section, remember that your goal is to find these parameters and change them in order to customize your UNIX system.

What Happens When You Configure and Install a UNIX System

Now that you have the vital parameter names under your belt, it's time to discuss what a system configuration is and why it is so difficult to pin down a specific configuration method in UNIX.

Most UNIX computer systems are binary versions, and so the kernel is represented as a series of "dot o" files called object files. Once the parameters are changed and new devices are defined, the system generation takes place. A system generation makes a new kernel, and the system generation program is usually a fairly large script that, among other things, invokes a make file. The /bin/make command is a program that works in conjunction with a Makefile that tells how to preprocess, compile, and load all the code necessary for an executable binary file. The end product of the system generation is the creation of the new kernel as well as new or revised entries in /dev.[3]

At this point you have a new system, but the new system is not installed. The next step is installing the new kernel, called newsys on some systems. In the installation procedure, the existing kernel is changed to the old kernel. If it was /unix, it now becomes /ounix, for old unix. The new kernel has its name changed, and it becomes /unix, /vmunix, /xenix, or whatever the manufacturer wants to call it. The new kernel replaces the old kernel in the root directory. Device tables also are altered during the installation. While most systems simply make additions, deletions, or modifications to /dev, very large systems write an entirely new device directory during the installation, like /newdev.

Once the new kernel is installed and you have a new or modified device list, the system is brought down and rebooted under the new kernel. If your system comes up and

---

[3] Any new devices added must have new entries. Any devices removed also have to be removed from /dev. Hardware devices are covered in more detail later in this chapter.

runs, you are now running under a new kernel, and you have completed a reconfiguration and an installation.

There is always the possibility that the new system *won't* come up and run. To fail in the middle of a system generation is a disaster you want to avoid! If the worst happens and your system falls down and dies before it ever comes up, fall back, regroup, and boot it under the old kernel.

One reason your system generation might fail is that it has run out of free blocks or inodes, and so you must be sure to have plenty of blocks and inodes available to complete the installation procedure.

The /dev directory contents are special files, inodes with no body and no space requirements. When a new device list has to be created on large systems, normally done on the root disk, you will fail in the middle of a sysgen if you are short of inodes.

Since you're creating a new kernel, wherever that kernel is being created, you're going to have to have enough disk blocks. On big systems, if you have /usr/src, it will need to have enough blocks. On smaller systems, like XENIX systems, there has to be a large enough block count wherever /usr/sys/conf resides. Always make sure you have enough space.

In Search of Configuration Files

Now that you have a general idea of how a system generation and installation are done, let's look at some details that will help you locate important configuration files so you can change system parameters that aren't readily available on your machine.

Start with the Header Files

We already talked about searching through manuals for configuration information. The next logical place to look is .h include file source code, known as header or include files. Why? Header files are included in C code by the C preprocessor. A header file contains and defines data structures and variables, sizes and defines tables, and sets constants and conditional compilation parameters. Parameters are system constants, and some of the constants in these header files are system configuration parameters.

Most header files that are required by the system itself to generate a new kernel are stored in /usr/include/sys. Here are some common header file names pertinent to system administration:

```
config.h
param.h
types.h
sysmacros.h
io.h
conf.h
map.h
rtm.h
space.h
```

The space.h include file has a lot of useful size information. You can get excited seeing a file name like param.h, because its name indicates parameters, but don't hold your breath. On some systems it is a virtual gold mine of data, but on other systems it holds only a little useful configuration information. Also, `config.h` can be a valuable size data source if you can find it.

Now you have to be careful, particularly if you're relatively new to UNIX and don't yet know your way around the system. First of all, header files may have different names on different UNIX systems. Second, some of the files you find are not going to be the files you want, even though they have identical file names. Some files are simply duplicates of the files you want. Others are forward references to the files you want.

Let's say that you're relatively new to UTS V UNIX but that you know that header files are found somewhere around `/usr/include` and you want to find parameters. You do an `ls` and you see `param.h` listed. Bingo! You've found a valuable parameter file, guaranteed. Or have you?

Before you get excited thinking that you have even found a header file at all, look at the size of the file or pick it up in the editor to see whether you really did find it. On a UTS V UNIX machine what you've really found is a one-line file called `param.h` that reads:

```
#include /usr/include/sys/param.h
```

This is actually a forward reference to the real `param.h` file located in `/usr/include/sys`.

Use UNIX to Help Search

If you know your parameter names and you've found pertinent information in the header files, you can't do anything with this knowledge until you find the actual files used to configure the system, because that's where the parameters are changed. You might start looking for files with the words *conf* or *master* in them. Whenever you look for a configuration file or directory, use `find` in your search:

```
find /usr -name "conf*" -print
```

Knowing that configuration file names change from OEM to OEM helps prepare you for some frustration.

Once you've found the configuration directory, move there and do a `grep` for whatever parameter you're after:

```
grep NBUF *
```

You'll soon develop your own little tricks. UNIX has numerous tools to help you find things.

Even finding a parameter in a configuration file on your system is not an absolute guarantee that the parameter will be changed. There is still a remote possibility that it will be changed by having been found somewhere and copied to another location. To be sure, read your system generation `Makefile` and find out where the system expects the parameters to be set for the first time before they are copied off somewhere else. Be prepared for some difficulty in finding the information you want, because `Makefiles` are not very easy to read.

Different Configuration Methods

UNIX is entering a new era of system administration. Old timers who started out in UNIX years ago remember how parameters had to be set by hand, one at a time, to configure a system. As UNIX evolves, it gets more complex. Today system configuration on a large UNIX system is a long, difficult job requiring a great deal of knowledge, preparation, and experience to do it right.

For years the pressure has been on OEMs to make UNIX system parameters easier to configure. As UNIX proliferates on desktop computers, it is hardly realistic to expect everyone running those machines to be able to do the kind of sophisticated system administration required on the minis on which UNIX was created. As a result we're starting to see exciting developments in menu-driven system administration software, primarily on micros. It stands to reason that the OEMs who make the best system administration software for UNIX micros will sell more machines because they will be easier to administer.

In UNIX System V Release 4 we see the first consistent menu-driven system administration. The sysadm command first seen on AT&T systems at Release 2 was expanded and nationalized at Release 4. At the same time an administrative user interface was added. Administrative tasks handled by the interface are

- Applications management.
- Backup services.
- Storage device management.
- Diagnostics management.
- File system management.
- Machine information management.
- Network services management.
- Printer and terminal management.
- Port service management.
- Printer service management.
- Restore service management.
- System setup management.
- Software installation and information management.
- User and group management.

The first time I saw menu-driven system administration was on AT&T's little 3B2 machines running UNIX System V Release 2. Then along came SCO XENIX System V, which has a very impressive system administration software package. The menu-driven system administration program does most of the configuration you need to do. It tells you what is configured; it gives you a help menu; or it allows you to modify parameters. Its master device configuration file is called master, and it's located in /usr/sys/conf.

Some systems, such as UNIX Version 5 Release 2 on the AT&T 3B2, do their system generations from *firmware mode*. The 3B2's configuration data are in /etc/master.d. Parameters to be changed are in the dozen or so files in the master directory. After changing parameters, the kernel, /unix, is copied to /ounix. A bootable object file is made for each file in /etc/master.d and is altered, and then the system is brought to the firmware mode and /etc/system is booted.

My favorite configuration system is the single configuration source file on UTS, a mainframe version of UNIX. You go in and make the changes in /etc/devicelist. Although devicelist is not the central configuration file, it supplies data to change the configuration files. A quick glance at the configuration file /etc/devicelist tells you what you need to know about most of the system configuration, a handy benefit with this kind of configuration method.

The Burden Is on You

Obviously, OEMs don't design their UNIX systems with universal system administration in mind. Although an OEM might defend these differences by saying, "It's a matter of implementation," the way that a system is administered also depends to some extent on the whims of the OEM. Regardless of the reason for the system administration differences from UNIX system to UNIX system, it's up to the system administrator to overcome any inherent difficulties and get the job done in spite of them. We can only hope that the efforts of the POSIX System Administration 1003.7 committee and the Sun AT&T consortium for System V Release 4 will bear fruit in future releases and that there will be uniformity.

By the way, once you find the configuration files you need, don't get the notion that you can move them to a more logical location so it will be an easier machine for you to administer. Don't even think about moving these files unless you are up to rewriting all the configuration file code and the corresponding Makefile code for the kernel on your system!

Talking to Hardware

Sizing buffers and tables is only half the battle. Defining the devices so that they will be *genned* during the sysgen and installation is the other half.[4]

You wouldn't think it would be hard for an application to talk to hardware devices, but it is a lot more complicated than you might first imagine. Think of a solid line from user to hardware device:

The user interface is through the /dev entry. The device driver has one foot in the hardware bus and the other in the kernel. The catch is that some devices are fed information

---

[4] The term *genned* is system programmer jargon for "generated." If VM system programmers need to add more addresses, they can *gen* the addresses without having to do an entire system generation.

in finite, uniform blocks (block devices). Others take a character at a time to a stream of characters of program-defined size: These are character (raw) devices. Terminals are character devices. Disks and tapes are used as block devices in conventional operation, but they can be both block and raw devices. The character form is used for formatting, and the block form is used for normal reads and writes.

The kernel has device switches to toggle between block and character I/O. There is a bdevswitch for block devices, and it has a series of block buffers at its disposal. The number of block buffers is configurable. The cdevswitch is for character streams, which have a set of very small buffers strung in the clists. Its size is also configurable. We've already discussed the parameter, NCLIST.

The special files in /dev are the system interfaces to the device drivers and therefore to the devices themselves. By definition, these device special files are different from all other UNIX files. In fact, they actually are special in a very interesting way. Although they have a directory entry and an inode of sorts, there is no file information. The inode information has time stamps and permissions as other files do, but the important difference in that inode information is major and minor device numbers.

Whether block special or character special files, the major and minor device numbers for special files are the key to understanding what's happening with devices. The major device number actually identifies a specific device driver that is triggered by the device switch. Everything in /dev with the same major number runs with the same driver. The minor number is a parameter that is passed to the driver, and there are no guarantees beyond that point. A minor number may mean something special to the device driver itself, say the number of a disk or the number of a port within a specific board, although there is no UNIX standard that requires this.

The following is a listing of a XENIX system's hard disk entry points to the hard disk driver:

```
$ ls -l /dev/h*
brw-------   1 sysinfo  sysinfo    1,   0 Mar  4 07:59 /dev/hd00
brw-------   1 sysinfo  sysinfo    1,  15 Mar  4 07:59 /dev/hd01
brw-------   1 sysinfo  sysinfo    1,  23 Mar  4 07:59 /dev/hd02
brw-------   1 sysinfo  sysinfo    1,  31 Mar  4 07:59 /dev/hd03
brw-------   1 sysinfo  sysinfo    1,  39 Mar  4 07:59 /dev/hd04
brw-------   1 sysinfo  sysinfo    1,  47 Mar  4 07:59 /dev/hd0a
brw-r-----   1 dos      sysinfo    1,  55 Mar  4 09:46 /dev/hd0d
brw-------   1 sysinfo  sysinfo    1,  64 Apr 30 18:52 /dev/hd10
brw-------   1 sysinfo  sysinfo    1,  79 Apr 30 18:52 /dev/hd11
brw-------   1 sysinfo  sysinfo    1,  87 Apr 30 18:52 /dev/hd12
brw-------   1 sysinfo  sysinfo    1,  95 Apr 30 18:52 /dev/hd13
brw-------   1 sysinfo  sysinfo    1, 103 Apr 30 18:52 /dev/hd14
brw-------   1 sysinfo  sysinfo    1, 111 Apr 30 18:52 /dev/hd1a
brw-r-----   1 dos      sysinfo    1, 119 Apr 30 18:52 /dev/hd1d
$ ls -l /dev/rh*
crw-------   1 sysinfo  sysinfo    1,   0 Mar  4 07:59 /dev/rhd00
crw-------   1 sysinfo  sysinfo    1,  15 Mar  4 07:59 /dev/rhd01
crw-------   1 sysinfo  sysinfo    1,  23 Mar  4 07:59 /dev/rhd02
crw-------   1 sysinfo  sysinfo    1,  31 Mar  4 07:59 /dev/rhd03
crw-------   1 sysinfo  sysinfo    1,  39 Mar  4 07:59 /dev/rhd04
crw-------   1 sysinfo  sysinfo    1,  47 Mar  4 07:59 /dev/rhd0a
crw-r-----   1 dos      sysinfo    1,  55 Mar  4 09:46 /dev/rhd0d
crw-------   1 sysinfo  sysinfo    1,  64 Apr 30 18:52 /dev/rhd10
crw-------   1 sysinfo  sysinfo    1,  79 Apr 30 18:52 /dev/rhd11
crw-------   1 sysinfo  sysinfo    1,  87 Apr 30 18:52 /dev/rhd12
```

```
crw-------   1 sysinfo   sysinfo    1,  95 Apr 30 18:52 /dev/rhd13
crw-------   1 sysinfo   sysinfo    1,103 Apr 30 18:52 /dev/rhd14
crw-------   1 sysinfo   sysinfo    1,111 Apr 30 18:52 /dev/rhd1a
crw-r-----   1 dos       sysinfo    1,119 Apr 30 18:52 /dev/rhd1d
```

Field 5 is the major device number, and field 6 is the minor device number. Notice the first character of the first field: It is either a c, for character special, or a b, for block special. The major device number points to the device driver, and the minor device number is an argument passed to the driver.

Special files in /dev point to different devices. As a system administrator you need to understand that individual OEM conventions are different. There are subtle differences that might confuse you at first; for example, on an AT&T 3B2 an ls -l on the file /dev/tty10 shows the following:

```
$ ls -l /dev/tty10
crw-rw-rw-   1 karen   bin    1, 0 Sept 6 12:45 /dev/tty10
```

The 1 in field 5 means driver 1, and it corresponds to I/O board 1. The 0 in field 6 is port 0. These are clever AT&T touches that happened to fit well on this machine. But on other UNIX systems the major and minor device numbers won't necessarily tie in so neatly.

The Transformation

The configuration process is generated by some exceptionally complex Makefiles. Regarding device entries, the magic of configuration is that it creates a number of successive files. As the file gets closer to the /dev entry, the data generation becomes less and less readable by humans. It starts out innocuously enough in /etc/devicelist on a UTS system:

```
110 dasd /usr
```

Then something like this is generated in iotab.c:

```
struct unit un110;
```

By the time it gets to conf.c it looks like this:

```
/*   0 */ MDISK(  0,       0,    FULL, "110s0")
```

The first zero in the parentheses is the minor number, and the second is the major number. All these examples have in common the number 110. A similar entry appears in conf.h. Notice that the minor and major devices appear for the first time when the configuration process gets closer to the /dev entry and thus the hardware.

Hardware Hints

Configuring the system doesn't mean only getting the internal kernel tables and buffers at a size that both the system and your users can live with. It also means partitioning the disks to make up for the hardware you don't have and getting the machine to recognize the hardware you do have.

Creative Disk Partitioning

Don't ever forget that as the system administrator you have the right and the means to customize your machine. Just because you have only two hard disks but wish you had four doesn't necessarily mean that you have to configure for two hard disks and save your pin money until you can buy two more. You do have the power to make four virtual disks from two hard disks by creatively partitioning the hard disks into four *virtual disks*.

The concept of virtual disks is not new to UNIX, but it has strong roots in mainframe UNIX systems, particularly Amdahl's UTS running under VM. VM is an acronym for *virtual machine*, and it is not so much an operating system as an operating system platform. Running on 370-architecture mainframes, it permits one mainframe to run several different operating systems simultaneously, a common situation at many installations. On an IBM 3090-600E, VM can easily support 12 UTS UNIX machines, 300 CMS machines, and half a dozen service machines.[5] Each UTS, CMS, and service machine is a virtual machine, but all behave as if they were physically separate machines. Incidentally, this is only one possible combination of machines you can put together on an IBM mainframe running VM. The combination depends on the type of installation you have and the applications you run there.

VM is also good at creating virtual disks, smaller virtual disks from one larger physical disk. A small conventional IBM 3380 hard disk has 880 cylinders of 150 blocks per cylinder and 4098 bytes per block. Because of the enormous size of mainframe disk packs, partitioning them along cylinder boundaries has been customary for a long time. The disk is cut up into as many pieces or partitions as required, anywhere it suits the system administrator's fancy. Even 20 to 30 partitions on a single large disk is not unusual. You can have as many virtual disks as you have disk cylinders or disk addresses. On mainframe installations you may be accustomed to partitioning your disks to meet your current special needs, but the virtual disk concept is exclusive neither to mainframes nor to VM. In their OEM versions, all contemporary UNIX systems can create disk partitions. A rose by any other name will smell as sweet, and virtual disks are only another name for disk partitions.

Sometimes microsystem managers can use mainframe and minisystem techniques. Let's say that you have an Intel 301 PC with two hard disks but that you want to divide them into six separate and mountable disks:

- / (root)
- DOS partition.
- A swap area.
- /local.
- /u.
- /backup.

SCO XENIX comes with a program that allows disk partitioning. It is located on one of the installation diskettes. Since you can't partition a hard disk when you're on the hard disk, the disk partitioning is done from a freestanding floppy version. By partitioning your hard disks, you make up for hardware you don't have by creating six virtual disks that behave just as if they're real.

---

[5] Service machines provide special functions, such as networking or timing, for the entire system.

A good example of a partitioning program is SunOS's format utility, which allows each physical disk to be divided into separate partitions. Both SunOS and ULTRIX are limited because they allow partitions a through h with addresses overlapped. This isn't enough partitions for most system configurations, aggravated by one or two addresses encompassing other partitions. The good side of the overlaps is that they allow more flexibility without having to repartition. Two overlaped 250M partitions can be used as one 500M partition. The c partition is the entire disk, and it can be used as one partition or ignored while the smaller partitions are used.

Whatever the size of your machine, each virtual disk has its own device address. It is important to develop a logical, consistent address protocol for all your device addresses.

Disk Address Protocol

You don't need to get fancy about naming conventions on a small machine. When you have four devices and four addresses, it's like remembering the names of your own children. You can't forget them. It is as simple as that. But on a large machine with hundreds of addresses, trying to remember every address is like a school principal's trying to remember the names of all the students at the school. It simply can't be done.

What you want to do is pick ranges of addresses for specific purposes so that the address range tells you something about the disk. If you set up a naming convention that is consistent, just looking at an address should tell you what kind of disk device it is. Let's say your root disks are always at address 220. Then if you see a disk numbered 221, without seeing the contents you will automatically know that this disk is added directly to root for some root-specific purpose.

The following is the addressing protocol that I use on mainframe system disks:

- Addresses 110, 220, 330, 550, and 660 are reserved for system disks: /dev/dsk/110s0 is /usr on a 370 mainframe, and /dev/dsk/220s0 is root.
- Subranges like 111, 221, and 331 are reserved for mounting to system disks. If you have to mount a disk on top of /dev/dsk550s0, the spool disk, then /usr/spool/console will be 551.
- Addresses 400 through 4ff are reserved for terminals (ttys). A typical terminal address is /dev/tty400.
- Addresses aa0 through aaf are for page disks when you've filled memory and have to page memory to a disk to get more room in memory.
- Addresses ff0 through fff are for temporary disks. Disks in this category are used only briefly.
- Addresses 700 through 7ff, 800 through 8ff, and 900 through 9ff are for user systems.
- Addresses b00 through eff should be kept in your pocket until absolutely needed.

These ranges are typical of a mainframe's addressing range. These addresses are in /dev or /dev/dsk and /dev/rdsk, and they are accessed by the kernel's mount table. You are free to make up your own addressing protocol, so use whatever works best for you. You'll be glad you did.

Your Goal: 20 Percent Free Disk Addresses

So much depends on the type of installation your system serves. On a system that has a large pool of disks available, you will be courting disaster if you run out of disk addresses. If you know that you will need 100 disk partitions in /dev, to be on the safe side, plan for an additional 20 partitions.[6] A 20 percent margin of free addresses should keep you covered.

Dos and Don'ts on Limits

A word here on limits. Many limits are set by OEMs, and some definitely cannot be configured. If the OEM recommends that you do not configure certain limits, listen to its warnings. You may find the magic button to exceed a specific limit, particularly on a source code machine, but don't risk it on an installation of any size unless you are given no choice. Expect your system to thrash and ultimately crash when experimenting with new parameter configurations (see Chapter 13). When you expand all the tables you think you will need to get the result you want, and to your dismay other tables often overflow unexpectedly, then you're in a world of trouble.

UNIX can be a hacker's delight, but don't experiment unless you and your users know what you're getting into and unless you're prepared to dig yourself out. If you must experiment with the system, make a full backup of the system files, and be prepared to do a full restore as a backout. *PROCEED WITH EXTREME CAUTION.*

Support Groups

The success of a UNIX version can be largely measured by the strength and availability of its support group. Frequently the biggest value-added item of a VAR is the support itself.

The reason that you pay for support services is so you can call the support group. When you administer your first UNIX system, get to know everyone at the support group. I predict that you'll not only come to know them on a first-name basis but you'll also know the names of their children before you become expert enough on your system to run it alone. Don't be afraid to ask questions! That's why you pay for support.

Before you buy a specific system, call the vendor and have him or her give you the names of satisfied customers. For example, if your company wants to buy ULTRIX, call DEC and ask who is running ULTRIX in your area. Then talk to those companies' system administrators and find out how good DEC's ULTRIX support has been.

Above all, if you find out that a vendor's support is poor, no amount of money saved will be worth buying that machine. It will cost you and your company way too much money trying to solve system problems for which there is no ready answer.

Monitoring the Tables

Watch the size of the system tables at peak usage, and you'll know what to expand and what to shrink at the next configuration. Use your system administration tools at

---

[6] This is /dev/disk on larger systems.

peak usage periods to analyze what's happening on your machine. (For more system-monitoring information, see Chapter 16.)

THE CONFIGURATION OF THE BSD 4.2 AND 4.3 SYSTEMS

It's much easier to configure a BSD machine. Every OEM adds its own special configuration touches, but in my experience, the Berkeley-based UNIX system configuration is relatively consistent from version to version. As we saw in the last section, System V UNIX derivatives take completely different system configuration approaches. In contrast, Berkeley systems have one configuration file, and the layout of that file is similar from version to version. Sun and DEC configuration files are comparable. You'll see a lot of devices and a few tunable system parameters. A Sun configuration file has more devices, and a DEC configuration file has more parameters.

You do give up some fine-tuning control on Berkeley-based systems. System V provides several pages worth of table-sizing parameters, such as NPROC, MAXPROX, and NUSERS, but BSD 4.2 gives you just a handful. For example, in a Berkeley UNIX configuration file, you can't size your system buffer cache large while keeping the process table small. Fortunately, most system administrators don't have to fine-tune their systems to this extent.

Sun and DEC use maxusers in a clever way. Rather than keeping it as a parameter that designates the maximum number of users, it is used as a multiplier. Then kernel table sizes are keyed to correspond proportionately to the maxusers setting. ULTRIX has a few more tunable parameters than does SunOS, and these parameters are found in the options section of the configuration file.

Where Is the Configuration File?

Trying to find the configuration file on a workstation for the first time is a trying experience, mainly because that file usually isn't on the system. Naturally, diskless systems rely on the server to hold their kernels and everything it took to build them, but dataless systems, with small disks of 90 to 300 megabytes, don't have a configuration section. Indeed, they may not even have a C compiler. The configuration files—about half of the administrator's command set, as well as the programming, partitioning, and formatting software—all are shoehorned onto the installation tapes or diskettes.

To do the installation or configuration work on a workstation like this, you will need to halt the processor and boot from the installation tape or diskette. Most of these systems boot from the prom prompt to the diskette or tape if either are present:

```
# shutdown -h now
 .
 .
 .
> b
```

Sun 2s, Sun 3s, and Sun 4s have two UNIX kernels on tape. One is memory resident, and the other resides in the swap area. Both allow you to do a lot of heavy-duty work, like partitioning and configuration. You can even recover a system with a damaged root disk. The Sun 386i is not quite so flexible, but only because its diskette is smaller.

Locating the Configuration File

The first thing you need to do is to find out where the system configuration information is stored. This information is easier to find from Berkeley system to Berkeley system. The configuration file is in places like /usr/sys/conf/*system_name*. For example, if *stalker* is a DEC system's name, its configuration files will be located in /usr/sys/conf/stalker. XENIX has a similar configuration file location called /usr/sys/conf/*. On systems that must serve multiple architectures, the location is more complicated. For instance, Sun has shared system files, and so for starters you should search for configuration files in /usr/share/sys. Choose the appropriate machine, and go from there. The configuration file for a Sun 3 called *cj* is in /usr/share/sys/sun3/conf/cj.

For lack of a better place to start, a configuration file called GENERIC is provided. The good news is that everything you'll ever need is in there. The bad news is that everything you'll never need is in there also. Make a copy of the GENERIC configuration file and edit it to remove references to things you don't need. In other words, if you have a high-end server with SMD disk controllers and hard disks, you won't need a kernel reference to SCSI controllers and drives. Having to remove everything you don't need from the configuration file also assumes that you are intimately acquainted with every hardware device on your system. If you aren't, you have some homework to do.

Know Your Hardware

System administrators *should* know all about the hardware they are running, but often software people tend to ignore the nuts and bolts of the system. Ask any hardware person. You can get away with hardware ignorance on PCs and mainframes. Whatever the PC hard disk and controller are, it's a PC bus, and you know that the UNIX configuration files have taken everything into account. On mainframes you have to know your disk types and tape types, but the hardware end is handled by the mainframe field engineers.

Midsized systems present the largest system administration challenge as far as hardware is concerned. System staffs are usually small, and hardware specialists are few and far between. More often than not it's up to the system administrator to answer the following questions about the machine:

- What kind of bus does the machine have?
- What kind of adapters does it have?
- What kind of disk controllers are on the machine?
- What kind of disks do you have, and how many?
- What kinds of tape controllers and tape drives does the machine have?
- What kinds of I/O devices do you have?

The list is often a lot longer than this.

You must know not only what hardware devices you have but also what sorts of device mnemonics the OEM uses for them. At the device special file end, the tape drive may well be designated as /dev/rmt0, but the actual tape on your DEC 3600 is a klesiu0 controller for a uba0 device in the configuration file that ends up being a TUB81+ tape drive in the flesh. Similarly, /dev/rmt0c may designate your first disk, but for the configuration file you also need to know that it is an RA 80 type disk on a uq0 controller. "How do you know that?" I hear you exclaim in exasperation. You deduce that information from knowing that you're running a Q-bus. Isn't it obvious?

As the system administrator of a midsized system, you are between a rock and a hard spot. Without full knowledge of your hardware configuration, you dare not comment out or remove any hardware lines. On the other hand, if you don't, you'll be running MCD controllers with SCSI controller code in the kernel and wondering why your kernel is so large. If you want your systems to run at maximum efficiency, you *must* know every hardware detail, for this will enable you to remove unnecessary devices from the configuration code, the only way to get a lean, mean machine.

Another good incentive for knowing your hardware well is to understand performance differences. I maintain two pairs of file servers, both approximately the same size and cost. One pair are DECs, and the other pair are Suns. When I run dump, the Sun is already rewinding its tape before the DECs get much past the leader. Why? The DECs have an SCSI controller, fine for small systems without time constraints on backups, but not ideal for the high output requirements at our site. Knowing the difference before I ordered the units would have been helpful.

Removing Unwanted Hardware References

In the process of getting rid of unwanted devices, administrators of file servers hosting several architectures should take care not to remove references to all the supported architectures. For example, a Sun 3/280 server supporting Sun 3/60s should leave in lines referencing "SUN3_60."

The GENERIC configuration file is heavily commented, and all comments should be read before deciding to remove a device, flag, or constant. The rubber hits the road when you get to controller choices. Here you *must* know precisely what controller types you have in your system. Remove everything except those you do have. You also must know the names and types of all optional goodies you purchased with the system, such as graphics and floating-point accelerators. Other add-ons to know are mouse interfaces and cipher and Ethernet chips.

Configuration File Formats

Configuration is divided into two broad tasks. First you define the system, and then you define the devices and parameters. Sizing system tables and buffers controls the size of the kernel and therefore the size of available memory. Defining the devices has a twofold purpose: It creates entry points to the device drivers in /dev, and it limits the list of devices to the ones on your machine. More of the configuration task is defining miscellaneous items—such as time zone, system node name, and similar characteristics and values—to system parameters, also known as tunable parameters.

To make configuration files more orderly, a BSD configuration is divided into four definition sections:

- Global definitions
- System image definitions
- Device definitions
- Pseudodevice definitions

The order varies in the file, depending on whether your system is a Sun or a DEC.

Global Definitions

In our lifetimes each of us probably fills out several thousand forms. When we see

name ....

we automatically fill in the blank. Making your global definitions is similar to filling out a form. You fill in the blanks. Fill out three lines like this on a DEC,

```
machine
cpu
timezone
```

so that they look something like this:

```
machine    vax
cpu        "VAX785"
timezone   8 dst
```

Like all system information, global definitions should be researched before starting your configuration. It's helpful to send the GENERIC configuration file double-spaced to the printer and then to use it as a configuration prototype.

A note on the timezone parameter. Some systems define time zone constants like PDST and PST, but all systems support the number of hours from GMT. California is 8 hours away from GMT, and so it is defined as

```
timezone 8 dst
```

with dst showing that daylight saving time is observed.

On a Sun you see things like

```
machine        "sun 3"
cpu            "SUN3_160"
cpu            "SUN3_260"
cpu            "SUN3_110"
cpu            "SUN3_60"
cpu            "SUN3_E"
```

Although it is tempting to rid the system of everything other than SUN3_260,[7] if this is a server, be careful to leave in the systems that you will need to serve, such as SUN3_60 for Sun 3/60 workstations.

On a Sun you next see the ident line. Replace GENERIC with the name of the system:

```
% ed GENERIC
/ident
ident          GENERIC
.s/GENERIC/fancy/
w
q
%
```

After altering ident, move to maxusers. On Sun systems maxusers is a multiplier for most of the system tables. If you make this too large, you will sacrifice available memory,

---

[7] The Sun 260 is identical to the 280 in board and bus, but the 280 is a rack mount. Twenty years ago that would have made it a mainframe!

and if you make it too small, you will hang or crash the system. If you're not sure, a little too large is better, but after the configuration, be sure to use your system diagnostics to monitor table sizes during periods of peak usage. If you have gone overboard and made the tables way too large, resize `maxusers` and reconfigure the kernel.

System Image Definition

The system image definition is the shortest and easiest part of the configuration because it is a one-liner that defines the kernel. Here is its form on a DEC:

```
config  filename  config_clause  config_clause...
```

The file name is the name of the kernel. It may be `unix`, `vmunix`, or whatever the convention is on your system. When compiled, the new kernel resides in a directory other than `/`, and there will be no name confusion until you transfer it to `/`. The trick is to rename the old kernel to something appropriate before bringing in the new one:

```
# pwd
/usr/sys/conf
# mv /vmunix /Ovmunix
# cp vmunix /
#
```

No one can take for granted where `root` and the swap devices will be, so their locations are put on the system definition line. The location of `dump` must be defined as well. If you have no room for a dump partition, dump to the swap area. With `root` on `/dev/ra0a`, `swap` on `/dev/ra1b`, and `dump` on `/dev/ra4b`, the system definition looks like this on a DEC:

```
config vmunix root on ra0a swap on ra1b dumps on ra4b
```

The word `on` is optional. Notice that `swap` can use the word `and`:

```
swap ra1b and ra2b
```

On a Sun the generic line that starts it all is

```
config          vmunix swap generic
```

Although `vmunix` is the conventional name for the 4.3 kernel, if you want something different, now is the time to make the change. In addition, `swap` is the name of the swap disk on Suns. Typically it looks like this:

```
swap on xy0b
```

It is also time to find a home for `root`:

```
root on xy0
```

When finished, the line should look something like this on a Sun:

```
config vmunix root on xy0  swap on xy0b dump on xy0b
```

Remember that `and` can be used with `swap`. I recommend having multiple swap devices if the system is going to swap frequently.

Device Definitions

In this section, if you don't know your hardware, you're a dead duck, for this is where you eliminate unwanted devices from the generic configuration file and add any new ones. On all systems you must know the mnemonics for all your devices, the bus, and all adapters and controllers. Look in BSD manual(4) to get a list of the devices.

Here's a painless way to get device mnemonics on the system:

```
% man -k tape ¦ grep '(4)'
```

In this, man -k does a string lookup, and handing it a device type like disk, tape, or terminal will get the top line of the manual pages that have the keyword. It will also get too many pages, so cut your list to an intelligible size by greping on (4) for manual section 4. Take it a step further to get the device types only for the tape and disk devices for your machine. Let's say you're on a DEC:

```
% man -k tape ¦ grep '(4)' ¦ cut -f1
mtio
mu
stc
tm
ts
tu
ut
uu
% man -k disk ¦ grep '(4)' ¦ cut -f1
dkio
hp
ra
rb
rd
rk
rl
rx
urx
```

Some OEMs, like DEC and Sun, publish manual sections of device mnemonics in the back of several of their system administration reference volumes. If you still can't find device information, your last sources of hope are the purchase order for the computer or the catalog that you used when you bought it.

The device definition section of the configuration file describes every device on the system and every device that the OEM ever thought you would buy. In spite of this there may be some device that you want to add that is not there. If so, you will have to add it and its driver.

The device definition section for real devices resembles this for a DEC 3600:

```
adapter      uba0     at   nexus ?
controller   klesiu0  at   uba0
controller   tmscp1   at   klesiu0   csr 0174500      vector tmscpintr
tape         tms0     at   tmscp1    drive0
controller   uda0     at   uba0
controller   uq0      at   uda0      csr 0172150      vector uqintr
disk         ra0      at   uq0       drive 0
disk         ra1      at   uq0       drive 1
disk         ra2      at   uq0       drive 2
```

```
device       qe0    at  uba0    csr 017440    vector qeintr
controller   klesiu1 at uba0
controller   tmscp2 at  klesiu1 csr 0160404   vector tmscpintr
tape         tms1   at  tmscp2  drive 0
```

Note that each line of the real device section starts with a device keyword. The devices are

adapter   A connection to the system bus.

master   A (DEC) MASSBUS tape controller.

controller   A real or virtual device controller, a device that controls and connects
             to nonbus devices.

device   A device connected directly to the bus rather than to a device controller.

disk   A disk drive, hard or floppy, connected to a controller.

tape   A tape drive connected to a controller.

Beware of the keyword nexus. Although it made sense on DEC Vaxen systems, it has been carried over to most BSD systems and the original meaning has been lost. Bus interfaces such as adapters use the nexus keyword.

Control lines in the device definitions have the following form:

```
keyword device_name at connection_dat csr
    address drive drive_nbr flags
    number priority vector vector_name
```

Not all are used at once, but this is the order. Here is a typical line in the DEC 3600 device definitions section of the configuration file:

```
0device  qe0 at uba0 csr 017440 vector qeintr
```

The device name is qe0, the connection is uba0, the csr address is 017440, and the vector name is qeintr. Let's go into these device categories in a little more detail.

Device Names

Device names are mnemonics for the device, and usually are accompanied by a logical unit number. The most familiar one is the disk device name, such as ra0, in which ra is the mnemonic, and 0 is the device number. Thus ra0 is the first hard disk.

Drive Number

The drive number comes after the device name:

```
tape  mt0 at drive 0
```

This is pertinent to tapes and disks. When the ? wildcard is used for a drive number, the number of the drive is assigned at boot time.

csr

The csr stands for *control status register*, and it must be passed an octal address. As such, csr is the specification that precedes the address.

Flags

Flags are passed to the driver, and they have no fixed meaning. This is not unlike minor device numbers, which are also passed to the drive once the major numbers are known. Frequently both are used for bit patterns to pass a maximum amount of information.

Priority Levels

Priority levels are established for interrupt processing. Unless you are sure of what you're doing, don't change them.

Vector Interrupts

Some systems use few channels for interrupt handling: PC architecture is infamous for this. Some use only one channel. To identify from what device the interrupt is coming, a hardware interrupt vector must be assigned. There are integer values, but most often the vector has a constant assigned to it. Let's examine another line of the configuration file device section:

```
controller  tmscp1  at klesio0 csr 0174500 vector  tmsintr
```

Here we see the vector interrupt `tmsintr` assigned the controller `tmscp1`. Note the construction of the vector name:

```
device_name + interrupt_name
```

A DEC Device Section

Now let's discuss the real device section of the DEC 3600 again and trace some of the dependencies. By *dependencies* I mean the chain of devices, where this device depends on that device and so on down the line. A device chain doesn't jump out of the device section of the configuration file. Rather, you have to go in and dig for it.

The hard disks are `ra` devices; for example, a `man` on `ra(4)` tells you that the drive is an MSCP disk interface. These devices are attached to the `uq0` disk controller, which is a Q-bus controller. Its control status register, `csr`, is octal 0172150. The interrupt vector is `uqintr`, with the `uq` a direct reference to the controller type:

```
adapter      uba0     at   nexus ?
controller   klesiu0  at   uba0
controller   tmscp1   at   klesiu0   csr 0174500    vector tmscpintr
tape         tms0     at   tmscp1    drive0
controller   uda0     at   uba0
controller   uq0      at   uda0      csr 0172150    vector uqintr
disk         ra0      at   uq0       drive 0
disk         ra1      at   uq0       drive 1
disk         ra2      at   uq0       drive 2
device       qe0      at   uba0      csr 017440     vector qeintr
controller   klesiu1  at   uba0
controller   tmscp2   at   klesiu1   csr 0160404    vector tmscpintr
tape         tms1     at   tmscp2    drive 0
```

Notice the last line. You travel all the way back to the bus. Here tape `tms1` is attached to tape controller `tmscp2`, and the tape is at drive 0. The controller's control status register is 0160404 octal, and its interrupt vector is `tmscpintr`. The controller interfaces with controller `klesiu1`, which is attached to `ub0a`, the Q-bus adapter. The adapter `uba0` is the end of the line, because it is on the Q-bus. When you see `nexus ?`, you've reached the end of the device chain.

Sun Devices

The devices section of a Sun system `GENERIC` configuration file is three pages long. You need to choose the devices you have on your machine, but no more. The place to start is with your bus. What is it? That depends on the machine. The Sun 3/280 has a VME bus with 32-bit addresses and 32-bit data devices. In the configuration file this bus is a `vme32d32`.

From there, move to your controllers. Remember when you buy your system to get a list of all the devices used and a map of their location on the backplane. Sun has charts for the latter, but your own sketch will be better. Knowing what you have allows the editing of the `GENERIC` configuration file to go more quickly.

Look for devices like the Ethernet card, which is usually an Intel device with the mnemonic `ie`. No networking is possible without it. The rest of the Sun devices section includes graphics devices, color support, print controllers, floating-point accelerators, ciphering devices, and accelerators of all kinds. Know what you have on your system, and remove the rest.

Pseudodevices

Pseudodevices are the product of a device driver with no lower end. The classic driver has a high-level top end, written in C, and a low-level low end, written mostly in assembly. The low end talks directly to the bus.[8] A pseudodevice has no real device to talk to, and so it doesn't need to communicate directly with the bus or channel.

Memory is not a device in the classic sense. It is not directly attached to the bus, and so it doesn't need a driver to negotiate with the bus. However, in a larger sense, memory is the grandest device of all. It is the heart and soul of the machine. If you divide a computer into two conceptual working parts, you will have memory and the CPU. Thus `/dev/mem` and `/dev/kmem` can be classified as pseudodevices; `/dev/pty` is a pseudoterminal; and `/dev/ether` is an Ethernet pseudodevice. Similarly, windows and remote terminals also are pseudodevices.

Pseudodevices need no prolonged specification, so the keyword `pseudo-device` and the name of that device are all that are needed. Sometimes a number follows to specify the number of instances of that device; you will see a lot of windows and remote terminals. The following are some pseudodevice specifications for the DEC 3600:

```
pseudo-device    pty
pseudo-device    loop
pseudo-device    ether
pseudo-device    ufs
pseudo-device    inet

pseudo-device    nfs
```

---

[8] One exception to this rule is 370 architecture, which has no bus. Instead, the driver makes its deals directly with the channels.

```
pseudo-device    rpc

pseudo-device    lat
pseudo-device    lta
pseudo-device    dli
pseudo-device    decnet
```

Note that the pseudoterminals used for remote logins, `pty`, are followed almost exclusively by network pseudodevices.

Sun places pseudodevices ahead of real devices in its generic configuration file. If the system is networked, then the network lines will be left in:

```
pseudo-device       pty
pseudo-device       ether
pseudo-device       loop
```

There are pseudoterminals for remote logins, Ethernet devices, and loopback devices. All must be present.

Most Sun installations run Sun workstations like the SunX/60 to 260 and a Sun 386i attached to file and network services. Almost all users want to run `sunview`, even if they run X windows as well. Although 128 windows is the default, that might be excessive:

```
pseudo-device    win128
pseudo-device    dtop4
pseudo-device    ms3
pseudo-device    kb3
```

In this, `dtop` is for screens, and `ms` is for mouse.

A Sun server isn't likely to be used as a direct-dial system except for the console, so `sunview` support may not be necessary for the server itself. Rather, `sunview` is needed when the server supports diskless clients.

The `options` Section

Now let's look at a DEC `options` section:

```
options       QUOTA
options       UFS
options       NFSCLIENT
options       NFSSERVER
```

`QUOTA` is necessary if you think you may want to use disk quotas. If in doubt, comment it out, but don't remove it, as you might want it later. You leave `UFS` in because it is needed for local disks. If the machine is a server, `NFSSERVER` will be needed.

The following two options require a decision:

```
options       SYSACCT
options       SYSAUDIT
```

`SYSACCT` should stay only if you want system accounting. BSD accounting is not the best I've seen for bill-back purposes, but if you need it, it is better than nothing. It is always a good diagnostic for the system administrator. `SYSAUDIT` is for Sun's optional C2 security package. It creates a shadow password file similar to System V Release 4 that removes password encryption from /etc/passwd. It is a very tight security package, and you should use it if you feel the need for this level of security.

You will need the following if there is a DES encryption chip present (USA only):

```
options     CRYPT
```

Otherwise, it is clearly excess baggage.

Making and Installing the 4.2 Kernel

Once you have copied the GENERIC configuration file to a file named after your system and have edited it, you are ready to create a new kernel. All you need do on most systems is run /etc/config, and the new kernel will be created and written to the configuration directory. For a Sun it looks like this:

```
# /etc/config stalker
```

The config command handles all the dependencies and brings together all the intermediate files. It compiles the files you have changed and caused to be changed, and it creates a new unix, usually under the name of vmunix.

Copy your old kernel to another name, such as ovmunix, vmunix.old, or Ovmunix. If anything goes wrong, you can boot off the old kernel version. Now copy the new kernel from the configuration directory to the root directory.

The configuration directory is /usr/sys/conf on a DEC. Let's say the new configuration made from the GENERIC file is STALKER. It's best to be cautious, so copy the new configuration file to a backup copy before running config.

```
% cd /usr/sys/conf
% su
password:
# cp STALKER S.STALKER
# /etc/config STALKER
```

Now move to root and move the kernel to a safe name.

```
# cd /
# mv /vmunix /ovmunix
# cp /sys/STALKER/vmunix /vmunix
```

Now it is time to bite the bullet, bring the system down, and reboot the new kernel. Plan enough time in case something goes wrong. If it is a small system, like a user's desktop, first do everything you need to short of the shutdown. Take an early lunch break so that you can shut down and reboot the systems during the users' lunch hour. That will give you a full hour to bail out if need be. If you prefer to save your lunchtime for eating, schedule this sort of maintenance during a user's meeting time. Large systems are best done in the evening after prime time. Give a full week's notice for a weekend downtime.

It's Window Shade Time

The last thing you do when you have installed a new kernel or modified rc or rc.local is bring the system up and down several times before accepting it. You do it so many times it's like pulling a window shade up and down. Note all the console errors on the way up, especially unlabeled disks, mislabeled disks, any kind of shell error, the rc family of scripts, and anything else that shows up on the console. Run your system diagnostics, and be careful to check the size of the kernel tables. Once the system is up and back in the users' hands, recheck the table sizes to see that you sized the system correctly.

Sun Kernel Installation

DEC stays close to the 4.2 distribution. At this writing Sun is at 4.3, most noticeable in the newer file and directory locations. Sun is more cognizant of the role of the file server, and so it has more code and file systems that are intended to be shared. DEC doesn't provide kernels for diskless workstations, but Sun provides kernels for all of its architectures.

Sun configuration files are stored in /usr/share/sys/sun[2,3,4]/conf. If the system is a Sun 4/280, use /usr/share/sys/sun4/conf. Since 4.3 is consistent, cp GENERIC to a file named after your system. Once you are happy with the configuration file, make a copy of it and run /etc/config. A new configuration directory will be made with the name of your system. Let's call ours STALKER again. Then cd to this directory and run make:

```
# cd STALKER
# make
```

Servers for Diskless Clients

If you are running diskless clients, their kernels must be created on the server system and put in separate directories. The names are

```
/export/exec/sun[2,3,4] /sys/sun [2,3,4] /conf
```

In addition to the Sun 2, 3, and 4 architectures, there are 386i machines to consider if you are also running them diskless.

Say you are supporting a SPARCstation (Sun 4 architecture) named edmoura. Its client kernel has to be installed in its client directory on the server. The kernel goes in this way:

```
/export/root/edmoura
```

The client system does not have to be shut down to *make* the change, but it has to be rebooted to see the change.

```
# cd /export/exec/sun4/sys/sun4/MONO
# cp /export/root/mono/vmunix /export/root/mono/ovmunix
# mv vmunix /export/root/mono/vmunix
```

The actions of moving to the configuration directory, saving old unix, and copying new unix to the client's root area are the same as in an ordinary kernel installation, but the path names are longer.

Stand-alone systems don't seem that hard to configure after you've had to configure a file server for clients with different architectures. You could easily have a single server serving kernels to three or four different architectures and three or four different kernels for each one of those architectures. Keep the OEM's manual set close by, and check every step. Only one system is at risk when testing a kernel for a diskless client, the test client.

MANAGER'S CORNER

Tuning ROI

One big question for which you always need an answer is how much system performance can be bought by reconfiguring the system. A poorly configured and untuned system is a waste of money. When bus or channel contention blocks four out of five system-level transactions, your system is paging too much, and that's a bigger money drain than taxes are. On the other hand, time spent in system tuning continues to pay off.

How do you find out whether the UNIX system is properly reconfigured? Ask your UNIX system administrator for a simple breakdown of the following system statistics:

head and channel contention
page rate
load balancing
hit ratio

Also find out the amount of time the system is halting execution of your users' jobs by being in involuntary wait state.[9]

Have the system manager write a weekly report on these activities in nontechnical terms, with technical data supporting the conclusions in an appendix. You'll always have current system statistics on hand to make management decisions. Also, by requiring reports on the status of the system, you show your interest and commitment to system efficiency. Your staff will respond positively to your expectations, and the system will run better.

---

[9] The application makes requests of the system, and the system responds with "Not now, I'm busy!" This is called an *involuntary wait state*.

15

Sample Configurations

No one area in UNIX needs standardization more than configuration does. There is a tremendous diversity of file locations, command differences, and configuration methods. Once there seemed little hope of seeing even a vague semblance of a configuration standard, and so it was a great day for UNIX when the POSIX IEEE P1003.7 System Administration Committee was created. When its work is complete, configuration will be easier and more straightforward on all UNIX machines.

There are many UNIX configuration examples in this book. System configuration takes place when you install a new system, when you do system migrations and rollovers, and when you periodically tune a machine to get optimum performance, and there are chapters that touch on each of these categories. The purpose of this chapter is to get away from UNIX theory for a while and consider two actual UNIX system configurations.

You can read UNIX theory forever, but nothing will give you a better idea of what's involved in UNIX system configuration than observing the real thing. There is no way to fit into one chapter a sample UNIX configuration for every type of machine and every version of UNIX. System configuration methods vary a great deal across a wide spectrum of computers, from micro to mainframe. I have chosen the two UNIX configuration examples in this chapter because they're just about as different as they can get!

The reason for both system configurations is the same—a rollover to a new system version. One is a mainframe UTS system rolling over to a new UTS 1.1.3 operating system version, and the other is a VAXserver rolling over to a new ULTRIX-32 3.1 operating system version. But that's where the similarities end.

One reason the two examples are so different is that one is a mainframe configuration and the other is a mini configuration. Another reason the two configurations differ is that one is a Berkeley-based system and the other is an AT&T System V version of UNIX.

UNIX configuration varies with the version of UNIX. There are fewer tunable parameters on Berkeley UNIX systems than on AT&T UNIX systems. Most minis run Berkeley-based UNIX versions, such as SunOS and DEC ULTRIX, and so if you oversee one of these machines, you won't be tuning many system parameters. UTS UNIX system administrators are very busy tuning their systems because UTS UNIX is AT&T System V. These versions of UNIX give system administrators a wealth of system parameters to tune and configure to their heart's content.

UNIX configuration varies with the type of computer. System administrators really need to know their hardware for configuring minis, but they can get away without knowing much about hardware on mainframes, because the devices are *virtual*.

Enough introduction. Let's get down to the nitty-gritty.

A RELEASE MOVE OF A LARGE SYSTEM

Moving a system and its users to a new version or release of the operating system is seldom a breeze. As a rule, the larger the system is, the more complex the move will be. Moving an entire system is called a *migration*, an apt term, because it implies a major move. To illustrate the complexity of a release move of a medium-sized UNIX system on a huge IBM 3090-600E, we will move from Amdahl's UTS 1.1.2 to UTS 1.1.3. While some of the information in this subsection is relevant only to mainframe systems, everyone can learn more about system migrations and the manipulation of system files.

Point releases are mostly bug fixes, and they bring no major features. Because a point move has no significant impact, this migration is used to implement a few major features that have already been installed, Wollongong's TCP/IP and a purchased backup product, Ubackup from Unitech. The incorporation of additional system software add-ons during a migration is somewhat like Congress's tacking a bill onto another bill to slip in a new law. If done quietly enough, you can slip new software in without the hassle of calling a downtime for the system. But never put in anything like new, untested software with a major release of the operating system, as tracking the bugs will cost you dearly. Stick to X.X.X versions to keep your sanity.

The beginning of the move is creating an engine, although you can skip the engine process if you have only one system. On the other hand, even with one system it isn't a bad idea to make your basic engine with purchased and local software and no user directories. Save it to tape or diskette for future use.

The original system used to make the engine is taken off the vendor's distribution tape and is then moved to file partitions that are sized according to what you've done before on the machine. The OEM system is merged with Wollongong's TCP/IP software, and then local software such as CAD tools and local administrative programs and subsystems are added.

First you need a full disk pack (880 cylinders times 150 blocks per cylinder times 4096 bytes per block). The basic engine takes at least half the pack. Copy the engine to the disk by a mainframe utility called DDR. It is a byte-for-byte copy method somewhat like `volcopy` or `dd`. At the host OS level a VM directory for the UNIX system is created, mapping the start and length of each disk partition or minidisk.

Give the new system a name and install it with the VM `dirmaint add` command. The infant system is then booted for the first time. Clear its file system with `fsck`, and bring it up to `init s`.

Let's say the system uses an Ethernet device made by Intel, called a Fastpath. Test it when the system is allowed to come up to `init 2`. The machine can be considered alive. With the exception of the installed software, at this point the system is no different than if it had been taken from a distribution tape.

A large accumulation of software for this system is on shared disks. These are the executable (*read-only*) CAD files, manual pages, and local commands. The system's source code is on a shared disk, but it is made inaccessible to nonprivileged users by turning off the x bit on the `/usr/src` directory and making it owned by `bin`. Therefore, it cannot be reached at any directory level:

```
drwx------
```

To make the new machine have a real identity, it must have user file systems and all the files in the system file structure that make it unique. Here are the initial files to be copied over:

- `passwd`
- `identity`
- `local.rc`
- `cron`
- `devicelist`
- `group`
- `hosts`
- `networks`

This is minimal, but it is a start. Make the file transfers across the local network.

The `devicelist` file is unique to UTS. Although `/etc/devicelist` is similar in purpose to `master` and `config.c`, it is easier to use and understand. A typical entry:

```
$ grep '/usr ' /etc/devicelist
110 dasd /usr
```

This says that the disk address `110` becomes `/dev/dsk/110s0` and `/dev/rdsk/110` becomes `/usr`. An entry like

```
a00-aff dasd
```

creates raw and block special files for the range of `/dev/dsk/a00s0` to `/dev/dsk/affs0`, but no specific directories. When the machine is *genned* with the `sysgen` utility, `devicelist` is the blueprint to make the device files, mount lists, and the entire kernel. The generated mount list entry for the first (110) disk address is

```
$ grep '/usr ' /etc/mountlist
/etc/mount/dev/dsk/110s0 /usr
```

To make the system look as much as possible like the system it will replace, the user disks are attached *read-only*. When complete, there is no difference between this system and the one it replaces, except for the release differences and the add-ons. The mount list takes this in hand:

```
/etc/mount /dev/dsk/cc0s0 /net -r
```

The -r flag makes the mount *read-only*.

The engine has only a token page disk. For this working system, two page disks of 100 cylinders each need to be taken from the disk pool and given addresses in the range predefined to page devices aa0 and aa1. They are formatted and brought on line with the UTS pagdev command. The system, knowing them to be page devices, has them in the mount list in this way:

```
/etc/pagdev /dev/dsk/aa0
/etc/pagdev /dev/dsk/aa1
```

Now all the /etc files are checked and installed. Take your time here, and copy the original file to a safe place before installing the new one:

```
# cp passwd Opasswd
# pwck Npasswd
# cp Npasswd passwd
```

Never install Npasswd without first checking the new password file with /etc/pwck.[1] If you receive no reply, there are no errors. If there are errors, pwck will report each line with which it has problems and tell you why.

The step before a sysgen is to check to be sure that there is enough room to create a new kernel and /newdev. Both the root disk and /usr/src need breathing room on UTS. A few thousand inodes are required on /, and around three thousand free blocks are needed in /usr. These are big blocks, because on UTS V there are 4096 bytes per block. Failure to make room will create an aborted sysgen and much frustration. The device list is checked for the third and fourth time, and the system is sysgened. If it survives, a newsys will be done to install the new kernel. The new /dev is renamed. Save most of the old files in case you need to back out.

The reborn system is now booted, and the root and spool disks are cleared of all transient files. In theory it should come up clean, but in fact a new system always has a flaw or two in the root inodes. Run fsck a few times.

Now it is kludge time. Until the system takes *read/write* ownership of the user disks, they have to be linked either from the VM directory or in /etc/rc. My choice is rc. A set of link statements is added for removal when the system is on its own:

```
for addr in 772 773 774 775 776 777 778 cc0
 do
   cpmd link \* $addr $addr rr  password
done
```

The asterisk in line 3 is escaped to prevent it from being acted on by rc's shell before passing it to VM. If not, it will give VM an argument list of every file and directory in /etc.

---

[1] Note that /etc/pwck is System V only.

Now give the userless machine a purpose in life. Moving to `root`, add the user directories with some freehand programming at the command line:

```
# for dir in 286 386 486 fmd smd cmd tech cad net
>do
>mkdir $dir
>chown bin $dir
>chgrp bin $dir
>chmod 777 $dir
>echo "$dir done"
>done
#
```

Now all the user disks are attached *read-only* to test out the system at this point with the following `for` loop:

```
# for addr in 772 773 774 775 776 778 cc0
>do
>cpcmd link utsvi1 $addr $addr rr password
>done
#
```

They are now manually mounted with each disk attached to the machine:

```
# /etc/mount /dev/dsk/772s0 /286
# /etc/mount /dev/dsk/773s0 /386
 .
 .
 .
# /etc/mount /dev/dskcc0c0 /net
```

At long last the uprooted `passwd` file can be tested and installed:

```
# cd /etc
# pwck Npasswd
# cp passwd Opasswd
# cp Npasswd passwd
```

Had this been attempted before the user file systems had been mounted, there would have been three screenfuls of error messages.

The larger directories are now copied by the system administrator from the old machine to the new one. On conventional machines these directories would be taken off by `cpio` tape and read into the new system. But UTS UNIX has the advantage of living on VM, so again use its ability to link *read-only* to another machine's disks. Here the `accounting` and `admin` files and directories are copied with the `cpio` pass option, `-p`.

```
# cpcmd link utsvi1 440 ff0 rr password
# mount /dev/dsk/ff0s0 /mnt0 -r      #don't forget r (read)
# cd /mnt0
# find . -depth -print!cpio -pdvlmu /usr/adm
# umount /dev/dsk/ff0s0
# cpcmd det 440
```

With most of the necessary files in place on the new system, it is ready to boot, known as IPL in IBM jargon.

Always read all messages printed to the console when booting a system. This precaution is doubly necessary at this stage of machine building. Look with care for the following:

- `cannot mount...` error messages.
- Undefined addresses.
- Network errors.
- `mounted read only` error messages.

With the intermediate system up, it is time to compare the new with the old. A window terminal is a blessing here, but if you don't have one, two terminals side by side will suffice. Go to the base of each user file system and do an `ls -l` on the same directory on the two different machines simultaneously. Run the results to the printer and double-check them. After checking each, go to the transferred file systems like `/usr/adm` and `/usr/spool` and do the same. Check for the presence of all files and directories and also the size and time stamps. Make sure all the data really made their way to the new home.

It is also time to check the parameters *genned* into the system. How many `gettys` really are present?

```
$ ps -ef!grep getty!wc -l
48
```

Is `mountlist` what you had expected? All of these must be checked at this time.

All is well? If so, remove `/olddev` from the `root` disk. The system will never take another *gen* with this monster directory in existence. It is the inode hog of the world:

```
# cd /
# rm -rf /olddev
```

This removal takes time, even on a mighty mainframe with close to 100 MIPs at its disposal. It frees almost two thousand inodes.

All this work is done ahead of time. You will want to do most of it *before* the actual shutdown, because most installations have negotiated downtimes. The new system has to be installed during a designated downtime, but with preplanning and the wind at your back, the installation will take about two hours. Request a four-hour window to be on the safe side, for if anything goes wrong, you'll need the extra two hours. If you are not a VM wizard, have one on hand. To avoid the pressure of editing the new VM directory for the system migration during the downtime, create the new directory in a privileged VM account in advance, under a name that is unnoticed by VM's `dirmaint` to escape having VM try to install it. The UNIX system's VM directory is where all its minidisks are defined and allocated as well as dedicating devices, setting the system's share of the CPU, setting privilege, and placing the initiation password. In the case of `utsvil`, the file is called

```
UTSVIL NEWDIR A0
```

to avoid confusion with the real VM directory file

```
UTSVIL DIRECT A0
```

Cut and paste with the greatest care the VM `direct` files of both the old machine and the new one. This is brain surgery! The system disks of the new are joined with the user disks of the old. Check and double-check all device addresses. One slip and you will be trying to talk to a device that doesn't exist. The system will crash before ever seeing its first legitimate login.

By the time you have suffered through all this and checked everything, your eyes will be as red as the corrections you have marked and entered. Fortunately, you are ready to make your final moves. Come in rested and ready to go on the morning of the downtime. You may notice that you are the only one in the office working. That is the price of being a system administrator. That is also the point. No one is on the machine. With both the old and new systems up, make final copies of critical files like `/etc/passwd` and `accounting`. Remove the mounting kludge from `rc`. Remove the `-r`, *read-only* flags, from the user disks in the device list. Edit `/etc/motd` to the new system, and add a note about how you have been kind enough to put them on a new release:

```
$ cat /etc/motd
<=============================================>
        Welcome to UTSVI1
          a UTS V 1.1.3 system
<=============================================>
$
```

Make `motd` different enough from the last one to catch instant attention. Check the system's node name for the last time, and do the final `sysgen`.

Now is the moment of truth. Bring both systems down. All the magic for the next hour will be done in VM. First change the name of the old system to something that won't get you into trouble:

```
dirm chg utsvi1 to utsvo1
```

Here `utsvo1` stands for "UTS V old one." The user disks must be removed by editing them out of the VM directory:

```
UTSVO1 DIRECT
```

Using `dirmaint` again, issue

```
dirm get utsvo1
```

The `dirmaint` command deposits the directory in the reader of your privileged account and locks on it. Receive it into the work area and edit out all user disks for a while. There will be conflicts if you don't. Keep the system disks. You may need them if you forgot to copy anything. Now put the directory back:

```
dirm repl utsvi1
```

Get a copy of the old system for posterity in case you ever need to reconstruct it:

```
dirm get utsvt1 nolock
```

The next step is destructive. The temporary machine must be purged:

```
dirm purge utsvt1
```

The old system is now gone.

The directory that had been prepared the night before and checked more often than Santa's list is now copied to its final name:

```
copy utsvil newdir aO utsvil direct aO
```

You hold your breath for the last step:

```
dirm add utsvil
```

At this point you can see the light at the end of the tunnel. Bring up the new system. Do your final checking. Exercise

- lp
- vmread
- vmpunch
- The network

Long-list each of the user trees. Is it all there? If so, call your significant other, and tell him or her that you are on your way home.

VAXSERVER CONFIGURATION

There is an emphasis on setting system parameters in the configuration just seen. System V has quite a few tunable system parameters, and the configuration took full advantage of that fact. On the other hand, you didn't need to worry about setting devices, because although mainframe UNIX systems have many devices, they are *virtual*, not real, so the system administrator needs to know only the type of device and its address.

It's another story for minis. There are few system parameters, but *all* devices must be strictly set. Minis have too many devices to leave to default settings, but Berkeley UNIX takes that in stride. Devices vary greatly from one system to another, even on the same installation. One mini may use SCSI drives and controllers, and the other, MCDs. Nothing can be taken for granted or left to defaults. Each specified device becomes a specific device driver in the kernel, so the configuration of devices is a precise business.

System administrators of midsized systems must know their hardware. The master configuration file, usually called GENERIC, is either too short to have the devices you need or it has so many devices that it would make the kernel unnecessarily large if you kept them all in. The trick is to create a configuration file from your master file that has precisely the same devices that you actually run on your system.

We are going to configure a VAXserver 3600 in this chapter. The occasion is a move from ULTRIX-32 version 2.2 to version 3.1. You have been plagued daily by a fatal bug in the tape-drive driver that brings down the system every time you write more than one tape. Version 3.0 still has problems with the driver, but in version 3.1 you have high hopes for a stable tape-drive driver.

The system has two massive disk partitions for tools, but because both are nearly out of space, it is a good time for a disk expansion. It takes you one week to put a plan together. There is going to be a special trick to this migration. You have a spare RA 82 drive that you are putting on line to become the new root disk. Devices called *unit plugs* will be swapped. A unit plug tells the system the disk's hardware address, allowing the root disk to become drive ∃ and the new disk to become drive ◻.

The disk juggling protects the old root disk from being written over. What better backup can you have than the original disk? File writes can be made almost at bus speed, and the tape copies of the root disk can be saved just in case. Some more disk juggling on the system's two larger RA 90 disks also permits new areas to be created and data moved to them again on a disk-to-disk basis. Always try to keep at least one free disk drive in your back pocket. It allows both system and user areas to be enlarged while you have the users buy more. The trick is not telling anyone that you have a free pack. If you do, it won't be free any longer.

Preplanning is key to any move. List the system files to be saved beforehand. Make full backups the evening before the move. Pay particular attention to the /usr disk when you precalculate each partition. Partition sizes are based on historical information, such as the previous size of the user and tool disks. The root and /usr disk sizes are taken from the distribution notes, and /usr is calculated according to how much of the supported and unsupported software will be loaded from the distribution tapes.

The actual installation is no time to break out a calculator, so calculate the partition tables ahead of time. DEC partitioning is not as clean as Sun's; Sun allows you to cut up a disk cleanly on cylinder boundaries. DEC tells you only how many bytes you lost after you made your best guess on a clean cut.

The actual rollover starts by bringing down the system (halt) and leaving it on the boot prompt. The stand-alone tape is loaded, and the system is booted from that tape:

```
>>> b mua◻
```

The installation starts once the system is read from tape to memory. The DEC installation procedure is interactive. The partitioning and the installation of the new software are done from the installation dialogue, and the installation culminates with the creation of the new kernel that lies in /sys/conf/*machine_name*.

Copy the old kernel to /vmunix.old before moving the new kernel to /vmunix. The system is rebooted to the new kernel:

```
# shutdown -r now
```

Once up, the system's kernel configuration file, /sys/conf/FM◻2, is checked with vi to confirm that all devices are in and no new ones are left out. The identity information and the config line are double-checked. The devices section is checked and double-checked. Here's a list of the devices you're putting on the machine:

- 1 TUB 81+ reel-to-reel tape drive
- 1 TK 70 cartridge-tape drive
- 2 RA 82 disk drives
- 2 RA 90 disk drives

Kernel Configuration

The kernel configuration starts by moving to the /sys/conf directory and finding the GENERIC file. Copy it to a file with the name of your system.

The Global Section

Several items are identified and set in the global section of the configuration file. This machine is *fm02*, so you name it FM02. Start with the identity section of the file. Our system is a 32-megabyte, 32-user VAXserver 3600 located in California. Here is an excerpt from the global section of /sys/conf/FM02:

```
ident           "FM02"
machine         vax
cpu             "VAX3600"
maxusers        32
processors      1
maxuprc         50
physmem         32
timezone        8 dst 1
```

Notice that timezone is Pacific Standard Time, 8 hours from GMT. The vax system has a single processor. The maximum number of user processes, maxuprc, is set to 50, and maxuser is set to 32, which might seem like overkill for a system that is a server. After all, servers don't have users, right? At the most they may have three system support people logged on at a time, two administrators and one operator, and they are there only to do caretaking work on the machine. However, maxusers does not indicate the maximum number of users but is a multiplier for sizing the system tables, and so 32 is generous but not excessive. Setting it from 32 to 64 allocates 32 mbuf pages.

Additional parameters not shown include maxuva, the maximum amount of aggregate virtual address space that the system permits, and maxsiz, the largest text segment allowed.

Options

There are a few kernel feature options that must be specified in the configuration file. If the name of an option is present in the configuration file, the service will be present in the kernel. The following is part of the options section for our machine's configuration:

```
options         QUOTA
options         INET
options         UFS
options         NFS
options         RPC
options         LAT
options         DECNET
```

LAT stands for local area transport, necessary for the terminal servers for the machine. NFS is the network file system option. There wouldn't be a server without that. RPC stands for remote procedure calls, and it is needed by network software like YP and NFS. INET gives the basic internet protocols, needed for just about everything networked. UFS stands for ULTRIX file system. The system will be seen as diskless without this option.

Configuration Section

On our machine the `root`, `swap`, and `dumps` disk partitions are mounted whenever the system is up, so the disk addresses and the name of the kernel must be placed in the configuration statement:

```
config  vmunix  root on ra0a  swap on ra0b and ra1b dumps on ra1b
```

Notice that the keyword `and` is not only permissible but necessary for listing multiple swap devices.

Device Section

Here is where you must know your hardware. SUN gives you a fits-all-do-all `GENERIC` file that covers every conceivable piece of hardware that ever fit or ever will fit on any Sun system. DEC's `GENERIC` file is spartan. If you have VAXserver equipment not listed in the `GENERIC` file, you will have to find out the necessary information you need in order to put it in. Specific information can be found in manual(4) under the mnemonic name for the device, such as ra(4).

In this section of the configuration file you don't need to specify the bus, but you must know it in order to specify which controller types to use. Our VAXserver 3600 uses a Q-bus. That tells you it also needs a disk controller of type uq. The `adapter` is a `uba` device. It was originally intended for a UNIBUS, but because you know your hardware so well, you know that VAXservers use Q-bus and UNIBUS boards interchangeably.

Most device chains run *device* to *controller* to *controller* to *adapter* to *bus*. The adapter is a device because by definition it is the entity attached to the bus. The bus end is the terminator, and it uses the keyword `nexus ?`. At the other end the disk drives are type `ra`. The drives RA 82 and RA 90 were already specified in the global section of the file. RA drives are mass storage control protocol drives. One physical controller card services a number of drives, so the drives `ra0` through `ra3` are at controller `uq0` in this file. Remember that the reason you are in this section of the kernel configuration file is to change the number of drives from three to four, drives `0` through `3`.

The device section of the configuration file deals with both real and not-exactly-real devices. We see two controllers in the `ra` device-to-bus chain. One is the controller board itself, and the other represents a device on that board. Similarly, you see two controllers on the tape device chain, but only the `klesiu` device is real.

We have two kinds of tape drives, reel to reel and cassette. The configuration file treats them both as `tms` tape drives with `klesiu` controllers. The `tms` tells you it is a tape mass storage control protocol magnetic tape interface. The TK 70 tape drive is the first drive and the system default drive, `/dev/rmt0`. The reel-to-reel unit is the second drive, `/dev/rmt1`.

Here it all is in black and white:

```
adapter        uba0        at  nexus ?
controller     klesiu0     at  uba0
controller     tmscp1      at  klesiu0    csr 0174500    vectpr tmscpintr
tape           tms0        at  tmscp1     drive 0
controller     uda0        at  uba0
controller     uq0         at  uda0       csr 0172150    vector uqintr
```

```
disk        ra0       at  uq0       drive 0
disk        ra1       at  uq0       drive 1
disk        ra2       at  uq0       drive 2
disk        ra3       at  uq0       drive 3
device      qe0       at  uba0      csr 0174440    vector qeintr
controller  klesiu1   at  uba0
controller  tmscp2    at  klesiu1   csr 0160404    vector tmscpintr
tape        tms1      at  tmscp2    drive 0
```

Pseudodevices

The preceding device section deals with real devices. Each chain of *device* to *controllers* to *adapter* to *bus* creates a device driver and a file in /dev. Pseudodevices also have drivers and entries in /dev, but that's where the similarity ends. There is no hardware involved, nor do pseudodevices talk directly to the bus. Their drivers have no *lower end*, that assembly section of the driver that negotiates with the bus.

A device needs to be present in the pseudodevice section to create its spot in the kernel and /dev. Here are some of the listings for our configuration:

```
pseudo-device   pty
pseudo-device   ether
pseudo-device   inet
pseudo-device   nfs
pseudo-device   rpc
pseudo-device   lat
pseudo-device   decnet
```

The pty is a pseudoterminal, used for windows; ether is the Ethernet device; inet is the internet device; nfs is the NFS device; rpc is the remote procedure call device; lat is the local area transport device; and decnet is the DECnet device present on DECs.

Once the configuration file is thoroughly checked and modified, the kernel is recompiled and installed. The heaviest part of the install is over. While the old root disk is still mounted to /mnt, critical files are copied over, including the following:

- exports
- crontab
- fstab
- group
- hosts
- hosts.equiv
- inetd.conf
- networks
- passwd
- printcap
- sendmail.cf
- termcap
- ttys

The sendmail software must be reinstalled to our local configuration. The network must be shaken down thoroughly, and each workstation served by this system must be rebooted. Disks have been moved, and the old NFS mounts cause stale file handle errors. All of this goes away on the reboot. Enough detail has been taken care of to have business as usual the next morning.

Most of the real time on the installation is spent copying data from disk to disk. Nearly three hours go into this task. The installation starts at 17:00 Friday and is over at 00:30 Saturday. No TV time for the administrator this evening. It's worth it, though, because the 3.1 tape-drive driver works.

MANAGER'S CORNER

Major Migrations

A major release of the operating system is marked by changes in the C compiler itself and additions to the system calls and libraries. Both Releases 2 and 4 of System V are typical. There are numerous other changes, to be sure, but none as far-reaching as the change to the compiler and libraries. Code is usually forward compatible but not backward compatible. That is, the old code runs on the new system, but code from the new system doesn't run on the old one.

A major release is always accompanied by the additions of milestone software. The move to System V Release 4 is significant. SVR4 is a merge of System V, XENIX, BSD, and SunOS, with csh and ksh added. POSIX becomes the guideline, ANSI C is real, and the unreasonable open-file limit of twenty files per user is removed forever. Streams become the answer for almost everything, and TCP/IP networking as well as NFS and RFS are part of the standard distribution. The Applications Binary Interface becomes a new standard, and graphical user interfaces change the face of UNIX forever.

All sorts of problems must be faced with a new release of major proportions. Not only users but also operators and the system programming staff must be reeducated. There are no schools to teach the new system at the time of a release, so time must be allowed for system staffs to learn the system, prepare a migration, plan differences documents, and create their own in-house classes.

Sometimes large, critical software packages do not survive migrations without changes. Major releases always take longer than expected to nationalize within a company. To pull it off, they require commitment on the part of management, users, system staff, and tool and applications groups. Companies allow major outlays of money and time to install a new network or a new system, and major operating system releases should be treated in the same way.

When a major operating system migration is in order, *planning* and *commitment* must be coordinated at all levels. Inducements must be large, penalties larger, and all bridges burned after the migration. The most vocal manager in the migration must be the UNIX manager.

The creation of a migration machine is a genesis. An initial system at the new release level should be created as quickly, but as carefully, as possible. The system must be long-haul networked to give outside vendors access.[2] If possible, local networking should be

---

[2] A long-haul network is a network involving the telephone system's lines.

installed for access to in-house applications and system and tool developers. Once you've done all this, it's time to turn the heat up all the way on the software vendors. Now they don't have any excuse not to perform. The system staff must write and rewrite the system's software with equal speed.

As all the software pieces drift in, they must be installed and tested immediately. The key point comes when the system is thought to be usable. A single user-group should be selected for a test site. Pick the group well, because their buy-off of the system is the trigger for the nationalization of the release throughout the company.

Small stand-alone systems do not have to follow all these steps, but the system manager's responsibility is the same. Whatever purchased software is supported must be followed up to see if and when the vendor will have a release for that version.

A final note of comfort. You will seldom see a UNIX system release as far-reaching as UNIX System V Release 4.

CHAPTER

16

Tuning

Tuning is the art and science of making a system's hardware and software act in concert to give the best possible performance. It's hard to separate configuration and tuning. The first time you size and customize a new system, it's configuration, but every time you configure it thereafter, it's tuning.

Tuning is done by adjusting the size of system parameters based on data taken with system activities diagnostics. Reconfiguration is done by adding and removing devices, altering the size and location of partitions and other structural modifications intended to alter the architecture of the finished system. Before tuning a system, you must have solid statistics on the current machine's condition, and for that you need to know what information you are looking for and what to do with it when you get it.

The standard AT&T command for performance statistics is sar, the system activity reporter. For BSD and XENIX, use pstat and vmstat, as they will tell you most of the information you need. More information can be extracted from crash, a memory formatter created for examining system core dumps, but also useful for many other applications. Some OEM-specific commands also are helpful, such as Amdahl's stats command.

The information required to reconfigure a system is the fullness of the primary critical system tables and the performance figures for system I/O. We discussed some of the tables in Chapter 14: the process table, the inode table, the file table, and the text table. The text table controls the stored, executable portions of programs. Since they can be shared, knowing their location in relation to other processes is important. As we saw in Chapter 14, the buffer tables to analyze are clists and the system buffer cache.

Seeing table sizes is simple enough; size is reported as a percentage of fullness or as a fraction. Thus if there are 300 slots in a table and 128 are full, the fraction is 128/300.

The function of the system buffer cache is to allow disk reads to be taken in full blocks for the purpose of a *read-ahead*. Writes similarly are delayed for a time convenient to the system, and they become *write-behinds*. The *hit ratio* keeps score of the effectiveness of the buffer cache. The formula is

$$\left(1 - \frac{\text{real reads}}{\text{virtual reads}} \right) * 100$$

If there are 1 million virtual reads but only 100,000 real reads, the hit ratio is 90 percent, not a bad percentage to shoot for.

Before looking at tunable parameters, let's examine the diagnostic commands, as system administrators rely on them for configuration and tuning information.

AT&T SYSTEM V'S sar COMMAND

System V's sar command is supposed to be the do-all-fits-all system activity reporter. It doesn't do a bad job, but some information is not readily obtainable. The sar command either yields data back to some historical period or can be invoked to give data at a specified time interval, thus giving statistics repeatedly over some brief period. Watching activity at 5- to 10-second intervals on a busy machine is enlightening. Longer periods give very large numbers, and some important data will be skipped, falling between the cracks of the longer time period. For example, you may miss large page spikes or fleeting periods of involuntary wait.

−a Flag

The −a flag means *all*, and that is exactly what it reports. Pipe sar −a to the printer or to more, to tell you everything you need to know.

Be sure to use commands like vmstat, pstat, or sar at peak levels of activity to get useful data. Don't wait until you have time to get around to it. If necessary, write a monitor script that gathers useful data with only a single command:

```
sar -a 300>>/usr/spool/log/sar.dat
```

This can also be run automatically by script at intervals during peak time. Be sure to clean out periodically the log file created by the script, either manually or with a cleanup program. A good technique is to write it to OLDsar.log and to start sar.log again at line 1. Do this daily to be on the safe side.

−b Flag

The −b flag yields buffer activity, the tool required for sizing the system buffer cache. Among the columns of data are the hit ratios, %wcache and %rcache, the *write* and *read* hit ratios. Both reflect the amount of time the system was able to read or write at its convenience, as opposed to being forced to do I/O.

−u **Flag**

The −u flag tells how the CPU is spending its time. This is important to know. There is a point when the system gets so heavily loaded that the system itself takes more time in overhead than it gives to the users. Then you know you need to think about buying additional resources.

−d **Flag**

The −d flag gives disk activity. The output helps in tasks like seek centering for better disk performance, but there are better OEM programs for this sort of data collection, such as VM's vmmap.

−q **Flag**

The −q flag stands for *queue*, and it tells the length of the run queue and the percentage of time it is occupied.

−w **Flag**

The −w flag reports swapping activity, which you will want to know at peak loading, for then you can see how system performance is handicapped by paging and swapping. Paging slows down the machine. It increases disk I/O, because paging actually *is* disk I/O. When it is time to buy more resources, remember that there are several ways to deal with high page rates:

- More core memory.
- Faster page devices, such as small-diameter, quick-access hard disks; extended dedicated memory used as a disk emulator; and solid-state "disks" like the now-defunct Intel fast disk.
- Another computer.

With the per-byte cost of incore memory dropping faster than the per-byte cost of hard disks, and addressing going to terabytes, solid state is a good answer.

−v **Flag**

The tuning jackpot is the −v flag. It indicates the size of the text, process, inode, and file tables, given as fractions: used slots over available slots. Thus a text size of 33/64 is a text table that is about one-half full. Gather these numbers at peak loading. If the tables get close to full, the system will thrash, I/O will be held up, and new processes won't run until there are slots for them.

The XENIX configure command gives you the same information that sar −v does. It interactively gives you the current values of system parameters, and it also allows you to change them.

There are other flags for semaphore activity and character rates. If your users or applications programmers are taking advantage of IPCs, watch your semaphore tables.[1]

---

[1] IPC: Interprocess communication, or semaphores, shared text, and message queues.

All are useful, and none should be ignored. Here are most of the IPC constants and flags:

SEMA	Turn semaphore code on or off (1 or 0)
SHMEM	Include shared memory, yes or no (1 or 0)
MESG	Include message queue code, yes or no (1 or 0)
SHMMAX	Maximum shared memory size, 8K default on 3Bs
SHMMIN	Minimum shared memory size, 1 on 3Bs
SHMMNI	Maximum number of shared memory segments
SHMSEG	Maximum number of shared memory segments per user, 4 on a 3B
SHMALL	Maximum amount of shared memory for the entire system, 250KB for DEC UNIX
MSGMAX	Maximum message size
MSGMNB	Maximum byte count for a message queue, 16K for 3Bs
MSGQTL	Number of system message headers
MSGSSZ	Message segment size
MSGSEG	Total number of system message segments
MSGMAP	Message map size
MSGMNI	Maximum number of system message queues, default 10 on DEC and 3B
SEMMAP	Semaphore map entries, default 10 on 3Bs
SEMMNI	Number of semaphore sets
SEMMNS	Total number of semaphores on the system
SEMMNU	Number of undo structures
SEMUME	Number of undo entries per structure
SEMMSL	Maximum number of semaphores per identifier
SEMOP	Maximum number of semaphores per semop(2) call

SYSTEM CALLS

The number of occurrences of file calls like iget and namei may not move you, but they are good indicators of the type of work being done. If namei is called more often than any other call, chances are you have a lot of file system activity. All of this is helpful in understanding your system, as the types of calls are indicative of the types of activities.

crash

In a perfect world the sar command would be available on all systems. Not only is it standard UNIX, but it is also the easiest AT&T activity command to work with. Lacking AT&T's sar command or BSD's pstat or vmstat, you are forced to look inside the kernel while it is running. The crash command has the default of using memory as the file to read. It therefore looks at the living machine. Although crash is not an easy utility to use, it will get anything *if* you know how to walk through memory and read hex.

Note that crash is an interactive command. Initially it tells you nothing but instead gives you a simple **>** prompt and an eh? when it fails to understand or is interrupted. It gives you data that sar cannot, like statistics on the callout table [2] and mount table. It also gives you data that sar does on the process table, text table, file table, and any other table you can format. The data aren't as readable as sar, pstat, or vmstat data and cannot be redirected to the printer.

With the crash command, you have to calculate fullness, the ratio of the size of a table to the number of entries. One of its best tricks is to give a list of tunable parameters, which is a good sanity check against what you think you have or the configuration tables led you to think.

BSD 4.2 AND XENIX TUNING DIAGNOSTICS

Any good auto mechanic will tell you that a water pump can't be repaired. If it fails, he will advise you to throw it out and get a new one. This is good advice for everyone except the rare master mechanic who is also an accomplished machinist. Someone with that kind of skill can safely disassemble that water pump and repair it. Without that skill and training, forget it.

Berkeley systems do not yield easily to tuning by parameter. Administrators who are familiar with internals and know their way around the kernel files can change parameters on BSD systems, but if you don't have that training, you'd probably be better off not trying it.

This chapter emphasizes System V tuning, because the parameters are more readily available on System V UNIX systems. People on Berkeley systems will benefit from learning about these parameters, even if they never change many parameter settings. Knowing about system parameters helps you understand how UNIX systems work. Berkeley's diagnostic commands give the administrator plenty of information about the system.

iostat

The iostat command is simple, with equally simple output. It gives the number of characters read and written to terminals and to each disk, and also system (CPU) time as a percentage in four modes: user mode, user mode at low priority (niced), in-system mode, and idling mode. The command's output looks like this:

```
% iostat
      tty         ra0        ra1        ra2        cpu
time  tout    bps tps    bps tps    bps tps    us ni sy id
 0     3      1   0      4   1      5   3      3  0  2  95
```

---

[2] Parameter NCALL.

The disk rates are in kilobytes per second and average seek time in milliseconds. Terminal rates are in simple bytes per second.

The iostat command has optional *interval* and *count* arguments, *interval* being the time to report each interval in seconds. Since this puts the command in a continuous output mode, *count*, the number of screen displays, limits the total number of reports. For example, if I set an *interval* of 6 and a *count* of 10, I'll get 10 pictures over a 1-minute period. The *count* argument would be a welcome addition to many System V and OEM diagnostics.

The iostat command is particularly useful for giving *metrics* for repartitioning and redistributing disk loading. Metrics is manualesque for measurements. The goals are to arrange seeks about the disk's center tracks and to spread the load evenly. Pay particular attention to your swap disks and partitions.

uptime

The uptime command is relatively innocuous. It displays the current time, the amount of time the system has been up, the number of current users, and the number of jobs run in the last 1, 5, and 15 minutes:

```
% uptime
10:34 am up 11 days, 35 mins, 9 users, load average 0.90 0.80 0.60
```

The command rolls up who!wc -l, date, and a look in the accounting log, and this is an advantage for the system administrator. What if the system goes down in the evening, and your night operator forgets to tell you? Perhaps it went down unattended on the weekend, and it autobooted. Then uptime keeps your operators honest, because it tells you how long the machine has been up.

XENIX's version of uptime is somewhat different:

```
% uptime
The system has been up for 1 hour 20 minutes and 31 seconds.
```

It doesn't have as much information, but it is certainly easy to read.

vmstat

The vmstat command reports virtual memory statistics and process, disk, trap, and CPU activity. BSD and XENIX have no sar command or crash utility, and so you need to rely on pstat and vmstat. Like sar, vmstat gives you either a history or your work done over a time period. Called without a flag or argument, vmstat does its best to set a record for putting the most information ever written on a single line. It outputs information in four major categories: process, paging, system, and CPU. Because it is a memory reporter, it doesn't give critical data like hit ratios or table percentage full, but it does offer you some good system statistics and paging and swapping information.

Most of UNIX's memory-related activity takes place in virtual memory, /dev/kmem, as opposed to real memory, /dev/mem. The vmstat command is designed to deal with the analysis and reporting of virtual memory activity and to put out a massive amount of information in a single line:

```
% vmstat
procs     memory            page            faults           cpu
r b w   avm   fre re at pi po fr de sr s0 s1 s2 f0  in  sy  cs us sy id
0 1 0     0 1044 0  0 64  0 16  0  8  0  0 20  0  82 128  66  3 24 73
```

The output is reminiscent of iostat.

XENIX also has vmstat, but its output is slightly different, as seen in Figure 16.1.

```
% vmstat
    procs         paging                        system      cpu
r  b  w  si  so  ch  cm ffr swr sww rec shf shc cpy pf   in   sy   cs  us su id
1 21  0   0   0 393 333 333   0   0   0 893   0 751 9450 7657 22509 2723  1  1 98
```

Figure 16.1.

The first area of concern is procs, which reports the following process states:

r processes in the run queue

b processes blocked for resources

w runnable processes or processes in a short sleep of less than 20 seconds, but swapped

I/O and paging are the kinds of resources that block a process. Process table information is essential to know, particularly at peak loading. When you are out of process table slots, you are dead in the water until a slot opens up for the next process.

The next area vmstat examines is memory, both virtual and real. Memory is measured in *pages*, which are implementation dependent and architecture dependent. Most systems running BSD 4.2 and BSD 4.2 derivatives, such as DEC ULTRIX, have a 1024-byte page size. Items reported under the category of memory are

avm active virtual pages

fre free list size

In the vmstat output there are 155 active virtual pages and a free list size of 25,000. Output is scaled with the suffix K for 1000 and M (not shown) for 1 million.

Page information works with both page faults and regular paging activity. A page fault occurs when the system tries to access an unmapped page. It is a trap to the operating system indicating that there is no more memory, at least for now. In most systems the data are averaged over 5 seconds and are given in pages per second. The following are page's cryptic headers:

re page reclaims

at pages attached

pi pages paged in

po pages paged out

fr pages freed per second, a rate

de memory shortfall anticipated (short term)

sr pages per second scanned by the clock algorithm

By now, some of you must be wondering, "What does vmstat show that df doesn't?" The system's page disk or disk partition is not always shown by the df command. SunOS's df command shows the swap disk at 109 percent, as full as it can get. ULTRIX doesn't say anything about the swap disk. But either way it makes no difference, because paging activity is so dynamic that it can't be caught by df-type commands.

You must catch the "high-water" paging mark to get enough information for it to be useful for resizing your page area on the next system generation. A heavily paged system slows down considerably, as it is simultaneously memory bound and page bound. The system is taking page faults because no real memory is found. Real memory is then read out to the paging disk, and the memory image of older processes is brought back into memory from the page disk. Thus the disk I/O goes up. The system can become disk bound if it is in competition with user applications.

Although our vmstat output shows zeros under the page headers, that reflects the condition of the machine at one fleeting moment. Paging requirements vary greatly, and the paging differences from machine to machine show up only at peak loading periods.

Let's compare two desktop 386 systems. One is engaged in text processing and small program development. It supports four users, and it has an average of two users on at all times. This system has 2.5 megabytes of real memory and a 5-megabyte swap area. It might page as often as once a week. Compare that with another system, a 386 workstation with one user running CAD applications. It has 12 megabytes of real memory and a 50-megabyte swap space. It is paging more often than not. Paging requirements are application specific. Watch your page activity, and size both real memory and the page disk accordingly.

Under faults, trap/interrupt rates are given in events per second. The information-gathering period is 5 seconds. Here is the cryptic header information:

in   interrupts per second for nonclock devices

sy   system calls per second

cs   switches per second, CPU context

The interrupt rate has no direct bearing on system table sizing for configuration or tuning, but it is an excellent indicator for showing how taxed the CPU is. When a CPU is taking a constant beating, the only sure cures are buying a larger, faster machine or offloading the present system.

The last category reported by vmstat is cpu, whose reporting categories are

us   user time (normal and low-priority processes)

sy   system time

id   idle CPU time

Like iostats, the data are output as a percentage.

Knowing how to analyze the breakdown of system states is critical to understanding your system. To a point the system gives more of itself to the user than it takes in overhead. Somewhere around 80 percent CPU usage there is a marked change: The system starts taking the lion's share of the resource, 80 percent for overhead at 100 percent usage, whereas at 50 percent usage it takes only 20 percent for itself. This is usually aggravated by high memory usage and accompanying high page rates, inducing a higher-than-normal disk I/O rate. In short, everything goes to pot. This is the time to switch from administrator to politician and start lobbying for more resources.

pstat

The pstat command generates more statistics than the Census Bureau does. Like System V's sar command, pstat has many flags and functions, but its overall task is to report system table information. A thorough description of the command could run to one hundred pages, so we'll look at only a few areas.

BSD 4.2's pstat with the i option shows *gnode* information. A gnode is an NFS-equivalent of an inode. Inodes must occur on the local system, but a gnode gives equivalent information for remotely mounted files. The pstat command formats and reports on the process table and other kernel tables. Be warned that issuing pstat -i to the screen will only lead to frustration. It will output several pages of data if you let it. You can use more to read the output, but your best bet is sending the output to the printer:

```
% pstat -i
116/356 active gnodes
 LOC    FLAGS  CNT DEVICE RDC WDC GNO  MODE NLK UID SIZE/DEV
800c2000       44  9, 0    0   0    2  41ff 13   0    512
        .
        .
        .
```

Here are the header meanings:

LOC	the core memory address of the specific entry
FLAGS	state variables
CNT	the number of open file table entries for the gnode
DEV	major and minor device numbers of the file system where the gnode originates
RDC	gnode lock reference count
WRC	exclusive lock reference count for gnodes
GNO	I-number within the device
MODE	mode bits (as used in ls and chmod)
NLK	gnode link count
UID	user-id number
SIZ/DEV	byte count for regular files, major and minor numbers for device special files

The p flag prints process table activity, and its output looks like this:

```
% pstat -p
32/276 processes
  LOC    S PIOP   PRI  SIG  UID SLP TIM  CPU  NI  PGRP   PID  PPID
  ADDR   RSS SRRS SIZE WCHAN LINK   TEXTP  CLKT
800d7118 1  3     0    0    0  0   10 127    0  20   0      0  0
     .
     .
```

This command's staggered headers lead to much confusion, and the output is voluminous, because it prints everything in the process table.

The fraction 32/276 tells the table slots used over the full size of the table. For example, if you divide a 276-slot tale by 32 slots in use, you'll get the percentage of use, in this case 12 percent.

Let's look at the what a few headers mean:

LOC	the location or address of the table slot
S	the run state
PRI	priority
SIGNAL	signals received (refer to signal.h)
UID	user ID
NI	nice (refer to priority)
PID	process id
PPID	parent-process ID
channel	called the wait channel, the event or process waited for

When you use ps -l, you see a lot of these categories. The ps command is another way to look at the process table, and the third way is with a crash formatter.

Use the fullness fraction for system sizing. If you consistently see fractions like 270/276 at peak loading, it's time for a larger process table. On the other hand, if you consistently see fractions like 11/276 and 15/276 at peak loading, the tables should be smaller. Large tables waste precious core memory.

XENIX has its own version of pstat. Figure 16.2 is a heavily abbreviated look at its output.

```
% pstat
49 active inodes
   LOC    FLAGS CNT DEVICE   INO    MODE NLK UID  SIZE/DEV
  130f0          5  1, 40      2  40755  13   3       288
  13154     T    1  1, 40     47 100700   1   3     13858
  131b8     T    1  1, 40   2225 100711   1   0     60208
  1321c          1  1, 40    297  10600   1   0         0
  .
  14284          1  1,106    188  40755   2 201        64
  142e8     A    1  1, 40    115  20600   1  10      4,  1
  1434c          1  1, 40    114  20600   1  10      4,  0
  143b0          1  1, 40      6  60600   1  10      1, 41
10 text segments
   LOC FLAGS    CADDR   IPTR  CNT CCNT
  b0c0  W        c4d4  13154    1    1
  b0d4  W        cabc  13924   10   10
  b0e8  W        c6cc  132e4    1    1
  b0fc  W        c624  1353c    1    1
  b110  W        c81c  135a0    1    1
  b124  W        c8c4  1385c    1    1
  b138  W        c96c  131b8    3    3
  b14c  W        d14c  13e9c    1    1
  b160  W        c57c  141bc    1    1
  b174  W        d1f4  14220    1    1
```

```
22 processes
    LOC  S     F   PRI  SIGNAL  UID  TIM  CPU NI  PGRP  PID  PPID   ADDR  WCHAN  LINK
    c42c 1 403         0      0    0 127    0 20     0    0     0     46   9df0     0
    c4d4 1 101   30    0      0    0 127    0 20     0    1     0     70   c4d4  cb64
    d0a4 1 101   28    0      0    0 127    0 20    51   51     1    1f3   bdc4     0
.
    d14c 1 101   28    0    201   48    0    0 20    39  380    39    219   8e54  c4d4
    d1f4 31501   90    0      0    1   80 20    38  403    38    282      0     0
35 open files
    LOC  FLAGS CNT    INO    OFFS
    9704 R       1   13348      0
    9710 RW      3   13dd4     18
    971c R       1   133ac      0
    9800 RW      3   13f00     18
.
    980c RW      3   13b18     18
    9818 RW      3   13f64     18
    9824 RW      5   13be0   7542
    9830 RW      3   13d70     18
    983c RW      3   139ec     18
    9848 R       1   1402c      0
    9854 RW      1   14090   1940
    9860 RW      3   13ab4     18
    986c RW      1   140f4   4096
    9878 W       1   14158   5120
    9884 R       1   142e8  38660
    9890 R       1   1434c      0
    989c R       1   143b0      0
```

Figure 16.2.

These useful XENIX `pstat` flags do the following:

-i   prints the inode (not gnode) table

-x   prints the text table

-f   prints the open file table

Two other useful 4.2 diagnostics are `netstat` and `nfsstat`, which are network-oriented commands (see Section IV).

UTS'S stats

UTS's `stats` is one of my favorite OEM statistics programs. It graphs CPU activity—giving user and system time—I/O activity, I/O waits, and involuntary waits. An *I/O wait* occurs when the system must wait for I/O activity, like a disk `read` or `write`, before the CPU can go any further. An *involuntary wait* is peculiar to a guest/host system like AIX-370 on a VM host. The UNIX system asks for the equivalent of a system call from the guest system, and the guest system makes it wait, thus the term *involuntary wait*. UTS's `stats` command shows memory usage information, such as paging and swaps. Most important, it shows the high-water mark for critical system tables (like clists), the process table, the file table, `ioq`, and the inode table. Equally important, it shows system buffer cache information, particularly the hit ratios and the numbers that created them.

Like sar and vmstat, stats is either historical or time based. With a multiwindow terminal, the output resembles a hospital analog display of critical body functions like heartbeat and blood pressure. If any OEMs are looking for a good program to emulate, stats is the one.

TUNABLE PARAMETERS AND THEIR EFFECT ON PERFORMANCE

A lot of people think that system tuning is an arcane art practiced by a few "true" wizards. In truth, the majority of effective tuning is done by mundane analysis of available system statistics and reconfiguring to correct any abnormalities.

Hardware tuning cannot be neglected. Disk seek centering helps enormously in reducing I/O contention. Onboard memory and hardware caches also work wonders. Enough real memory to reduce or eliminate paging is a gift from heaven, and a solid-state paging device is the next best thing.

UNIX System 5 Release 4 marks a number of significant changes in the internals of the system, including dynamic kernel table allocation. Now many of the kernel tables can expand and contract with system needs. Bear in mind as you read through the following parameters and constants that because many of the tables are dynamic on SVR4 systems, the associated constant has gone away.

Tunable Parameters

Theoretically, any parameters can be changed on a source code system, but for the sake of discretion, you should leave many parameters alone, and fortunately those parameters are commented in the header files or C source. Some of the comments are gems. On some systems in /usr/include/sys/param.h I've seen comments like "Probably should not be altered too much" and "Cannot be changed easily." Although we talked about tunable parameters in Chapter 14, in this chapter we will go into more detail.

NBUF

NBUF is the number of system buffers, specifically the size of the system buffer cache. Its size is an important tuning parameter, because if the number of system buffer blocks is sufficiently large, the disk *hit ratio* will increase to a point.[3] The buffer cache holds disk data taken from each physical read. It acts as a *read-ahead* buffer, anticipating the next request. Similarly, the buffers hold data on a *write* until it is convenient for the system to physically write the data to disk. Taken to a logical extreme, *read-aheads* anticipate what will be wanted, and *write-behinds* delay disk seeks. Both reduce the number of disk accesses, thereby improving performance.

The number of actual buffers recommended is as low as 25 to 60 in PDP-11s and 80 to 400 in VAX 750/780s. XENIX starts at 250. UTS sets NBUF to 300 and up, enhanced by its block size of 4096 bytes.

---

[3] Remember that a hit ratio is one minus real reads divided by virtual reads. This yields the number of times that the system is able to get data from the buffer rather than the disk.

To get optimal performance, NHBUF, the number of hash buffers, should be changed when NBUF is changed. The hash buffers service the system buffer cache. NHBUF is set at about 64 on most machines for a 1:4 ratio to the buffer cache.

NPROC

NPROC is the number of process table entries known as slots. It is best analyzed with pstats. It holds not only active processes, *runable* and *sleeping*, but also the dead children of living parents, colloquially known as *zombies*. If this table is too small, everything will stop until one of the processes finishes up. Nothing new can be started, not even su or root.

NPROC is as small as 20 on PC-size systems; the manual recommends 50 to 200 for DEC PDPs and VAXs; and it is set at 300 and larger on mainframes. It can go much higher, but the other major tables, such as the inode and file tables, must grow proportionally with it. On many machines it is a multiplier of the number of ttys (terminals) configured. Amdahl uses a 3X multiplier (NPROC = 3 * NTUBES).

Closely watch the percentage of fullness of the process table when the system peaks. When there are no vacant slots in the process table, no new activity can start. Worse yet, everything else seems to slow to a standstill. Note that NPROC is not to be confused with MAXUP.

MAXUP **and** MAXPROC

MAXUP is the maximum number of processes a regular user can have. The number of user processes cannot be bigger than NPROC, the size of the process table, and so it's best to keep MAXUP to some reasonable limit, like 20 to 30. Any larger number of processes for a single user running simultaneously is a very special condition and probably would benefit if run with a "batch" scheduler like Berkeley's.[4] Even the largest machines default MAXPROC at 25. MAXPROC is the maximum number of system processes. Smaller desktop computers use 20 processes maximum, but there may be only one user on a workstation. With 300 users (and abusers), and each one trying to get 30 processes going, a 9000-slot process table would be required if each user used his or her limit at the same time. Be prepared to fight with users over this one. Users don't like limits, particularly on the number of open files and active processes they can have.

NCLIST

Character minibuffers are called clists. Even raw character I/O needs some sort of buffer. This is the I/O where serial asynchronous devices, like terminals, are stored. They are small buffers, originally around 24 bytes each on PDPs, but now they are set from 64 to 256 bytes apiece. Five to ten buffers per tty are required, and 100 to 300 total are typical, from PC to mainframe.

---

[4] Berkeley has a batch scheduler that creates short and long run-queues and forces jobs to be run "in batch," one at a time.

There must be a slot in the inode table for each file and device in the kernel inode table. There is close (but not equal) correspondence between the inode slots and the file table slots used. For each file there can be only one inode, but there can be several links, opens, and reopens; therefore, both the inode and file tables are set at the same number. The number of inode and file table slots defaults from 100 on the smaller systems to 400 and up on the larger.

TEXT

TEXT is the number of places or slots in the text table. Each slot exists for a *read-only* text segment, with a range of 25 to 60. Again, the workable number for your installation is determined by examining the system running under stress.

NSWAP: **Paging and Swapping**

Runnable processes are swapped out from memory to a swap device. The swap device is usually a disk, but it can be a solid-state device or an extended area of memory. Swapping a process is simpler and has less overhead than demand paging does. It is used on many System V Release 2+ machines in lieu of paging, as these systems still page memory for program data, but not for the programs as processes.

A separate disk partition is set aside for swapping, paging, or both. Many systems are configured with multiple page devices for faster and more efficient paging. Some smaller systems like XENIX set aside an area for swapping within one of the regular disk partitions, usually root's. Make sure that the addresses of either don't conflict.

The size of the page device should be at least the size of memory. My larger systems have well over 300 megabytes of paging disks. Workstations running CAD applications take 50 to 75 megabytes; the application's size determines the size of the page area required. Fourth-generation languages and software, such as data base systems and spread sheets, are memory intensive and take a substantial amount of real and paged memory. When you are out of memory, you see the out of memory message sent to standard error, the user's screen. This error message applies to both real and paged memory, and vmstat is an ideal diagnostic for paging.

FILES **and** INODES

The file and inode tables are interesting system tables. The file table stores information about each open file, and therefore there can be no more open files than there are slots in the file table. Remember that each shell and therefore each new process, except those in the background, has three open files at birth. They are standard in, standard out, and standard error. A point to ponder: If the number of open files per user process is expanded, what should be done with the size of the file table?

The range of FILES is from 100 to 300 and up on very large systems. When the table runs out of slots, no processes can run until the other processes close open files. It is sometimes necessary to initiate user education on points like closing files as soon as they are no longer needed.

MOUNTS

The mount table holds hands with the file and inode tables, as there is an entry for each mounted file system. Imagine the size of the mount table on a system with disk addresses going from /dev/dsk/110s0 to /dev/dsk/fffs0. Large systems require large mount tables, whose size is calculated from the number of disk, swap, page, and memory devices.

CALLS

The callout table is a bit difficult to understand. It is UNIX's attempt to operate in as close to real time as possible for some limited applications. The clock handler "calls out" a function to be handled at a later time. Each has a slot in the callout table, with terminal delays being typical functions requiring callouts.

Don't skimp on the size of the callout table. If this one fills, the system will crash. The normal range is 100 to 300, and if you have the slightest hesitation, go for the larger number.

MAXPROC

MAXPROC is the maximum number of processes that a nonprivileged user can have. Traditionally it was twenty-five, and most systems hang on to the twenty-five open processes per user. Like the per-user open-file limit, be prepared for a few arguments with your users over this one.

Setting Table Sizes

Setting tunable parameters the first time can be a guessing game; after that it should be a science. The system activity reporters are the number one tools in gathering tuning information. AT&T's sarg, saf, and tplot commands are very handy, and so are the pstat and vmstat commands seen on Berkeley and UNIX systems. OEM utilities can give additional information.

Tuning by altering the size of system tables and buffers is more than a match for expensive hardware additions. Excessively large tables and buffers are wasteful of vital resources because they increase the size of the kernel at the cost of the memory available to the user. But skimpy tables and buffers are worse because they cause the system to thrash, and then the system can give very little of itself to the user.

The basic information you need is the fullness of critical system tables and buffers at peak loading. The process table, file table, and inode tables are the most important to consider. On the buffer side you have clists and disk buffer cache information. Paging data are equally important. The bottom line for instantaneous system performance is a breakdown of the percentage of time spent in user, system, voluntary, and involuntary wait states.

AUXILIARY HARDWARE: TO PURCHASE OR NOT TO PURCHASE

Managers make a primary contribution to the organization by being discriminating purchasers of peripherals and computers. It is common practice to take the word of "sales engineers" as the absolute truth. But remember that they are salespeople first and engineers second. They will not tell you how to get a better product than the one they are selling, for that would contradict the reason for their employment. Taking 100 percent of the advice of your users and staff can also be misleading. Beware of brand prejudice. If you are surrounded by a lot of DEC groupies, you will probably have a DEC house, but there may be a better option at half the cost.

Your first thought should go to extending your existing hardware before buying new. If a desktop with a purchase value of $5,000 is bogged down because it is paging ten times more often than it is computing, a $400 to $1000 purchase of more dynamic memory can head off the purchase of a $15,000 supermini to replace it. A heavily paged mainframe may be unable to address the memory it does have. If the operating system has an addressing limit of 24 bits, you will live in the world of 16 megabytes until hell freezes over or until you can find an operating system that can address the memory the system came with. Contemporary mainframe UNIX and VM systems address 31 bits. These systems were a long time in coming, but they are here, and not using them is the same as sending your posttax profit to your competitor.

Solid-State Paging Devices

There are many intelligent purchases that greatly improve system performance and postpone the acquisition of new systems. Solid-state disk buffer-caching devices are a good purchase for MVS or VM, but they may conflict with UNIX's own buffer caching. Insist on running your own benchmark before committing to such a device.

Solid-state paging devices are worth their weight in gold. They increase page rates by a factor of 6 to 10, and that is an 800 percent improvement in performance average. It is not uncommon for a fully loaded large system to run sandbagged at 80 percent to 90 percent overhead. If you take the paging load off the system and take advantage of the memory that you do have, or purchase more if there is the need, the system will go from 80 percent system overhead to 80 percent user availability.

When you need to ask your manager for more computers or more memory, you will be asked, "Can you do anything to improve current performance?" When you can answer that you have done everything possible, you know you have done optimal tuning and configuration and shown intelligent purchasing of peripherals. There is nothing else left to do but buy more computers or memory.

LEARNING HOW TO CONFIGURE

How do you learn how to configure? Where does the information come from? The first place you may think of turning is your OEM, but you might be disappointed. Your OEM's coding group wrote the code and put the tools in, but that doesn't necessarily mean they know how to use them.

Years ago when I was with an aerospace fluid carrier manufacturer, I ran into the engineers from DuPont who manufactured the raw material the company used in hose core. I asked the DuPont engineers for information on how to process the material, and their answers surprised me. They told me that we were the experts on processing, not them. They didn't know about processing. They found out about processing from people like us.

The UNIX world is no different. The people who know how to tune are not the OEMs and the support group but the system programmers, managers, and administrators who have been out there in the trenches doing it for years. Granted, not everyone knows how; most machines are very poorly tuned. However, there are some who know how to tune very well indeed.

Real knowledge of tuning comes from years and years of experience and commitment. It comes from a substantial number of crashes. It comes from having to live with problems between system generations when you suffer and bleed severely. When you sit and watch the machine for days because you're not in a position to take it down and you see the clists hitting 100 percent and performance degrading, you agonize over the condition of your machine. You can hardly wait for the first opportunity you have to bring it down and make your clist tables larger.

You learn that you can't play with some parameters. When all of a sudden your machine goes belly up on you for what you figure is no known good reason, you read the core dump and find out that you've got a `broken page chain` message. Up until that point you probably never heard of a page chain, and now you own one, and it's broken. By the time you trace through all the table indirection involved, you will not only know what a page chain is; you will never forget it.

The people who do know about tuning are the ones who have been doing it the longest. You can get a lot of helpful information from the OEM. Its support group will tell you where to find the parameters, and often they will be able to tell you what these parameters govern. If the support group can't track down the information, have them put you in direct contact with an engineer who can. But how specific parameters behave on your machine is something you will have to find out yourself through hard experience. There is no other way.

MENU-DRIVEN SYSTEM ADMINISTRATION

There have been several menu-driven, interactive system administration programs generated by companies like SCO and AT&T. Before system administration programs existed, old timers like myself who started back in UNIX Edition 7, and later System 3, had to set all the parameters by hand, one at a time. Obviously UNIX is not going to survive the marketplace if it's necessary to hire some guru to configure the machine. As UNIX continues to proliferate on desktops and midsized machines, no one can afford to hire an army of gurus. They're expensive, and there aren't enough of them.

Consequently, for years the OEM has been faced with making parameters easier to tune. It took the biggest part of the 1980s. It is interesting that this innovation did not occur on mainframes; rather, the first good menu-driven system administration programs were on the micro. I first saw them on System 5 Release 2 AT&T 3B2s. There are smoother versions, and the SCO XENIX programs stand out as classic.

XENIX is ported by Microsoft, but SCO is a value-added reseller. It adds features to systems that originally came from AT&T via Microsoft. Its program tells you what you have, and it even gives you a help menu. You can modify it as well. Since menu-driven system administration is an integral part of System V Release 4, eventually we'll see it across nearly all UNIX machines.

CLASSIC TUNING ADMINISTRATION

Even with menu-driven administration, knowledge of *longhand* tuning and configuration is imperative for a professional administrator or system programmer. The point of knowing internals is knowing which parameters you are actually going after. That is the one thing consistent from machine to machine. The highly experienced, ace administrators usually won't bother with menu-driven administration, but will go directly to where the code is. If they do use menu-driven system administration programs, they use them in terms of what they already know. When the menu-driven program asks, "What is the maximum number of processes you want on your machine?" they immediately know it's really asking, "How do you want to set NPROC?"

Even if there is a menu-driven system administration program on your system, a good administrator won't try to avoid learning internals. The cost of your menu-driven system administration programs is that you have tens of thousands of machines configured very large. They are oversized of necessity, and having to tune them eventually is a distinct possibility.

MANAGER'S CORNER

Tuning Saves Money

Whether mainframe, mini, or supermicro, you don't casually run out and buy more memory. The minute you hit a dollar restriction, you need to wait until a new fiscal period starts. You're stuck with whatever you got at plan, usually an annual affair.[5] You may be maxed out. You may have no more memory to work with. You may have the memory but not the addressing capability. When you're faced with real-world restrictions, like money or addressing, the only way you're going to save your neck is by being very knowledgeable. Your system administrator has tools to see what is really required of your machines. Then you can tune and configure to real needs.

---

[5] *Plan* is the corporate ritual of middle management's rolling up their financial requirements to upper management for the next fiscal period.

If your system is still down on its knees even after tuning all possible parameters, it's management decision time. There are alternatives to simply going out and buying a bigger machine or another machine.

Your system's activities reporter can show you that your machine is I/O bound. When you're out of memory and you're I/O bound, normally that's the kiss of death. You've pushed this poor machine just as far as it's going to go. Historically the only way to go larger has been to make a bigger machine. If you're on a Sun4/180, you go to a Sun4/280. If you're on a 3090-200, you go to a 400. If you're on a 3090-600E, you have to buy another 3090.

Before you sign the purchase order, get some hard answers. Why are you in constant I/O wait? Why are you out of memory? If you addressed all the memory, what's happening? If your system administrator looks at your system statistics and system activity reporters, she may find that you're running out of memory and paging. If you're paging fast enough, you're spending most of your time reading processes on and off a rotating disk, because that's where you page to. By spending a twentieth of the money of a new machine on a solid-state disk or extended storage, you can increase your page rate substantially. If you were paging 40 times a second, a solid-state disk can give you up to 450 pages per second. With this increase in performance, you will pick up speed, and your I/O performance will pick up noticeably.

Being out of memory may point to disk I/O. If you're paging, it is disk I/O. Your lack of memory forces a high degree of disk activity. If you can speed up your disk activity by means of solid-state devices and if you can aid it by additional caching, then you can pick up your performance. Solid-state devices were first seen about 1982 or 1983 on the little machines with a RAM disk, but the idea has been carried all the way up to the mainframes.

In short, if you and your system administrator put your heads together, you may be able to postpone buying an additional machine by optimal system tuning and efficient use of peripherals.

17

Crashes and Dumps:
□□□□ □□□□ □□□□ DEAD

Few things get a system administrator's heart going faster than the statement "The system's dead." A human being is irrevocably dead only when there is no heartbeat, no breathing, and no brain waves. Medical personnel are trained to check thoroughly, because often people who seem dead can be revived. Upon seeing what appears to be a dead system, the system administrator also needs to find out whether the system is really dead or whether it can be revived.

The UNIX system has a variety of user-unavailable situations, from *dead* and *dying* to *gravely ill*:

- Dead, no CPU activity, no usable kernel in memory.
- D & D, down and disabled.
- Disabled wait state.
- Console up, terminals down.
- System hung.
- "Stuck in the mud," paged to death or the process table is full.

DEAD

The first situation is □□□□ □□□□ □□□□ DEAD. You can't get much clearer than the hex message "dog easy able dog" written to the program status word. The kernel panicked and killed itself. When the kernel senses that it, the kernel, is not in order, it immediately opts for an honorable dispatch rather than risking further corruption. It issues an internal panic call and writes DEAD to the PSW. On sophisticated machines it writes a suicide note to an internal buffer, sometimes called the osm buffer. (This is an internal circular buffer intended to store errors and console-type information.) Then the kernel takes its last breath and dies.

A dead system is one of the easiest situations to handle. The word *dead* means exactly what it says. Reboot the system. Once up, read the console log. Look over the system's last complaints. Then list /dump/dump, /var/adm/crash, or wherever your dump is written. No matter how large or small your UNIX machine is, every well-planned machine is prepared to leave a core dump when it dies. Well-planned machines either dump to a space especially provided for dumps, or they dump to their own swap space. If you have done your job and provided a dump area, you will have a body on which to do an autopsy. The next move is to read the dump with crash or the OEM's dump formatter. Now go immediately to the console log or osm buffer, and read the kernel's last words.

When you find the problem, fix it and reboot. You may not be able to put your finger on the exact cause of death. Deduce what you can from the system error file, the console log, the osm buffer, the process table, the last few stack traces, and the remains of the last run process. Point them out in a memo. Tape the dump and the kernel—/unix, /vmunix, or whatever your OEM calls it—and send the memo and the tape to the OEM. Call its support staff before and after the receipt of the tape. Walk them through the dump as far as you understand it, and that will get their attention enough to get them going. The rest is up to them, but keep after the support group until you get an answer.

D & D

D & D stands for *down and disabled*. This is a difficult situation. On conventional UNIX systems the system is available only to the console. On large systems that are the guest of a host operating system, such as UNIX running on VM, you can reattach to the virtual console to get to the system. The virtual console is normally detached while the system is up and is reattached only when necessary. You will find the system in *CP state*, meaning that you are in the host operating system, not UNIX. Type in B to interrupt and to bring back the UNIX console. You should see the message

```
disabled wait state
```

and a program status word. If you are a VM guru or have close access to an IBM SE or FE, copy it down for further reference. He or she can decipher the PSW and the error messages.

The system is not dead, but it is very, very close. It is only waiting for the *coup de grâce*. The trick for you, the system administrator, is to get a dump. Without it, you will never know what brought the system down. Issue a system restart:

```
# cp system restart
```

The system will come back with the message dumping.

Now the procedure is the same as for DEAD, because your machine is truly dead now. Bring it back up, read the dump, and correct the problem.

HUNG

The hung machine is the biggest problem in the dead and dying category. It is neither dead nor in a disabled wait state. The console is alive. The kernel is alive. All the user processes are "normal" from the machine's perspective, but from the users' point of view the machine has gone off to Valhalla. If a user types in a command, nothing will happen.

There are many reasons for a system to get hung, but most are some form of overloading. A full process table is one typical cause. No new activity can start until some of the old processes finish and release slots in the process table. The processes that caused the process table to fill are huge jobs, either memory intensive or I/O intensive, or both.

The usual situation is two or more massive jobs taking all the core memory and then spilling into the page disks. Paging gets so high that page-ins and page-outs make the machine I/O-bound. This is an important point to remember. A job can be construed to be CPU intensive with little or no I/O, such as simulations or large computational programs. If their jobs exceed core memory, they will get page intensive, and then they will be I/O bound. The thing to look for is how memory intensive the process is.

What happens is a huge job is paged in. Having filled memory, it starts to execute. Crunching along but producing no visible output, it exceeds its time slot in the scheduler. The scheduler has no concept of program size, nor does it care. There is another job out there, and when its turn comes, the scheduler ruthlessly pages in the next huge job, paging out the old one without the slightest remorse. The new job also takes time to page in, but before it can produce any noticeable results, it is time for another job to get back into the address space. Technically the system is not hung, but for all practical purposes it is.

The cure is to kill at least one of the competing jobs. Call the owners and give them a hand in the decision, but have at least one major job killed. The long-term cures are a better scheduler, machine offloading or moving work to another machine, or batch processing. Fair-share schedulers and similar contemporary schedulers take into account job sizes and group priorities. Small jobs come and go quickly, getting small pieces of the system often. Large jobs get a much larger time slice but are run less frequently.

Machine offloading is simple if you have the resources. Large jobs tying up smaller machines get moved to larger machines. Desktops offload to minis or mainframes. Minis offload to mainframes. The buck stops there.

Batch processing is associated with the old IBM machines of twenty years ago and current MVS systems. It brings back memories of JCL and RJE. UNIX is a multiuser, multiprocessor system, and batch processing is a single-user, single process that runs close to real time. A dedicated batch system has *no* users at all. It just takes jobs, queues them, and runs them one at a time. Nevertheless, batch processing is done on UNIX machines. The Berkeley batch system maintains batch queues on the local machine. It has been modified at sites like Intel to offer a remote batch queue. There is also a version that uses the BSD printer facility to dispatch jobs to remote machines. In both local and remote schemes, the batch daemon queues jobs and does not allow them to be executed until the first job in the queue is finished. They are executed one job at a time. Since they get nearly all of the resources, they don't compete with one another, and overhead is reduced from as much as 70 percent to as little as 5 percent.

It is incredibly difficult to get a word in edgewise on a hung system. The first problem is getting onto the virtual or real console. You must keep trying to take control of the system. The second problem is that the ailing system won't even listen to root because it is so busy processing and thrashing. If you are persistent, you may get a command wedged in and acted upon. On the other hand, you may get nowhere, and then it is time to take down the system and start over.

The worst thing you can do is a power down or a hardware boot on a live UNIX system. Doing a force from the host system is the same as a hardware boot on large systems. Thus every effort must be made to bring down the system gracefully. The system must sync and write its files. Unmounting the disks is frosting on the cake: then /etc/mnttab will make sense when you bring up the system again. The disk copy of /etc/mnttab will show the system's multiuser state unless all disks are unmounted on the way down.

If all else fails and the system must go down the hard way, fsck will have to be run twice on the root disk, and the spooler will look like the city dump. The lost + found directories will be full. The reason files wind up in lost + found is that they have no directory entry and therefore no file name. They are stored with an inode reference for a name. Now you have the job of calling the users and finding out whether they want their nameless files.

PAINFULLY SLOW

The painfully slow system is all too familiar. It is a long way from dead. It is not even sick. It is just overloaded. It is ironic that as the demand for user time on multiuser operating systems goes up, the system time also goes up, but it does so disproportionately. If a single user with a midsized job runs that job on a UNIX system without any other jobs in competition with other users, he may be surprised to get nearly 100 percent of the system, and his job will finish with astonishing speed. As tens of users run up to hundreds of jobs, the machine goes to 100 percent capacity. When the system gets 75 percent for overhead, that leaves only a paltry 25 percent for the users.

Until the system becomes nearly hung, there is little to do but keep an eye on interactive system statistics like sar, vmstats, or pstats that watch the condition of the buffers and tables. When the situation becomes severe enough, you have reason to step in and take action. Here is where you gather tuning and configuration information. Which tables and buffers need to be enlarged? Which ones can afford to be made smaller so that you can free more memory for users?

This is also a good time to get involved in the politics of running a system. Go to the users' managers or representatives and have them make the deals among themselves determining who gets job priorities and who will pay for further resources.

READING DUMPS

When you read a dump, you are looking at the kernel internals of a dead system. As a matter of fact, you should have a reasonable knowledge of internals before you try to read a dump. You should be familiar with the major system tables, the queues, and the associated data structures. Fortunately, there are many excellent books available on internals.[1] The structures defined in /usr/include/sys are the second source of internals information. Those with source code systems not only have more files in /usr/include; they have the source code as well. The place to start learning is in /usr/src/uts/*/sys and /usr/include/sys. Configuration files associated with system generation are another good place to get information. Look for master, master.c, config.c, or config.h—the names vary with the implementation.

A knowledge of the system's architecture is also helpful. Some mainframe UNIX operating systems *require* hardware internals knowledge to read a dump, because 370 systems talk to the system's channels, controllers, and devices rather than to a bus. Knowledge of the bus, adapters, controllers, and devices on conventional machines is important, but it may not be required for reading dumps.

You definitely want to know about the system's processor. If nothing else, you need to know about the processor's program status word, stack pointers, and registers. The stack pointer often points to where the trouble lies.

All events are handled on interrupts. An interrupt is required to make anything happen on the machine that requires a device, such as writing to disk or reading a tape. Interrupts and traps are required knowledge for dump reading. System calls are the user's entry into the system, and they round out the picture of required internals. The kernel's own calls are difficult to understand because they are internal to the kernel and so they are never seen by the system programmer. Thus they have no manual entry and no mention in the standard tutorials. So what is a system administrator supposed to do when dump, error messages, and some diagnostics refer to kernel calls? An example is the reference to grow.c, given when memory cannot be allocated.

Another prerequisite for reading dumps is understanding the system's memory management scheme. It is hard to understand a broken page chain error when you don't even know what a page chain is. A broken page chain is a break in address indirection, making it impossible to reach a data location. A good place to start learning about the system's memory management scheme is by constantly watching system diagnostic tools like sar. After constantly watching the healthy machine and checking all the critical system tables, the sick condition characteristic of a dump will be easier to recognize.

---

[1] Maurice J. Bach, *The Design of the UNIX Operating System* (Englewood Cliffs, NJ: Prentice-Hall, 1986); Andrew S. Tennenbaum, *Operating Systems Design and Implementation* (Englewood Cliffs, NJ: Prentice-Hall, 1987); Douglas Comer, *Internetworking with TCP/IF* (Englewood Cliffs, NJ: Prentice Hall, 1988). Please note, however, that these books do not cover System V Release 4 internals.

CAUSES OF CRASHES

When the kernel senses it is being corrupted, it will use a simple mechanism to protect itself from further corruption—it will commit suicide. It will attempt a dump, and then it will kill itself. We've looked at a broken page chain, a common cause of death. Memory is allocated to processes discontiguously. Wherever the kernel can catch memory while moving forward through the address space is where you will get it. Memory locations are mapped through segment tables to page tables. Region tables are also involved with memory allocation for text, data, and stack regions, depending on the UNIX version. If the links that join these virtually contiguous areas of memory are broken, the system will be corrupted, and out it goes.

First it writes its death note to the osm buffer, which resides in a fixed area of main memory on some systems, records all kernel errors, and time-stamps them. The same errors eventually find their way to the console itself, the console or error log. If the system crashes, the console or error log and this buffer will be the only places the system's death statement can be found. The final message may not even make it to the console, and to read the osm buffer you need to get a kernel dump.

The system dies when reacting to an event signaled by an interrupt, exception, or trap. Typical interrupts are

- Service call—the result of a system call.
- Page translation exception.
- I/O.
- External clock event.
- Hardware machine check.
- Panic—the last breath—the system dumped.

Interrupts are hardware events, which are things like disk reads and writes, data entered to a terminal, and carrier detect from a modem. These hardware events can cause an interrupt. Software takes care of hardware interrupts as a trap, a software event.[2] Exceptions are caused by a process, typically zero-divide or illegal pointer.

The interrupt-handling flow is to a context switch from an interrupt usually generated at bus level. The old program status word is stored, and the new one is loaded. If all goes well, the interrupted process will restart when its turn comes to run again. Next a kernel process, lowcore.s, calls the trap appropriate to the interrupt. Then a common trap routine is called that branches to trap.c, and trap.c now calls the appropriate handler or makes a service call to respond to a system call. If it cannot handle events, it will call panic. In the last step, panic will initiate the dump.

Note that all of the kernel calls are part of the kernel code. They are not programs, processes, or even system calls. They are simply kernel routines.

---

[2] Refer to /usr/src/uts/*/sys/trap.c.

PREREQUISITES

A system dump must have a place to dump to, like the /var/adm/crash or /dump directory. You must create the dump directory, but the dump creates the dump file. On BSD systems, /var/adm/crash already exists. The dump and a kernel image are automatically dropped there on crashing. A succession of crashes fills /var, so it is wise to give /dump or /var its own disk partition. This guarantees that it will be large enough to hold a dump and that it will not be filled by other processes.

Because a dump is a copy of the memory version of the kernel as it existed the moment that the system died and dumped, the size of /dump must be at least the same size as the kernel. If a dump is already present as /dump/dump, the kernel will overwrite it when doing another dump.

I frequently leave enough room on /dump to hold two dumps. As soon as a dump takes place, I copy it to /dump/OLDdump. If the system is dying with some degree of regularity, I put the current dump and a copy of the kernel, /unix, on the same tape as soon as possible. You may have to send tape, along with a copy of the kernel, to the vendor that supplied the system, in order to get a full interpretation of the dump and thus an answer to your problem.

osmbuff, /dev/osm, AND /dev/error

When you examine a dump, the system's osm buffer is the place to start looking. The osm buffer is where the system complains about any detected errors. It is connected by /dev/osm to the console, and on larger systems it is sent to a console log. A small system puts its errors in files like /usr/adm/messages or /usr/adm/error. Read memory starting at about 300 lines before the osm pointer to the point where the osm pointer index was located at the time of the crash. If the system's dump formatter is worth its salt, the last events up to and including the dump call will be right there at your fingertips.

If the cause of the crash is not apparent, walk through the entire osmbuff from beginning to end. Because osmbuff is a circular buffer, when it hits the top of its address area, it will start back at the bottom again.

PROCESS TABLE

What was running when the system died? The answer to that question is in the process table. Move to the process table and format its contents. There is a pointer to the current process, often called curproc.

The last running process does not have to be the process that killed the system. However, this one is a good candidate if the system was killed by a user process. Get its process-ID number for more searching. The kernel is normally invulnerable to errors created by user processes. Write a process that deliberately destroys itself, and you will see that the process only damages its own address space. It may go up in a virtual cloud of smoke, but the kernel will never even feel its demise. That's the theory, but occasionally systems do crash from errors inflicted by user processes. I've seen it happen.

STACK TRACE

Stack traces are a wealth of information if you can make sense of them. Look for kernel calls on the stack, as they can be the key to the disaster. When you have our familiar broken page chain problem, the stack trace shows a call to grow.c, the call to increase the size of a memory. The crash stack command gives a kernel stack trace.

FILE, MOUNT, AND INODE TABLES

The file, mount, and inode tables all can be formatted by crash and other dump formatters. All are a good source of information when trying to trace crashed processes file I/O. While reading the dump, it is also a good time to check the size of all three tables to see whether they are adequate. There is no better time to reset the size parameters and generate a new system than when bringing it back up again, providing the machine is fast enough to make a new kernel without wasting too much time. This sort of a move is a judgment call. You are within your rights to do a quick expansion if the system tables are so small as to put the machine in jeopardy. This is clearly a Severity 1 problem, and the administrator should deal with it immediately without waiting for a scheduled downtime.

CALLOUT

You must check the callout table. If it fills, the system will crash, guaranteed. If your system diagnostic programs don't give you the size of the callout table, use crash to get its size. If it is so small that it is endangering the system, allocate more space immediately; otherwise, wait until the next scheduled downtime. Luckily System V Release 4 uses dynamic table allocation and relieves us of this problem.

WALLOWING THROUGH MEMORY

When formatting tables have given you good ideas but no conclusive evidence, you have no choice but to read memory addresses, formatting a few hundred lines at a time to try to find more clues. This is a desperate but necessary move when all else fails.

The keys to this treasure hunt are addresses taken from stack traces. Stack locations can also be found from memory. You will develop the knack of seeing the stack pointer when reading the unformatted hex of a memory location. Register contents are stored in succession. The address ranges and relative values are giveaways to which register is which. A sophisticated dump formatter breaks down registers for you.

MANAGER'S CORNER

Computer Education

Computer education for your staff is expensive. A good class on reading dumps runs about $2000, and the class usually should have as a prerequisite an understanding of internals and system calls. The internals class will cost you as much again. Also, classes on internals and reading dumps aren't that easy to find. Add to the cost of the course the additional expenses of travel and lodging, and you will have invested a pretty penny before you can get some of your staff to read a dump.

Now let's look at the high price of not knowing internals and not being able to read a dump. A large system costs roughly $10 a minute, or $600 an hour, to own and maintain, based on a 24-hour-day availability. Lose only two hours of availability, and you will have the cost of a major UNIX class. You will also have a user uprising on your hands. Thus you should have at least one system programmer on the staff who is capable of taking problem determination to the point that a kernel bug can be pinpointed. It is not necessary that the system programmer be able to fix the bug. That is the job of the OEM. But it is necessary that he or she be able to locate the bug, prepare a report, and make a tape of the crashed kernel's memory contents as well as the kernel with symbol table intact. If not, the vendor will be unable to help you.

Your users can live with a report truthfully stating that the bug has been isolated and the OEM is working on it. It will be even more acceptable if they are given some way to work around the problem until it is fixed. But the users will not live with "We don't know what the problem is, but we are working on it." In a nutshell, it more expensive *not* to train your staff in UNIX internals than it is to pay for training.

S E C T I O N

IV

Network Administration

CHAPTER

18

Network Administration

NETWORKS

For nearly a decade the expression "the net" automatically conjured up a picture of the UUCP network. Created at Bell Labs and therefore AT&T, it was only natural for the first network to be on long-haul lines. Old UNIX could just as easily be networked over a hardwire. In fact, hardwire was far easier than configuring a dial-up system. HoneyDanBer took some of the sting out, but an administrator's first installation of UUCP could take a week and cause a substantial amount of frustration.

THE ETHERNET

The concept of *local area networks* (LANs) was well known by the middle 1980s, but LANs were not an overnight success. There were many networking schemes competing for supremacy, and Ethernet–TCP/IP communication finally won. Ethernet was as much of a blessing as UNIX was for the garage shop computer OEM of the period. Whereas manufacturing a computer used to mean having to write an operating system as well, in the early 1980s you could get UNIX as an operating system for a mere $40,000 for a license and another $20,000 to $50,000 for a port.[1] Then Ethernet and NFS were introduced to UNIX and put in the public domain. Thus the technology existed, the port was easy and cheap, and it was the bandwagon to be on. Ethernet was *the* UNIX network method by the end of the decade.

---

[1] The cost of a UNIX source license doubled between 1980 and 1988.

What we now call Ethernet–TCP/IP merges two sources of networking applications. These are the Berkeley *R* commands and the operating-system-independent `telnet` school of software. Function is overlapped and duplicated, and in many cases choice is a matter of taste or prejudice. For example, `rlogin` and `telnet` have the same function—both get a remote login. Although `telnet` works on any operating system to which it has been ported, `rlogin` is UNIX specific. Neither one has UUCP's drop-and-forward service. Then again, at 10 to 100 megabytes per second, drop-and-forward is an anachronism best left for the voice lines of Ma Bell.

UNIX has strong roots in networking. Created at Bell Labs, UNIX soon picked up D. A. Nowitz's UUCP as its hardwire and long-haul form of networking. It took Berkeley to put the concept of LAN and WAN networking over the ether.

There is a lot of confusion about what the terms Ethernet, Internet, and Arpanet mean. I like this comment about the Internet best: "The Internet is a great research project plagued by its success." All the networks that connect the contiguous United States are basically research projects. The Arpanet, funded by the military, is the hub of most networks, and it was the central backbone of the Internet. The Internet is funded by many sources, private and public, and it is a research project to define and create an experimental network that will be the pattern for all future networks. The two names are used interchangeably in conversation and are often thought of as being synonymous. In fact, TCP/IP is a layering of two protocols above Ethernet. The IP stands for Internet Protocol and corresponds to the layer of the network that delivers network frame packets from the wire and transceivers, the physical network. Next is usually a protocol layer making *reliable* stream transmission, TCP, or *unreliable* datagram deliveries, UDP. The intended meaning of *reliable* and *unreliable* are important, and we will learn about them shortly. TCP is typically used for `rlogin` or `telnet` remote login network software, while UDP is used for mail delivery software.

Most local area networks are Ethernet using TCP/IP and UDP/IP protocols. If the LAN requires only a few hundred feet of cable, the entire network can exist on a single passive wire with no active devices other than each system's own transceiver. A small complication arises as the network grows in length to a thousand feet or so, because switches, such as repeaters, bridges, or routers, enter the line. The simplest devices are repeaters. However, repeaters, particularly multiple-port repeaters, can deliberately be used to create and, to a small extent, isolate legs of a local network segment. This aids in trouble-shooting and problem isolation. In time the LAN gets so large in size and wire length that it needs to "fall back and regroup." A group of Ethernet-linked computers then can become a subnetwork in its own right by using routers.

Networks are joined by special-purpose computers that are bridges or routers. *Routers* allow connections of networks and subnets. A *bridge* is a device that connects network segments to form a larger LAN. *Gateways* join major networks and can deal with unlike protocols, but bridges cannot. Whereas a repeater passes on everything, including electrical noise, the bridge connects Ethernet segments and stores and passes packets only. It arbitrates collisions and filters noise.

Network segments are thought of as being connected by coaxial cable, but in fact they can be connected by twisted-pair wire, thick or thin coax, fiber optics, or any technology that can pass intelligence. Every time you turn around there seems to be a new medium of Ethernet transmission. Currently, alternative methods of transmission include microwave, satellite, and AM broadcast. There is no restriction on what method of transmission may be used.

Glossary

Let's define a few terms:

router   Sometimes called a *gateway*, a *router* is a special-purpose network computer used to receive, filter, and route network traffic at the network level.

bridge   A *bridge* connects smaller network segments into a larger network segment and stores and forwards network packets at the link level.

subnet   A *subnet* is a group of systems using the same internet network address and subnet address.

internet   An *internet*, uncapitalized, is a group of packet-switched networks connected by routers. It comes from the term *internetwork*, to connect LANs into a wider area network.

Internet   The *Internet*, capitalized, is a national network. Internet gateways connect ARPANET, MILNET, and NFSnet using TCP/IP protocol suites.

The goal of a network is universal interconnectivity. To achieve this, networks or subnets are connected by routers or bridges to larger groups and by gateways into one huge network. To run networks like the Internet, you need an enormous cobweb of gateways connecting smaller networked segments to the larger network. Handling the problems of address resolution, routing, timing considerations, and a host of other problems is a science in itself. Conceptually, the network is considered to be one huge entity. When you take it apart, you see that it is composed of multiple networks and subnets joined by gateways. A gateway is used to connect a lesser network to a larger network, such as the Internet.

Packets

The packet is the heart of most networking transmission systems. Data are grouped into small, portable, bufferlike groups, and a header is attached ahead of the data. It's like putting a letter (data) into an envelope (header). The header contains routing data, checksums, and a total of the data sent in the packet, all massaged into a magic number, as well as other information. The routing data have both destination data ("mailing-address" data) and source data ("return-address" data).

Packets are created from raw data at the transport level of the network software. It is called the Transmission Control Protocol layer for ease of understanding, TCP for short. This layer or level is also shared by UDP and other protocol services. The packet is augmented as data leave the system and travel down through each layer of the network. Next the packet is built into a datagram, at the Internet Protocol (IP) layer, and it is built into a network frame at the network interface layer. Each step after the transport protocol layer adds another header.

Getting Out

The data start out with the packet header; the datagram header is added to that; and the frame header comes last. Each step is like putting the last envelope into another envelope.

Getting In

Each successive layer of the internet software strips the "envelopes" as data arrive at a destination. Each layer uses the header information to piece together the packets, datagrams, and frames into contiguous data.

There are no guarantees that any one packet will even arrive, much less arrive in order. By interpreting header information, a resend can be requested, and a packet can be retransmitted. The emphasis should be on the word *unreliable*. You can't rely on any one specific packet's arriving. The UDP protocol is unreliable by definition. If the sending and receiving hosts are there and the routers, bridges and gateways are alive, the success rate will be phenomenally high. TCP is the only major protocol that advertises *reliable* stream service. In fact, the reason that TCP exists is to provide *reliable* stream service.

Protocol Layers

The entire network scheme relies on layering. The internet layers are

application	User-level programs like `telnet`, `rlogin`, `ftp`, `finger`, and `rwho`.
transport	Transport-level programs such as TCP and UDP.
internet	internet protocols like IP.
link/physical	Local network protocols.

From the bottom up the physical net encompasses all the active and passive devices that bring data to the computer, including cables, fiber optics, transceivers, repeaters, bridges, and gateways. The network interface is where frame-to-datagram translation takes place. The internet (IP) layer does datagram-to-packet translation, and the transport layer does the final packet-to-data stream conversion. The application layer is the user software used to access the net, such as `telnet`, `rlogin`, `ftp`, `tftp`, `finger`, and `rwho`.

The transport layer is the home of TCP and UDP. TCP is the protocol used with `rlogin`, `telnet`, and other applications requiring reliable stream transmission. UDP is used by mail. IP stands for *Internet Protocol*, and so the internet layer is the *IP layer*.

The lowest layers are responsible for reading headers and examining checksums and time-out information. The lowest layers add this information on the way out, and they read and act on it on the way in. The actual details of multiplexing data, packet formation, protocols, and the hundreds of other steps required to make *unreliable* data transmission *reliable* are fascinating but beyond the scope of this book.

Client–Server Relationships

The client–server relationship is necessary for the network to function. A client program makes a request by way of the net to a server on another host system, and the server responds by fulfilling the request. Don't confuse this with daemon servers, which have different functions. Internet client servers rely on creating a number of "well-known ports,"[2] addresses that are reliably answered by a server. Thus a `telnet` client makes a request of a `telnet` server when it contacts the remote host system. The brunt of the work is done by the server. In terms of real software, the client and server are daemons, and in the case of `telnet`, the daemon is `telnetd`.

Network schemes lend themselves well to both Berkeley *sockets* and AT&T System V Release 3 *streams*. Both allow for interconnecting layers. For example, what we commonly call TCP/IP includes `sendmail`, but `sendmail` uses UDP/IP. With both sockets and streams, UDP is replaced by TCP to talk to IP, the Internet Protocol. The layered approach keeps protocol layers separate and easier to use, but writing the code becomes a larger and far more complicated task than with a more rigid system.

The TCP/IP family of applications software consists of

`telnet`	Similar to `cu` but over the Ethernet, a universal access method.
`ftp`	File transfer protocol, DOD's powerful file transfer system.
`rlogin`	BSD remote login, like `telnet`, but UNIX only.
`rcp`	BSD remote copy, copies between systems only remotely like UUCP.

Add to this network mail, BSD `sendmail`, and a host of utilities to go with the login and file transfer programs, such as

- `finger`
- `hostid`
- `hostname`
- `ruptime`
- `rwho`

This is the user's view of TCP/IP. The administrator's side is more complicated.

TCP/IP INTERNALS

Each TCP/IP user facility has a corresponding daemon. Most are written to take advantage of the daemon–server relationship. The daemon sits in the background waiting for a request for its particular service. When that service is requested, the daemon spawns a child process called a server daemon that does the actual work. Thus there is only one parent daemon, but there can be many server processes. Server daemons die just about as fast as they are spawned, but the parent daemon remains alive as long as the system is up. Should it die, as the system administrator, you must find out what killed it and restart it. The server is alive as long as the user needs it. When she logs on through `telnet`, she gets a `telnet` server of her own. When she logs off, that server dies.

Before System V Release 3, mainstream UNIX was not prepared to cope with the problems of network layering. Berkeley was always at the forefront of communications

---

[2] A *well-known port* is a port assignment. These protocol port numbers are used by such servers as `telnet`, `rlogin`, `ftp`, and `time` and `echo` (`ping`) servers.

experimentation. BSD uses sockets to get around the network layers, and eventually the Berkeley sockets were improved upon by streams. Sockets and related commands are library functions in manual(3), as opposed to streams, which are implemented at kernel level. A socket is very much like a named pipe joining together several layers into a whole. The following illustration depicts stream layering:

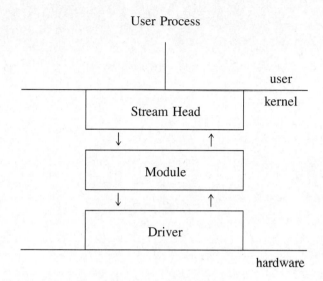

Streams work within the kernel by establishing a stream head just below the user level. Streams make a path to the driver and allow as many layers or modules as necessary to be slipped in between the stream head and the driver. The modules are under the control of ioctl(2) and can be switched with relative ease. If you picture the 7-layer ISO network model as five stream modules, it is easy to see how streams work well with any network protocol by stacking protocols as stream modules.

Sockets

There are several socket types. The one associated with TCP/IP is SOCK_STREAM, a name reference to socket stream. Its UDP counterpart is SOCK_DGRAM. The listen(3) call is associated with sockets forming a backlog for incoming connections. When watching the network status of an individual machine with netstat, the string shown for most connections is *listen*, the reference being the software's listening for activity. This is not unlike a getty.

IMPORTANT NETWORK FILES

The network uses several files for login validation, access validation, aliases, maintenance of local entries, and tables for hosts and other networks. These files are also used to start the network when the system comes up.

NETSTART

Berkeley networking is all one piece. There is nothing to add to set up a network, because the `inetd` daemon and the `inetd.conf` configuration file get you going. Networking is not built into AT&T UNIX machines that run UNIX releases before the 5.3 release. If you want networking on those machines, you have to buy it separately, and you will get a script to initiate the network, like `NETSTART`. The `/etc/NETSTART` file is called by `rc` and is used on systems with add-on networking, such as Wollongong's network package. A typical `NETSTART` script is

```
/etc/ifconfig fp0 stalker -trailers up
hostname stalker
/etc/telnet
/etc/fingerd
/etc/ftpf
/etc/rshd
/etc/tftpd
/etc/rececd
/etc/routed
/etc/rlogin
(cd /usr/spool/mqueue; /bin/rm -f [lnx]*;
/usr/lib/sendmail -bd -q30& )
```

The first thing to notice is that the `hostname` is made known before `sendmail` is run. The host name on this system is `stalker`; `ifconfig` enables the network interface; and `fp0` is the interface parameter for the Ethernet device, on this system an Intel Fastpath. The `-trailers` flag disables trailer link-level encapsulation. Note the `sendmail` startup in the last line of the preceding script excerpt: This task is performed by `rc` in BSD network systems.

NETSHUT

The shutdown counterpart of `NETSTART` is `NETSHUT`, which is called by `/etc/shutdown`. Here is an example:

```
echo "killing network daemons;"
kill -9 `ps -ae|egrep 'telnetd:rlogind:fingerd:rwohd:ftpd:
 ethsrv:netserv:ttylink'|awk -F" " '{ print $1 }'
```

If there are any local network cleanup tasks to be done besides killing daemons, this is the place to do it.

/etc/hosts

The `hosts` file contains the names of the systems your system knows. Each record in `hosts` has a minimum of two fields: Internet address and host name. Host name aliases are optional. Typical entries look like

```
128.213.109.115    glendoral    gl1
128.213.1.1        bridge3      br3
```

You won't reach a node if there is no entry for that particular host, and so it is important that `hosts` be brought up-to-date every time a new system is added to the "known worlds" of your network.

/etc/networks

The `networks` file is similar to `/etc/hosts` in that both files' records have two to three fields each. Networks can contain information about all the known networks on the Internet. These fields contain the (official) network name, the network number, and aliases for network names. A typical `/etc/networks` file starts like this:

```
#
# Internet networks
#
# network-name    address           alias
#
loopback net      128               software-loopback-net
acme-net          129.217           Acme-engineering-network
h1-net            129.217.1         Acme-H1-network
h2-net            129.217.2         Acme-H2-network
jj1-net           128.217.17        Acme-JJ1-network
japan-net         128.217.152       Acme-Japan-network
```

A crucial part of network administration is notifying local system administrators of *all* changes in the network, including additions and deletions. Most sites have one person or group responsible for keeping the `/etc/networks` and hosts files modified. As system administrator, you should keep a trilogy of `/etc/networks` files: networks, Onetworks, and Tnetworks. Do the same for `/etc/hosts`. Keep three files so you can pull a three-way swap like the `passwd` exchange seen in Section I. Here networks becomes Onetworks; the new `networks` is read into Tnetworks; and it is then copied to `networks`. Once you see that it works well, you can delete Tnetworks.

localhosts

As the name implies, `/etc/localhosts` is the local host file. A few entries are

```
#%%%%%%%%%%%%%%%%%%%%%%%%%%%%%%%%%%%%%%%%%%%%%%%%%
#    Acme Engineering TCP/IP NETWORK HOST DATA BASE
#               01/13/19
#%%%%%%%%%%%%%%%%%%%%%%%%%%%%%%%%%%%%%%%%%%%%%%%%%

128.1    localhost lcl me loopback

# @@@@@@@@@@@@@@@@@@@@@@@@@@@@@@@@@@@@@@@@@@@@@@@@@
# Rescue Host Data Base
# @@@@@@@@@@@@@@@@@@@@@@@@@@@@@@@@@@@@@@@@@@@@@@@@@

129.217.51.1     bear           FM-310-386
129.217.51.2     pointblank     SS-386-1
129.217.51.3     martin         GL-286-1
```

These network entries are localized and specific, the final destinations, not areas or gateways.

NETWORK TOOLS

There are several tools to help you work with the TCP/IP network. We have already seen `ifconfig`. Let's discuss a few others.

/etc/route **and the Kernel Route Table**

Getting beyond the local network requires the use of a router or gateway. The /etc/route command is used to add and delete entries from the network routing tables, which are located in the system's kernel. A route is a destination, host, or destination network as well as a known gateway to that host or network.

There are three commands to /etc/route: add, delete, and change. The syntax is

```
/etc/route [-fhn] add! delete  destination "gateway" metric**
```

The *destination* parameter is either a host or a network to which the route is directed. Be careful when you specify route destinations. Specifying a network gives access to the entire network, but specifying a particular host limits access to that host alone. Networks and hosts can be specified by the Internet address or the symbolic name referenced in hosts and localhosts.

The gateway parameter is the physical gateway through which network packet transmission must pass. The first UNIX lookup route is in the host name table, /etc/hosts, and then the network table, /etc/networks. The final parameter, metric, is the *hop count,* or the number of jumps required to get from source to destination. When adding a route, metric must be used. The -f option is used to flush all gateway entries from the routing tables.

The host table can be watched with netstat's -r option:

```
$ netstat -r
Routing tables
Destination      Gateway      Flags   Refcnt   Use      Interface
127.0.0          localhost  U       0        0        li1
acme-net         stalker    U       11       713425   fo0
```

The flag field has three states: U (for up), H (for host), and G (for gateway). Refcnt is the reference count, the number of active users on the system.

hostname

The hostname of the system is put in the kernel when the system is installed or regenerated by way of the system configuration file. It can be modified without doing a system regeneration. Local commands like nodename or hostname display or change the node name.

```
# /usr/bin/hostname stalker
```

Do not use any UNIX metacharacters in the host name. Rather, it should be a continuous name of fewer than 32 characters.

rwho

Just as who tells you who is on the system, rwho tells you who is on the network. But rwho is a known resource hog that is disabled on most systems by commenting out its lines in the local rc file. It displays all users on all hosts on the local network.

TROUBLESHOOTING THE LOCAL NETWORK SOFTWARE

Your most common LAN complaint is "telnet isn't working." The variation is "TCP/IP is broken." Either way, it is all the same to you, the administrator, whose job is solving problems. Even if you have a network specialist or network staff, first you must find out whether the problem is local. If you have several machines under your immediate local control, call from one to the other. Try calling it both ways, in and out; rlogin and telnet are probably the quickest. There is a ping utility that checks whether a node is alive or not.

If you cannot get in or out of the local system, try an internal loopback test. Call the machine from within itself. If it can log onto itself, the internal software is all right. Then ping another system. If telnet fails, try rlogin. If one local daemon is dead, are there any others? Do a ps on the individual daemons. Are they alive? When you are troubleshooting, it never hurts to make a shell script to find out quickly the process status of the daemons. The netstats utility also tells you the daemon status.

If all the daemons are alive and the loopback test passed, you can assume that all is well inside the system. Suspect the world external to the computer's bus, but do not rule out an internal Ethernet card. If the Ethernet device is external to the machine, it is safe to assume that the problem is external also. Try the same test from a sister machine. If the test fails to get out, then the local network can be suspected. At that point you have done your problem determination and can now safely blame the network itself. Call other system administrators on the network by phone and see if they are experiencing problems. Your last step is to call the network manager. Be tactful, but explain that you have already done your problem determination and that now it is his or her problem.

If you are in charge of your own network hardware, don't forget the obvious. Test the network hardware for loose, disconnected, or broken connectors and shorts. They are the major cause of failure. Test transceivers to see if they are warm and working. Test older external network devices like Intel Fastpaths, Spartacus boxes, and IBM DACUs to see whether they are alive or have to be *hardware reset*. Some units like Intel Fastpaths must be reset if the system has come down. It is imperative that the operators or techs have an SOP (see Chapters 20 and 21) that states precisely how to reset the device and why it is important to do so.

Daemons

Network daemons are usually robust. Like all daemons, they will kill themselves rather than live in a corrupt environment. Most are of the parent/server variety. The parent daemon listens for a request and then spawns a child to do the work. The parent is protected at all times. Like all daemons, network daemons must be started at system initiation, so they must have an entry in inetd.conf(5), rc, or in the rc family.[3] It also

---

[3] That is, /etc/rc, /etc/rc.local, or the rc directory rc.d.

pays to have a program that restarts daemons hidden away in your own `/local/etc` file:

```
for daemon in ftpd ftpd rlogin rchd telnetd fingerd rexecd rwhod
  do
    "etc/${daemon}"
    echo ${daemon} started
  done
  /usr/lib/sendmail -bd -q30m
  echo sendmail started
```

Make sure that all the network daemons are dead before doing a mass start like the preceding one. Never have two parent daemons running.

You can find out whether daemons are alive in several different ways. You can use `ps` and then `grep` for a particular daemon:

```
ps -ef!grep telnet
```

Or you can use a shotgun script made specifically for this purpose:

```
 for daemon in ftpd ftpd Brlogind rchd telnetd fingerd rexecd rwhod
   do
      ps -ef!fgrep ${daemon}!fgrep -v fgrep
   done
```

You can also use the `netstat` command:

```
netstat -a
```

There may be times when you need to kill a daemon. Get its process-ID number from `ps`. Use `netstat` to see if there are any connections using that daemon. If there are none, kill the process. *Be sure to get the parent daemon.*

NETWORK ADDRESSES, MASKS, AND BROADCASTS

Internet addresses are discouragingly mysterious to users and new network administrators. Written as four bytes, called `octets`, they look like this:

```
128.216.155.54
```

Each number, separated by periods, is a decimal representation of one byte. This may look confusing at first, but we'll soon see the rhyme and reason.

An internet address is a 32-bit number that is unique to a single host computer at some network location. The address has two to three different parts: a network number, a host number, and an optional subnet number. (A *subnet* is a subnetwork, a network within a network.)

Think of how you find a normal street address, like 1234 Alder Lane. The number, 1234, identifies a particular house, but if you don't have the street name, you aren't going to find that house. Having only the street name is a help, but without the address number, you're still up a creek. You definitely need the number *and* the street name to get to the right house. The street name corresponds to the network number, and the house number corresponds to the host number.

Network Address Basics

At this point you might be wondering, "If there are three parts to an internet address, why are there four bytes?" Here's where the plot thickens. There are three classes of networks: A, B, and C. Class A is intended for networks that have a multitude of hosts and only a few networks. It takes the following form:

```
net.host.host.host
```

Notice that it takes three bytes to form a host number in a Class A network. The range of the net number is 1 to 126. Thus, a Class A network number might look something like this:

```
126.5.40.215
```

Looking at all this from a binary point of view, the first 2 bits of the first byte of a 32-bit Class A internet address are 01. The number 127 is saved for a loopback address:

```
$ grep '127\.' /etc/hosts
127.0.0.1       localhost    lcl    me    loopback
$
```

Class B addresses are suitable for a medium number of networks with a medium number of hosts. Here is its form:

```
net.net.host.host
```

It takes 2 bytes for a host number in a Class B network. It also takes 2 bytes for a net number, and the range of possible Class B net numbers is 128.1 to 191.254. Again, it's handy to remember the binary perspective. The first 2 bits of the first byte of a Class B 32-bit internet address are 10.

The third and last form is Class C, which is a mass of networks supporting a few hosts each. The form is

```
net.net.net.host
```

Here it only takes 1 byte for a host number but 3 bytes for a net number. The Class C net number range is 192.0.1 to 223.255.254. The binary characteristics are easy to remember: The first 2 bits of the first byte of a 32-bit Class C address are 11.

All of this could have been made simpler with a larger address, such as a 48- or 64-bit address, but at the time the addressing scheme was conceived, no one imagined that the Internet would grow to its current gigantic proportions.

Broadcasts

A broadcast is the act of sending packets addressed to every host on the network. Let's imagine there is a special transmission for all *128.216* machines to read. To do so, the address normally occupied by a specific host becomes all binary ones,

```
1111 1111
```

or 255 for each byte. Thus, for our Class B network, 128.216, a broadcast address is

```
128.216.255.255
```

Why use all binary ones? Does anyone remember party lines? If you called your Aunt Rose in a little town of fifty people, everyone in the town would hear the special ring (two longs and one short), indicating that the call was for Aunt Rose. (Theoretically only Aunt Rose would answer it, but in fact a lot of other people would listen in if they had nothing else to do.) Broadcasting is kind of like that, only with a slightly different twist. Think of our broadcasting example as calling a huge party line at a curious little town called 128.216. The difference is that there is no special ring for any one number. Everybody's phone rings there, and everyone picks it up.

In a sense, all packets on a network are "broadcast," because they are received by every host on the wire. The network is not a filter; it is an antenna. It sends to everyone. The filtering takes place because each host knows its own internet address and accepts only those packets addressed specifically to it. The only exception is the network broadcast. Every host picks it up. All those binary ones are a dead giveaway.

Why is broadcast transmission used? The following is a real-life example: The ARP stands for Address Resolution Protocol. Sometimes a host needs to resolve an internet address into an Ethernet address. To do so, it broadcasts a special packet asking all host machines if any of them have that Ethernet address, and, if so, to respond with the physical internet address. RARP stands for Return Address Resolution Protocol, and it is similar.

Subnet Masks

Just when you think you're starting to get all this down pat, you run into some new wrinkle, like subnets. In order to set up a machine to join a network—even if you don't have a subnet on your site—you need to calculate a subnet mask. Let's take a look.

Class A and B networks have enough room in their host fields to support a subnet address. Class A networks have 24 bits of host space, so they work especially well for this:

```
net.subnet.host.host
```

Subnets act as networks within networks, and they are useful for organizing hosts within a network into logical groups. An engineering company could be divided into subnets for MIS, engineering, fabrication, and so on. Subnetting can assume a great deal of the load from any single network, thus picking up speed on the net by relieving an already taxed bandwidth. It is also handy for isolating parts of the network.

Subnet masks use the network bits of the internet address. Like network addresses and broadcast addresses, subnet masks are 32-bit numbers. The first step is knowing what a mask is. A mask is a template held over a piece of data that causes some of it to be read and some of it to be ignored. The bitwise operators *and* and *or* are used.

I once knew an old timer who turned off his hearing aid every time he didn't want to hear someone, and subnet masks can do nearly the same thing. For example, if you are using the bitwise *or* operator, you will use ones for what you want to hear, and zeros for what you want to ignore.

Here are the most frequently used network masks:

```
255.255.255.0      Class C
255.255.0.0        Class B
255.0.0.0          Class A
```

NFS

The Client–Server Relationship, Mounts, and Key Files

NFS stands for *network file systems*, but the explanation of the acronym doesn't begin to explain the significance of NFS in today's computer environments. NFS has revolutionized the world of UNIX computing, extending each UNIX machine far beyond its boundaries. The workstation–server relationship is possible because of NFS. Not only has it achieved high-speed data sharing, but it also has brought it to such a degree of perfection that the location of the shared files is totally transparent to the users. NFS has truly crowned the era of connectivity.

Conceptually, NFS is relatively simple. Under NFS any system can prepare file systems to be mounted to other systems. NFS client systems then can mount those file systems to their own file trees.

NFS creates a typical *client–server relationship*. The server is the *producer*, delivering a service, and the client is the *consumer*, receiving a service. The commodity being produced and consumed is the ability to extend a file system from one host to another.

Like network processes that deliver and receive services, NFS requires daemons and specialized files. The daemons provide services at both ends, the client machine and the host machine. The files tell what is going to happen to whom. There is also another layer of magic over and above ordinary networking. That layer consists of RPC services. RPCs are remote procedure calls, enabling one system to execute "calls" equivalent to system calls and library routines on another system.

Some system files are critical to networking. The principal system files are accessed at initiation, the files reached directly or indirectly by `rc`. Daemons are also initiated by `rc` and `rc.local`, and Wollongong provides the networking software for UNIX systems originally furnished without them. Berkeley and Berkeley-derived systems are more sophisticated, as they start a daemon, `inetd`, that reads which daemons to start from a file in `/etc` called `inetd.conf` and starts other network-related daemons.

A Manual Mount

The original `mount` command has been rewritten to allow network files also to be mounted with the same command. In other words, the `mount` command on a machine running NFS is not the same `mount` command you would find on UNIX Edition 7.

Let's review a typical local disk mount:

```
mount /dev/ra1g /usr
```

This says, "Mount device special file `/dev/ra1g` to file system mount point `/usr`."

More information must be passed to the `mount` command to mount a network file system. Here is a typical manual network mount:

```
mount -t nfs -o rw,hard,bg svr01:/usr/cae /usr/cae
```

What a difference! The mount type must be specified after the `-t` flag, and here it is `nfs`. The `-o` flag precedes several kinds of possible options. In this example the options are a hard mount for a read/write (rw) file system, with multiple retries in the background (bg) if the first mount attempt fails. The argument, svr01:/usr/cae, is the name of the server host and the file system you're going to mount. Note that the server's host name, svr01, must precede the file-tree name. The second argument, /usr/cae, is the mount point, the same as in a conventional disk mount. Note the use of file-tree names rather than device special file names.

If everything goes well, the mount will be immediate and will hold unless it sees a umount command, a network interruption, or a crash on the server.

We just saw a manual NFS mount, but manual NFS mounts are the exception, not the rule. Usually rc does the mount at initiation time. Before this can happen, two files and several daemons must be present.

rc: **Mounting with Network File Systems**

Conventional rc-driven mounting of NFS file servers requires that two files be present, one on the server and one on the client host. The server's file is /etc/exports. The client's is /etc/fstab. The /etc/export file tells the system what files may be exported for mounting to remote hosts. The /etc/fstab file tells the remote host what file systems to mount. The files shown for mounting in /etc/fstab are both local files and remote files.

The fstab files are used to do the mounts on all NFS machines. This clever concept of having a special table for the mounts has been seen in other UNIX systems. For example, UTS's /etc/mountab is a mount table with a list of all the mounts. However, UNIX system administrators should know that /etc/fstab is unique in syntax and not altogether consistent from one OEM's system to another.

Enough talk. Let's go right into a SunOS system's /etc/fstab file and look at a few entries:

```
/dev/xya / 4.2 rw,noquota 1 1
/dev/xy0b /usr 4.2 rw,noquota 1 1
svr2:/usr/cae /usr/cae nfs rw,hard 0 0
svr2:/usr/local/man /usr/lib/local/man nfs ro,soft 0 0
svr2:/home/scott /files/scott nfs rw,soft 0 0
```

The first two entries are for local mounts, called 4.2 mounts after the Berkeley BSD version number from which they originated. They are local because the mounts take place directly on the host. They start with the expected form:

```
device_special_file file_system
```

This is followed by a comma-separated list of options, and it ends with a pair of integers. The integers indicate two positional parameters, *frequency*, the frequency or interval between backup dumps, and *pass*, the pass in fsck to check the partition.

The last three entries in our /etc/fstab file example are NFS mounts. NFS mounts take place anywhere *but* the local host. Note that the *pass* and *frequency* parameters are used in both local and NFS mounts. The form is this:

```
host:file_system directory type options frequency pass
```

In SunOS these arguments are separated by blanks, but this is not consistent on all UNIX systems. ULTRIX uses a colon-delimited list:

```
/usr/users@server01:/homes:rw:0:0nfs:hard,bg:
/usr/man@caeserv:/usr/man:or:0:0:nfs:soft:
```

There are other differences as well. On ULTRIX the form is *filesystem@host* instead of *host:filesystem*.

In spite of the differences in `fstab` formats between SunOS and ULTRIX, a Sun 386i workstation can still be client to a VAXserver 3600, and everything will work. Similarly, a DEC MicroVAX can be a workstation host to a Sun series 2, 3, or 4 server. Whether Sun, DEC, Apollo, or HP, NFS works on them all. That is precisely the point of the NFS design. RPCs communicate via XDR, external data representation, and so the data format makes no difference. External data representation guarantees that the data will look the same in spite of the byte order, word order, or any other differences.

/etc/exports

No discussion about `/etc/fstab` would be complete without discussing `/etc/exports`, which tells what can be exported to which host. It can also open a file system to the world. The following illustration is taken from an `/etc/exports` file:

```
/usr/cae
/u/mcd/bhunter stalker
/u/mcd/sbrock cj
/u/mcd/gsimko daboss
/u/mcd/dhudock farside
/usr/cae/X10 fm1 fm2 fm3 fm4 fm5 fm6 fm7 fm8
```

The first entry, `/usr/cae`, is a computer-aided engineering tool directory, and it is open to any machine that cares to mount to it. The next four entries mount hosts to specific server file systems, and each line states that the named specific file system can be mounted only to the named host. Thus, `/u/mcd/bhunter` is mounted to `stalker`, and so on. The last entry opens an X Window, `X10`, area to hosts `fm1` through `fm8`. Clearly, a great deal of control is possible with `/etc/exports` file entries.

Let's back up and regroup some concepts. The `/etc/fstab` file is on each client machine and requests the mounts. The `/etc/exports` file is on the server and states what is allowable for export.

It should be noted that `/etc/exports` won't cross file system boundaries. If, for example, `/usr/man` is a mounted file system separate from `/usr` on the server, a separate entry will be required to mount `/usr/man`, even if one exists for `/usr`. Thus, `/etc/fstab` must be maintained for each file system that is added.

NFS Interaction

The typical NFS installation consists of one or more file servers and two YP servers, one a master and the other a slave. These servers serve up to a dozen workstations each. This system of servers and clients is not a loose federation of computers but is tightly coupled. Many workstations are diskless and rely entirely on the existence of the server. Workstations with their own disks rely on the file servers for the bulk of their data.

Most frequently these cluster systems rely on the Yellow Pages (now NIS) service to simplify administration. YP maintains a data base of administrative files for common access, such as /etcs passwd, hosts, and group. The master server has the only set of source files that is updated continually. The slave servers have replicated copies.

There are strong interdependencies on a system of workstations. Administrators can mount and dismount disk partitions at will on a stand-alone system, but they cannot on an active NFS server system. If it has been exported, the workstations will have it mounted. The clients react by filling the server's console with stale file handle messages and a similar complaint to their own consoles.

It is important to understand the cause and effect of an NFS mount:

- At boot exportfs is executed, usually by rc.local. This causes /etc/exports to be read. Now the kernel knows which directories are exported.
- The NFS daemons are executed by rc.local.
- The client's mount can now request that the NFS directories in /etc/fstab be mounted.
- The rpc.mountd daemon on the server handles the mount request.
- The server's rpc.mountd daemon sends a *file handle* identifier to the client.
- The exportfs file notifies the server's kernel of the export information.
- The biod daemon on the client is now able to handle data from the server in blocks and thus improve the client's performance.

NFS PROBLEMS

You've just seen the bullet list of what happens when everything goes right. What if your server "goes away"? Sometimes servers seems to go off to never-never land. When a server's file system becomes unavailable, even momentarily, the individual hosts bombard the server with error messages and tie up the console. The client hosts then send stale file handle error messages to their own consoles until the system is rebooted or the NFS daemons are killed and restarted.

The consequences are far less drastic when a YP-master server dies and a slave server is present. The slave server takes over the YP duties, and it is business as usual unless this is also the host's file server. Then the hosts that depended on that particular server for their files are out of luck. Even though client hosts can come and go without notice, servers cannot.

MOUNT TYPES AND RELATED PROBLEMS

A *hard mount* is done to cause the NFS mount to keep trying until a mount is successful. Hard mounts are usually done for critical file systems. The counterpart, a *soft mount*, simply will return an error if it cannot make the mount within a specified number of times. The rule is that if it is not a life-or-death file system, mount it soft. Diskless servers mount root and swap hard, and all hosts mount the man pages soft.

Error messages differ from hard to soft mounts. The hard mount message says:

```
NFD server stalker not responding, still trying
```

The soft mount gives up, writing this to the error log and the console:

```
NFS mount failed for server mcdserv, Timed out
```

If you get this message with the clients running, it is a good guess that the server either is not running well or is not running at all. I usually am logged onto most of my servers from my own workstation by way of X Windows. A quick `ps -qax` or `ps -lax` tells me what is alive on the server. The `-qax` flags give minimal information, whereas the `-lax` flags offer more information than is needed.

If you're working from the client, `rpcinfo` will tell you what's happening on the server and track the problem:

```
#  /etc/rpcinfo -p mcdserv
program  vers   proto port
  100005    2    udp 1035   ypserv
  100008    2    tcp 1023   ypserv
  .
  100004    2    tcp 2001   ypbind
  .
  100003    1    udp 2045   nfs
  100004    1    udp 1091   mountd
```

If any daemons appear to be missing or if the list seems too short, you then will have to attempt a login to the server. Don't give up just because a remote login fails. Head for the computer room, and try the system's console. If the server is down, you are in the right place to reboot it.

NFS MOUNT FAILURES

An NFS mount occurs either from a command-line invocation or from `mount` reading the mount table `/etc/fstab`. The latter is the more common. As a result, `/etc/fstab` is the first place you want to look when `rc.local` is unable to do a mount automatically on booting. The `mount` command calls the YP binding daemon `ypbind` on networked systems running YP. The `mount` command calls `ypserv` to get the IP address of the host. Without YP, the local `hosts` table must be consulted. Next, `portmap` comes into play, and `mount` calls the server's port mapper to get the port number of the mount daemon `mountd`. The server's mount daemon then checks `/etc/exports` to see if the mount is permissible. The server's mount daemon returns the *file handle* of the mounted file system. Should the mount be broken later, a `stale file handle` error will result. The local `mount` command now initiates the `mount(2)` system call with the `fhandle` given by the server. Last, a mount entry is added to the kernel mount table.

It is necessary to understand this chain of events in order to troubleshoot an NFS mount failure. Mount errors occur for the following reasons:

- Server down.
- Device busy.

- Illegal file system name.
- No such file or directory.
- Server not in `hosts` data base.
- Invalid directory name.
- `portmapper` failure.
- Access denied.
- Not a directory.
- Not owner.

Most of these problems are self-explanatory. A down server must be restarted, but first try to find out why it's down. A down server is apparent from the calls you receive from your users.

The `device busy` message is seen more often when trying to unmount a disk. Anyone logged on and using a file from the disk or with the shell path currently in a directory on a disk partition causes a `device busy` error.

The `nfs_mount: illegal file system name...` message is most often caused by forgetting to put the server name in front of the file name, such as `svr1:/usr/cae`.

The `...not in host data base` error message is straightforward. The name is not in `/etc/hosts` or the YP data base.

The `invalid directory name` message is caused most often by failing to use an absolute path name.

The `nfs mount ...server not responding: port mapper failure -- rpc timed out` message means that something is missing from the chain. Your Ethernet is marked `down` by `ifconfig` on the server or client host; the Ethernet is down somewhere along the wire (short, loose connector, break); or the server is down.

The `access denied` message occurs because your client's name is not in the server's `/etc/exports` export list.

The `not owner` message is caused by `root`'s not issuing the `mount` command. While seemingly self-evident, this is aggravated by `root`'s having a user ID of `-1`, rather than `0`, when logging on from another system. The only user with less power than an ordinary user is a foreign `root`.

Forget the technical details of NFS for a moment and think of the incredible advances it makes in computing. For the first time foreign files can be mounted to a local file system and treated as if they are on a local disk. All of this is accomplished without the replication of data required by the local system and also without the insufferable delays that came with using its much older predecessor UUCP. NFS makes the workstation viable.

A Walk Through `rc.local` on an NFS System

It takes a lot of daemons to run NFS. Some of these daemons already are familiar to many of you, such as `ifconfig` and `inetd`, conventional Ethernet/Internet daemons. The servers must run `portmap` and `mountd`. They are the first daemons started by `rc` on the system's way into multiuser mode.

portmap

The `portmap` daemon is the first network daemon to come alive. There is a general coding convention for the `rc` family of startup daemons. Rather than taking the chance that a daemon may not be present in the directory, its presence is tested. For example, the `rc.local` code looks like this when starting the `portmap` daemon:

```
if [ -f /etc/portmap ]; then
  /etc/portmap; echo -n ' portmap'  > /dev/cons
fi
```

The left bracket, `[`, is a link to the `test` command. The matching right bracket, `]`, is a no-op. The `-f` flag of the `test` command tests for the existence of a file. Thus the line reads, "Test for the existence of `/etc/portmap`. If it is there, start it and say *portmap* to the console device."

The code could be cleaner, since we see four lines of code crammed into two lines, but there are far uglier conventions in use. Take a look at this cryptic gem, also out of `rc.local`:

```
[ -f /etc/portmap] && { /etc/portmap
        echo -n 'portmap'>/dev/cons
}
```

To the average programmer who doesn't usually dabble in system programming, code like this is virtually unintelligible. Unfortunately, it is used in system scripts as often as not. Translated into plain English, either the `test` command or its link, `[`, will return a *true* if it evaluates true. The `&&` operator will execute the next line if it sees the *true* condition. The brackets, `{}`, are used for grouping and executing the enclosed commands in the same shell.

To the uninitiated, this kind of shorthand programming notation is confusing. At first it seems like a plot to confuse new administrators. Take heart. You will get used to it in time. Eventually code like this is a piece of cake to read and understand.

biod

The NFS daemon, `nfsd`, is followed by `biod`, which starts the NFS synchronous block daemons. It is used only by the client host, not the server. The `biod` daemon performs *read-ahead/write-behind* block moves, not unlike those used by the system's buffer cache, and for the same reason. This strategy allows the system to do reads and writes when it is best for the system, thus allowing better interrupt handling for other processes. Like `nfsd`, `biod` can run with several active duplicate daemons to speed service:

```
[ -f /etc/biod ] && { /etc/biod 4
  echo 'biod started'>/dev/cons
}
```

The number of NFS and block I/O daemons is a function of the system's size. Small systems usually use only four, but larger systems use at least eight.

nfsd

The next daemon in the chain is `nfsd`, which handles file system requests from client hosts. It is an unusual daemon because it can take an argument to create multiple copies of itself:

```
if [ -f /etc/nfsd ]; then
    /etc/nfsd 8        /* create 4 NFS server daemons */
    echo ' starting 8 nfs daemons'>>/dev/co
fi
```

Notice that `nfs` is run with four or more active, duplicate daemons to speed service.

rpc.mountd

The `rpc.mountd` daemon is next in line. The `rpc.mountd` answers mount requests by reading /etc/exports to see if it is permissible to do the mount.

Lock and Status Daemons

NFS provides a locking service. The stock default is to disable the NFS locking service and enable local locking. Add the following to /etc/rc.local to enable NFS locking:

```
[ -f /usr/etc/statd ] && {
    /usr/etc/statd & echo 'statd'                  >/dev/cons
}
[ -f /usr/etc/lockd ] && {
    /usr/etc/lockf & echo 'lockd'                  >/dev/cos
}
echo 'NFS locking enabled'                         >/dev/cons
```

The `statd` daemon is the network status daemon that monitors the client and server status of requests made by the local `lockd` daemon. If you have disabled NFS locking, be sure to disable `statd`, or its constant whining will fill the console with error messages. When `lockd` is active and `statd` detects a failure, `lockd` will recover the locked files or file regions.

As the name implies, `lockd` is the network lock daemon. NFS lock requests can be sent locally or by a remote host's lock daemon. The local `lockd` processes these requests.

Removing Daemons from `rc`

From time to time, you may have to remove a daemon from rc, but don't ever remove the lines. You may need them later. Instead, comment out the lines by putting a pound sign in front of them. Be very careful when commenting out the lines of a daemon from rc.local. Be sure to get *all* the lines, including the last `fi` or `}`. Then leave a comment line with your name and date:

```
#     removed rwhod    6/4/89   b hunter
#   if [ -f /etc/rwhod ];then
#       /etc/rwhod;echo 'starting rwhod'>>/dev/console
#   fi
#
```

Add a blank comment at the end to separate visually the omitted code from the rest of rc.local.

If you have the opportunity, by all means test the script. If it is not tested and there is a slight error, even one uncommented fi, the script will cause rc to hang, and you will be unable to come up into init 2 or multiuser mode. To test rc.local, run it with sh -x or with set x embedded in the code. Run rc in test mode from single-user mode.

Passwords Under NFS and YP

There are different kinds of servers. One machine may be a file server. The same machine or another machine may be the YP domain server. The same machine or another machine can be the sendmail master. Under YP, data are altered by logging onto the master YP domain machine and editing the /etc data bases. Password administration is done so frequently that the NFS command Yppasswd(1) is provided for the task.

At System V Release 4, NFS and RFS are part of the UNIX standard distribution. And since UNIX is no longer thought of as a stand-alone system, this addition is none too soon. There is a major difference in the NFS and RFS treatment of user IDs and group IDs. NFS uses common and consistent user IDs throughout its domain, whereas RFS uses the log name and does its own internal user-ID resolution. If you use both, you must use consistent user IDs and group IDs. If you use only RFS, you will be still better off using a central data base for user IDs, group IDs, and log names, since you will have confusion on file transfers if you do not.

UUCP

In the earliest days of UNIX, the UUCP family was the only UNIX network, and so AT&T long-haul phone lines made sense. UUCP is a drop-and-forward service, like CompuServe. The difference is that UUCP does the storage itself. Letters written and files transferred on UUCP are stored on the sending systems for transfer at a later time. Files set up within the UUCP system tell the system when it can and can't poll, so you can take advantage of phone rate changes.

UUCP can be run over a simple hardwire connection from one machine directly to another. It makes a very simple network over short distances. The cu command excels here.

When looking at early networks like pre-BNU UUCP, remember that modems and dialers were separate entities. To go from modem to modem was similar to an Ethernet connection using two repeaters.

In his original UUCP paper, D. A. Nowitz described UUCP as a series of communications programs by either hardware or dial-up service. UUCP is used for file transfer and remote command execution, a description that covers UUCP in a nutshell but fails to mention a major use for mail transfer. Sending mail through UUCP is only a bit harder than regular UNIX mail. Thus to send mail to my oldest son on the other side of the country, I invoke mail

```
mail apex!sphynx!necutc!linus!chad
```

and in a day or two he has my message. While this is not as fast as using the Internet, it still beats the U.S. mail.

UUCP installation was a nightmare back at Version 7. It required a specific dialer, a Bell 801, or source code modification. Early users of 68000 ports, particularly those ported by Microport, had UUCP but could not use it without substantial kludging. The HoneyDanBer[4] versions made installation and management of UUCP a reality.

Programs loosely grouped in the UUCP family are cu, uucp, uux, uucico, and uuxqt. One of the simplest UUCP commands is cu, allowing a connection from one UNIX machine to another. The uucp command puts together files and mail to be transferred along with a few uux commands to make it happen. The uux command makes work files that are executed on remote machines, and it also executes user command scripts on remote machines. Its counterpart, uuxqt, executes those files when they are received.

The uucico command is the workhorse of the UUCP system, since it does the actual data transmission. It has some handy debug flags for troubleshooting UUCP problems, and uucico performs the following functions:

- Scans the spool directories for work.
- Places a call to a remote site.
- Negotiates a line protocol to be used.
- Executes all requests from both sites.
- Logs work requests and work completions.

UUCP Tasks

UUCP is work intensive to the system administrator. It fills spool directories and log files and adds entries to cron and rc that must be maintained. Cleanup scripts can be run by cron to clean out system spools. Note that uuclean is standard UUCP for cleaning the spools. It trashes anything older than a set time, usually three days, which makes as many problems as it solves. Undelivered mail and files must be chased down by the administrator and touched to prevent them from being wiped out.

UUCP Files

UUCP scatters its files, by storing them in /bin and three other major areas. As a store-and-forward service, UUCP needs places to spool and finds them in /usr/spool/uucp and /usr/spool/uucppublic. The uucp directory stores work files, data files, and executable files for spool transfer, while uucppublic is a holding area for incoming files. On secure systems uucppublic is the only area that is accessible to a calling system.

UUCP stores its executables and configuration files in /usr/lib/uucp. All executables are in /usr/lib/uucp except for uucp and cu, which are in /bin. The original Nowitz version of UUCP was difficult to configure, partially because of its use of dialers and nondialing modems and partially because there was no apparent way to configure it without source code. But the BNU version recognizes the existence of dialing modems and caters to them.

---

[4] Also known as BNU, for basic network utility. This version of UUCP is the product of Peter Honeyman, David A. Nowitz, and Brian E. Redman. Note that Nowitz was the author of the original Bell UUCP.

The original AT&T 5.2 BNU version uses a file, /usr/lib/dialers, to establish dialing sequences for individual modems. The dialers file uses the following escapes:

Escape	Action
\c	suppress newline
\d	2-second delay
\D	phone number or token
\e	echo check disabled
\E	echo check enabled
\K	break
\n	newline
\p	pause
\r	carriage return
\T	send phone number or token
\nnn	octal number 0nnn

XENIX uses separately compiled C programs for each modem type. Both source and a.out files are in the /usr/lib/uucp directory.

Ports and devices must be defined for the system, which is done in /usr/lib/uucp/L-devices. Each port used for modem or hardwire communication must be defined as a direct device. Furthermore, each port with a conventional dialing modem must be redefined as an ACU with the port name and a reference to the XENIX modem a.out file or 5.2 dialers file. Both ACU and DIR entries must have the baud rate or rates specified. Here is what L-devices looks like on a XENIX system:

```
ACU   tty1A  /usr/lib/uucp/dialHA24       300-2400
ACU   tty1B  /usr/lib/uucp/dialVA3450     1200

DIR   tty1A  0     1200
DIR   tty1A  0     2400
DIR   tty1A  0     9600

DIR   tty2a  0     2400
DIR   tty2a  0     1200
DIR   tty2a  0     9600
```

The XENIX file has the system's ports with modem control, tty1A, and tty1B, defined as direct devices. A port without modem control, tty2a, is also defined for direct use only. Note that tty2a is a hardwire-direct port and that tty1A and tty1B are also defined as modem ports. Port tty1B is set up for a 1200, baud Racal Vadic, and port tty1A is set up for a 300- to 2400-baud D. C. Hayes or a Hayes-compatible modem.

Here is a Devices file used on an AT&T 3B system, typical of most System V Devices files:

```
ACU tty14 - 1200 hayes
Direct tty14 - 1200 direct \D
Direct tty12 - 4800 direct \D
```

In the AT&T file port tty14 is set up for a 1200-baud Hayes modem at 1200 baud. Port tty12 is set up for a hardwire-direct connection at 4800 baud, the maximum speed the AT&T I/O board can realistically handle.

The next most important UUCP file is L.sys, which is known as Systems on System V. Here is a typical System V Systems file:

```
apex   Any ACU 1200 12011980577 in:--in: Uhunter word: cb750a
stalker   Any ACU 1200 9854811 in:--in: Uhunter1
laidback Any 1200 14139868020 in:--in: Uhunter cb750a
interstate never
```

Let's pick apart the first entry. It means call apex at any time; apex is an ACU running at 1200 baud with the phone number 1–201–198–0577. Repeatedly wait for the prompt substring in:, the tail of Login:. When you receive it, send Uhunter and wait for the substring word, the tail of Password. On getting word, send the password cb750a.

The last entry is much simpler. If called by node interstate, don't allow a login. This is a simple but effective security method.

The XENIX L.sys file is similar:

```
apex Any ACU 2400 120111980577\
 ogin:-BREAK-ogin:-BREAK-ogin: Uhunter word: cb750a
```

This entry for apex is similar, but this time it is set up for a 2400-baud modem. The login sequence now requires sending a break to retry and reset the receiving modem's baud rate. The receiving modem is a 9600-baud-capable Telebit, and because of its complexity, it requires a bit more coaxing than does a simple 1200-baud modem.

There are less important /usr/lib/uucp files, like L-dialcodes or AT&T Dial-codes. This simple file has a code- and number-sequenced record:

```
LA   1213
SF   1418
NJ   1201
Sac  1351
```

There are the dial-code sequences for area codes or tricky internal code sequences like a dial-out on a PBX-internal phone system to the outside world:

```
SFout 91418
```

The dial code is substituted in the system's dial sequence:

```
apex Any ACU 1200 NJ9890574 in:--in: Uhunter word: cb750a
```

UUCP Administration Commands

The user command uucp is used to send files to other UNIX systems. Its syntax is

```
$ uucp -n joanna /u/proj1/back.door.doc apex!~
```

This means send the document called back.door.doc to apex, and put the file in /usr/spool/uucppublic. Send mail to user joanna that the file has arrived. The !~ is the uucppublic instruction telling the receiving system to put the file in /usr/spool/uucppublic.

The real workhorse of the UUCP system is uucico. While uucp or uux lines up the work and places work files in /usr/spool/uucp, it is uucico that does the actual transfer, and uucico scans /usr/spool/uucp for work files whenever it is invoked. In

BNU, uusched does the actual scanning and calls uucico to contact other systems. Using uucico directly is an excellent debugging method, with the -x flag used as the debug flag. There are nine levels of debugging, from one to nine. As a security measure the debug information does not show logins and passwords. The following is an example of uucico syntax with the -x flag:

```
# /usr/lib/uucp/uucico -r1 -x5 -sapex 2> /tmp/uubugs
```

Here uucico is called at the fifth level of debugging, -x5. The flag -r1 places the call in the initiating or master mode, where uucico initiates the work and does its own work first before asking the other system if it has any other work to do.

uuclean

The cleanup program for the UUCP system is uuclean. On XENIX it is an a.out C file, and on other systems it is a script. Usually uuclean is invoked by cron. Also, uuclean has options to allow it to scan for files with a specific prefix, clean other directories besides /usr/spool/uucp*, clean files older than "N" hours, provide debugging information, and send mail to the owners of deleted files.

uuqxt

The uuqxt daemon comes alive to scan the spool directory for outstanding requests from the calling system. It works in partnership with uucico: uuqxt reads the files in /usr/spool/uucp* and checks to see if the calling system has permission to execute any requested command. Then uuqxt will make transfer requests of its own if any files are needed from the calling system.

Making a Connection with a Port or System

There are only a few steps to make a link with the outside world:

1. Set up and initialize the physical port to be used.
2. Establish a node name for your own system with uname, hostname, or an equivalent.
3. Make an entry in Systems or L.sys showing the dial-out steps.
4. Make an entry in Devices or L-devices for a direct connection. If a modem is used, make an entry for a modem connection.
5. If necessary, make a file to describe your modem type. This is not required for known modems like Hayes.
6. Set up whatever security is necessary to prevent unauthorized entry into the system now that you have opened up the system for the world at large to call in.

MAIL

UNIX mail comes in a variety of flavors. There are currently three forms of addressing, local, location specific, and location independent. The original AT&T mail command simply gets mail from one user on the system and sends it to another. This gets mail to Dave Hudock on the local system:

```
$ mail dhudock
```

when Dave is on the same system.

With the advent of UUCP, `mail` became a little more complex internally, but to the user it changed only in that the invocation was a trifle more complex. To reach Dave at a remote system called `farside`, you do this:

```
$ mail farside!dhudock
```

Now the *bang* character is necessary to get mail across the phone lines to another system.

Forms requiring the name of a specific system are location specific:

```
$ mail dhudock@farside
```

To go to Dave at `farside` by way of `cj`, you do this:

```
$ mail cj!farside!dhudock
```

Mail sent out across the Internet poses a problem, because no one knows all the systems in between you and whomever. The solution is having the user send mail to a mail *domain*:

```
$ mail dhudock@folsom.apex.com
```

Here the commercial domain of `apex` routes to the local mail domain `folsom`, and no one needs to know the name of the system that Dave lives on or the name of the mail-master system that delivers it.

With simple local mail, one has only to keep the location of mail clean and writable. The location, of course, changes with the version:

Edition 7	`/usr/spool/mail`
System V	`/usr/mail`
BSD 4.3 and up	`/var/spool/mail`

Berkeley UNIX has enhanced sending system mail still further. It allows mail to be sent to the printer or return mail to be sent with a single mnemonic invocation. Most systems have both Berkeley and AT&T versions. The BSD version is `/usr/ucb/bin`, and the conventional version is `/usr/bin/mail`. The order of the search path is important. If a user wants BSD mail, the path will look like

```
% echo path
. /usr/ucb/bin /usr/bin /u/local/bin
```

The invocation of BSD mail is of particular importance, since some AT&T versions don't work with `sendmail`, a software mechanism to give `mail` access to the internet. In addition, `sendmail` also negotiates routing through UUCP.

The UUCP version of mail requires only that UUCP be set up and working. There is no more work required for mail that was not there for UUCP already.

The `mail`/`sendmail` **Model**

Before getting into the mechanics of the `sendmail` system, let's create a theoretical model of the system. The `mail` command acts as an agent to get mail from the user and to receive mail to pass to the user. As such, it is called a *user agent*. The mail user agent passes the message and the from-to information to another agent to deliver it, a *transport agent*.

The transport agent is now responsible to take the from-to information and create the mail-message-header information, finding the routing, adding the time, resolving addresses, and figuring out the correct mail domain so that you will know where to send the message (with header). The transport agent requires a data base of alternative names and name-address combinations for address resolution. It also needs its own built-in set of rules on how it is going to do all the things for which it is responsible.

Now that the tasks are separated, let's review them. The `mail` user agent does the following:

- Accepts messages.
- Verifies the existence of the recipient.
- Concatenates the message and the message header to the recipient's mailbox.
- Returns the mail if it can't be delivered.

The transport agent, `sendmail`, and its `/etc/aliases` data perform these tasks:

- Take mail messages and header information from the user agent.
- Interpret the *to* address and initialized routing.
- Send mail to local mailboxes if local, to a delivery agent if not.
- Get mail from delivery agents and deliver it to local users.
- Resolve aliases for rerouting.
- Create and distribute error messages if mail can't be delivered.

There is more to system mail than just the `mail` and `sendmail` programs and the `aliases` data base, as we shall see.

`Mail.rc` and `/.mailrc`

Edition 7 `mail` had few options. You sent mail, and you got mail. That was about it. Berkeley's `mail`, along with its transport-agent `sendmail` counterpart, offers so many features that you probably won't want all of them. Some degree of control over the number of features must be exercised by the local site and the individual user. This control is managed through special rc files. The system's control file is `/usr/lib/Mail.rc`, and the user's is his or her `~/.mailrc` file.

The `/.mailrc` file can be a simple one-liner:

```
% cd
% cat mail.rc
set append dot crt
%
```

The append and dot options are only a few of the many mail(1) set options available:

append	Appends messages to the end of the user's mailbox, not the beginning.
ask	Asks for a mail subject.
askcc	Asks for a CC (courtesy copy) message.
DEAD = filename	Saves undeliverable letters in the file *filename*.
dot	Uses a dot (period) for the mail-end-of-text character, usually a $^\wedge$D.
quite	Doesn't print the opening message when opening mail.
save	Saves the mail message being typed if interrupted (by EOT or kill).
VISUAL = editor	Sets the screen editor to *editor*, default vi.

An ignore operator is also provided, allowing the user to get rid of unwanted header information while preserving the from-to date information. An interesting feature of these rc mail files is the alternates option, which allows the user or system to define optional addresses, like this:

```
% grep alternates .mailrc
alternates bhunter@fms1 bhunter@fms2 bhunter@stalker
%
```

As the administrator you will use Mail.rc to create a default mail environment for your users. Teach them how to use their home /.mailrc file, and give them a default /.mailrc file when creating their login directory.

sendmail **IN PRACTICE**

Putting mail on the network created a new set of problems. The task of sorting out what was local mail, what was UUCP, and what was network was too much for mail alone. So a Berkeley student, Eric Allman, tackled the problem, and the result is BSD sendmail, although sendmail is not a mail program at all. It exists a level below mail and negotiates the routing of mail through the network, through UUCP, or for simple local delivery.

One of sendmail's major functions is to route mail between mail domains, and it does that very well indeed. The sendmail utility runs on every system on the network that uses mail, usually every machine. One system must take on the task of being the mail hub, called the *mail master*. Also, sendmail runs as a daemon on all systems using network mail. The sendmail daemon reads its sendmail.cf configuration file on invocation to see how to parse addresses, rewrite the mail's headers, set options, and even set the rules by which it will do all of this. The /etc/aliases file is read by sendmail and augments routing by allowing names other than the actual user and system names to be used for mail forwarding. Thus sendmail has built-in abilities to monitor itself, log itself, log its activities, and generate debugging information.

Each system must run the sendmail daemon, /etc/sendmail. When sendmail is run from rc with the aid of the -bd flags, sendmail goes from a command to a daemon:

```
if [ -f /usr/lib/sendmail -a -f /etc/sendmail.cf ]; then
    (cd /var/spool/mqueue; rm -f nf* lf*)
    /usr/lib/sendmail -bd -q1h && chat -n ' sendmail'
fi
```

The q flag ensures that saved messages will be processed at a noted interval, here one hour.

mqueue

The sendmail utility maintains its own mail queue, /var/spool/mqueue, whose contents can be seen with the malq command or sendmail with the -bp option. Several types of files live in the mail queue directory, including log files, data files, and queue files. Other types of files are known by their leading two characters as well. Here is a summary:

d   data file

l   lock file

n   a transient file created when a new ID is made to prevent a race condition

q   queue control file

t   temporary file

x   transcript file

A typical listing of mqueue:

```
% ls -l /usr/spool/mqueue
-rw-------  1 root       214 Aug 23 15:07 dfAA07863
-rw-------  1 root        40 Nov 15 15:32 dfAA07876
-rw-------  1 root       405 Nov 15 09:30 qfAA07863
-rw-------  1 root       416 Nov 15 15:32 qfAA07876
-rw-rw-rw-  1 root      7410 Nov 15 15:32 syslog
-rw-rw-rw-  1 root     19303 Nov 15 04:05 syslog.0
```

The data file names start appropriately with df and contain the mail message exactly as it is typed in. It is a pure ASCII file. The queue file names start with qf and contain the mail header, the *from* and *to* information. Here is the typical contents of a qf file:

```
% cat qfAA07876
P19450
T627686218
DdfAA07876
ADeferred
S<sbrock@cj.apex.com>
R<dhudock@farside.apex.com>
H?P?return path: <cj!sbrock>
Hreceived: from cj by svr02 (5.51./10/0i); Mon 15 Nov 89 15:32:18 PDT
Hreceived: by farside (5.51.10.01); Mon 15 Nov 89 15:32:59 PDT
Hdate: Mon 15 Nov 89 15:32:59
Hfrom: sbrock@cj (Scott Brock)
Hmessage-id: <8911200173O.AO7876@cj>
Hto: farside::dhudock@farside>apex.com
Hsubject: lunch
```

Just about everything beginning with an H is printed at the top of the message once it is delivered. The following are some other codes:

D   data file name

R   address of recipient

S   sender address

T   time of creation

P   message priority

M   message

Note that both forms of addressing are used in the qf file. Thus we see both S<sbrock@cj.apex.com and H?P?return path: < cj!sbrock>. The first method is the DARPA method associated with Ethernet, and the second is most often associated with UUCP.

If an old message or a queue file is stuck in mqueue, start your debugging by reading the qf file. Look at the routing. Is the destination a legitimate mail client? Was it routed through the mail master? Your answer should be here. If it isn't, look in the syslog error and log file.

The log file for sendmail is /usr/spool/mqueue/syslog. It is restarted every day in the early hours of the morning. The old log file is saved to a numbered suffix like syslog.0. The log file records everything, both good and bad: It tells of successful transmissions, and it holds sendmail error messages. Here is the beginning of one syslog file:

```
Nov 20 01:02:03 syslog restarted
Nov 20 04:05:02 localhost: 1387 sendmail: alias database out of data
Nov 20 04:06:02 localhost: 1387 sendmail: to=ibm08::chan@ibmvax.apex.com
```

There are three kinds of messages here. There is a simple announcement that the log restarted at the time set by cron. An error message announces an out-of-date alias file. Finally we see the result of a successful transmission. If there are transmission delays, they will show up in the log as well:

```
Nov 20 10:20:56 localhost: 14645 sendmail: AA14362: to=cj!sbrock, delay=00:00:03
```

Here is where you can track your network and see where mail gets lost on the line on an out-of-bandwidth network.

sendmail.cf: **The Configuration File**

The source of all information for routing and just about anything else that is going to happen in the process of mail transmission is sendmail.cf. The system allows the configuration file to define symbols, classes, priorities, and options.

Each system comes with a "generic" sendmail.cf file, which is heavily commented and as self-explanatory as an OEM can make it. The trick of the configuration is to read from the top down and to supply the needed value for each variable. In addition, sendmail defines macros. A macro looks like DA$w, with $w set to the name of the current host. A is the macro name:

```
#
DA$w
#
```

Be sure to set the mail domain, the D macros, the UUCP system that hubs UUCP messages, the U macros, and the relay machine, the mail master using the R macros.

The configuration file defines symbols, classes, and protocols as well as mailers, delivery programs, and address-rewriting rules. An orderly `sendmail.cf` file first handles its general *defines*, creating each macro as needed. All these macro definitions start with a D:

```
#
#
# macro decnet_relay = "fm2";
DAfm2
#
# macro my_domain = "apex.com"
DBapex.com
#
# macro uucp_gateway = "apexu"
DDapexu
#
```

Don't look for consistency among uppercase macro names because they are user defined.

To reiterate, the macro has the form D*cval*. Remember the example of $w? The D means define; *c* is some character, uppercase or lowercase, and it is followed by a value. Thus above the expression DAfm2 is macro A, which is set to the value fm2. This defines a DECnet relay host, a necessity for a UNIX system on a VAX running TCP/IP over DECnet. This combination has the advantage of allowing communications with VMS systems as well.

Typically you will have to do your first `sendmail` configuration from the generic configuration file. It is not usually as orderly as our example is. Generic files are heavily commented, so much so that only one line in five or so is functional. Looking at the A macro again:

```
#
#
# The $w macro is preset by sendmail to the current host's
# name. Here we simply capture the value in our own $A macro.
#
DA$w
#
```

There is no easy way to do the first configuration. You simply must slug your way through each explanation of the macro and set your value to it. There is a significant amount of variation from vendor to vendor and no fixed value for any uppercase macro. Lowercase macro names tend to follow Eric Allman's variables as defined in the BSD *Sendmail Installation and Operations Guide*.

The next section of an orderly configuration file is the options section. Options macros start with an O. Here the SMTP help file is located:

```
#
#   o_fsmtp = 'usr/lib/sendmail.hf";
OH/usr/lib/sendmail.hf
```

```
#
#
#    o_postmaster = "postmaster";
OPpostmaster
#
```

In addition, postmaster is set. Administrators usually set postmaster in /etc/aliases to whichever log name receives sendmail's mail complaints, usually themselves.

The next section of the configuration file is the *precedence* section, which sets mail delivery priorities:

```
# precedence
#    first-class = 0;
Pfirst-class=0
#    special-delivery = 100;
Pspecial-delivery=100
#    junk = -100;
Pjunk=-100
#
```

What the numbers signify is self-evident: 100 means *now*, 0 means *soon*, and -100 means "The check is in the mail."

In the *trusted* section the designated users are the only ones allowed to set mail's from name:

```
#
# trusted
#    { root, daemon, uucp, network };
Troot daemon uucp network
#
```

Now comes the *header* section.

```
#
#    for (f_return)
#            define("Return-Path:", "<$m{sreladdr}>");
H?P?return_Path: <$g>
#
```

These are the header lines we saw in the /usr/spool/mqueue/qfAA* files:

```
H?P?return path: <cj!sbrock>
Hreceived: from cj by svr02 (5.51./10/0i); Mon 15 Nov 89 15:32:18 PDT
Hreceived: by farside (5.51.10.01); Mon 15 Nov 89 15:32:59 PDT
Hdate: Mon 15 Nov 89 15:32:59
Hfrom: sbrock@cj (Scott Brock)
Hmessage-id: <8911200173O.AO7876@cj>
Hto: farside::dhudock@farside>apex.com
Hsubject: lunch
```

In the *class* section, where systems can be grouped, the class definitions look like

```
#
CW fw1 fw2 fw3 fw4 fw5 fw5 fw7 cj stalker farside
#
CS fs1 fs2
#
```

A *class* can be a grouping of all workstations or all servers.

In the *mailers* section the programs are described:

```
#
Mlocal, P=/bin/mail, F=rlsDFmn, S=10, R=10, A=mail -d $u
Mprog, P=/bin/sh, F=lsDFRe, S=10, R=10, A=sh -c $u
#
```

F sets flags, and A sets arguments.

The rules for rewriting mail headers are set in the final section of sendmail.cf. Very lengthy, the rules section is not for the timid. Rules are also covered in the BSD *Sendmail Installation and Operations Guide*.

It would be remiss of me not to point out that sendmail has extensive debugging facilities, and these debugging facilities are a major security gap. It was the sendmail debug feature that was used by the 1988 worm to break into Berkeley-based systems such as Sun and DEC. Accordingly, sites with source code remove this feature from the sendmail code. Others *zap* it out of the binary version by substituting a series of null bytes (\0) for the string DEBUG. Future UNIX releases will probably be free of this well-publicized defect.

There are precompilers for sendmail.cf; indeed, much of the clean output in our examples from sendmail.cd was from such a precompiler. Should you have occasion to use one, remember to change values in the source file only. The precompiled version will be overwritten at the next run of the precompiler.

There is a strategy to sendmail configuration. Create a simplistic sendmail.cf file for individual mail hosts and an all-encompassing file for the mail master. If a host is not able to cope with a mail delivery, it will send it back to the mail master, which then is able to deliver it or leave it sitting in /usr/spool/mqueue. The postmaster then has but one place to look for undeliverable mail, the mail master. An accompanying log file, syslog, contains logs of successful deliveries and error messages, where the administrator finds the clues to why some mail couldn't be delivered.

Create one version of each, a host version and a master sendmail.cf version. Distribute them to each system that you install thereafter. Creating sendmail.cf is not something you want to do twice.

/etc/aliases

The /etc/aliases file provides sendmail with a mechanism for rerouting mail with a minimum of effort on the part of the administrator. The mail-alias file is read by the sendmail program when it is invoked at startup. It can also be invoked manually by the newaliases command. Run newaliases whenever /etc/aliases is modified (newaliases simulates sendmail used with the -bi flag). The entries in /etc/aliases have the form

alias: user_name@system

as in

```
scott:sbrock@cj
```

A major use of the aliases file is to reroute all mail going directly to the mail master to the machines and users where they are most apt to read it. This is a handy technique on systems with workstations and file servers. Here is an `aliases` file set up for exactly that purpose:

```
#          Folsom Mail Server /etc/aliases
#
#
MAILER-DAEMON:postmaster
postmaster:bhunter@stalker
#
msgs: "!usr/lib/msgs -s"
rnews:"!usr/local/uurec"
#
bhunter:bhunter@stalker
scott:sbrock@cj
sbrock:sbrock@cj
achen:achen@fm1
shilo:shilo@fm2
gsimko:gsimko@fm3
.
.
jcroy:jcroy@fm33
```

Combine this with the mail master having the `host` alias of `folsom`, and no one outside the mail domain need know the real name of the mail master. All mail can be sent to `folsom` and reach the user:

```
% mail scott@folsom
```

instead of

```
%mail sbrock@cj
```

which requires that the sender know the name of Scott's system or at least the name of the mail server serving `cj`.

Notice in this example that commands can be aliased as well. The `MAILER-DAEMON` and `postmaster` aliases must be present.

The users have a file with capabilities similar to those of `/etc/aliases`, called `~/.forward`. It is wise to advise your users to use `.forward` for transient changes in addresses. The entries in `.forward` have the form

```
username@system
```

and look like this:

```
scott@stalker
```

Mail normally sent to Scott at his workstation `cj` is forwarded to the system `stalker`.

Also, `/etc/aliases` needs to be changed when users are added or moved. Be sure to run `newaliases` at each change, as this will cause `sendmail` to reread the file.

Setting Up `sendmail`

Setting up `sendmail` usually takes a lot of effort the first time you do it. After that it's pretty routine. Like UUCP, each host system has its own autonomous version of `sendmail` commands, queues, and libraries. The main point to remember about the sendmail system is that although it acts as one unit, it is actually a series of independent programs and files. Each host system must be set up separately and tested on its own. That is, sendmail does not magically come up when the mail master comes up.

The first step in a network mail setup is to get everyone's hosts file to give out the name of the mail master. The simplest system is to run YP to give everyone the same hosts file. In that file give the master mail machine the alias mailhost:

```
$ ypcat hosts ! grep mailhost
128.213.69.55 stalker mailhost folsom # Folsom mailserver
```

Another thing you can do is put the real name of the mail master in each client's sendmail.cf configuration file, but this would be tedious if the mail master's duties were shifted to another system. Also, you would have to log onto each client in the network and alter its sendmail configuration file. The stalker system is aliased as both mailhost and folsom, so other sites can reach it without knowing the name of the mail master. In this way it's necessary to send it only to the site name:

```
% mail gsimko@folsom
```

When the mail reaches the Folsom mail master, it is rerouted by way of the aliases file to Mr. Simko.

The next step is to modify the sendmail.cf file shipped with the system to create a sendmail configuration file compatible with and customized for your site. Although sendmail is supposed to be patterned after termcap and printcap, its mnemonics are terse and far from self-descriptive. Thus it is best to take the time to create one good sendmail.cf file and extend it to each system in your mail network. Sun has two sendmail configuration files in /usr/lib, sendmail.subsidiary.cf for mail clients and sendmail.main.cf for the mail master. Note that /etc/sendmail.cf is a *soft link* to one or the other.

Remember that rc, not local.rc, must be modified by adding the sendmail lines to start the daemon:

```
if [ -f /usr/lib/sendmail -a -f /etc/sendmail.cf ]; then
    (cd /var/spool/mqueue; rm -f nf* lf*)
    /usr/lib/sendmail -bd -q1h && chat -n ' sendmail'
fi
```

Add these lines after the return from rc.local and just about at the very end of rc. Either reboot the system to start the daemon, or better yet, issue the line from the console manually.

The mail directory, /var/spool/mqueue, must be created if it does not exist already. To be secure, make it unreadable and unwritable to the public.

From time to time you will want to modify Mail.rc to clean out mqueue. Have it clean out files that are over some arbitrary number of days old; four to six is a good range. Anything less would allow a file lost on a four-day weekend to get blown away.

Once the sendmail configuration file is complete, the daemon is started, and the mail-queue directory in is place, you can test sendmail. Simply send a mail message to another system on your local network that has sendmail working.

Simple Debugging

Once you have installed the `sendmail` system on a host, test it by sending a mail message from that system. You can use a newly created user account to originate the message. That will test both `sendmail` and the new user's setup. If the mail reaches its destination, you will have done your job well. If not, start debugging. Did the mail make it to the mail-master system? Look in its `mqueue/syslog`. The log itself and the queue file `qfAA*` will give you quite a lot of information. If the mail made it that far and the log tells you that it sent it to the proper host, move to that host's mail directory. Is the mail there? I remember one instance in which the recipient would type `mail` and be told there was none, but her mail was in `/var/spool/mail` all the time. Her path searched `/bin`, first picking up a symbolic link to `/usr/bin`. Although she thought that she was getting UCB mail, she was actually getting Edition 7 `mail`, which knows nothing about `sendmail` or `/var/spool/mail`.

Your best tool in mail debugging is a good understanding of the mail system and `sendmail`. Use each new system installation and new user account to strengthen your knowledge of the mail system's internals.

MANAGER'S CORNER

Commitment to Network Support

Who owns the network, and how much of it is owned? Large installations have a network manager and staff. Smaller installations have at least one network technician who owns the network. The areas of argument are what belongs to the individual systems and what is clearly network. The need is for dual ownership. The computer system manager and staff should work as if they own the network software on the system, because they do. The network manager and staff should take the attitude that they are responsible for all network software. Indeed, if they don't act as the center of competence for the network software, who will?

Not long ago the only way you could buy a computer with full network software was to buy a Sun or similarly networked OEM system.[5] Otherwise you had to buy a network software package and glue it onto the system as best you could. For example, on UTS systems the only network software package is Wollongong's internet software WIN/UTS.

I know of one UTS site not long ago that developed a total UNIX strategy. The general plan was to link as soon as possible all machines with TCP/IP, from desktop micros to mainframes. This move was dictated by the engineering users to bring together all UNIX systems, a sensible, forward-looking approach to this site's working environment. The MIS plan was to hire a staff of TCP/IP people to support the system.

Good things take time, and it took a long time to implement this strategy. After two years of linking micros and minis and converting the minis to UNIX, they were

[5] This problem went away at Release 5.4 when network software, including RFS and NFS, was built in. This is one of the reasons that 5.4 was an important UNIX release.

ready to link the mainframes. The administrator installed Wollongong's Internet software on the mainframe, knowing that as soon as she did so, the engineers would beat down the doors to use it. They desperately needed to communicate with one another, and they had been waiting for two years. Neither the network staff nor the network manager had been hired yet, but the interviewing had begun.

Here's where a manager's lack of technical knowledge almost resulted in a fatal error. The MIS manager in charge of providing service to the engineering users was afraid to take responsibility for this new intimidating software. Thus he took the stand that TCP/IP, although installed and available, was officially unsupported until a staff was hired, trained, and in place. That would take more than four months.

Imagine yourself in this position. Would you give a tool as powerful as the Internet to the engineers who had been waiting for it for two years and then state, in effect, that they couldn't use it until it was supported, however long that might take?

The system administrator, knowledgeable about UNIX, took an opposing stance. She maintained that the MIS group must take ownership of the internet as soon as possible and support their end of the internet as best they could. When confronted with new, revolutionary, unavoidable technology, one must face the task of learning as much as possible about it, and quickly. No matter how unsettling this new technology is, one must face the problem and grapple with it. There is no other solution in today's hard-driving, rapidly developing computer industry. Putting the department's collective head in the sand for four months would accomplish nothing positive, she maintained. She also felt that this approach would send a negative message throughout the organization, and it would be a slap in the face to the very engineering users whom MIS was supposed to support.

In the end she took temporary ownership of TCP/IP and kept it. The system administrators and system programmers took home the Wollongong manuals and pored over the heavy technical material. In true UNIX tradition, they shared their knowledge and had brainstorming sessions to speed the learning process. It was a challenging endeavor, and the more they learned, the more pride and excitement they felt about the product. In time a network staff was recruited and trained. By the time they arrived on the scene, a receptive, enthusiastic group of system administrators and system programmers was awaiting them. Consequently, the incorporation of the network staff as part of the MIS team took only a short time.

UNIX has a grand tradition. From its inception it has been shared. For a long time one of the few ways to learn about UNIX was by word of mouth. There were no books, only manuals and tutorials. As a result, people working in UNIX environments taught one another. By that same tradition, it is up to all of us who administer and program the system to take pride in ownership of our systems and associated networks and software. If there is no education available elsewhere, then it will fall on our shoulders to provide that education. If no one else is ready to take the responsibility of the system software and extensions, then let us do so.

S E C T I O N

V

System Management

19

Critical Services Administration: A New Approach

UNIX system administration involves more than a technical knowledge of the UNIX system and the ability to administer it. Part of the job of administering the UNIX operating system is communicating the needs of the system and its users to the management of your company. If your manager is not of a technical bent and isn't familiar with UNIX, he or she may have some preconceived notions.

DEFINING CRITICAL SERVICES

A *critical service* is any process or subsystem that will jeopardize the machine's availability if it is defective or absent.

System administration problems vary in severity, on a scale of 1 to 5. Severity 1 problems put the system in immediate jeopardy. The rule is fix it in a few hours or less. Severity 2 problems require action that day and represent a reasonable threat to the system. Severity 3 usually indicates a software problem that doesn't threaten the entire system but will harm part of its function. By the time you get to Severity 5, you have something not so vital, like a documentation error.

Some system problems are minor and can be handled hours later. Others stop the machine cold and are major catastrophes. Most fall somewhere between these two extremes. Because no two sites are identical, each site has its own set of critical services.

Since system administration problems vary in severity, the way you solve them will also vary. You can prevent some problems by writing automated software, usually daemons and cron-driven scripts. You can write a program activated by cron at regular intervals to clean system spoolers. Other problems don't lend themselves to software solutions. User-ID and login services must be done by hand. Still, you can avoid many problems by writing specific programs and procedures covering each task. The OEM and VAR programs `adduser` and `moduser` are fine examples, for they handle user administration more reliably than does longhand administration.

Put your system administration knowledge to work for you and streamline the running of your system. First, identify, enumerate, and describe the critical services on your site. This process should continue as a regular, ongoing system administration task, with the critical services list updated periodically. After you define the critical services on your machine, you and your system programmers need to write clear, concise instructions that identify problems and detail the necessary operating procedures either to solve them or at least to fix them temporarily until the system administrator can make a house call.

Make education an ongoing part of your job. Hold classes and educate your operators and support staff at regular intervals until they know enough about UNIX and UNIX system administration to handle some of these critical service tasks on their own. Have an open-door policy. Regardless of your level of expertise, the motto must be "The system administrator is in."

Now roll up your sleeves and write your own software to monitor as many critical services as possible. A typical script is our familiar `dfall` script:

```
:
df -t /usr /usr/spool/console /usr/spool /tmp /
echo "rdr:\c"
ls /usr/spool/rdr|wc -l
echo "console:\c"
ls /usr/spool/console|wc -l
echo "out:\c"
ls -a /usr/spool/out|wc -l
ps -ef|egrep 'vm|osm|cron|assassin'|grep -v 'grep'
echo "megafiles:\c"
ls -l /usr/mail/root
find /usr/spool -size +100000c -print
```

These scripts must be tailored to your specific site requirements. This script works fine on an IBM 370 installation running UTS, but your systems will be different.

Although some critical services can't be handled with software monitoring, identify the ones that can, and describe each problem carefully. Then design software that will monitor your system effectively, giving you the feedback you need to keep in touch with the health of your machine.

We shall explore all of these approaches to system administration in this chapter. Your system will stabilize dramatically when you perform all these steps. Instead of trying to fight an out-of-control system every day, you'll be in control. It's a good feeling.

IDENTIFYING THE SYSTEMS CRITICAL TO YOUR SITE

Before you do anything else, you must identify what is critical to your installation's survival. The following are some critical services common to most sites, including both distributed and local operating system commands and utilities:

- All spooler activity.
- General system daemons.

- Communications daemons and processes.
- Backup, restore, and archive activity.
- System boots and shutdowns.
- Bill-back accounting.
- lp printer spooler system.
- User-ID, group-ID, and other login-related services.
- File system consistency maintenance.
- All network facilities.
- The system event scheduler, cron.

There will be other critical services pertinent to your site. It is your job to identify them.
     All these services can be roughly divided into three categories:

1. Those handled with existing system software.
2. Those handled with your own scripts and programs.
3. Those requiring human monitoring.

Bear in mind that these categories always overlap one another to some extent.

Services That Are Handled by Existing System Software

Many critical services are already handled by existing system software. Software for
backup and archiving, software to format disks, and software to make file systems all are
standard administration software. Examples are fsck, pwck, df, sar, and ps. You can
add much more control by carefully documenting each procedure so that other people
doing these tasks will do them precisely the way you want them done.

Services That Need Software Protection

The second category covers critical services that are not under existing software protection. If one of these critical services fails, the machine will fall down and die. Disaster is
imminent on a large system when the spoolers or the tmp disk fills. When critical system
disks like root and /usr fill, they are Severity 1 problems, and you're immediately out
of business. There is no system software to monitor these functions. The dfall script
we saw is an adequate *ad hoc* monitor program that helps identify problems. But when
the problems actually occur, direct system administrator intervention is the solution.

Services That Cannot Be Monitored with Software

Some critical services cannot be monitored automatically with software:

- System boots and shutdowns.
- File system consistency checks.
- User-ID, group-ID, and other login services.
- Resource expansions and maintenance.
- Backups and restores.
- Network facilities.

A human being who knows how to program needs to sit down and take a look when one
of these categories goes out of whack. How effectively these areas are monitored depends

on the thoroughness of the system programmers and operators. There is no substitute for training, experience, and diligence, but having clearly written instructions is a distinct help.

DOCUMENTING YOUR SYSTEM

When you give documentation and training to operations and customer services, you quadruple your return in more efficient system performance. The best favor you can do yourself is record, immediately after they happen, how you handle all difficult system administration scenarios, so that you will have a record of what needs to be done when they happen again. The cost of not understanding history is having to repeat it.

You should keep a written record of your system administration problems and solutions. Some obscure problem that took you hours to solve might happen again in a year, and you don't want to waste time reinventing the wheel. You will gradually discover the best procedures to follow for your site, through both careful study and trial and error. These system administration procedures should be carefully spelled out so that others who are less skilled can handle them.

There are several good ways to document system administration tasks. List those tools that are needed to support the system but are not part of the standard distribution. Have system programmers and administrators write a manual page for every new command created as a result of their system programming. If a subsystem that you and your staff have created is large and complex, take the next step and describe its use and care. I have seen several fine subsystems discredited and abandoned for lack of good documentation.

SOPs and SAPs

Share your system administration knowledge through documentation. We all know that SOP is a military term for Standard Operating Procedure. At my site I've modified the meaning of SOP to stand for System Operations Procedure. SAP stands for System Administration Procedure. SOPs and SAPs help the system run more efficiently and are covered in detail in Chapter 20.

New Manual Pages

Each new local command created on your site should have a corresponding manual page written at the same time, or it should not be accepted. These manual pages should include the following:

- A clear description of the service.
- A list of all files and related commands used or affected.
- A table of diagnostics, system errors, abnormalities, and cures.
- How-tos on starting daemons, invoking diagnostics, and whatever else it takes to understand the software or service.
- The name and location of files and commands.

Don't skimp on manual pages. The an `nroff` manual macro is easy to use. Reading a manual page for a local command is as natural to UNIX people as coming in to work in the morning. Follow the same precedents set in standard UNIX manuals. If a command is peculiar to system programmers, it should go into Section 8. If it describes a file format, it should go into Section 4. Store them in `/local/man` with the same `u_man`, `a_man`, and `p_man` subdirectories as with standard manual files. For example, a local system administration command called `mkfoo` is stored here:

```
/local/man/a_man/man8/mkfoo.1
```

Change Control

Change control is a written notice that something on the system was changed or is going to be changed. Change control should be signed off by everyone in the organization affected. Its purpose is to warn everyone of new or coming changes and allow an installation time for the change during a downtime.

No local software of any kind should be put into production on system without a manual page in `/local/man` and formal *change control*. If the current manual page does not completely cover the situation for which the procedure was written, an SAP, SOP, or both need to be created and distributed.

Tutorials

Whereas manual pages give information and SOPs and SAPs give step-by-step instructions, tutorials go one step further and provide all this, in a well-rounded educational approach using theory and background material to illustrate concepts. Brian Kernighan's "A Tutorial Introduction to the UNIX Text Editor," Bell Labs, September 21, 1978, is a good example of a tutorial.

Tutorials usually are written only when a subject is so complex that it requires thorough documentation to understand it. Recently I was involved with an in-house software program that nearly was scrapped for lack of clear documentation. The code was good, and the manual pages were equally good, but the documentation stopped short of providing written tutorials. The program was quite complex, and without tutorials it could not be adequately supported by anyone but its author. In time the necessary documentation was written, and the subsystem was saved.

SOLUTIONS TO CRITICAL SERVICE PROBLEMS

It is unreasonable to expect systems to have software for every need, but critical services can be met

- With existing commands.
- With purchased software.
- By replacing or augmenting existing commands and utilities with local scripts.
- By creating new commands and utilities.

There are several ways to solve critical service problems. Some need only software, such as monitor programs to keep you in touch with your machine; however, there is no one definitive software method. Other problems need a joint approach: You write monitor software and couple that with specific SOPs or manual procedures for operators to follow.

Let's examine some actual system administration problems in the way you would on the job. As you encounter problems, you consider possible solutions, including software.

Watch Programs

A watch program keeps an eye on critical services. It can be a free-standing program or a daemon that watches an event and then acts. A cron-watching daemon watches cron by looking for its entry in the process table. If it doesn't find the entry, it will tell you so and then restart cron.

Imagine that you have a rather complex local program at your site. It needs to be run at a few minutes after midnight, at 00:15 on Sunday, and on the first few minutes of the first day of the month. If this program fails to run at any of the specified times, the entire software group will be up that well-known creek. This is clearly a critical service. Let's say you have a grace period of eight hours and after that the problem is Severity 1.

One solution is to write a watch program that checks each time the program runs and then reports its completion. The results can be listed in tabular form by machine and function. A quick scan will tell you if the program didn't run or lost function.

If extensive SOPs have been written for our fictitious program, the operations staff will know how to recover the program if the watch program fails. A typical scenario is operations failing to bring up the machines until a few minutes after their weekend downtime ended at 23:59. The delay causes our program not to be run on time. By following clearly written SOPs, the operators check to see if the program ran. Upon discovering that it didn't run, the operators run it according to SOP instructions. Our program is recovered.

Certainly, a check program can be written to check automatically all phases of our program and correct anything that goes wrong, but who or what is going to watch the check program? As the administrator, you can draw the line at whatever degree of complexity you want to live with. What if our program is so complex that it will be difficult to recover if it stops in mid-program, unless you read through a thousand lines of code to find the problem? Do you want to read through another five hundred lines of a check program on top of that?

Password Administration and Critical Services

Let's take a look at password and group administration, as quite a few programs aid in this activity.

- `/bin/passwd`
- `/etc/pwck`
- `/etc/grpck`
- `moduser`

- `adduser`
- `deluser`[1]

Things can still go wrong, even with these tools to aid your password administration. In all but the smallest installations there are multiple machines, each with its own `/etc/passwd` files. If left to chance, each user who has logins on multiple machines in this environment will have a different user-ID number, one for the workstation, another for the mainframe, and still another for the VAX. Someday someone is going to need to make file copies across machines by `tar` or `cpio`. After a file system move or migration, without the same user-ID number on each file, she will have the wrong ownership, and you will face an unbelievable amount of work to get file ownerships back to where they belong.

A central data base of user log names and user IDs would solve this problem. The data base is not standard UNIX, nor is anything like it distributed with the system, although Yellow Pages comes close, but it will not cross YP domains. Thus a data base system must be created by system programming. Software must also be created to access the data base and tools like `adduser`, modified or rewritten by the programming staff to force the use of the data base. The end result is a password administration system that is responsive to the needs of the installation.

In any system in which there are multiple UNIX machines, each user must have a user-ID number. The ideal solution is to have an employee's ID number be within the user-ID range. Regardless of what number is used, all the machines in one system have to access user-ID numbers from a central data base. That central data base should be available not only to all administrators but also to all support personnel who give out logins. Even if users leave the system, their old user-ID numbers can be restored when they come back.

Daemons: It Would Be Heck Without Them

Daemons are high on anyone's list of critical services. The name daemon may be unique to UNIX, but the concept is not. Daemons sit around waiting to be called to do a specific task. They are started by `root`, usually in the `rc` initiation script. Once called, a daemon "does its thing" and disappears, only to return again when needed. The daemons listen at a port or channel, waiting for an event and an incoming request.

There are two forms of daemons, the stand-alone, do-it-all daemon and the *daemon server*. The stand-alone daemon is invoked by `root` as a background task. It is not attached to a terminal, so it runs in the background. It listens for an event and performs the needed task.

The daemon server splits tasks. The parent daemon waits, listening for a request. It then spawns a child server to do the actual work. The server inherits the connection made by the parent daemon. As each server finishes its task, it dies, but the parent daemon lives on. Internally the daemon parent forks the child. Network daemons like `telnetd`, `fingerd`, and `ftpd` are good examples of the daemon–server relationship.

---

[1] Note that `moduser`, `adduser`, and `deluser` are vendor-added commands and are found on a great many systems. If these commands are absent, they frequently are coded by the system programming staff.

Death of a Daemon

Many critical services are driven by daemons, and so function is lost whenever a daemon dies. A daemon dies for one of two main reasons. It either kills itself in self-defense or it is deliberately killed by an interrupt or a system programmer. The first occurs when a daemon shuts itself off, reacting to a situation it cannot handle. For example, if a daemon created to write to a file finds that file's disk full, the daemon will do itself in.

When you find a dead daemon, restarting it isn't a good idea until you find out what killed it. If it is a daemon that is associated with the spooling system, first use the df command to see how full the spooler disk is. Is it full? Read root's mail. Did the dying process write a death note? Check the console log. Does it show the spool disk full? If it's 20 percent full, there is no need for concern, but if it's 80 percent full, suddenly that's the most important thing you've got to do. Discover why the daemon died, and *then* restart it.

When you restart a daemon, watch its progress for a while. The ps command issued at short intervals shows when a daemon gets into trouble, for ps is the process table formatter. It tells the status of various and sundry processes. One of the fields that the ps command outputs is the amount of actual CPU time that the command it is monitoring has accumulated. Watch to see if the daemon is accumulating CPU time, as noted in the eighth column:

```
$ ps -ef|grep lpsched
lp    29    1  0 Sep 11  ?  1:39 /usr/lib/lpsched
```

Be suspicious if the time is excessive. Bear in mind that you're working on a machine that does tasks in nanoseconds, so if you see something that has taken 50 to 60 seconds, that's an enormous amount of time in computer terms.

Consider a command like UTS's vmread, which reads files from the 370 reader into the machine's spooling system. That command normally accumulates 2 or 3 seconds at the peak of its running time. Then it's done, and since it is a server daemon, it zeros itself out. If you see close to a minute's worth of time accumulated, you will know immediately that this daemon is in trouble. And when you see 500 or 600 seconds of accumulated time, then it's not only in deep trouble, it has been in deep trouble for a long time.

Do not start an unfamiliar daemon without reading the daemon's manual page. Some daemons are started by a process other than rc; an example is UTS's vmpunch's vmpunchd daemon. This is a daemon server, not a daemon parent, and it is started by anyone issuing the vmpunch command. Kill the daemon, and *then* go in and purge the VM reader. The daemon is restarted by issuing vmpunch. Then there's nothing for it to choke on. The VM reader cannot be purged until that daemon is dead, so it is important that all steps be followed in sequence.

A documented system administration procedure (SAP) is as good as money in the bank. Often you may run into an obscure problem, solve it, and eventually forget about it. But if the problem comes up one year later and if you haven't written an SAP, you might have to go through the whole process of solving the problem again simply because you can't remember how you did it. If you have written an SAP, however, you will know immediately how to deal with the problem. Document the problems you solve, and you'll have your SAP to fall back on.

Let's look at a scenario in which a daemon is deliberately killed. We find that the console log, /usr/spool/console, is filling to the point that reading the current console with the editor will soon be impossible. Now is the time to start a new console log file. On some machines the daemon is /etc/osmcat, which takes the output of /dev/osm and cats it to the console log. To start a new console log file, simply find osmcat's process-ID number, kill it, and restart it:

```
# ps -ef!fgrep osm
root 59  1 18:26  ?  00:03 cat -U /dev/osm.all
# kill -9 59
# /etc/osmcat
#
```

Now that there is a new console log file, check the old one to see what filled it.

When Your Critical System Disks Runneth Over

Critical services that are neither cron timed nor daemon related must be run frequently, either manually or by software. Like any critical services, they will damage the system if left unmonitored.

The following system disks stop a system cold when full: /, /usr, /usr/spool or /var, and /tmp. Spooling processes and processes that write to /tmp are particularly troublesome.

The order is as follows: mail fills /usr/mail, /var/spool/mail, or /usr/spool/mail; uucp fills /usr/spool/uucppublic; lp fills /usr/spool/lp; and /tmp is filled by everything and everyone.

Handle these critical file systems by first identifying them. Write a script that does a df -t on all file systems identified as critical. This script is a short version of the dfall script shown earlier in this chapter:

```
# dfall  b h hunter 1/23/86

df -t / /usr /usr/spool /usr/spool/console /tmp
echo
ps -ef!egrep 'osm!cron!telnetd'!grep -v grep
echo
echo "console files:\c"
ls /usr/spool/console!wc -l
echo
exit
```

Use the grep filter to see whether the osm, cron, and telnet daemons are alive. Last comes a count of the number of files in the console log directory.

It is wise to tailor the size and quantity of critical file system disks to suit your needs. Don't allow your /usr or /var disk to be filled by spool or log files. Make /usr/spool a separate disk partition. Better yet, also make /usr/spool/console its own disk or disk partition. Then when /usr/spool/console fills, /usr/spool will still have space, and the system will continue to function.

Making a disk larger is a temporary solution to a filling-disk problem, but it is not necessarily good. Disks of any size will fill if left unchecked. Let the users use /tmp as their own temporary disk, and it will never be large enough, even if you make it 100 megabytes. Do not let users use /tmp for their files, file systems, or directories. Enforce that rule, and you will have far less trouble.

The /tmp directory may or may not have its own disk. On smaller systems it's just about guaranteed that it will not have its own disk. In cleverly written system code, the same program that writes to /tmp erases the data when the program execution is through. If well-trapped system code fails in mid-execution, its dying act will be to remove all the files it created from /tmp.

Unfortunately, not all code is well written, so streetwise UNIX system administrators put code in their cleanup scripts that scours /tmp at least once a day. Poorly written code drops a file in /tmp, hoping that another process will eventually pick it up and remove it. Poorly written code makes no provision for trapping interrupts. If the program fails, it will leave trash sitting in /tmp like some nasty litterbug. If /tmp is not well enough protected by permissions, users will find it and write entire directories to it. Because a very large part of the system software relies on writing small files to /tmp, if it is full, the software will receive a disk-full error and not be able to run. Part of your critical service scheme thus includes monitoring /tmp. If you find it filled, rm the whole thing short of the lock files and files written in the last few minutes, blasting it clean to the base directory.

Keep system disks cleaned and small. Don't leave console and error files unread and unerased. Read the error file and console file, if you have one, and send them to the printer if you need a permanent copy. Then erase them. The exception to the rule is /dump. Read dumps as quickly as possible. If necessary, copy them to /dump/OLDdump if you have made room. There is no need to erase /dump/dump, because the next dump will overwrite it anyway.

PERIODIC CRITICAL SERVICES

Some critical services have to be fired by cron at periodic intervals. The system's cron file, /usr/spool/cron/crontabs/root, contains many of them. Tasks triggered by cron are

- Running the weekly full backup.
- Running daily incremental backups.
- Running accounting.
- Running bill-back accounting.
- Running the clean-out scripts.
- Writing time and date to the console and console log.
- Running the uucp processes: uudemon.hour, uudemon.cleanu, uudemon.spool, and uudemon.admin.
- Doing disk-to-disk /etc/passwd and etc/group backups.

To reiterate, if a critical service is not performed periodically on the system, the system and its users will be in trouble. These periodic services can be checked manually or programmatically. If done programmatically, human intervention is still required. An immediate solution is to write a single daemon to check them or to have cron initiate checking programs. If cron or the watch daemon dies, the service will not be watched.

A commonsense solution is to check cron manually from time to time, similar to the way the dfall script does. Then have cron fire the rest of the watch programs.

The system administrator defines periodic critical services not driven by cron that must be done at specific times. For example, if you're dependent on bill-back accounting to return revenue, that becomes a periodic critical service. Now if any of these critical services die, you're in deep trouble. Write a daemon that wakes up every now and then in order to verify that a periodic critical service is alive. On one site we even had a daemon called cron_watch that woke up from time to time to see if cron was still running. This daemon not only checked to see if cron was running, but it also restarted cron if it had to. Then it notified the console that it had fired and done its job.

Don't be complacent just because you have a watch daemon watching cron and every other critical service. Who's going to watch the watch daemon? The whole point is, don't rely on programs as ultimate solutions. Human intervention is necessary. You watch cron, you let the watch daemon watch cron, and you watch the watch daemon.

DEALING WITH CRITICAL SERVICES

When a daemon dies, part of the system's function dies with it. Whatever service it performed, once the daemon is gone, that service is no longer being carried out. For instance, if you forget to get out bill-back accounting, you will lose the system's revenue.

When a critical file system disk fills, daemons writing to it die in self-defense. Then system and user programs that would write to the disk fail. The system may hang for lack of room or services. Perhaps it is not dead, but it is unavailable. Periodic services left undone jeopardize the system. If you leave the file systems unchecked and unrepaired long enough, eventually the machine will become so badly brain damaged that you will have no choice but to take it out and shoot it. It is the system administrator's responsibility to see that all critical services are performed and to do this by whatever means necessary.

CRITICAL SERVICES MONITOR

The purpose of a critical services monitor is to watch from a single console or terminal all those functions defined as critical on *all systems*. The output must be refreshed periodically. To save confusion and avoid errors of omission, run the monitor from a single-configuration data base. Then only the data base need be updated, as opposed to changing hard-coded items in the code. In multiple machine environments, the machines' data are kept in a data base, just as password data are kept in a central data base.

Ideally, a monitor not only watches critical services but also provides corrective action wherever possible. Upon detecting that cron has died, the monitor should not only report the death and time, but it should also restart the daemon and report the time of the restart. The monitor should write to both the console and a log file.

Just be careful not to carry this too far. Remember that most daemons should not be restarted until a programmer has had an opportunity to find out what killed it. Similarly, when a program detects a full system file disk, it should not erase any files programmatically. Rather, human intervention is required to identify noncritical files for erasure. User programs should not be erased without notification except when the user has violated a service-level agreement.

RELYING ON COMMON SENSE

We who administer UNIX systems are used to writing software to automate system tasks, and so wanting to automate critical services completely is a natural inclination. But it's not a good idea. Most of us have seen the skit in which two robots attempt to dance with each other. After a few graceful moves together in perfect synchronization, they get slightly out of sync and are no longer holding each other. With frozen smiling faces, each robot goes its own way, still dancing with arms outstretched, oblivious of obstacles in the way. They knock over lamps and coffee tables until eventually the male robot dances out the window. While this is all very funny, it is also a sober reminder that fully automated tasks without benefit of process synchronization are doomed to disastrous ends.

At the other end of the spectrum is the fully manual critical services administration system. We've all worked in environments like this. A more descriptive term for it is "firefighting." Living with an out-of-control system that requires frequent patching just to keep it going makes for an anxious work environment. There are other problems with doing everything by hand. The first is procrastination. When you are overwhelmed with numerous system problems, you tend to put off fixing things until they get pretty bad. The second is error determination. You can't fix it if you don't know it's broken. Without the benefit of watch programs and monitors, you find out the system is sick only when the situation becomes critical.

It's best to attack system problems with a combination of approaches. Use automation for diagnostics, error detection, and monitoring. Fix the things that can easily be caught and fixed with software. Most other problems can be detected with software, but human beings need to fix them with the aid of good documentation.

THE BOTTOM LINE

The bottom line of critical services administration is that there is no one simple way to deal with them. They can be handled by interactive watch programs, watch daemons, monitors, and periodic manual checking. All must be covered by procedures, manual pages, or tutorials. Only the smallest systems can afford to escape critical services administration.

MANAGER'S CORNER

Critical Services Management

I used to have long discussions with an old-style MIS manager who didn't understand why UNIX couldn't be run by the operations staff, with minimum intervention by UNIX system administrators. We were frequently at odds on this issue. He was a veteran of over a decade of CMS/VM administration in MIS environments, and he simply could not understand why an exception had to be made for this upstart UTS UNIX system running on a VM host!

There are many managers out there today who acquired their technical computer skills before UNIX became commonplace in business environments. UNIX is very different from older operating systems, and managers should continue their technical education so they understand why. Fascinating as it is in design, UNIX is an extremely complex operating system that is still developing, and it has a way to go before system administration becomes standardized and routine enough to leave to operators alone.

On the other hand, the new guard often can learn from the old guard. My MIS manager had a good point: A well-run organization *should* be able to do a lot of day-to-day UNIX system administration using second-line support staff and operators. Even though UNIX is rather complex, a lot of routine system administration chores can be taught to operators. It not only isn't necessary for the system administrator to do all the hands-on work, but most of the system programming staff need be on call only for system emergencies. In this way they will be free to do what they were hired to do: configuration, programming, and software installations.

I developed a new approach to UNIX system administration in an attempt to reconcile the old guard with the new. I call it *critical services administration*. My staff and I wrote carefully detailed instructions that explain step by step the vital system administration chores for our UNIX systems. I trained both support staff and operations to take over as much of the system administration workload as possible without putting the system at risk. Education became as big a tool as software.

After two years of continuous grooming, the systems showed dramatic improvement in stability, and it took a much smaller technical staff to run the machines. My old MIS manager had the right idea, but it took a lot of work to make that idea a reality.

CHAPTER

20

SOPs and SAPs

The small, single system, owned and run by one person, can easily live without a set of procedures to administer it. The manual set and a few good books suffice. But for large UNIX systems the system administration staff needs to create common system rules and procedures to keep the work environment orderly and sane. System administration procedures not only define *expectations* but also provide ongoing *education* for everyone on the staff. It's a good way to share acquired knowledge with one another.

I worked on one mainframe site where the system administrators could count on a minimum of one call a night from operations, with some system administration or operations problem. The problems were usually minor, but the people in operations were unable to handle them because of the relative complexity of the UNIX operating system. After the system administrators wrote a fairly complete set of operations procedures for various system administration scenarios and I taught classes to the operators at our site, however, the operators rarely needed the help of a system administrator after hours.

STANDARD OPERATIONS PROCEDURES

Anyone who has served time in the military is well acquainted with standard operating procedures (SOPs). Not only the military but also many corporations survive and thrive on SOPs. On our site SOPs are standard operations procedures, step-by-step information for operators, help-desk personnel, and junior system programmers to help them perform day-to-day system administration and maintenance tasks.

SOPs should be as short and nontechnical as possible. The following SOP explains bringing up the local Ethernet (TCP/IP) on multiple-mainframe UNIX systems:

SOP

Initializing the TCP/IP Local Ethernet

B. H. Hunter
February 4, 1988

The current implementation of TCP/IP to UTS production systems has created a number of additions to the IPL procedure.* UTS requires that the Internet devices (Fastpaths) be present and active for the system to be able to go into multiuser mode (init 2). This SOP describes the procedure.

Standard IPL After Shutdown or Crash

Conventional IPL after a VM host or hardware failure must be preceded by a hardware reset of the Intel Fastpaths. If the system crashed and VM just came up, do this:

- Hardware-reset the Fastpath (push the reset button).
- Log on to each UTS machine and IPL them per SOP.

Fastpath Errors on Initiation

If UTS systems cannot contact the Fastpaths, they will not be able to go into multiuser mode. The system will go through all the motions, but eventually it will hang and go into a disabled wait state.

Device or Address Off Line

On initiation, VM will send a message to the UNIX virtual console if there is a Fastpath error. The console will display four addresses (220–223) as offline. The recovery is

- Hardware-reset the Fastpath.
- Vary the lines on "vary on 220–223."
- Attach these lines:

1. att 220 uts1 320
2. att 221 uts2 321
3. att 222 uts3 322
4. att 223 uts4 323

---

* IPL, initial program load, means "boot."

This must be done from a privileged CMS account. The UNIX virtual console will display the "attached" message on completion. It is now safe to IPL.

Path Not Operational

When a path is not operational, a message appears on the console as it enters initiation level 2 that resembles this:

```
0 - path 0310 not operational (CC3)
fp_sense_done: non ceti channel address 0x0 ignored
```

These lines appear for each Fastpath system combination. If the machine IPL is allowed to continue, it will become disabled and either come up briefly or dump. The trick is to interrupt the initiation and go to the CP state where the system can be logged off. If the system should make it to `init 2` before you can stop it, log on immediately as `root` and initiate a graceful shutdown. Only as a last resort should you CP force the system.

Dos and Don'ts

Reiterating the SOP:

- On recovering from a shutdown, VM crash, or hardware crash, reset the Fastpath every time.
- On recovering from a `UTS Fastpath not available` error, reset the Fastpath every time.
- Do not go to multiuser mode if the Fastpath is not available.

Note the form of this SOP. It uses clear, simple language familiar to operators. Terms like *IPL* are preferable to *boot*, because the targeted reader in this SOP is a mainframe operator. *IPL* is alphabet soup to people on minis and micros and isn't suitable, so for them you should use the word *boot*. *Know your audience.* Don't be afraid to use phrases like "push the button" in preference to "do a mechanical reset." In the preceding SOP, however, *mechanical reset (push the reset button)* is used so that the operator won't try a software reset, which in this case won't work.

Avoid dense technical prose that no one wants to wade through. A straightforward thought, such as

> Don't boot until you have pushed the button on the Fastpath.

can be turned into the following, truly tortuous technical statement:

> Initial program load should not be accomplished until after establishing a hardware reset with the system internet device that is channel attached to the physical system that the virtual system guest resides upon.

A sentence like that should be illegal.

To keep it short, use bullet lists wherever possible. Have headings make points, and keep your descriptions brief. It is all right to refer to another manual page or another SOP if you don't overdo it, but avoid going beyond a depth of one forward reference.

Here is an SOP for recovering a local accounting system:

SOP

dayacct: *Running Day Accounting Manually*

B. H. Hunter
March 24, 1988

When a UTS system has been out of service during the time when `cron` should have run daily accounting, `accounting` has to be run manually. To verify that `accounting` has been run, use `/local/etc/uwatch`:

```
$ uwatch uts1 uts2 uts3 uts4
```

If today's date does not show on the `dayacct` line, `dayacct` must be run. The command invocation is

```
/local/etc/dayacct
```

and you must be `root` or `su` to use it.

For further information, see manual page 1L, `dayacct`.

SOPs should be an ongoing part of UNIX system administration. If someone in operations has ever asked you how to do something, chances are you need to write an SOP!

SYSTEM ADMINISTRATION PROCEDURES

SAPs are system administration procedures, which outline intermediate to advanced system procedures. The audience consists of system programmers and fellow administrators, so SAPs are more technical than SOPs. They assume a higher level of knowledge and experience.

In a perfect world, SAPs already would be written for every challenging or difficult procedure normally encountered on your systems. They all would be available in neatly indexed manuals, and you wouldn't have to write them. Although in the real world, you end up writing all the SAPs, the time is well spent. When everything goes wrong at once, you often end up relying on your SAPs for guidance.

The following SAP is for an ordinary `cpio` tape archive. It is short and sweet, but its language is technical. The SAP gives options and explanations, relying on the expertise of the system programmer and administrator to make intelligent choices.

SAP

---

cpio Tape Archives on UTS

B. H. Hunter
January 5, 1988

cpio: **File Copy to Tape**

This SAP is for archiving file systems to tape in cpio format. It is best to
archive mountable file systems separately. Path names should be relative,
not absolute. For example, /u should not be archived from **root** (/) but,
rather, from /u. Thus /u/foo is ./foo and can be moved anywhere without having to fight with the path.

Archive with the following steps:

- Estimate the size of the file system to be stored.
- Label the tape both internally and externally.
- Look for files bigger than the tape volume limit.
- Attach a tape drive to the system.
- Establish a system-to-tape drive interface.
- cpio

Estimating File System Size

The size of a file system is best estimated with the df command. The following displays both the size of the disk and the number of blocks used:

```
df -t filesys
```

On this system, blocks are 4096 bytes per block. On 3380 DASD there are
150 blocks per cylinder.

Tape Label

Tapes must have an external label, specifically the label stuck to the reel.
An internal label is also necessary to keep the tape from being mounted as
the wrong tape and overwritten. The UTS command for tape labeling is

```
label -w tape_name
```

where tape_name is the name used for the tape mount. Use the -i flag if
you have to give a name to the tape that is different from the mount name:

```
label -i label_name tape_name
```

(continued)

Look for Files Bigger Than the Volume Limit

Files larger than the tape volume size are a problem. Although cpio is capable of crossing volume boundaries, you have to hold its hand. The capacity of a new 10-inch reel of ½-inch tape is over 250,000 blocks. To find files larger than 250,000 4096-byte blocks, use find:

```
find -size +2500000 -type f -print
```

This is calculated with eight logical 512-byte blocks to the 4096-byte block.

Attaching a Tape Drive and Making an Interface

The UTS tape command must be used to get a tape mount from the tape operator. The command also creates a file in /dev/tape associated with the physical tape drive. The tape must be mounted as writable:

```
tape -w -s label_name tape_name
```

This creates a /dev/tape/tape_name and makes a request at the system console asking the operator to mount a writable tape.

Using cpio to Tape

Writing out to tape with cpio requires the -o option. The -v option is used to give a visible output of the file names going to tape. ASCII header information is needed for portability, so the -c option is used. The largest possible block size is used to save tape and time, the -B option. All the necessary options are -ocvB:

```
cpio -ocvB
```

But cpio needs an input list, and find and ff, fast find, are the best sources of an input list:

```
/etc/ff -I /dev/dsk/NNNs0!/bin/cpio -ocvB>/dev/rmt/drive.n
```

or

```
/etc/ff -I /dev/dsk/NNNs0!/bin/cpio -ocvB>/dev/tape/tape_name
```

NNN is the disk address. The -I option of ff suppresses the inode number output.

Although find is used similarly to ff, the name of the root directory being copied is used rather than the device special name. The option -print must be used or there will be no output, and -depth guarantees that the directory will be fully searched.

```
find /dir_name -depth -print!/bin/cpio -ocvB>/dev/tape/tape_name
```

Notice that SAPs cover areas more in the domain of the system programmer and that a deeper understanding of UNIX is assumed. For example, the cpio archive example assumes that dot notation (./) for the current directory is understood by system administrators and system programmers. An operator who understands some VM and some UNIX but is not expert in either might not know information of this nature, and so an SOP for this scenario would have to be worded differently.

The next SAP explains a disk or inode expansion under UTS UNIX. Running an operating system on top of an operating system (UTS guest on a VM host) adds complexity. Few UNIX programmers are fluent in VM, and so this SAP gives them a hand.

SAP

Disk and Inode Expansion

B. H. Hunter
November 9, 1988

Disk and inode expansions can be difficult. The simplest system is to copy from the old minidisk to a permanent new minidisk. When DASD is limited and an inode expansion is needed, you won't have a permanent disk to copy to. In this SAP a temporary disk is used.

The Basics

The basics of an expansion are

- Prepare the temporary disk.

1. VM-attach the disk.
2. VM-link the disk.
3. UNIX-format the disk.
4. mount the disk.

- Make the file system unavailable to the users.

1. unmount the user disk from the system.
2. mount the user disk to a temporary mount point.

- Copy the old file system to the temporary disk.
- Verify the copy.
- Format the old disk.
- Make a file system (mkfs) on the old disk.
- Copy the data back.
- Verify the copy.
- Unmount both disks.

(continued)

- Mount the reformatted disk back to its original mount point.
- Release the temporary disk from the system.

Example

In this example a user disk at VM address 774 is having its inodes expanded. The file system is /u/fmd. Its virtual address is 774, and it is an 180-cylinder minidisk living on disk pack A042. The system is UTS4.

With UTS4 in multiuser mode, prepare a temporary disk. First VM-attach a temporary disk of 180 cylinders at VM and UTS reserved address ff0. Then link and verify:

```
# cpcmd link \* ff0 ff0 mw passwd
# q v dasd:grep ff0
```

Now (from UNIX) format the disk:

```
# format ff0
```

In this example we are trying to expand the inodes for a 4:1 block-to-inode ratio (note 150 blocks per cylinder):

```
# mkfs /dev/dsk/ff0s0 20000:5000 3 150
```

Now mount to the temporary mount point mnt0:

```
# mount /dev/dsk/ff0s0 /mnt0
```

Make 774 unavailable to users.

There is a problem here. If volcopy is used, the minidisk must be attached where /etc/mountlist has it listed. The requirement can be overridden, but not without some trouble. If the disk can be unmounted, cpio will be the better choice. Another option is to change the ownerships and permissions of the source mount point.

Unmount and remount the disks:

```
# umount /dev/dsk/774s0
# mount /dev/dsk/774s0 /mnt1
```

Now copy to the temporary disk

```
# volcopy /mnt1 /dev/dsk/774s0 a42 /dev/dsk/ff0s0 fmatst
```

and verify the block count:

```
# df /dev/dsk/774s0 /dev/dsk/ff0s0
```

volcopy or cpio

Should you use volcopy, cpio, or tar? In theory, volcopy is faster, but it is a lot pickier. What you gain in copying speed may well be lost floundering with mount checks and syntax verification. The strategy of a disk copy is to do a quick copy in one direction for the sake of time and a tight recursive-descent copy in the other for the sake of compaction and reorganization. The compaction removes disk gaps, reconstructs the inode tables, and removes slotting from the directories. Finally, cpio with the −o option on the way out and the −i option on the way back accomplishes the desired reorganization.

Now back to the business of expanding 774's inodes:

```
# cd /etc
# fuser -uk /dev/dsk/774s0
# umount /dev/dsk/774s0
# format /dev/rdisk/774s0
# mkfs /dev/dsk/774s0 26975:6750 3 150
```

If no cleaning and compaction are necessary, use cpio with the pass option:

```
# cd mnt1
# find . -print!cpio -pdlm /mnt0
```

Next verify the copy:

```
# df -t /dev/dsk/774s0 /dev/dsk/ff0s0
# ls -l /dev/dsk/774s0 /dev/dsk/ff0s0
```

If all has gone well and you get a block-count verification as well as a listing verification, detach the temporary disk:

```
# umount /dev/dsk/ff0s0
```

Put the cleaned disk back to its own mounting point:

```
# mount /dev/dsk/770s0   /u/fmd
```

and release the temporary disk back to the system.

MANAGER'S CORNER

Establishing Solid Intergroup Relations with Documentation

It is essential to the success of your organization that a solid relationship be created and maintained with operations and the support organizations. It is all too easy to get into an *us*-and-*them* relationship. By providing organizations with both standard operating procedures and training, you will establish a closer relationship and have the side benefit of all organizations knowing exactly what is expected of them.

Just how well you prepare procedures and training will be in direct proportion to how well you are perceived. There is a second benefit to providing education. When system administrators give a class to the operations staff on the care and feeding of UNIX, they create a person-to-person relationship with each operator present in the class, who will now not only respect such administrators but also will learn more about their point of view and group, and the administrators will learn about theirs. The operators will feel more comfortable about calling the administrators with questions in the future. More open communication between groups is the desirable result.

If you are a nontechnical manager of technical personnel, I strongly recommend that you encourage system documentation by requesting a courtesy copy of each SOP and SAP as they are distributed. Take the time to read them at least once. You will understand much better the technical operations of your department and how the groups interact with one another. The more technical material you understand, the better you and your technical staff can communicate with each other.

C H A P T E R

21

The Organization

We see a lot of management books on the market today, but all of them are written from the perspective of those who manage, not those who are managed. Since not all system administrators are managers, in this chapter we shall approach the organization primarily from the system administrator's perspective.

COMPUTER ORGANIZATIONS

Computer organizations vary in size, charter, and style. The duties of the UNIX system administrator vary with the type of computer organization. Single users who are totally responsible for their own system are the smallest computer organization of all, and for them, system administration is a minor task. The next step up is small-system administrators and users. Their first job is doing applications programming and whatever other departmental workload their schedule permits, but they also are responsible for administering the system for their group or department. On larger machines or numerous clustered computer systems, system administration is a full-time job, and the system administrators are often system managers, with a staff of system programmers and operators.

Beyond this individual autonomy is the *organization*. Depending on its structure and charter, there are many different kinds of work environments for system administrators, too numerous to go into here. However, in your career as a system administrator you will probably work eventually for one of the most common computer organizations, *MIS* or *engineering*. As caretaker of the computers, you will seldom be in the unique position of working for both organizations simultaneously, but sometimes you will find yourself having to straddle the fence between both groups. Because each has different ways of doing business, it is to your benefit to understand both.

Management Information Systems (MIS)

Management information systems is classically business oriented and conservative by nature. Because it prefers technological safety to technological leadership, its software, including the operating system, is chosen for dependability. MIS managers prefer to run software one or two releases behind in preference to risking the potential bugs in a new release.

System availability is of paramount importance to MIS. All end users on all networks are expected to be able to access all systems and have everything working all the time. Anything less than 98 percent availability, including network downtime, is considered intolerable.

Users are not the prime directive in the MIS organization. MIS is where you often find applications groups and software. Applications, such as payroll or inventory, usually take priority over users' needs.

The Engineering Organization

The engineering organization is liberal by nature, prefers technological risk to technological safety, caters to its engineering users, and rides the bleeding edge of technology. This is where you often find the tool groups.[1]

The engineering organization is driven by its engineering users. The newer the release, the better. If someone has a new system in the offing, the engineering organization will want it for its features. Bugs are not only tolerated, they are expected as normal in new releases, and they are soon known by word of mouth. There may be some user complaints about system crashes, system hangs, and network burps, but engineering users tend to take them in stride because they understand the technical reasons for them.

Reconciling MIS and Engineering

As a system administrator, your first obligation is to your users, whether MIS or engineering. How can you effectively serve both sets of users when they have such different outlooks?

The single most effective way to appease the conservative MIS side while also satisfying the liberal engineering side is for the system administrator to implement a test system. A test system will not endanger the status quo, but it will provide an experimental software and hardware laboratory for your engineering users. MIS won't see anything wrong with new software, provided that it has been thoroughly tested and approved at your site's test system.

---

[1] Risking oversimplification, *applications* are software for users, and *tools* are software for engineers. A compiler can be called a tool, and a data base program can be called an application.

As long as the hardware is the same architecture, you can use an older system for test work. DEC organizations can retain older, depreciated systems like VAX 750s as test systems. Desktops are cheap enough to always have at least one spare test machine around. The mainframe organization running its systems on top of VM can make virtual test systems any time they need them. They can even run a different version of VM as a VM guest, such as a VM/HPO guest on a VM/XA host.

Running a new operating system is the ultimate test for any site. I have worked in organizations in which I was paid to test new OEM systems. In other places I gladly volunteered to take a beta system. The usual reason for entering a test-site agreement is to develop a system for eventual site use. When you and your users know that you are suffering through an alpha or beta release, bugs are better tolerated. By the time the alpha system you are struggling with reaches the beta stage, it's going to be exactly what your company needs, and all groups will benefit.

The test machine concept is handy and safe for all your users. You can run parallel systems until the system you are testing is released and fully supported, so test machines are your users' best protection, whether MIS or engineering.

ORGANIZATIONAL DIVISION

UNIX system administrators coming from smaller computer sites are often at a loss when they start working on large-scale systems. For example, when you go from one site with twenty users working small UNIX systems and networked PCs to a mainframe organization with multiple sites and hundreds of users, culture shock sets in. Where are the printers? How do data get to the printers? How do you get backups, and who does them? Who handles networking, and how many networks are there? How do the users get in touch with you, and are they allowed to? How do you communicate with the users, and are you allowed to? Who are the system programmers, and where are they? This section clarifies the standard organization structure of larger computer sites.

Large computer sites may not only service several building floors; they also may consist of multiple computer sites worldwide. Although all the sites probably communicate with one another, each has a varying degree of autonomy. Each has something similar to the following computer organization model:

- Operations.
- Networking.
- The help desk.
- The system group.

Operations

Operations provides the first-line interface between system hardware and software. On large computer sites the operations center resembles the bridge of the starship *Enterprise*. The entire area is secured, and you need special security clearance to enter. The center usually consists of an operations area, the machine room, the tape library, the tape drive area, and a print center with several printers in its own area and print bins accessible to users.

Operations is a glassed-in area with numerous state-of-the-art plasma display consoles that monitor all the systems in the machine room. Clocks on the wall are set to times at other sites worldwide, and some terminals can be used to contact any company-owned terminal or data center in the world. The operations center also contains the network center, which has its own diagnostics displays, such as LAN analyzers and network-monitor workstations with network maps. There are hundreds of technical manuals, and several operators and technicians sit at their stations keeping a watchful eye on the health of the machines and networks.

Windows in the operations center look out into the tape library and into the machine room, where thousands of lights show frenetic modem activity. To enter the machine room, you go by way of a separately secured door. Once inside, you enter the realm of magnificent machines, the latest and greatest that current technology has to offer.

The machine room on large sites occupies several hundred thousand square feet and is filled with computers and terminal, disk, and network controllers. There are separate cooling units, banks of modems close to the network controllers, and channel-to-bus adapters for the Ethernet networks. The floor is raised to make room for coolant pipes and miles of cables and power lines. The temperature is kept well under 70 degrees, and it is not unusual to see operators working in ski jackets. There is a steady 90-decibel noise from cooling units and hard disks. You may see an FE or operator, but most of the time the machine room contains only machines.

On large computer sites there may be multiple mainframes of impressive size in the machine room. An IBM 3090-600E runs an incredible 75 MIPS. Each physical hard disk, called a spindle, holds a minimum of 1 ½ gigabytes, but it can hold over 4 gigabytes of data. These physical disk drives are clustered into *strings* of hard disks, all on a single controller. Multiple strings of hard disks form a *DASD farm*.[2] DASD farms are measured in gigabytes, but they can run into terabytes. In short, there is an incredible array of machines and devices processing an incredible amount of data.

Operators work in this dramatic environment, and their job is vital. They watch the system consoles, do whatever system maintenance they have been trained to do, run backups, provide tape mounts, and handle the print centers. Operations is limited only by training and available procedures. A qualified, well-trained, and well-managed operations staff can offload much of the work traditionally done by system programmers and analysts.

The Networking Staff

The networking staff keeps the network alive. They maintain it, extend it, and add value to all phases of its operation. Network technicians are trained in all aspects of diagnostics and troubleshooting. Your network, and therefore your system's availability, is no better than your network staff.

In the past the networking group has always been separate from the system group, but TCP/IP Ethernet and the local internet changed that. Although network administrators are usually limited to very large sites, today more companies are hiring network administrators to handle the proliferating networks on their computers. It is also becom-

---

[2] DASD is an acronym for direct access storage device.

ing more common for system administrators to add network administration to their list of system chores. Because BSD and System V Release 4 make networking part of standard UNIX, UNIX system administrators might as well resign themselves to learning all they can about networking if they haven't already. That's where UNIX is today.

As network availability and transmission speeds increase, networks become more extensive, and network technology becomes more complex. A comprehensive understanding of all networks is for the rare few, so don't be afraid to hire network professionals. Some firms specialize exclusively in networking. If a company is going to add a major network or revamp its current networks, don't reinvent the wheel. Do yourself and your company a favor and get professional network help.

The Help Desk

The help desk is the user interface. Frequently the help desk is part of an applications or tool group, and it exists to service the questions of users. Large sites have hundreds of users, each of whom must have his or her own login created, own .profile or .login, and so on. The help desk can do all this with the help of an adduser program created by the system programmers. It also helps provide work space for new users.

The help desk provides relatively simple answers to questions like "How do you get a listing?" and "How do you access the printers?" It also takes requests for restores and more storage. The help desk can provide temporary disks and even do disk expansions. It passes on any problems it can't handle directly to more experienced personnel. The help desk is so effective that many organizations have a second-level help group that is a part of the systems group. The first-level help group takes all problems, but it gives the more difficult ones to the second-level help group. The second-level help group is directed to pass on really tricky problems to the system administrators or system programmers.

Although the help desk is often staffed with semitechnical personnel, it must be thought of as part of the computer group so as to avoid an *us*-versus-*them* relationship. You all are in this together. Besides, any organization that helps the users helps the system administrators as well, because your users are your customers. The internal customers are as important to your organization as the external customers are to the company's sales group. Show your appreciation for the help desk often. Know that if managed well, the help desk can be the glue that holds a computer organization together, because they take questions and requests from operations and users alike.

The System Group

The system programming staff can have many titles, but their functions are the same. The following are the duties of most system programming staffs:

- Administer the systems.
- Apply updates and fixes to the system.
- Do problem determination.
- Be a vendor interface for software and hardware.
- Add value to the system.
- Train operations and provide education.

- Create operations SOPs and write other system documentation.
- Write and maintain system software.

Chapter 22 discusses the specifics of the system group and the systems organization.

WORKING AS A SINGLE ORGANIZATION

If a computer organization is broken down into too many separate, autonomous groups, it cannot adequately provide the services for which it was created. Thus it is important for the groups to communicate with one another frequently during the course of the business day. If some of their functions overlap, so much the better, because they will be more sensitive to one another's needs. As system administrator, you are in charge of the systems, and in that role it is possible for you to help the groups work together. But if, as a system administrator, you are also a system manager, there are specific management strategies that you can use so that the *systems*, *operations*, *network*, and *help* groups can act as a single organization: organization structure, matrix management, and technically oriented management.

Organization Structure

Organization structure joins or divides. If you place operations in a separate tree from systems, eventually they will respond to user problems with a *not-my-job* attitude. If the system staff is not encouraged to give customer support and to aid the help desk whenever necessary, the people at the help desk may become reluctant to ask the system staff the questions they need to aid the users properly, and the users will be cut off from the answers they need to do their best.

The following is what happens when a computer organization is fragmented by management into entirely separate groups: I know a company in which TCP/IP Ethernet was brought to the mainframes by the CAD tool organization, also instrumental in bringing TCP/IP to minicomputers and desktops. Although the MIS management knew that the software and hardware were coming, they failed to provide staff or management for TCP/IP networking. The CAD tool organization wrote a TCP/IP driver for a Wollongong TCP/IP package and delivered the product to the mainframes, in their words, as "a done deal." There was no ownership and no support. The network group had no experience with either TCP/IP or the Ethernet because they were SNA oriented. Only the dedication of the UNIX system programming staff kept TCP/IP alive until management finally responded with a TCP/IP group and manager.

How could this scenario have had a happy ending? Management could have planned ahead of time for the arrival of the software and hardware. A support staff and trained manager could have been ready to go. The managers of the MIS organization could have urged the managers of the CAD tool organization to encourage both organizations to work together for the benefit of both sides. The network group and the system group could have been been educated in TCP/IP ahead of time to prepare for the new networking on the mainframes and the new networking support staff as well.

A computer organization should be structured so that individual managers in various computer areas are cross-trained to some extent. If a UNIX system runs on VM, its manager not only should be proficient in UNIX but also should be encouraged to survive in VM. Similarly, VM system and software managers should be able to survive as UNIX users. Without sensitivity to different environments, there can be no synergy, no magnification of one another's efforts, and therefore no overall success.

Operations and the systems group can work well as a team. For example, the systems group can be encouraged to take some responsibility for the success of operations. They should offer training for operations and keep operations well supplied with written procedures for the care of the system. If system programmers are coming in nights and weekends to keep the system alive because the operators don't know enough about UNIX to keep the machine going, the fault lies not with the operators but with the system group for not adequately training operations and establishing standard operations procedures. Operations, in turn, can be encouraged to take responsibility for the systems they operate for the systems group. If operations works willingly with the systems group by making staff available for system training, both groups will benefit enormously.

Several years ago I was asked to train an operations staff in the care and feeding of mainframe UNIX. Operations made attendance voluntary, and so I had only three or four operators reluctantly show up at 7:00 in the morning, and a few more made their appearance at 5:00 in the evening. With that attitude, I knew my teaching was doomed to only limited success. Two years later I was asked to do the same thing, only this time I was streetwise. I provided a training outline but stopped short of teaching until I was guaranteed a large, wide-awake audience at a reasonable hour. An operations staff member took the responsibility for organizing all operations staff (forty operators and shift supervisors) to show up for two sets of four-hour classes lasting three days each. Attendance was mandatory. The classes were not only a success, but the emergency evening and weekend calls I used to get from operations went from one a day to one a month. This example shows how systems and operations can work together to enhance both organizations and improve and add value to the system.

Matrix Management

In matrix management, managers report to more than one manager at the next level. Matrix management can be an effective management tool, or it can inflict another useless layer of management on managers and supervisors already overloaded with excess administrivia. Combined managerial and technical knowledge of how a computer organization works provides the key to effective matrix management in any computer organization. The more computer services that are matrixed with technical insight, the better the computer organization should run.

A good example of technical matrix management is having the supervisor of a second-level help group report to the manager of MIS help groups (customer support) as well as to the systems manager, who is now interfaced with two environments to serve.

A bad example of matrix management is having UNIX system administrators report long distance to their actual direct engineering manager in another state while also having them report to a local MIS manager with no knowledge of the UNIX system and no interest in the activities or welfare of the engineering customers. Just because the two managers are at the same level doesn't justify using mere proximity as an excuse for matrix management.

Technically Oriented Management

The effectiveness of the management of most computer organizations is directly proportional to the amount of the individual managers' technical knowledge. There is a popular management belief that good managers need only to know how to manage. By carefully gathering information and making good decisions, they can pilot their organization through anything. Every nontechnical manager I've ever met is convinced that this is true. In some rare cases it actually is true, but most of the time it's not. All nontechnical managers should ask their technical staffs to give them an honest appraisal of what it is like to be managed by people who aren't technical. They will have to brace themselves for some unpleasant, myth-shattering truths.

The Disadvantages of Nontechnical Management

How can nontechnical managers make good business decisions based on technical innovation? Consider an example pertinent to UNIX system administrators: Many managers without UNIX backgrounds see UNIX as some vague, homogeneous operating system, not much different from any other operating system. Will they be able to recognize the significant differences between UNIX System V and another operating system that only claims to meet the System V Interface Definition and the proposed POSIX standard? Of course they won't.

Managers who are technically uninformed are inherently insensitive to the real needs of their technical staff. Often I have seen nontechnical managers blithely dictating what they want their technical people to do without even remotely considering that what they are demanding is impossible. All the staff can do is look at one another grimly and wonder how on earth they can get through to these turkeys. Lack of knowledge leads to unrealistic expectations. No matter how adept your technical staff is, they can't perform magic.

As a nontechnical manager, you might feel uncomfortable about saying to your technical staff, "I don't understand." You shouldn't. Your staff needs someone who keeps on asking until he or she finally learns enough to provide knowledgeable direction and decisions. If your technical staff is going to give the best service, they will need adequate technical leadership.

All too frequently, nontechnical managers try to avoid or ignore technical issues. They become part of the problem rather than part of the solution. But if managers take the responsibility for learning as much as they can, and if they listen well to their technical staff, eventually they will learn a great deal about the underlying technical issues. Accordingly, their management will reflect the technical needs of their group, and their company will benefit from solid decisions.

HOW MANAGERS CAN BE MORE EFFECTIVE TECHNICALLY

Knowledge is power. Those who use it have it. There are two messages here. The first is that knowledge must be used in order to be of any value. The second is that knowledge must be possessed in order to be powerfully used. It is imperative that managers' technical skills do not diminish, and yet they must still devote time to their people skills and exercise them. Maintaining the level of technical knowledge needed to manage a technical staff while simultaneously performing effectively as a manager requires as much balancing skill as walking a tightrope does.

For you, as a UNIX technical manager, this means keeping a hand in the day-to-day operations of the system, release installation and evaluation, and system programming. Keep close to your staff by making *floor time*, time spent with workers while they are engaged in their day-to-day activities. Ideally, you should be able to cover adequately for absent, individual contributors. Your hands-on technical work should be deliberately varied. Don't be afraid to tackle some programming, user administration, installations, and new system creation.

System administrators who are also managers must push for enough employees so that they don't throw themselves so much into the running of the systems that they neglect their managerial duties. They should also push for a reasonable meeting schedule. Technical managers' meeting schedules must be kept at a tolerable level so that they have time to function well and keep their technological knowledge up-to-date.

NONTECHNICAL MANAGERS CAN INSPIRE A TECHNICAL STAFF

Several years ago we were faced with a hard-disk error on a critical disk pack. My manager was nontechnical, but he knew how to gather enough information from his group and eventually find a solution. He immediately called an on-the-spot, *ad hoc* committee meeting. In five minutes everyone involved knew who was responsible for what actions, when we would meet again, and who was to coordinate our plan of attack. The words *blame* and *fault* were never mentioned. All he wanted to do was solve the problem. After a couple of hours of problem determination, we eliminated software as a possible cause. An FE looked at the pack, and sure enough, he found out that the evening before, he had left it, by accident, switched in diagnostic mode. This manager provided an inspiring role model. He took charge immediately, acted decisively, and took responsibility for the problem, no matter what the cause or circumstance.

A year or so later, the same group had a different manager. We were hit by the 1988 worm incident, a disaster potentially far greater than the failing hard disk. The new manager hid from responsibility in the safety of his office until the crisis had passed, hoping that the technical staff would provide their own direction. Fortunately, we did, but that is not the point. As a role model, this manager inspired nothing but nausea.

Managers Must Actually Know What Each Employee Does

Managers cannot either direct activity or sit in judgment of others' activities when they don't understand what these others do. Good managers go out and observe the activity of each staff member. They ask questions and become familiar with their work. If you are a manager of technical people and you have staff members who do nothing but programming, read their code and documentation, watch the software work, and only then you will be able to pass judgment on their performance.

The activity of getting involved, taking regular floor time, and learning about what is done and how long it takes enhances a manager's ability to estimate how long other, similar jobs should take. I had one programmer who claimed he could program *anything* in a few hours. A nontechnical manager ignorant about programming might believe this nonsense. Since I had programmed for a living for years, I knew right away that this programmer was not capable of doing accurate time estimates. Even small programs take about a half-day to code, test, debug, and correct. Besides, I knew from direct observation that standard company projects had taken this young programmer months to complete, just like everyone else. He was a legend in his own mind. The longer a project took, the more he blamed everyone around him for inhibiting his "genius." A veteran staff programmer would have told me that he could deliver code and documentation in a reasonable amount of time, say 60 days, and I could count on him to deliver.

Managers of programmers must know enough about programming to be able to calculate realistic time schedules for programming projects. They must also realize that a 40-man-day project takes one programmer two months, with the proviso that the programming job is the *only* job he does in that period.

Managers Must Be As Technically Current As Possible

You can't manage System V Release 4 if your last real experience was in UNIX Version 7 or VMS. I have seen UNIX badly mismanaged by operations managers and supervisors who assumed that if it ran on a mainframe, it must be like VM or MVS. I actually had an operations manager ask for VM programs (called *execs*) to bring up (boot) the production UNIX systems so "it would not take so much time to IPL them." It is this kind of manager ignorance that causes the staff to lose confidence in the entire management structure. If you are ignorant about the technical aspects of the group you are managing, take the responsibility of learning enough to provide adequate direction. Managers who can provide adequate technical answers and direction not only earn the respect of their technical group, but they also inspire their employees to emulate their example and keep on learning.

MANAGER'S CORNER

The Crisis of Technical Management

It is unfair to lay the blame for inadequate technical management solely on the heads of nontechnical managers, for there is a crisis in technical management today. One classic advancement route in technical companies is for individuals to be promoted to management on the basis of their superior technical skills. Here's where the crisis begins. They now must spend time acquiring managerial skills at the expense of time formerly spent on honing their technical skills.

There is a relatively short honeymoon period, during which the managers' technical knowledge remains relatively current while they spend time refining their managerial skills. Unfortunately, the managers' technical knowledge eventually becomes dated, and their technical skills lose the edge. Although their peer managers and senior managers respect their background and technical knowledge base, their direct employees, all technical, soon sense their lack of current technical knowledge. The technical staff's confidence in their technical management ability starts to erode, and not without good reason. Their ability to make intelligent technical decisions diminishes as a function of the time elapsed since they were "hands-on" technical.

Managers are usually swamped with administrative duties. I know many technical managers who take fierce pride in staying abreast of current technology while simultaneously handling their people-management duties, but this is done by working 60-hour weeks, postponing vacations, and getting old at an early age. Often there seems to be no alternative short of a 125 percent solution.[3]

I maintain that this situation is unhealthy not only for computer organizations but for American business as a whole. Time and time again I've seen the pursuit of technical knowledge fall victim to the belief that functional management—the nontechnical management of ongoing tasks—is ultimately the most important issue for managers. It makes sense to them at their level of managerial development. Success in higher management *is* being a functional manager. Whereas previously such managers' role models were technical people, now their role models are nontechnical managers. However, in technical companies this reasoning is faulty. The real strength of technical managers lies in their technical ability and its preservation and enrichment.

Almost 100 percent of the educational budget for the technical staff is spent on technical training. Nontechnical managers tend to spend whatever educational budget they allot to themselves for managerial courses. They confine their reading to managerial subjects and an overall view of "the field." While their subordinates read the *Bell Technical Journal* and *USENIX Conference Proceedings*, they read *Computer System News* and *Infoweek*. The subordinates go to the core, while the managers view the skin.

When it comes to decisions, the managers may have the "big picture," but they fail to understand the underlying technical issues. The managers are forced to rely on the opinions of individual contributors who may have the wrong focus, be uninformed themselves, or suffer from prejudices. Thus nontechnical managers often make decisions based on erroneous or slanted information.

Here's how management's technical ignorance resulted in considerable trouble for one Southern California defense company's mainframe UNIX strategy: The original plan for a $300 million military contract was mainframe UNIX, no language choice specified. During the planning stages it was decided that Ada would be the project programming language. The Ada decision was based on management politics, stemming from the desires of a handful of programmers who thought it would be "neat." They were a minority, but they were vocal and they had a persuasive but technically ignorant manager as their champion. He liked Pascal, and he viewed Ada as some kind of Pascal superset.

The upper management staff was also technically ignorant about UNIX, so they never understood why this might be a bad idea. They found out soon enough. During this period the Department of Defense had just announced its commitment to Ada, and so polished, bulletproof Ada compilers weren't available yet. The compiler that this company finally purchased was scandalously inadequate. It was barely at alpha stage and should never have been offered for sale. It was so slow that "real-time" computing was impossible. These

---

[3] Intel initiated the 125 percent solution in a period of survival when it asked its employees to work an additional 10 hours a week without compensation.

problems ate into project schedules to such a degree that the UNIX mainframe strategy was eventually scuttled. There were internal shakeups, reassignments, and redistribution of resources. I often wonder how much face this company lost with the government.

If one member of senior management had read anything remotely technical about UNIX, she might have asked some of the right questions, like "Why use Ada when we can use C?" All this time the tremendous programming power of the C language was going to waste on their mainframes and other UNIX systems. Other ground satellite–positioning contractors had gone to C without a second thought, but not this site. The persuasive but technically ignorant engineering manager sold management on an idea that should have been nipped in the bud.

CHAPTER

22

Service-Level Agreements

This chapter is for anyone who manages UNIX systems, including system administrators, system managers, and nontechnical managers of technical people who run UNIX systems.

Many organizations leave the relationship between the users and the computer support staff to goodwill and faith. If there are problems, they will be *worked out somehow*. In the private sector, supplying a service on a continuous basis is always handled by contract. For example, to buy a year's worth of weed control for $250, you sign a contract with the weed-control company. This protects you and the company by specifying when it will spray and when you will pay. Corporation divisions allot tens of millions of dollars a year to be supplied with computing services. Why should a corporation supply computing services to its users without a contract? There are such contracts, and they are called *service-level agreements*.

A service-level agreement is an in-house contract between the users and the suppliers of a service within the company. It is deliberately specific so that both sides know what is expected.

Almost everything in a service-level agreement affects the system administrator in one way or the other. You must know the entire document and all the potential ramifications for your organization, or you will find yourself stuck with responsibility for problems you don't want or need.

DEFINITIONS AND MEASUREMENTS

The first section of a service-level agreement defines all acronyms and words apt to have unknown, multiple, or ambiguous meanings. Specifically, terms like *hot line*, *backup*, *UNIX*, or *VM* should be clearly defined. Lawyers make their fortunes and diminish those of their clients by debating the meanings of words and phrases that, had they been clearly defined in the law, regulation, or contract, would have never left room for litigation.

So be extremely specific with words like *work week*, *prime time*, *severity level*, and *availability*. For example:

> Prime time is 07:00 to 18:00 Monday through Friday.
> Nonprime time is 18:00 to 07:00 Monday through Friday.
> Weekend is 18:00 Friday through 07:00 Monday.

DOWNTIMES

The hottest issue in a service-level agreement is downtime scheduling. Neither machine nor software can withstand continuous usage without relief for preventive maintenance. Some organizations have a daily downtime in nonprime time. Most have weekly downtimes, normally on the weekend. Some shops, particularly MVS houses, have a midweek downtime. A few sites have one software and one hardware downtime per month.

Consider the choices well. If you have a reasonable cushion in your downtime, you can always give back the machine to the users early. But if you negotiate away all of your cushion, you will be the bad guy when you continually run over your time window.

UNSCHEDULED DOWNTIMES

Do not forget unscheduled downtimes, which will happen regardless of your best intentions. Deal with them on paper first. How much notice must be given to the users when announcing an unscheduled downtime? At what level of severity are you justified in calling one?

SEVERITY LEVELS AND ACTIONS

Severity levels equate to *pain*. They can be defined on a scale of 1 to 5. At the first level, the highest severity level, you can define the threshold of pain as a problem that disrupts most of the system's service. A Severity 2 problem immediately threatens less than some arbitrary level of total availability, say 20 percent to 40 percent. An example is a major piece of software that doesn't stop all work but kills 20 percent of possible output. At the opposite end is the Severity 5 problem, which is trivial, such as a manual error, an additional feature, or a bit of foo foo to be added to a program.

You decide how to cope with the different severity levels in a service-level agreement. Since you are defining expectations, now is the opportunity to *quantify* those expectations. You can state that Severity 1 problems must be solved within six hours, which gives the administrator the right to bring down the system for an unscheduled downtime if necessary. This is your chance to get *your* wording, and it might be the only chance you will get for a year.

OPERATOR AND PROGRAMMER COVERAGE

Coverage is as important as downtimes. Are you offering 7×24 service?[1] Does that coverage involve separate service groups such as customer services and hot line, operations, and technical services, systems, and programming groups? Be specific about which groups will provide which services. A broad 7×24 statement has at least one system programmer and one operator working in-house on every shift, including weekend shifts. Would a system programmer work a second shift, let alone a weekend fifth shift?

PRINT CENTERS

Who is going to maintain the printers? If operators do it, will they maintain user print bins? How often will the printers be emptied and bins stuffed? This may sound trivial to a senior staff manager, but it is a fighting issue for both users and operators.

USER IDS

Will users be allowed a choice of user ID? Do you want *wizard*, *jeff*, *stinky*, and *oz* on your print banners? Can you track down *biff* when he has taken 100 mainframe CPU hours and you want to know why? The running convention in the industry is first initial concatenated to the last name and truncated at some reasonable limit, say eight characters max. Thus Tom Schulte becomes tschulte. Tom Bradford becomes tbradfor or tbrad.

USER REQUESTS AND PROBLEMS

If a hot line has been established, when is it active? Does the operations staff take calls when the hot line is not active? If so, are they ready to commit staff? Service-level agreements are not only for users but for operators, too.

TAPE MOUNTS

Tape mounts are a hot issue. How much lead time is required for a mount? Is five minutes unreasonable? Who is responsible for storing and archiving tapes? Will users be allowed to take tapes out of operations? As manager, you may have to budget for tapes, a tape librarian, or a tape operator.

---

[1] That is, 7 days a week by 24 hours a day, or 100 percent coverage.

TAPE RETENTION

In addition to tape mounts, tape retention must be covered. How long are tapes to be retained? Where are they to be stored? How quickly can they be expected to be retrieved? You should already have a general idea, but drawing up a service-level agreement will force you to decide on specific answers.

TAPE SECURITY

Tape security is another hot issue. Should you let tapes out of the computer room? No is an easy answer, but is it realistic? Many sites network between unlike machines with *Sneakernet*. Sneakernet is data transferred by making a tape, putting the tape under your arm, and jogging across the street to another computer system to get it read. Can users keep tapes? Sometimes, but it depends on the user, the nature of the data, and the procedures on your site. Allowing managers to retain tapes of deleted user files gives them confidence. They know they can get the files back if they need to, and you will get more space on disk without a major hassle.

There are as many good reasons for a loose tape policy as there are for a tight one. *The integrity of your data can be guaranteed only by the integrity of your users and your willingness to prosecute those who lack it.*

BACKUPS

Service-level agreement items relating to backups go far beyond the issue of retention. How long is a reasonable time to wait for a restore? Which organization is contacted for a restore—operations or the hot line? Are users billed for restores, or are the costs to be part of overhead? You may want a punitive clause for restores. UNIX accounting allows for it.

TEMPORARY DISKS

Does the organization provide for temporary storage, and if so, how long can you hold on to a temporary disk? Are temporary disks backed up? If so, how long will that particular tape retention be? Temporary disks can save you money by offloading files that would otherwise get written to a permanent place in storage, but it will cost you initially for the disk space required to initiate it.

RESPONSE TIME

Is response time going to be in the contract? What is a reasonable response time? Response time can be measured in fractions of seconds or in an *expansion ratio*. If a trivial job ran in 6 seconds on an unloaded system (03:00, January 1, New Year's Eve) but takes 36 seconds to run on a loaded system, its expansion ratio is 6 to 1. As you can see, sometimes the expansion ratio is a bit misleading. It is not always a precise indicator. If an expansion ratio is used, it should be monitored by a local program and written to a log.

One final point on expansion ratios: If you define a maximum expansion ratio and it is exceeded, what will the organization do about it? Don't create expectations that cannot be backed up by some action.

PROBLEM RESOLUTION

The service-level agreement must be very specific about problem resolution. Broad statements can get you into a world of trouble:

Technical support will be responsible for problem resolution.

You just promised the world with this one. If a CAD, applications, or network tool breaks down, your system programmer will go down in smoke. Be specific. It is not unreasonable to make the technical support staff responsible for first-level problem determination, but it is unreasonable to make them automatically responsible for their resolution.

Imagine this scenario: A user calls with "Telnet doesn't work!" It can be a network problem, or it can be local software. You don't automatically turn it over to the network group. The system administration staff must first demonstrate conclusively that the local software is working. First run a software loopback test. Next either ping or call another machine within the local cluster. If that goes, it is a safe bet that the problem is outside of the local node. It is definitely a network, not a software, problem. Now it's clear which group is responsible for the problem.

RESOLUTION OF HARDWARE PROBLEMS

The operations staff, or certainly the data center staff, are responsible for reporting hardware failures and taking immediate steps toward their resolution. Put this in writing in your service-level agreement. Otherwise, operations will call a system programmer, report an outage, and expect the programmer to get on the phone with the vendor.

SPECIFIC SOFTWARE SUPPORT

Who supports what must be in black and white. Is there a data base group? If so, then be sure its end of the contract is the support of that data base and its software. If you have VM on your site systems, specify that VM system programmers, *not* UNIX programmers, are responsible for problem determination and the resolution of VM problems. Similarly, tool groups should support tools, and network people should support the network.

HOW OFTEN SHOULD SERVICE-LEVEL AGREEMENTS BE REVIEWED?

Yes, even the service-level agreement itself is in the service-level agreement. How often should it be reviewed, and who will be responsible for it? Will technical groups co-chair with user groups? Is there to be a separate computing council?

WORDING

A service-level agreement is no different from any other technical writing. It must be worded as clearly and concisely as possible. Clear wording generates clear understanding and leaves little open for interpretation. Every company department concerned in the agreement will know who it is and what is expected of it. Say it right the first time in your service-level agreement, and you won't get into major interdepartmental disputes. And then you'll have more time to do what you were paid to do in the first place, UNIX system administration.

MANAGER'S CORNER

To Thine Own Staff Be True

Often nontechnical managers fall back on canned responses to cover their lack of technical knowledge. When you don't know what to say, it's human nature to come up with something safe and innocuous until you figure out what's going on. Whenever the system stumbled on one of my mainframe sites, I used to have a nontechnical manager who responded with annoying predictability, "What changed?" It seemed like an excellent question the first time I heard it, but after a few repetitions, the novelty wore off.

Your technical staff needs solid guidance, not worn-out phrases. "You have to understand corporate policy" is not an answer. It tells the employee that you don't know the answer now and never will. How many times have I groaned inwardly when I heard, "Be proactive!" Don't subject your staff to the clichés of current corporate management jargon. Save them to impress other managers.

The computer industry is notorious for its technical jargon and numerous acronyms, irritating to those outside the field who don't understand them. Nontechnical managers may be confounded by all the UNIX technical terms, but corporate jargon is equally as irritating to nonmanagement personnel. When technical and nontechnical people want to communicate, they both should rely on plain English.

A fine American gentleman named W. Edwards Deming developed some revolutionary management principles in Japan over the last 40 years, and one of those principles emphasizes that hiding behind empty phrases and overworked acronyms demoralizes employees. The keyword here is communication. Level with your staff; they will respect you for it.

SECTION

VI

System Administration Scenarios

CHAPTER

23

System Administration Scenarios

We have studied pedestrian UNIX system administration, UNIX subsystems, system creation, system configuration, system tuning, networking, and system management, but even all that doesn't give a complete idea of what it's like being a UNIX system administrator. As the author of this system administration text, it is my job to categorize and neatly outline all the events that the reader may encounter in system administration, and yet there are some events that defy categorization. Administering a UNIX system is an ongoing adventure, and in time you will have many unexpected experiences. To help you anticipate some of the problems that you will encounter and to demonstrate real-world methods of problem determination, I have put together the following collection of system administration scenarios.

It is said that a historical action cannot be judged accurately without understanding the perspective of the event at the time it occurred. With this in mind, analyze each scenario for the method of problem determination. Do not rule out instinct in the process of doing your own problem determination. In time you will develop an intuitive feel for what is happening and how to cure it.

System administrators are generally overworked and underappreciated. Frustration levels will hit record highs, and eventually you will run out of time and energy. When you get to this point, you may either quit in disgust or learn to work *smarter*. The only substitute for time is knowledge.

THE FILES THAT WOULDN'T DIE, AND WHY

I have had a number of files that were annoying because they could not be removed. Most had hidden characters in their names. One file appeared as bar but was actually named foo^H^H^Hbar. Another file was only called *. An octal dump of the parent directory

```
$ od -xc snark
```

uncovered the real name, but think about the difficulties in removing that file! I used

```
$ rm -i ?
```

When it asked me if I wanted to remove *, I agreed, and it was gone without putting anything else in danger.

This scenario is one of a kind. A user came to me with a handful of night-of-the-living-dead files. They all were in the same directory. In fact, an ls showed all of them as directories themselves. They all ended in .o. File-oriented commands like ls, du, df, file, and rmdir couldn't deal with the strange files. The owner explained that they were originally object files but that somehow they became mutant directories.

I had the gut feeling that the object files had their thirteenth through sixteenth bits in the mode field flipped in the inode structure. I tried to get the inode number with

```
ls -ilb *
```

because the i flag gives the inode number and the b flag forces the printing of nongraphic characters. That didn't work either. Only an octal dump of the directory gave the inode number of the bizarre directory.

Luckily I am a UNIX old-timer, and I remember some of the older commands that have fallen into disuse in newer versions of UNIX. Thus I knew that the inode could be cleared with a very old command, clri. Once the inode was cleared, the directory was easily removed with a simple rm. When the bit fields in the thirteenth through sixteenth positions become corrupted, the system is not able to talk to the file or the directory. There is little choice but to clear the inode with clri and to remove the directory entry. That's what was done with the files that wouldn't die.

lp WON'T WORK, AND WORSE

One day someone from the help desk came to me with an unusual problem. The lp command wouldn't work for him. He was in his own account created a year ago. An examination of his .profile showed that LPDEST was set to a reasonable printer. Sitting at his terminal I tried to send his .profile to the printer with the lp command. I failed in the attempt.

Then I tried

```
pr .profile|lp
```

That worked: pr does not do the directory checking that ls does.

I changed to su and tried lp directly again, but that didn't work. This told me that the *read* permissions in .profile were not affected. I changed file paths from relative to absolute, but that didn't help either. My intuitive feeling was that lp could not resolve the file path.

The next step was to access the user's account from my own login. His home directory was inaccessible. It couldn't even be accessed by root. A listing of his home directory showed the following permissions:

```
$ls -l /mis/griffin
drw-rw-r--  10 griffen mis    272 Sep 1986 griffen
```

Notice that there are no x bits turned on in his home directory. To a regular executable file, such as an a.out file or shell program, x bits mean *execute*. However, to a directory, x bits indicate *traverse* privilege. When they are turned off, no one can traverse the directory.

Although this user's account was a year old, it was obvious that he had not used his UTS account for much of anything until now. One of our less-senior system programmers had set up his account a year ago. I later found out that she had set up other accounts in this way but that they had been fixed by more knowledgeable operations personnel.

Once you solve the problem, the cure is usually simple enough:

```
$ su
password:
# chmod 775 /mis/griffen
```

This scenario reminds me of a permissions horror story I picked up at a system administration conference. A system administrator did a chmod 666 recursively from root to the end of the branches. With no traverse privilege anywhere, wherever she was logged in was where she was doomed to stay. That was the end of that system!

df SHOWS NO DISK SPACE BUT...

I came in at 8:00 one morning and hardly had time to put down my briefcase when I got a frantic phone call. A user had an out of disk space error on his screen, but he suspected there really was a lot of space left on disk. Most users with out of disk space errors are not ready to come to grips with the fact that they have actually run out of disk space, but I knew this user. I trusted his problem determination ability.

A df -t of the minidisk confirmed that there was no space. The console log showed the system complaining about it:

```
$ sed -n '$p' /usr/spool/console/Dec27      # print the last line
22:36:16  W os/alloc.c(alloc)(1.16.11) no space on /dev/dsk/77fs0
$
```

Further investigation showed more than 7000 lines of no space messages in the console log.

Only 74 inodes were taking up 66,000 4K blocks, or 365,000 bytes per file. That didn't make any sense. I used the `find` command to look for large files:

```
find -type f -size +100000c -print
```

but it failed to display any files whatsoever. A recursive descent listing showed only a handful of small files in about twelve directories.

I suspected that either the kernel's inode table was corrupted or some process was holding captive the in-core inode table's free list, pending a disk write that was never to come. This happens when the system is attempting to do a massive write to a space that is too small, such as trying to write 40 megabytes of spooled console errors to a 10-megabyte disk partition.

I issued a `fuser` and a `umount` command on the disk partition. It failed to allow the disk to be unmounted. I ran a `ps -ef` piped to `grep` in the user's name to see if there was a parent process spawning processes faster than I could kill them. I tried the `fuser`/`unmount` command pair again, and this time it took:

```
# (fuser -uk /dev/dsk/77fs0;umount /dev/dsk/77fs0)
```

The disk was unmounted.

Once unmounted, I used `fsck` to check the disk for corruption:

```
# fsck /dev/dsk/77fs0
```

No corruption was found; the disk version was good. When I remounted the disk, `df` showed only a few hundred blocks in use. The operation was a success. Apparently, the in-core inode table had been corrupted, but unmounting and then remounting the disk caused that part of the inode table to be rewritten correctly.

TERMINAL WON'T GET PAST PASSWORD

This is one of the strangest problems I have seen. A Wyse 30 terminal was added to a small system. The terminal port was defined in `/etc/ttys` as requiring no modem control, so it took only a few minutes to configure it and get the login prompt. When I entered the log name, the terminal behaved just fine, but when I entered the password and hit the return key, nothing happened. When the login program timed out, the marred login cycle repeated.

I reattached the terminal to my 3B2, where it worked like a dream. I brought it back to my Intel 301, and the same login problem reappeared. I reset that terminal to every imaginable combination of data and stop bits, emulations, and parity, but I succeeded only in getting worse results.

Wyse terminals have the ability to map characters. For example, an asterisk can be mapped to an ASCII null to deliberately prevent a user from wildcarding. I suspected that the user had inadvertently modified the mapping of a character in the process of setting terminal characteristics. I reset the terminal to its defaults. It came up and worked just fine.

WRONG TERM SET IN THE USER ENVIRONMENT

A serial board had been added to a XENIX 386 system to accommodate some Wyse terminals and other peripherals. User profiles were modified quickly to identify the terminal at a specific port. Once done, the constant TTY was set and exported. Then a curious thing happened. When the nonmotherboard ports were used, vi came up strangely. It was virtually unusable. The terminal came up as the monitor default of ansi. Here is a part of the user's .profile:

```
:
PATH=/bin:/usr/bin:/u/local:.
MAIL=/usr/spool/mail/eric
EXINIT="set wrapmargin=10"
export PATH MAIL EXINIT
umask 022
nbr=`who|grep eric|wc -l`
if test $nbr -eq 1
    then
    setcolor lt_cyan
    elif test $nbr -eq 2; then
        setcolor lt_cyan blue
        else
            setcolor yellow
 fi
setcolor -c 8
tty=`tty`
if [ "$tty" = /dev/tty2c ]
 then
  TERM=tvi925
  TERMCAP=/etc/termcap
  export TERM TERMCAP
fi
```

The .profile has an entry for the Televideo 925 that the Wyse was emulating, but I overlooked the XENIX tset statement. Because tset is unique to BSD and XENIX, it is easily ignored by a UNIX System V purist. The fix was to invoke tset in .profile:

```
:
PATH=/bin:/usr/bin:/u/local:.
MAIL=/usr/spool/mail/eric
EXINIT="set wrapmargin=10"
export PATH MAIL EXINIT
umask 022
tset -m ansi:ansi -m tvi925:925
nbr=`who|grep eric|wc -l`
if test $nbr -eq 1
    then
    setcolor lt_cyan
    elif test $nbr -eq 2; then
        setcolor lt_cyan blue
        else
            setcolor yellow
 fi
setcolor -c 8
```

While it is tempting for someone used to UNIX System V to preserve that environment, there are differences in BSD and XENIX that can't be ignored; /etc/ttys, /etc/ttytype, and /bin/tset are glaring examples.

FAILED MODEM

This scenario starts with a modem connection that worked fine for four years until one day when it suddenly stopped working. Obviously something had changed, but what? The hardware had been moved, so it was immediately suspect. Port assignments were checked, and all devices were on the right port. The modems were turned over and switch settings checked. Nothing had changed there. These solutions would have been too easy.

Now desperation time was approaching. A modem was disconnected from another computer and attached to the system that wasn't talking to the modem properly. It also failed. By now it was looking like a software problem.

Next I did a listing of the tty devices:

```
# ls -l /dev/tty??
crw--w--w-  1 bhunter     edit 1,  0 May 20 19:31 /dev/tty11
crw--w--w-  1 root        root 1,  1 May 20 19:40 /dev/tty12
--w-------  1 root        bin 14    July 4 18:11 /dev/tty11
crw--w--w   1 root        root 1,  2 May 20 19:44 /dev/tty13
crw--w--w   1 root        root 1,  3 May 20 19:48 /dev/tty14
```

Notice that the third line has no major or minor device number. In fact, it is a *regular file* with the same name as /dev/tty11, the modem port. Eureka!

I had discovered the problem. Now to work out a cure. It wasn't that easy. A

```
# rm -rf /dev/tty11
```

removed the legitimate node, but it didn't touch the file, which had obviously been put in by the devil himself. Now each device was presented for removal:

```
# rm -i /dev/tty1?
```

The answer to all files but one was no. Eventually, the nonspecial tty11 file showed up:

```
/dev/tty11: ? y
```

Next the device special file had to be remade:

```
# mknod /dev/tty11 c 1 0
```

The fix was successful, and all was well.

How on earth had this odd file been created in the first place? Obviously by accident. There is a good chance that someone tried to send something to the device while superuser, perhaps something like this:

```
# echo AT>/dev/tty11
```

ETHERNET CAN'T GET OUT

A junior system programmer logged onto a UNIX test system to exercise his knowledge of the internet. He was able to telnet out, but he could not telnet in.

I checked the telnetd daemon with a loopback test. I saw the loopback test fail for the first time in my experience as a system administrator. All daemons were alive and well, and `netstats` showed nothing unusual. The machine knew its node name. The `networks` and `hosts` files were in agreement with their sister machines on the same subnet.

Listen to your intuitive feelings about what is wrong. I had a feeling that the internet addresses were not being resolved. I asked another system programmer if anything had changed. She informed me that she had installed new `hosts` and `networks` files on all machines one day earlier. However, nothing had been done to force the system to reread the network-related files. The system was a test machine, so it was immediately taken down and rebooted. Then Ethernet was able to work in both directions.

Rebooting the system is the poorest way to fix a problem. Although it gives you a cure, it doesn't give you an answer. Analysis told me that the shutdown executed `NETSHUT`, which killed the network daemons, and the startup executed `NETSTART`, which restarted the network daemons. Thus the `hosts` and `networks` files were reread. The lesson here is that `NETSHUT` and `NETSTART` must be run every time the networking files are modified.

THE UNMOUNTABLE DISK PARTITION

A system programmer approached me with a puzzling problem. She was ready to do a file system space expansion, but she couldn't unmount the disk. She had `walled` the users and used `fuser` to get all users off the disk, but the system kept coming back with a

```
disk busy
```

message. She did a `who` to see who was on the system and then `greped` /etc/passwd to see if any of the current users had that disk partition as a home directory. I double-checked with `fuser`.

The system in this scenario is a large mainframe UNIX system with disk addresses starting at hex 110 and going all the way out to fff. A file, /etc/mountlist, is used by `rc` to mount each minidisk disk partition when the system comes up at `init 2`. I suspected that another file system attached to the system had refused to unmount, and so I `greped` `mountlist` for the file system that was so tenaciously hanging on:

```
# fgrep 'tech' /etc/mountlist
/etc/mount   /tech /dev/dsk/cc6s0
/etc/mount   /tech/grp2 /dev/dsk/992s0
```

Notice that with /tech/grp2 mounted to /tech, the cc6 /tech disk would stay busy until address 992 was detached.

The situation was complicated because system users were logging back on and had shells running accessing grp2 directories. Killing them before attempting an `fuser` was futile. Faster than a system programmer could type commands, the shells were back running processes using the disk system. The trick was simultaneously to kill user processes and unmount the disk. Fortunately, UNIX allows multiple commands on one command line and allows them execution in the same subshell:

```
# (fuser -uk /dev/dsk/992s0;/etc/umount /dev/dsk/992s0)
# (fuser -uk /dev/dsk/cc6s0;/etc/umount /dev/dsk/cc6s0)
```

This time there was an unmount.

The lessons are

- Never assume that a file system is the top of the tree.
- Never assume that a user process is the only thing keeping a disk busy. Error messages are not always literal.
- Don't waste time between dependent commands when you have spawning processes. Type two or more commands per line and keep them in the same subshell.

IS YOUR SYSTEM REALLY HUNG?

A dead system is truly deceased. All processes are stopped, and the kernel is gone. The system writes the address □□□□ □□□□ □□□□ DEAD to the program status word, and then it departs this world.

A "hung" system and a "down and disabled" system, however, are neither up nor down. They lie gasping for breath like mortally wounded villains in a grade B film. A hung system is kernel resident with noticeable kernel activity but no measurable results. A D & D system is kernel resident, but it has no kernel activity.

Sometimes a system appears hung, but technically it is not. A system can be in a perpetual paging situation in which it pages in one enormous job after another. Each job is so big that by the time its context is loaded, process execution barely gets to a point that any results can be obtained, and so the scheduler pages that job out and allows another huge job to page in.

An overpaging system doing no useful work is technically alive. It isn't hung, but it certainly appears to be. Here is a useful script that finds time hogs:

```
:
echo "time hog:"
ps -ef!sed -n 'lp'
th=`ps -ef!egrep  v 'getty!defunct'!
sed 's/[0-2][0-9]:[0-5][0-9]:[0-5][0-9]//
s/[A-S][a-z][a-z] [0-3][0-9]//'!awk '{ print $6 }'!
sed -n '2,$p'!sort -n -r !sed -n 'lp'`
ps -ef!fgrep $th!frep -v 'grep'
```

The sed command strips out time and date fields to guarantee that the accumulated CPU time will be in the proper field location so that it can be picked up by awk every time.

A different version of the same script uses the -ae flags to eliminate the time/date field problem, with -ef flags used later in the code for fuller output:

```
:
set `ps -ae!fgrep -v getty!awk '{ print $3 }'!sort -n -r!sed -n '1,5p'`
ps -ef!sed -n 'lp'
for time
 do
    ps -ef!grep $time!grep -v grep
done
```

The set command is used to put time values from the ps command into the positional parameters $1 through $5. This line simply gets the top line of output from ps:

```
ps -ef!sed -n 'lp'
```

The output looks like this:

```
$ /local/etc/th
UID    PID   PPID   C   STIME     TTY    TIME   COMMAND
root  14831   153   0   Dec 22   ttyp5  131:28 /etc/telnetd
root  21622   153   0   Dec19    ttyp4   7:55 /etc/telnetd
root      2     0   0   Dec15      ?     4:56 <pagedaemon>
root  22049     1   0   10:54:36   ?     0:00 /etc/getty tty605
```

The kernel is alive in a hung system. Sometimes it is possible to get back onto the system console. Ideally, the system console is not disconnected and is watched constantly by an operator or system programmer. There are times you have to keep trying to log on or to execute a command when logging on. The trick is to "slip a word in edgewise." Should you succeed, kill the page hog or whatever job has the system hung. A ps -ef shows accumulated times, and the hog is evident.

On large mainframe UNIX systems with a multiple-domain feature or with operating systems like UNIX running as a VM guest, diagnostics external to UNIX are used to show system activity. One hundred percent use with no viable output shows you that you are in some sort of a loop condition, like our page-in/page-out scenario. With no activity, you're either D & D or DEAD.

If the possibility of getting the system back on its feet again seems slim, there is little choice but to reboot. Always let down the machine as gently as possible. If the system can execute its shutdown script, sync the machine and issue a quick shutdown.

THE PRINTER WON'T WRITE

In this scenario my trusty AT&T 3B had been worked on by an AT&T field rep. I had just gotten it home and was bringing it up with a brand-new motherboard when the lp command failed to give any output. I checked the cables, connectors, and ports. It was clearly time for deeper problem determination.

Then I bypassed the lp system and went straight to the printer:

```
$ su
password:
#
# echo "testing 1 2 3" >/dev/lp
```

This successfully sent the test message testing 1 2 3 to the printer. This told me that the port was active, the printer worked, and the cables were good, and so the problem must be in the lp system.

An lpstat showed the scheduler running and the queue enabled. The printer was not accepting. Because the system was not being used by any users, I returned to init s. Every time you change init levels, the system goes to innittab and does everything that innittab has labeled for that level. When I went back to init 2, I knew that rc was fired, so lp should be working. Sure enough, lpstat showed all systems go.

Unfortunately, when I submitted a job to lp, I received this error message:

```
can't write to /dev/lp
```

Here the `lp` spooling system plainly could not write to the printer, but I had already showed that `root` could. This told me that the device permissions must be off. Time to check the file mode:

```
# ls -l /dev/tty13
cr--r--r-- 1  lp   bin   1, 3 April 15 17:20  /dev/tty13
```

Notice that there are no *write* permissions at any level. Although `root` could write to it because `root` can write to anything, other users, even `lp` itself, could not.

The port was turned on by doing this:

```
# chmod 622 /dev/tty13
```

Why were these permissions changed? The lesson here is not to assume that anyone will leave your machine the way he or she found it.

NO GETTY

On the same little AT&T system, the console came up, but the `ttys` would not show a login.

Initially I checked for the following:

- Cable-to-port connection.
- Cable-to-`tty` connection.
- `tty` baud setting.
- `/etc/inittab` entry.

In the incident preceding this one, in which a tech had replaced a motherboard, apparently the technician had also set the `inittab` entry from `respawn` to `off`, thus disabling the `getty`. Be prepared to find significant changes on a repaired machine.

USERS CANNOT LOG ON: EQUIPMENT CHECK

I tried to log onto one of the UNIX systems first thing in the morning for maintenance, but I couldn't get on. A call to operations confirmed that users were not able to log on. Logging onto the disconnected console confirmed that the machine was on its deathbed. As a matter of fact, it died and dumped as soon as I said hello.

Rebooting the machine caused it to generate errors regarding disk addresses 775 to 778 and aa1. Reading the kernel dump confirmed the initiation errors. Before it died, the last few error messages in the kernel's `osm` buffer showed page-read errors, equipment checks of the addresses noted, and the keyword `dumping`. Reading `/usr/spool/console/cons` and the console log `/usr/spool/Mar21` confirmed the `osm` buffer message.

A disk map showed virtual addresses 775 to 778 as residing on the same physical disk pack. Address aa1 was also on the same pack. The rest of the pack was unused disk space known as a *gap*. Since aa1 was a spool disk, the `osm` errors would make sense if the disk were physically damaged or unavailable. A field engineer was called in to examine the disk. It was a hardware error, and it was corrected without loss of data.

On rebooting the system, an alternative page device was used. Addresses 775 to 778 were verified with a query command and found to be available. Each was mounted manually and tested one by one. All were good. Finally the aa1 address was brought back up as a paging device. The machine lived.

Looking back, all the steps were taken properly. The page device was unstable, and this is what brought down the system in the first place.

CORRUPTED PASSWORD FILE

This war story started just before lunch one winter morning. Customer services called to report that some users could log on while others could not. To compound the confusion, ls was giving user-ID numbers rather than user names for some users:

```
$ ls -l mosim
-rw-rw-r--  1  1211 ilcd   94  Dec27 15:34 mosim
```

On my systems I save passwd to files like Opasswd, OLDpasswd, and old.passwd. Also, /etc/passwd is automatically backed up daily to a central password data base. They all should be close to the same size, but a

```
$ ls -l /etc/*passwd
```

showed that /etc/passwd was the smallest *passwd file. The difference was 6548 bytes for passwd and 17461 for Opasswd. When /etc/pwck was run on /etc/passwd to confirm password file corruption, it showed a missing colon after the group-ID number of one of the users. The passwd file was truncated at this entry.

The system in this scenario is very large, with many local features for critical service protection (see Chapter 19). To failsafe the system's passwd files, each passwd file is copied from each machine to a central passwd file on a central administrative machine. At 08:00 that morning I found a mainframe-specific network daemon called vmpunch stuck. It had accumulated considerable CPU time, a sure indication of trouble. I killed the daemon server and restarted another by issuing a command to exercise it. Before restarting it, I cleared the vmpunch spooler, /usr/spool/out. There was a real possibility that the password-file protection daemon was writing to it when I rudely interrupted it and inadvertently caused *writus interruptus*.

The moral of this story is to do an ls -l on any spooler files before doing a blanket cleanup. A check of the time would have shown the spool file to be current. Additional checking with ps could have shown the active process working on passwd.

An additional helpful hint is that /etc/passwd is delimited by the semicolons separating each field. One colon too few or too many, and /etc/passwd cannot be parsed by the login-password process beyond the record with the mismatched fields. Here /etc/pwck is a helpful tool.

APPARENT DIRECTORY CORRUPTION

The site of this scenario is a UNIX/VM installation running on 370 architecture. Operations called to tell me that minidisk address 771 was unavailable. With a VM host for the UNIX system, a limited number of VM commands are available from UNIX. The VM query command is capable of telling a vast amount of information about both real and virtual devices. In this case I needed to know what VM knew about its virtual disk address 771. From UNIX I did the following:

```
# query 771
771 FMD037 R/W 884 cyl 8520
# fgrep 771 /etc/devicelist
771 dasd /m8n
```

Here query showed that the host operating system knew about address 771. It not only was legal, but it also had plenty of space—the entire 884-cylinder pack (884 cylinders times 150 blocks times 4095 bytes per block). The disk was *read/write* and lived on disk pack FMD037.

The /etc/devicelist is the configuration file used by sysgen, the system generation software, and greping it showed that 771 was mounted to /m8n. A grepof /etc/mountlist would have shown similar results.

The mystery deepened when a listing of /m8n showed nothing. Attempting to

```
# mkdir /m8n
```

gave an error, and ls didn't give any information about /m8n, so one of the few options left was to do an octal dump of the directory itself:

```
od -c  /m8n
............
\0 \0 m 8 n \0 \0 ......
```

Obviously, UNIX knew about /m8n. Remember that in UNIX every mountable file system has its own base, called root or /. If you have ten mountable file systems, there will be eleven roots on that UNIX system. This particular file system's root file system was corrupted, and so it was time for further diagnostics.

An fsck -n of the root disk showed an unreferenced inode, a missing block, and a bad free list. Clearly, not all was well. The unreferenced inode, 3175, was cleared manually:

```
# clri /dev/dsk/220s0 3175
```

This line cleared inode 3175 from disk 220.

The unreferenced inode was one problem cleared, but there were other problems to solve. The inode should not have caused the loss of a directory. Permission was obtained from the users to bring down the machine. With due notification to operations, the system was taken down and then back up to init s. The root file system was then cleared with fsck. Now coming back up to init 2, /m8n was available. The file system consistency checking and repairing worked.

Another problem solved, and one more to go. In spite of all these maneuvers, 771 was still unavailable. All attempts to mount the disk were unsuccessful, but query showed the disk to be available to the system.

At this point it was now safe to point the finger at VM, the hardware, or both. The disk was detached and turned over to an FE for diagnostics. It was found to be inaccessible to VM because of a hardware fault. It was repaired, linked to the UNIX machine again, and found to be workable.

This story clearly shows that you should never blame the hardware until you have exhausted every software possibility. One job of the system administrator and his or her staff is problem determination. Be sure to check the software before pointing the finger at hardware.

SYSTEM GENERATION FAILURE

By the time I was knowledgeable enough to do system generations[1] on an ongoing basis, I figured I had finally reached the stage at which I wouldn't make careless system administration errors anymore. That was my first mistake of the day.

I needed to add to a machine more disk addresses (/dev/dsk/*), another page device, and a few other goodies. I was trying to figure out how to survive until a downtime weekend to get this sysgen done. The site service-level agreement forbade unnegotiated downtimes, except for Severity 1 problems, those that have an immediate effect on 60 percent of the system's use or availability.

Meanwhile, as a separate event, the system crashed for lack of sufficient paging area. The politics of the situation allowed me to declare a Severity 1 situation and thus keep the machine down for a few minutes to make corrections.

As long as the machine was down for repair anyway, I decided to *gen* that new page device. On large machines you grab whatever downtime you can get. I had already allocated the disk, and it needed only to be linked and formatted. I hastily brought up the machine into single-user mode, init s, and started a sysgen. Much to my dismay, the system responded by failing the sysgen.

A good system administrator does not get discouraged easily. In my haste to get the sysgen done, I had forgotten to check the remaining space on both my root disk and the source disk /usr/src. The remains of an earlier sysgen still cluttered both disks. The machine's system disks were deliberately sized for only enough room for a sysgen, providing that the installation procedure following the sysgen and a newsys cleaned up the remains.

A sysgen creates an entirely new and separate /dev called /newdev. The sysgen eats up inodes more rapidly than any other system activity does. Remember that a device node or *special file* is actually an allocated inode and a directory entry without any file blocks allocated. After the sysgen, /usr/src, /etc, and / are scattered with files called *Othis* and *Othat*, which are old files replaced by the last system generation and

---

[1] A sysgen involves the recompilation of the kernel and any other code that has been affected by the changes, addition, or deletion of devices (/dev/*), installation of drivers, and so on.

installation, sysgen, and newsys. And /usr/src is filled with intermediate files that are cleaned out at each successful installation.

The recovery was to manually clean out /usr/src, /, and /etc of all O* files and other interim carnage. The newly created /dev temporary files had to go as well. When a df -t showed 3000 blocks free on both systems disks, the amount needed for this system, the sysgen was rerun successfully.

This story has a few morals:

1. Always clean up after a system generation, successful or not.
2. Always check and maintain room on all critical system disks.
3. Fully understand system generation and installation internals.

This scenario led to the creation of the dfall script that I used every morning on my mainframes to observe the condition of all system files and critical daemon conditions.

TCP/IP FAILURES

This is an imaginary scenario to show what to do with TCP/IP failures. Let's imagine that a user complains that ftp, the TP/IP file transfer program, doesn't work. Your first impulse might be to test for the presence of ftpd, the ftp daemon, but don't take the user's explanation literally. If ftp is not working, what else is not?

Start with the basics first. Is TCP/IP working? Do a telnet *loopback test*. Log onto the machine in question, and log in again with telnet from the same machine. This loopback test will show whether the software is alive and well. Next, telnet or rlogin to another node. After that, ping the system from another node. If this works, the hardware level is intact.

TCP/IP software is unusually stable. If a daemon dies, it is a rare event, and it will die in self-defense. Drivers and hardware are far more likely to cause problems. Look for loose connectors first. Next look for newly made connections. The good news with thin-wire Ethernet is the ease of making a connection. The bad news is that an amateurish user with a do-it-yourself connection can take out the entire local Ethernet. Careful branching of nodes off multiple-port repeaters will localize the damage.

If the Ethernet device is separate, such as a Spartacus K200 or an Intel Fastpath, look to see if the box has been down for any reason. If it had a power hit or if the UNIX machine was booted, it has to be reset before an IPL can be successful (see Chapter 18).

UNIX/VM SCENARIOS

UTS UNIX has run for most of the decade, and AIX is IBM's major UNIX system strategy. Mainframe UNIX is interesting to study because it runs in both native mode and as a guest of VM. Native mode offers some advantages in efficiency. VM guest systems have more flexibility and better diagnostics.

Just as the appendix is a vestigial intestinal extension, and a coccyx is all that remains of our primate tails, 370s have vestigial card punches and card readers. They are no longer real, but they live on as virtual. Virtual punch and reader files are made of 80-character records, all that remains of the 80-column punch card. There is also a virtual printer that has 132-column records.

Why doesn't someone can these old relics? Because they have been put to good use. They are the interprocess communication of the 370. Files can be spooled by punching to readers or printers. Since they are delightfully virtual, they are actually memory devices, and so they are perfect buffers for all sorts of things. A VM system consists of many separate operating systems, all running on the VM platform. There can be many UNIX virtual machines, dozens to hundreds of CMS single-user systems, and one or more MVS systems, all on the same VM host, all on the same hardware. They communicate with one another by sending data via the punch of one system to the reader of another virtual system. From my machine, I punch you a file. You log on to find the file in your reader. It is just that simple.

UNIX on VM takes advantage of the punch and reader mechanism. Granted, you can use TCP/IP to move files, but if you use a simple mail or fetch command, the files will go by way of punch to reader. TCP/IP Ethernet displaces some of this traffic, but local transfers are much faster, running at channel speed via the punch-to-reader system.

Contemporary mainframe UNIX systems spool through both internal and external spool files. Each UNIX system has its punch, reader, and printer supplied by VM. Internally it has additional spoolers. A typical system has /usr/spool/rdr paired with its VM reader, and /usr/spool/out is paired with its punch and printer. When the machine is running quietly and below capacity, all of this works rather well. When the machine is running "with the needle pegged" at 100 percent, there can be problems, particularly when any of the spoolers fill. In fact, 370 system spooler problems are frequent and sometimes severe.

I should mention that commands to VM (CP/VM) can be executed from UNIX by the administrator. When you see commands like q (query), ind (indicate), or smart, they are VM commands executed from UNIX. Also, cpcmd prefaces all other VM commands, so a VM link of a disk is

```
LINK * 440 440 -MW
```

This is executed from UNIX as

```
# cpcmd link \* 440 440 mw
```

Note that the asterisk is quoted with a backslash to escape the shell. Also notice that the VM command line is in uppercase characters, whereas the UTS UNIX command line is in lowercase characters.

Filling punch Scenario

Files sent out of the machine by mail or vmpunch are not going anywhere, let alone to their destination. The UNIX spooler /usr/spool is filling rapidly. If it fills completely, it will hang the machine. By the time the system administrator is informed about the situation, it is already a crisis. Very little salvage time is left.

If the machine goes D & D with full spoolers, it won't come up again into multiuser mode without considerable work by the system administrator while still at init s.

The first step in problem solving is diagnostics. The following yields many data but little information:

```
ps -ef!fgrep -v getty
```

On the other hand, this yields a little information that goes a long way:

```
ps -ef!fgrep vmp
```

The daemon you want to see is vmpunchd. Thus the substring vmp extracts good information with a minimum amount of time wasted.

Because vmpunch is a server daemon, its visible presence with any amount of noticeable time accumulated is an indication of trouble. Inspection of the spooler's punch file /usr/spool/out will reveal multiple files. Normally it is empty because it is only a buffer. Its function is similar to /usr/spool/lp because it holds files only until they can be sent somewhere else. Because punch fills /usr/spool/out, it has many files with today's date and a recent time stamp.

The first step is to kill the vmpunch server, vmpunchd. It obviously is more dead than alive anyway. Since vmpunchd is a server, issuing a vmpunch command starts it cleanly. Do something trivial:

```
$ vmpunch -v mframe2 -i bhunter /etc/motd
```

Then punching motd to another machine is always a good trick to start the daemon. Now do this:

```
$ ls -l /usr/spool/out!wc -l
```

Each successive listing of the spooler piped to word count, wc, should show the number of files diminishing. In a very short time they will reach 0. Now it's time to party.

Hung Reader Scenario

In this scenario the spool disk was full, but a df -t didn't show enough blocks to come close to filling the disk. An ls -l showed the same condition. Nevertheless, the system continued to give disk full errors on the spooler disk address. A ps showed vmread active and accumulating time.

This is the sort of problem that makes you wonder whether you're in the right line of work. Nothing seemed to make sense. Running UTS on VM was an advantage, because I could use VM for diagnostics. By querying the virtual UNIX machine's reader—not to be confused with /usr/spool/rdr—I found a few files, one of which was enormous. The UNIX machine had bitten off something larger than it could swallow. UNIX had allocated all the available blocks in /usr/spool/rdr. Although both ls and df recognized this, they had no way to tell me that the allocated blocks were not a file yet. Worse yet, it never was going to be a file. This was a true standoff.

The fix was to clean out everything that was expendable on the spool disk. It was a good excuse for a major housecleaning. The console log, /usr/spool/console, was full of 550s0 out of disk space errors. The log was clearly expendable. I killed vmread and restarted it. It took a while for the file to get from /usr/spool/rdr to the user, but at that point the machine was free.

Whether the system is a VM host system or a native one, the problem is the same. Fill the system's spoolers, and everything will stop. There is a way to keep /usr/spool from filling when your troubled spool directory gets full. Let's say that the console log fills in the evenings. Users have software that beats on the system and sends errors to /dev/osm and consequently to /usr/spool/console. Perhaps the processes run in the background and fill their own users' disks, sending disk full errors to the console and thus the log. It has happened to my machines often enough. Give the problem directory its own disk. If, for example, /usr/spool/console or /usr/spool/uucp has its own disk and it fills, it won't take the machine down. Its daemon will die out of self-defense, but the system will continue. As long as the root disk / and /usr/spool are breathing, the machine can continue to function.

Filling the Console Log Scenario

This scenario is similar to the filling spooler, but it is specific to /usr/spool/console. If the console directory is on the spool disk, as opposed to having its own disk, the machine will be prone to hang. Errors filling the console log file are repetitive. They are frequently disk full or some hardware diagnostic.

Once we had a severe problem with an obscure language package. It would write its own internal stack, not the process stack, right down out of its stack area. Then it would keep right on going, eating up its data and text areas. It would continuously send stack too large messages, filling the osm buffer and the console file in short order. It didn't act on the error; it just complained about it.

The first step was to kill the daemon writing the console file. Next I found the process writing the error messages and filling the disk, and I looked for any of its children. Last, I notified the user both out of politeness and to keep him from doing it again.

On a VM guest UNIX system, I queried the machine's punch:

```
q f
```

Do this at reasonable intervals to observe growth or lack of it. If necessary, query the machine's virtual printer:

```
q prt
```

to see what is filling. You may have to close and purge the virtual UNIX machine's console:

```
# cpcmd close cons purge
```

VM's close does just that. In closing, it terminates spooling. The purge option of close empties the VM spool to the corners.

MACHINE FAILS TO COME UP TO MULTIUSER MODE

This was a frightening situation for a system administrator. Operations called in the middle of a Saturday afternoon because one of the UNIX machines refused to come up into multiuser mode. It would come up in single-user mode, but on attempting

```
# init 2
```

it failed to issue the usual messages from rc and the local.rc scripts. Instead it popped back to the console with

```
console login:
```

This was disconcerting, because on that particular machine the local.rc script was supposed to disconnect the console. Obviously, that wasn't happening. I was unable to resolve the problem over the phone, so I drove to the plant to take a look. The file systems were not mounting, so from init s I issued

```
# sh -x /etc/mountlist
```

This is a file containing all the mount commands for this system. Everything mounted. All seemed well.

On Sunday morning, operations called again. This time it was the same scenario, only worse. I drove to the site half-asleep. This time there would be no rush. The problem would be researched and fixed. I had operations look up the last root restore tape, just in case. Watching the console messages closely, an error message was picked up concerning /etc/mnttab. Doing an ls on /etc/mnttab showed no file. Where had it gone? Why had rc failed to create it? Closer investigation showed *execute* permissions missing on /etc/mountlist. There was no way for the shell to get the file systems mounted.

When looking for a command line to make something happen, it is best to grep it from rc, cron, or wherever it exists. On a 3B the line for setmnt is

```
# fgrep -n 'setmnt' *rc*
1: /etc/devnm / ! grep -v swap ! /etc/setmnt
#
```

It can also be trickier, as on this mainframe:

```
$ grep -n mnttab rc
12: if [ ! -f /etc/mnttab ]
$ sed -n '12,15p' rc
if [ ! -f /etc/mnttab ]
  then
    /etc/devnm / !egrep -v 'swap!root'!/etc/setmnt
fi
$
```

Although the line and the location vary from machine to machine, the idea is the same: /etc/mnttab must be created. It contains the name of the place where the device special file is mounted, the name of the special file, date, and permissions. It is best seen with an octal dump, since it is data and not a human-readable file. The setmnt line was typed in and executed. Next *execute* permissions were added to /etc/mountlist. The machine was brought up to multiuser mode.

Next came a game I call window shade. The system was taken down gently and then rebooted. All error messages were noted and errors fixed. This was done until (1) the system booted without error messages, and (2) I felt confident that the machine was OK. I call it *window shade* because you bring the system up and down until you're satisfied.

There were two good reasons that Saturday's work failed to bring permanent results. First, I was in too much of a hurry. The second reason was that in using

```
sh -x /etc/mountlist
```

to get debugging information, the shell executed a file that had no execution bits. Had I done the *window shade* on Saturday, the lack of permissions would have surfaced.

Problems with `rc` and initiation procedures are severe, and for this reason I have given them their own chapter, Chapter 12.

LOST CURSOR CONTROL IN X WINDOWS

Some system administration situations are so strange that the administrator doesn't even know where to start. The following is one of them.

A user came to the system administrator with an unusual problem. The cursor movement in the `vi` editor became erratic when used in X Windows. The left arrow, `L`, moved the cursor left as expected, but suddenly it would move the cursor down one line. At first this sounded like a classic `termcap` problem, but the `termcap` entry was OK. Cursor movement was all right when used outside X Windows.

What would you do at this point? Fortunately, the administrator who lived through this scenario knows X Windows well, and he had the idea of trying to alter the window size. Sure enough, the window was too small for the combination of X Windows and `vi`. Once the window was opened enough to give both the X Windows and `vi` enough room to breathe, the cursor behaved itself. Thanks to MCD's Scott Brock for this one.

BOY SCOUTS

We all have a favorite horror story. Some we tell, but others we are ashamed to tell anyone. This horror story is all mine. It is tempting to pretend it happened to someone else, but I won't. The story starts with my thinking of myself as the system's Boy Scout. An administrator should be trustworthy, reliable, and courteous to all his users, I thought. He should never tell anyone no. I was in the middle of a very nasty day, doing all kinds of human multitasking, but this image of myself as Helpful Human Being kept me going.

I was hanging in there just fine until the first-line help desk called to tell a bizarre story. They not only listened to a user's request to copy all of `/etc` and `/bin` to a user's disk partition, they actually did it. Now the two clone system directories needed to be removed. Although the help desk had copied the directories without a second thought, a surprising feat in itself, they felt uneasy about removing them.

We all know what a good system administrator does at times like this. You hang up the phone, and then you calmly write down what has to be done. Having formed your plan, you move to the user disk, find the wrong `etc`, and suavely remove it with a full path name, like this:

```
rm -rf /usr/schmuck/illegal/etc
```

That is what common sense tells you to do, but that is not what the system Boy Scout did. Carried away with the image of being helpful and necessary, I soothingly reassured the hot-line person, "Just hang on, and those directories will be gone in a second." With the phone still cradled between my neck and left shoulder, I changed the directories to where the illegal etc directory was and quickly typed:

```
rm -rf /etc
```

How many thousands of times had I typed in /etc? It was an automatic reflex. But /etc is an absolute address and etc is a relative address, and so there I was with a throwaway system.

That is the end of the story. The rest of the day was an exercise in system restoration and seeing just how good our tape storage and catalog system was. The moral? Summer camp is the place for Boy Scouts, but the system is the place for cool-thinking, cool-acting professional system administrators.

THE UNKILLABLE PROCESS

Sooner or later we all discover a "night of the living dead" process that won't die. This particular one was uncovered when I came back from a recent seminar on a Friday and found a job that had been running on ftp for almost a week. I was up to my neck in work, and I hastily issued a SIGKILL against the process. It didn't return an error, so I went about my business, thinking the problem was solved.

The following Monday, the system response was noticeably slow, with ps showing an ftp process with a large accumulation of time. Doing a grep on ftp gave the following output:

```
$ ps -ef!grep 'ftp'
bhunter  29532  24610 0  14:12:25  tty600  0:00  grep ftp
root       150      1 0  Dec 4         ?   685:23  /etc/ftpd
root       154      1 0  Dec 4         ?     0:1   /etc/ftpd
```

The date was December 12, but the process had been there since December 4. Besides the large amount of CPU time, the parent process ID was unusual. A user process has to invoke tftp. Normally only an initial user shell has the PPID of 1, *except* for root-initiated processes. A PPID of 1 could only happen if the real parent process had died or been killed, and then init inherits the process.

Obviously it was time to get more information about the process. The output of ps -elf showed the process as swapped (F is zero) and in the sleep state (under the S category is an S):

```
F S  UID    PID  PPID  C  PRI  NI    ADDR  SZ  WCHAN   STIME     TTY    TIME    CMD
3 S  root     0     0  0   0   20  5000330271 1ecc38  Dec 20      ?    0:26   <system>
1 S  root     1     0  0  39   20  ffe000 22  ffe000   Dec 4      ?    1:35   /etc/init
3 S  root     2     0  0   5   20  ffc000  0  1aac18   Dec 4      ?    0:44   <pagedaemon>
0 S  oyama 16932     1  0  29   20  d28000 37  1ef0ce   Dec 7   tty1p  695:07  ftp -vn jjcad
```

The last process's priority is 29, and its nice value is 20. Its processor utilization for scheduling is 0. It is not only sleeping; it hasn't taken any CPU time in recent history.

A who showed no one on ttyp1, a remote terminal. Trying to kill the process had no effect, and a no such process would have been generated on a typo or nonexistent process.

Putting It All Together

Because the `tty` is a remote terminal, it is assumed that the user logged in by way of `telnet` or `rsh`. He executed a file transfer via `ftp` and disconnected at some time during its execution, leaving his login broken while `ftp` was in the sleep state.

The `ftp` process is at priority 20. In this system, `PZERO`, the threshold for interrupts, is set at 25. Therefore, the process can be interrupted. There is a catch, however. Either the `kill` command or the `kill` system call can send a signal, but a system failure or fault can cause a process to *ignore the signal*. The process sleeps, waiting for an event (`wchan`); `sleep()` takes an argument `disp`, which is used to set the process's priority during its sleep. If the event never occurs, the process can never wake up to take the signal. Thus, it was clear that the `ftp` process had lost all ties with the world when the tube went away. Nothing short of a reboot would change its state.

TERMINAL IN OPEN MODE

A XENIX system had just been rolled over to change its hard disks. The standard distribution had been restored from the distribution diskettes, and the changeable system files had been restored from backup. Everything seemed to be going well and all files were restored. It was business as usual until a user logged in using an old Adds Viewpoint terminal and came up in open mode when using `vi`. Immediately her `.profile` was checked and it appeared to be OK. Next the system administrator logged in on his account. His account not only knew of the port, but he also came up in open mode.

The `termcap` file had been changed to make an entry for an Epson FX-850 printer to print italic and boldface in draft mode. It was instantly suspect. With no `vi` available, `grep -n` was used to isolate the lines with the word epson, and `sed` was used to read the entry:

```
% grep -n epson /etc/termcap
33:epson|Epson FX-1000 or Panasonic 1595 printer:\
% sed -n '33,36p' /etc/termcap
epson|Epson FX-1000 or Panasonic 1595 printer:\
    :hc:am:co#80:is=\E@:so=\EG:se=\EH:ul:hd=\EJ\022:hu=\Ej\022:\
    :us=\E4:ue=\E5:
```

Everything looked fine: `ansi` followed epson, and `ansi` was working well.

The `termcap` file was copied to `Otermcap`, and a compact version was made with only the devices currently on the system. It would be fast if nothing else.

The new `termcap` file did nothing. If not `termcap`, what could be different? Then `tty` was run from the wayward terminal to get its address. It was `tty2c`. The new suspect could only be `/etc/ttytype`. On BSD and XENIX, `/etc/ttytype` is a file that lets the system know what kind of terminal to expect at any port. The file looked like this:

```
ansi    tty11
ansi    tty12
unknown tty1a
unknown tty2a
dialup  tty1A
dialup  tty2A
dialup  tty1B
```

```
dialup    tty1C
dialup    tty1D
unknown   tty1b
unknown   tty1c
unknown   tty1d
dialup    tty2B
dialup    tty2C
dialup    tty2D
unknown   tty2b
unknown   tty2c
unknown   tty2d
```

Do you see it? The `tty2c` terminal port was `unknown`, so it would throw the login into unknown mode. The cure was to change it to read

```
adds tty2c
```

There is no magic in these stalk-and-fix scenarios. The requirement is to be familiar enough with the system to know the internals of the events that you are dealing with. In this case the user's environment learned of the terminal type from `/etc/ttytype` at login time. At login the terminal type is passed to the environment from the user's `.profile`, `.login`, or `.cshrc`.

The terminal type would be used for the first time in that login when the user used a `termcap`-dependent command like `vi`. As a result, the three links in the chain are

- `/etc/ttytypes`
- `~/.login` or `$HOME/.profile`
- `/etc/termcap`

Knowing the events offers an opportunity to investigate each element until the cause is found. *Work smarter, not harder*.

AND THEN EVERYTHING WENT WRONG

Ever have a day when everything goes wrong? This was one of those days. The setting for this drama was a cluster system consisting of several Sun workstations running SunOS 4.0 networked to a pair of DEC-dedicated file servers running ULTRIX 2.2. Full NFS and YP networking were in effect. It was a startup installation, and the users were just getting used to NFS.

The slave server recently had a file system appended by adding another disk partition to it to allow for more room. One of the workstations attached to it became upset when it was unable to reach a file system at the address it was supposed to, and it started to generate `stale file handle` error messages to its server. The `stale file handle` message is NFS for "The address I was looking at used to be good. What happened?" These errors flow fast and furious to the unattended console, and they quickly fill the error-log files.

Noticing the system performance had degraded, the administrator started to investigate. No one was logged onto the server, and no processes were running to take time from the system, but it was running slowly nevertheless, dragging three out of four wheels. One look at the console in the machine room and the answer was clear as could be: The console was too busy getting swamped with error messages to allow a word in edgewise, let alone any instructions from root. It was time to bring down the server. At the time, the administrators thought the workstations attached to it would have to come down first. Unfortunately, workstations were in the process of being added every few days, and no script yet existed to do a mass shutdown. In fact, the system was *so* new that no single person even knew all the workstations attached to the servers!

After all known workstations were shut down, one Ethernet address hung on like glue. It was a new workstation added unobtrusively a few days earlier, and none of the staff present at the time of this disaster had known it existed. By the time the new workstation was found and its host name was deduced from its Ethernet address, everyone was getting pretty rattled.

Here our horror story takes a turn for the worse. The workstation host name was only one letter different from the server's, and naturally Murphy's law predominated. The server was shut down by mistake. Now there were more dead systems around than dead actors in a Shakespearean tragedy. With heavy hearts, both the UNIX system administrator and the system manager took off to the machine room to work directly on the consoles.

Both systems started coming up side by side, but they core-dumped at the same point in the boot procedure. They came up to single-user mode all right, but they died about 60 percent of the way through rc on the way up to multiuser mode. In fact, they unceremoniously died and dumped, as close to crash and burn as a computer can get without actually emitting smoke and flames.

Now it was time for some hard questions. What had changed since the last boot? File servers usually don't go down this often. The last shutdown and reboot had come when they were created several weeks earlier. A printer had been added, but that wasn't life threatening. There was also a partial repartitioning, but that was a trivial affair. All other changes were minor.

When the system came up, rc executed past the point where it called local.rc. Starting at the invocation of rc.local, the code looked like this:

```
sh /etc/rc.local
.
.
/etc/update
/etc/cron
/etc/accton /usr/adm/acct;    echo -n 'accounting'   > /dev/console
[ -f /etc/inetd ] && {
   /etc/inetd;                echo -n 'network'      > /dev/console
}
# [ -f /etc/rwhod ] && {
#   /etc/rwhod;               echo -n 'rwhod'        > /dev/console
}
cd /usr/spool
rm -f uucp.LCK.*
```

The notation

```
[ -f file ] && { command1 ; command2 }
```

means test for the existence of file. If the test command returns a *true*, it will execute the commands in the curly braces in series without generating a new subshell. The left bracket, [, is a link to /bin/test, and the right bracket,], is a no-op, necessary to preserve balance. This is *not* easy syntax to read. A simple if-then-fi would have been far easier to read and understand. Perhaps if the guy who commented out the code had been more familiar with this particular syntax, it would have been easier to avoid this error.

It had been a long day, and it was getting late. When rc appeared to execute to the point where inetd was executed and the network message put to the console, the system manager and the administrator went out for supper and a much-needed cup of coffee. They thought that they were in for a very long indoor weekend.

Another administrator came over to take a look while the captains of this UNIX ship were away. With a fresh eye, he immediately noticed that the last curly brace was unmatched. He commented it out and booted the systems successfully.

In the process of commenting out the rwhod daemon, a notorious CPU pig, the last curly brace was overlooked. The result was a syntax error that halted the boot process and generated a dump. The system cannot come up if rc or rc.local fails. The correct code looked like this:

```
[ -f /etc/inetd ] && {
    /etc/inetd;                echo -n 'network'      > /dev/console
}
# deleted rwho 5/19/89 DWH
# [ -f /etc/rwhod ] && {
#   /etc/rwhod;                echo -n 'rwhod'        > /dev/console
# }
#
cd /usr/spool
rm -f uucp.LCK.*
```

Don't ever feel ashamed about making dumb system administration mistakes. They often are informative learning experiences. Sometimes it seems as if you learn more from mistakes than from reading the manual!

What are the lessons here? The first is that rc and rc.local should have been tested with the tools available—the -x and -v debug flags of /bin/sh—found even on these Berkeley-based systems:

```
# sh -xv rc|more
```

The -x flag shows every line that is executing, and the -v flag echoes every single line. The rc and rc.local scripts can have a set -x embedded at the top of them. This also would have been handy for debugging.

Second, the rc script should have been tested after it had been altered:

```
# sh -vn /etc/rc|more
```

This causes the shell to parse the script but not actually execute it. Unfortunately, this is seldom practiced because it requires a shutdown to test properly. The rc and rc.local scripts must be executed from single-user mode, so that executing rc while the system is up causes a doubling of the system daemons and risks erasing critical dynamic system files. However, *not* testing has its disadvantages also. In this case it gave the system staff some serious moments. Had this scenario not occurred on late Friday afternoon, there could have been a major system outage.

Cluster systems running NFS and YP have an Achilles heel when it comes to testing rc or a new kernel. The key YP daemons, ypserv and ypbind, tie server to workstation irrevocably. If the file system is disrupted, the workstation host will quickly complain stale file handle. As a result, alterations to server file systems must be done with the workstations down.

The only remaining option is to have at least one slave server defined to Yellow Pages. Then one of the servers can come down and be altered while the other is up to care for the workstations' file system needs. The catch is that if the files needed by any of the workstations are on the server that has to come down, they are in trouble anyway unless the disks can be switched. What is gained is that fewer systems have to come down. YP servers exist to provide access to the YP data base, not to ensure user data availability.

File system maintenance must be carefully planned and orchestrated. A downtime is required, and everything that can be done in advance should be, to minimize the length of the downtime. Here, detailed, step-by-step planning is an absolute necessity.

What are some other lessons? Back up your root partition daily, and be prepared to do a root restore at a moment's notice. Be familiar with the restore command so you don't have to learn it at an inconvenient time, like when you have to use it! Automatically back up critical files disk to disk when you modify them:

```
# cp rc Orc
# cp rc Trc
# ed Trc
.
.
w
q
# sh -xvn Trc
.
.
# cp Trc rc
```

A little caution at this point saves a lot of grief later.

A final point. The workstations can stay up when the server goes down. All this comes with experience. A special thanks to Dave Hudock, the Lone Ranger who saved this situation.

FULL root DISK

A lot of scenarios hit us sooner or later, but the root-full syndrome always seems to come sooner. Here are the gory details: You log on and change to su to do some useful work as only root can do, but you find out that the system won't allow you to do anything. Hastily you do a df -t \ of your root disk, and you find no space. Now what?

Remember that root needs room to breathe. Small files are created and erased constantly, and room is required to do this. Always make extra room on the root disk so you have enough elbow room to work.

Personally, I hate to see /usr cluttering the root disk, but small systems have a lot of baggage on their root disk, and often /usr is one of the suitcases. Larger systems tend to partition heavily, so the root disk may contain only /dev, /etc, /bin, and a minimum number of root files such as /unix itself, the kernel. Workstations are configured with volatile file systems sharing the root disk. For example, Sun workstations place their /var directory on the root partition. And /var is the home of files that breathe, such as the spooler files, traditionally kept in /usr/spool on earlier systems.

Before you can free up some room on the root disk, you must find expendable files that can be removed. The best bets are spool directory files, like the files in /usr/spool. Spool directory files are in different locations on some UNIX systems, such as /var/spool. The main point is that only if you know your system well and have spent enough time cleaning it out will you know where to find the dust under the rugs. Mainframe systems fill /usr/spool/rdr, /usr/spool/out, and /usr/spool/log with amazing regularity, but /usr/spool/console will fill the fastest.

If you are not yet familiar with your system's hiding places, let your system do the looking for you. Since wandering about the UNIX file system creates confusion and frustration for novice administrators, why not let the find command do the looking for you until you get your bearings? The find command has some of the strangest syntax in UNIX, but it is worth the effort of learning it. Here we tell find to look for files of 50,000 or more characters and to print the names it locates:

```
$ find / -size +50000c -print
```

Start the search at root (/). You have to tell it to -print, or it simply will return a true to your shell, and you will never know that you got results.

You can narrow the search a little by telling find to look for files only and ignore directories:

```
$ find / -size +50000c -type f -print.
```

Now limit the search even further by having find look for files over 50,000 characters that have been made in the last day or two:

```
$ find / -mtime -2 -size +50000c -print
```

Some UNIX versions do not have the c modifier for the size option. Then you must use blocks as a size, the old 512-byte-per-block size at that.

Now let's finish the search from root for system files that have grown too large too fast. The final act is to get the output from the ls command. Use find's exec option, which fires another command. This one has really tacky syntax:

```
$ su
password:
# find / -size +100 -mtime -3 -type f -exec ls -l {} \;
```

The brackets, { }, pass the find output to ls as an argument. The \ is mandatory to escape the semicolon.

If at first you think find's syntax is too nasty to face, copy the find command line to a shell script to use later when you need it. The main point here is to shorten the search whenever possible. You don't have to search from root unless you want to search the entire system. Once you get to know your system, you can start at var, spool, or wherever your searching experiences tell you the hiding places are on your system.

Once you have found the recently created files that appear to be clogging the system, you will have to determine whether they are expendable. Console files, log files, error files, and other files that report errors are expendable. Eventually you will become intimately acquainted with the special characteristics of your own system. As you gain more experience, before sending these files off to UNIX Valhalla, check them to see just what the major complaints are. You may find thousands of identical error messages with a specific hardware complaint in the error or console log file. Investigate it, and make note of the complaint before removing the file. Be careful, because some files, like log files, must exist. You can either empty or shorten those.

The quickest way to empty a file without removing it is write over it with nothing:

```
# cd /usr/spool/log
# >sendmail
```

Now /usr/spool/log/sendmail is an empty file. The C shell counterpart is to touch the file.

In time your skills will become more polished and you will move to suspect directories instinctively, but for now become friendly with find and a few of its options.

THE root **PARTITION IS FULL, OR IS IT?**

This horror story started innocently enough. A file server system started grinding to a halt. The root disk was filling, and very little useful work was being done. Because this system was a file server, its less-than-ideal condition was not immediately obvious to the users. The site was composed of "dataless" workstations and several servers, all using NFS.

Once alerted, the system administrator did a remote login to the server and executed a df. The system was running SunOS, a Berkeley 4.3 derivative. It showed 109 percent disk usage on the root partition, as full as it ever gets.

The normal procedure at this site is to run find from the base of the troubled directory and look for large files. The longer you do this, the more things you will think of for find to do:

```
find / -size +100000c -type f -mtime -2 -exec ls -l {} \;¦
  egrep -v 'usr¦cad¦var¦homes'
```

This says, "Have find look for all files starting from root with a size of 100,000 characters or more made today. Make a long listing of them, and filter out those from /var, /usr, /homes, and the cad directories." Note that cad is a local tool directory.

The huge file we were looking for wasn't present. There were no large files other than the few that are always there. Here's where an ordinary scenario starts to look like a horror story. As far as df is concerned, the disk is full. So where are the files?

If a process is attempting to write a huge file, it will effectively hold captive the superblock. The free list is no longer free, and a process's perception of the file system is that it is full. When you suspect this is happening, how do you pin down this condition? Logging into the system, a ps -axq showed an unimaginable amount of time taken by an error-logging daemon, syslogd. This daemon reads system messages and forwards them to whatever files the system administrator specifies in /etc/syslog.conf. A mainframe would have sent them to the console log and a micro to /usr/adm/messages, its error log.

The immediate cure is simple enough. Use the process-ID number to kill the process:

```
kill -9 nnn
```

Here nnn is the process ID taken from the ps command's output.

The root disk fills often enough to warrant creating a monitor program both to watch for legitimate filling and to look for runaway processes and daemons. Here is a short version:

```
:
find / -size +100000c -type f -mtime -2 -exec ls -l {} \;|
  egrep -v 'cad!usr!var!homes'
set `ps -axq!awk '{ print $4 }'!sed -n '2,$p'!
  sort -n -r ! sed -n '1,5p' `
ps -ax!sed -n '1p'
for time
 do
   ps -axq!grep ${time}
 done
exit 0
# root.mon
# 4/21/89 bhh
```

A colon starts the first line to make it execute in Bourne shell, even in this C-shell environment. I don't have any particular preference for either shell, but Bourne-shell programs are more portable.

The set command is used to pass the initial filtered ps output to the positional parameters $1, $2, .. $5:

```
set `ps -axq!awk '{ print $4 }'!sed -n '2,$p'!
  sort -n -r ! sed -n '1,5p' `
```

The Bourne shell's for loop construct has a default condition:

```
for time [in $#]
  do
```

The positional parameters are understood when not written.

The crux line filters out the third field of ps's output, the time:

```
ps -axq!grep ${time}
```

Then sed removes the first line, the ps header line. Its output is then filtered by sort and sorted in reverse numerical order:

```
sort -n -r
```

One last pass through sed again, and the first five lines are printed:

```
sed -n '1,5p'
```

Passed to grep by way of the set command, the original full lines are again picked up. The result is the five worst CPU hogs on the system.

Exercised with sufficient frequency, this little monitor script keeps the system out of trouble. Keep an eye on troublesome processes or daemons. If you have multiple systems of the same type, whether stand-alones, workstations, or servers, look at the same daemon on all of them. Does it draw a disproportionate amount of time? If so, suspend use of the daemon while you investigate the problem.

root IS FULL—AGAIN

The most common system administration scenario is a critical disk partition filling. No disk partitions are as important as root. This particular root full problem occurred one Monday morning when I was already up to my console in problems. One by one, every user of one of the Sun workstations wandered over to my office with variations on the following theme: "The machine is so slow that it's not doing anything." Finally, one knowledgable user came in with the unvarnished truth: "The root disk is at 100 percent."

Indeed, everything had come to a halt on that machine. A user login on the console was frozen. I did a remote login as root and used the find command to get a listing of files created or modified in the last two days:

```
# find / -type f -mtime -2 -exec ls -l {} \;
```

Nothing remarkable came to light.

At first I thought the problem must be a hung daemon attempting to write, holding captive the root superblock free list. I had certainly seen this kind of situation often enough. I understood that the users had processes running, so I didn't want to bring the systems down. However, a ps -lax showed no massive user process running. All it showed was the usual shells and X Window stuff, as well as a page full of network daemons. I asked the users if I could bring down their system. Workstations belong to those who use them, and it is common courtesy to ask their permission to bring it down. There were no objections from the users. After all, the machine was virtually inoperable anyway.

Like most workstations, this one ran a Berkeley-based UNIX system. There are no init states, and so the system had to come all the way down:

```
# shutdown -h now
```

This is a BSD shutdown to the halt state. Once fully down, I booted off the prom into single-user mode:

```
> b -s
```

Now the system was up in single-user mode with its disks unmounted.

The problem was apparent immediately. SunOS configures /home on the root partition. The /home space is actually root space; in fact, it is the root partition. It is intended either to be a mount point for users' home directories taken from the server or to hold only "precious" files. In this case, our users had been overly ambitious and used far too much space.

To aggravate the matter, problems bringing up DOS Windows under X11 had left DOS directories in each of the users' home directories in /home with more than 300 blocks apiece. This is a bug/feature of sunview.

Using du from root on a workstation that is using a file server leads only to frustration. It will size *all* files and directories, not only on the server machine but on the clients' as well. However, on a system in single-user mode, with all disks unmounted, du gave only one or two screens full of very valuable information. Then du showed up the total block usage of each user and also the DOS directories. DOS had left its footprints all over the place. My original find command line failed to find this information because I used -type f:

```
# find / -type f -mtime -2 -exec ls -l {} \;
```

Normally this is a good approach, but it looks only at files. In this case I needed directories, too.

One quick rip through /homes to rm -rf the DOS directories, and the disk was back to 82 percent full in less than a minute.

What can be learned from this scenario?

- Put the users on their own partition at all times. *Don't share* root!
- When looking for disk killers with find, look for directories as well as files.
- Keep as much of the users' work on the server and as little on the workstation as possible.

The last point is critical. Unless your workstation is blessed with 300+ megabytes of disk space, save the available space for system work.

I wish you wouldn't have to face scenarios like the ones in this chapter, but unfortunately, you will. Keep cool, and make your plan quickly, not hastily. The goal is to rescue your system. Learn as much about internals as you can, learn from past experience, examine the facts, make your problem determination, and then seek the answer. Keep your sense of humor, if you can. The longer you administer UNIX system, the easier it will get.

MANAGER'S CORNER

Hire with Care

System managers often select their own staff. If you are the one who hires and fires, it is up to you to evaluate what individual contributor does well and what his or her weaknesses are. When you hire a programming specialist and you find out that she doesn't administer well, you are right to show her how to administer, but you are wrong if you fault her for her lack of administration skills; that is not what she was hired for.

The hire is far more important than the fire. If you hire well, you should never have to fire. Be fussy about whom you hire, interview well, and make your points before a contract of employment is made. If you need someone desperately and you can't find a good candidate, bring in a contractor until you do find the right person. Advertise exactly what you are looking for. Be equally precise about what you are not looking for. The morale of the rest of the staff drops drastically when someone is fired, so hire with care.

INDEX